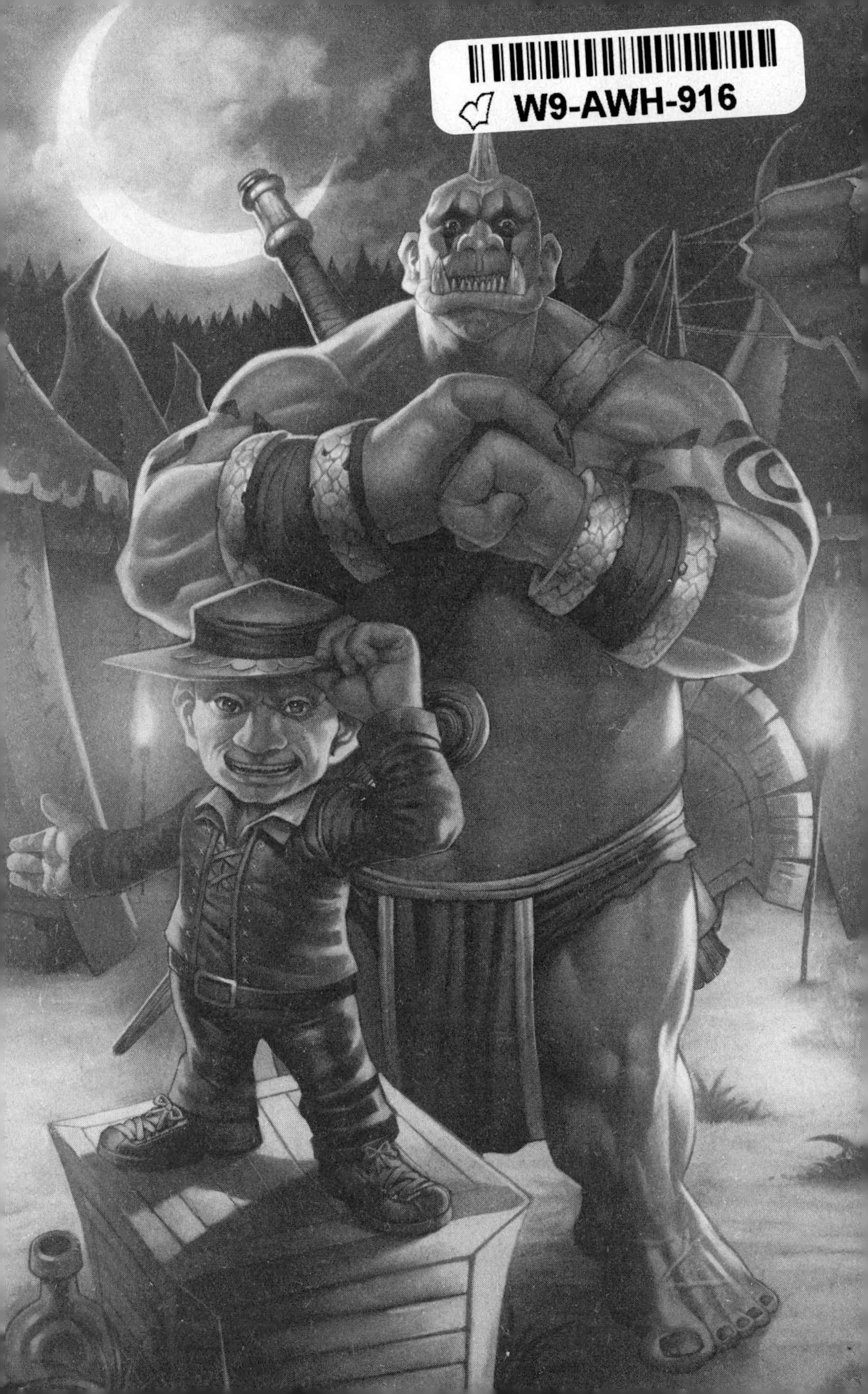

Warcraft: Legends Vol. 4

Contributing Editors - Hyun Joo Kim & Janice Kwon
Layout and Lettering - Michael Paolilli
Creative Consultant - Michael Paolilli
Graphic Designer - Louis Csontos
Cover Artist - UDON with Saejin Oh

Editor - Troy Lewter
Print-Production Manager - Lucas Rivera
Managing Editor - Vy Nguyen
Senior Designer - Louis Csontos
Art Director - Al-Insan Lashley
Associate Publisher - Marco F. Pavia
President and C.O.O. - John Parker
C.E.O. and Chief Creative Officer - Stu Levy

BLIZZARD ENTERTAINMENT

Senior Vice President, Creative Development - Chris Metzen
Director, Creative Development - Jeff Donais
Lead Developer, Licensed Products - Shawn Carnes
Publishing Lead, Creative Development - Rob Tokar
Senior Story Developer - Micky Neilson
Story Developer - James Waugh
Art Director - Glenn Rane
Director, Global Business
Development and Licensing - Cory Jones
Associate Licensing Manager - Jason Bischoff
Historian - Evelyn Fredericksen
Additional Development - Samwise Didier and Tommy Newcomer

A **TOKYOPOP** Manga

TOKYOPOP and ⊙ are trademarks or registered trademarks of TOKYOPOP Inc.

TOKYOPOP Inc.
5900 Wilshire Blvd. Suite 2000
Los Angeles, CA 90036

E-mail: info@TOKYOPOP.com
Come visit us online at www.TOKYOPOP.com

ISBN: 978-1-4278-0830-1

First TOKYOPOP printing: June 2009
10 9 8 7 6 5 4 3 2 1
Printed in the USA

WARCRAFT

LEGENDS

VOLUME FOUR

HAMBURG // LONDON // LOS ANGELES // TOKYO

WARCRAFT
LEGENDS
VOLUME FOUR

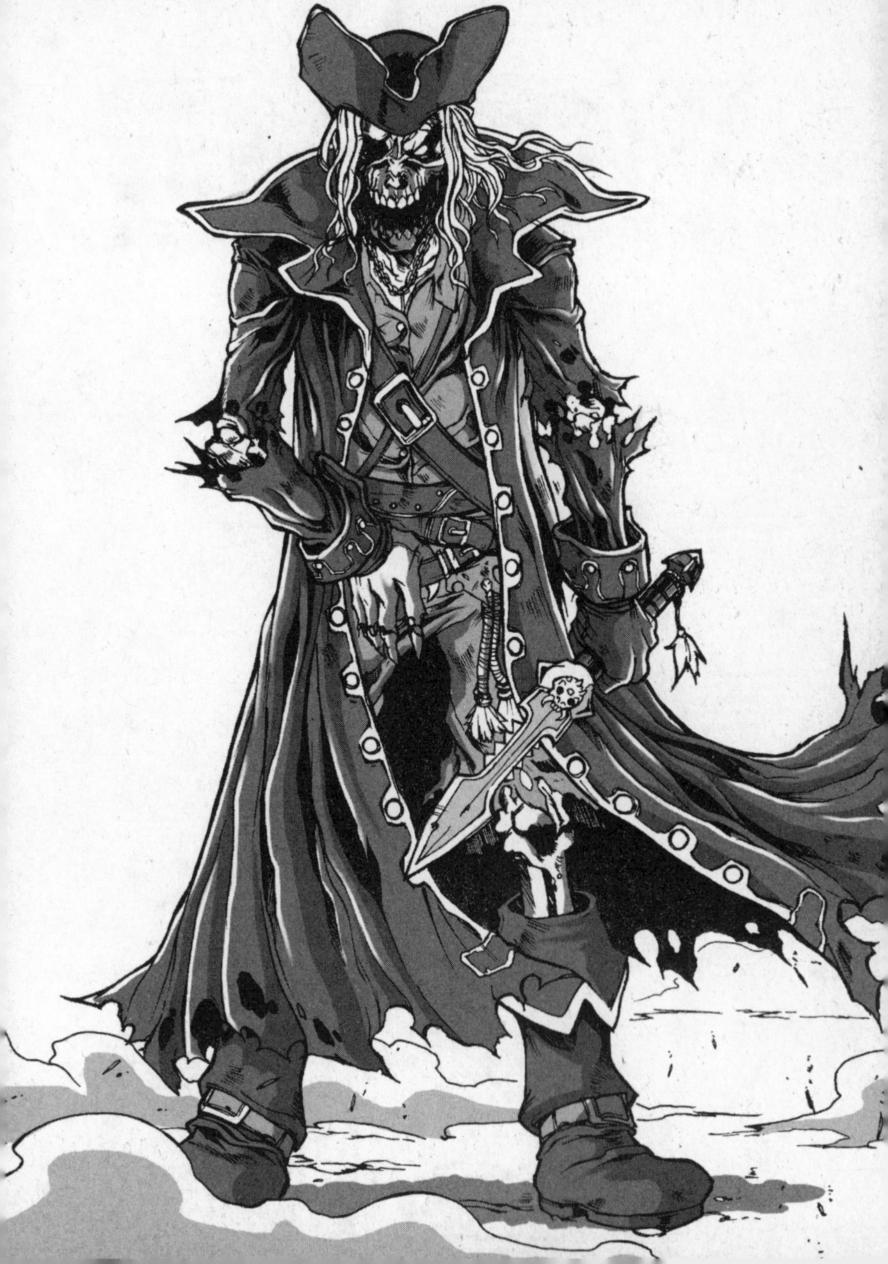

WARCRAFT

LEGENDS

VOLUME FOUR

FATE

WRITTEN BY RICHARD A. KNAAK

ART BY JAE-HWAN KIM

CONTRIBUTING EDITORS: HYUN JOO KIM & JANICE KWON
LETTERER: MICHAEL PAOLILLI

STORY SO FAR

The undead walk the lands of Azeroth as rotting nightmares, vicious and unyielding in their brutality. They are broken into two factions: the Forsaken, led by the Dark Lady, Sylvanas Windrunner; and the Scourge, commanded by the dark lord of the dead, the Lich King. For the living of Azeroth, to become undead is to be damned for all eternity.

Trag Highmountain, the courageous tauren who sacrificed his life in *Warcraft: The Sunwell Trilogy – Shadows of Ice*, found himself reanimated as one of the undead. However, Trag's condition was unique: his mind rebelled against the carnal bloodlust typical of other undead. Nevertheless, his thoughts were clouded with visions of a foreboding kingdom of ice and snow, and his ears were filled with the Lich King's rancid whispers urging him to kill...

In Trag's desperate search for answers, he sought help from the tauren shaman Sulamm. However, unbeknownst to Trag, Sulamm was conspiring with his kinsmen to kill the undead tauren, and Trag barely escaped the flames in which he was thrown. Betrayed and alone, Trag could no longer control the Lich King's incitement to mindless mayhem...until Thrall, warchief of the Horde, sensed Trag's suffering and shared his own story of triumph in the face of the dark urge to kill. Thrall's words and noble intentions helped Trag regain control of his mind, and with renewed resolve Trag journeyed to the frozen tundra of Northrend. He befriended a taunka named Akiak, who agreed to lead Trag to the Dragon Wastes. It was there that Trag found a bone fragment from the ancient proto-dragon Galakrond. Trag hoped to harness the fragment's mysterious power as a weapon against the Lich King.

Yet Trag's victory was short lived, because the anub'ar--fierce undead minions of the Lich King--attacked Akiak's village. During the ensuing battle, Trag fell into the anub'ar's underground tunnels and managed to stop the fiends from sinking the taunka village. Although separated from his allies by the resulting cave-in, Trag pressed on through the tunnels beneath the tundra, finally emerging aboveground outside the gates of his final destination: Icecrown.

His long journey at an end, Trag must now confront the Scourge's maleficent ruler...or risk losing his soul forever.

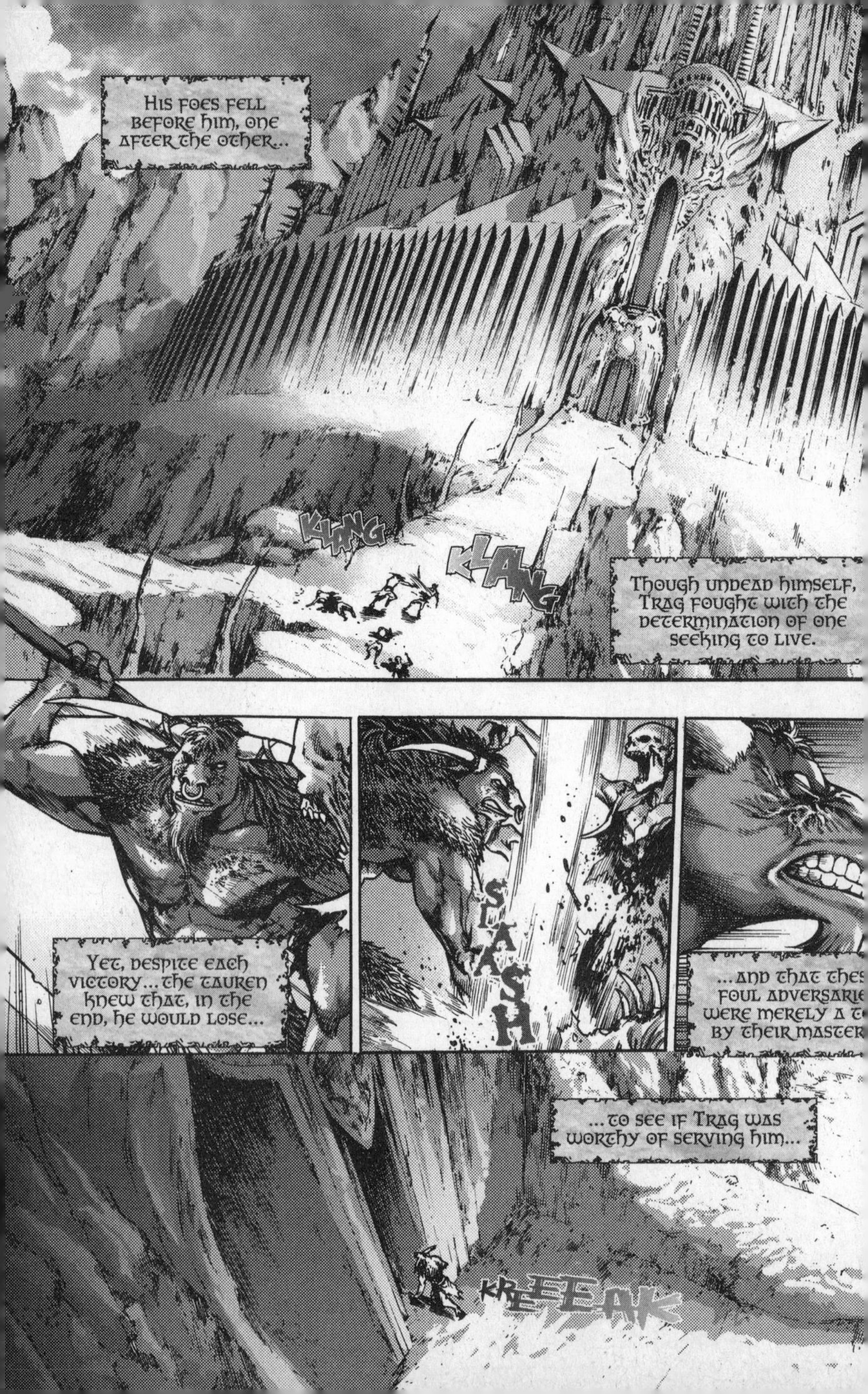
His foes fell before him, one after the other...
KLANG
KLANG
Though undead himself, Trag fought with the determination of one seeking to live.
Yet, despite each victory... the tauren knew that, in the end, he would lose...
SLASH
...and that thes foul adversarie were merely a t by their master
...to see if Trag was worthy of serving him...
KREEEAK

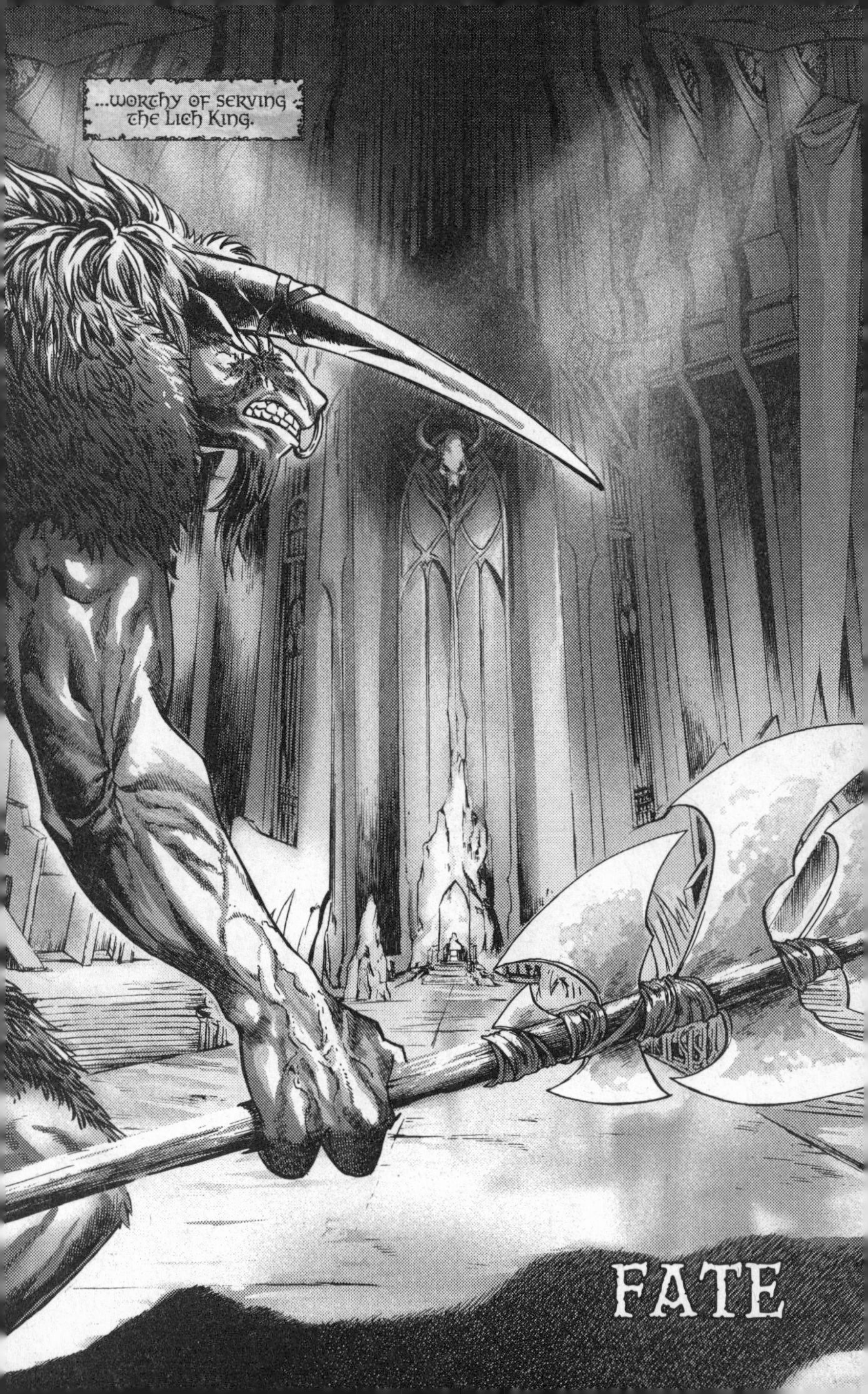

...worthy of serving the Lich King.
FATE

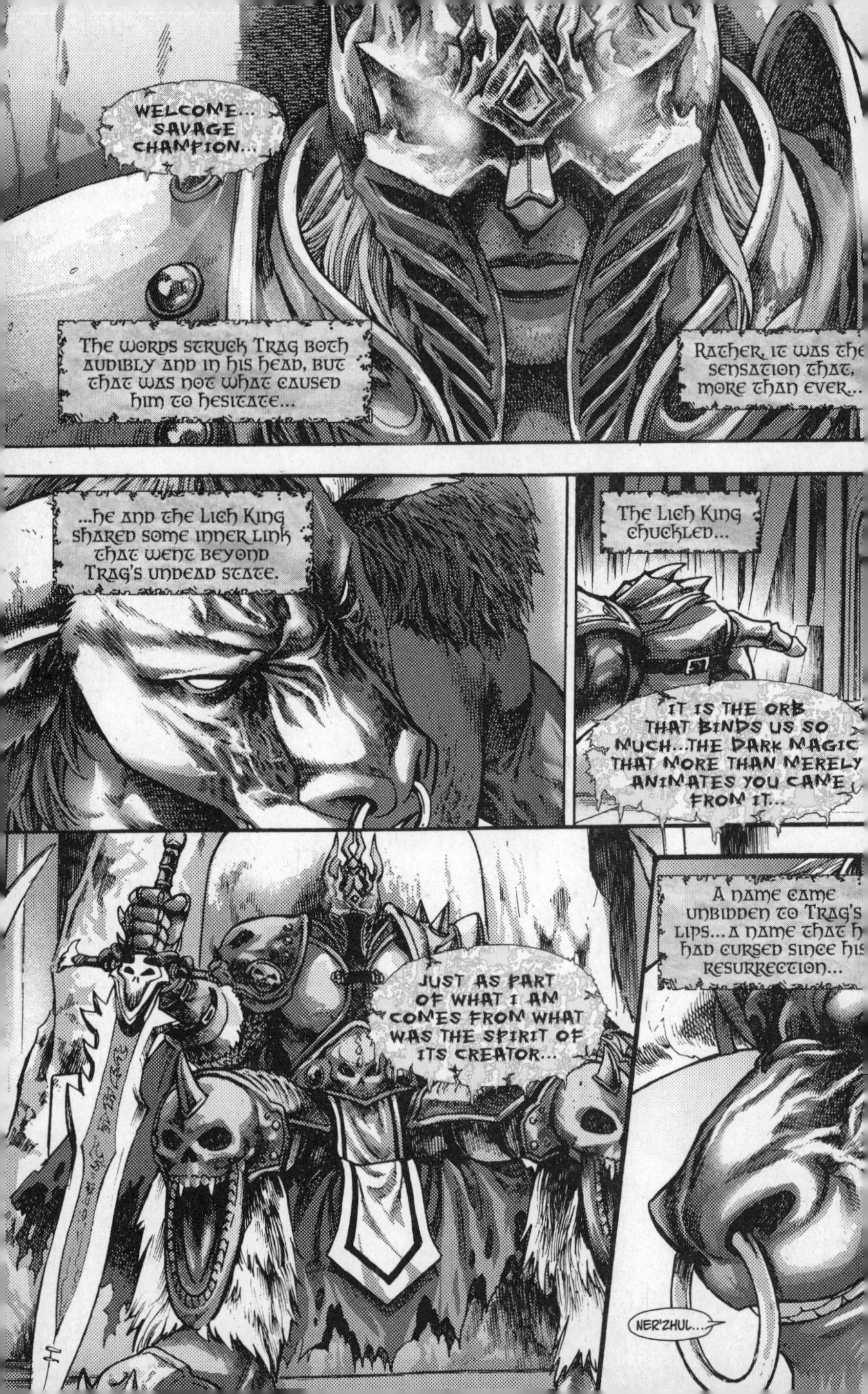
WELCOME... SAVAGE CHAMPION...
The words struck Trag both audibly and in his head, but that was not what caused him to hesitate...
Rather, it was the sensation that, more than ever...
...he and the Lich King shared some inner link that went beyond Trag's undead state.
The Lich King chuckled...
IT IS THE ORB THAT BINDS US SO MUCH...THE DARK MAGIC THAT MORE THAN MERELY ANIMATES YOU CAME FROM IT...
JUST AS PART OF WHAT I AM COMES FROM WHAT WAS THE SPIRIT OF ITS CREATOR...
A name came unbidden to Trag's lips...a name that he had cursed since his resurrection...
NER'ZHUL...

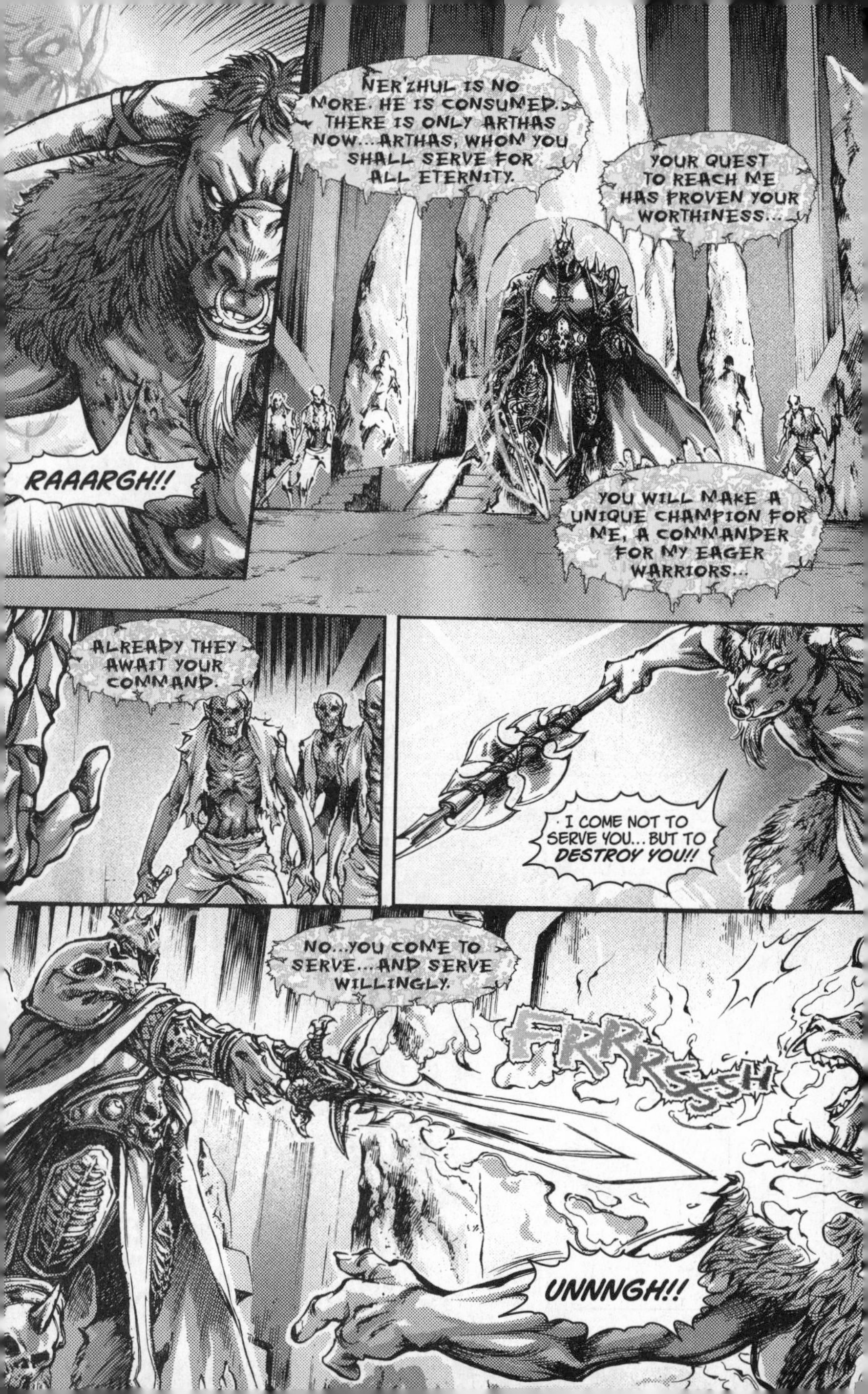
NER'ZHUL IS NO MORE. HE IS CONSUMED. THERE IS ONLY ARTHAS NOW... ARTHAS, WHOM YOU SHALL SERVE FOR ALL ETERNITY.
YOUR QUEST TO REACH ME HAS PROVEN YOUR WORTHINESS...
RAAARGH!!
YOU WILL MAKE A UNIQUE CHAMPION FOR ME, A COMMANDER FOR MY EAGER WARRIORS...
ALREADY THEY AWAIT YOUR COMMAND.
I COME NOT TO SERVE YOU... BUT TO DESTROY YOU!!
NO... YOU COME TO SERVE... AND SERVE WILLINGLY.
FRRRSSSH
UNNNGH!!

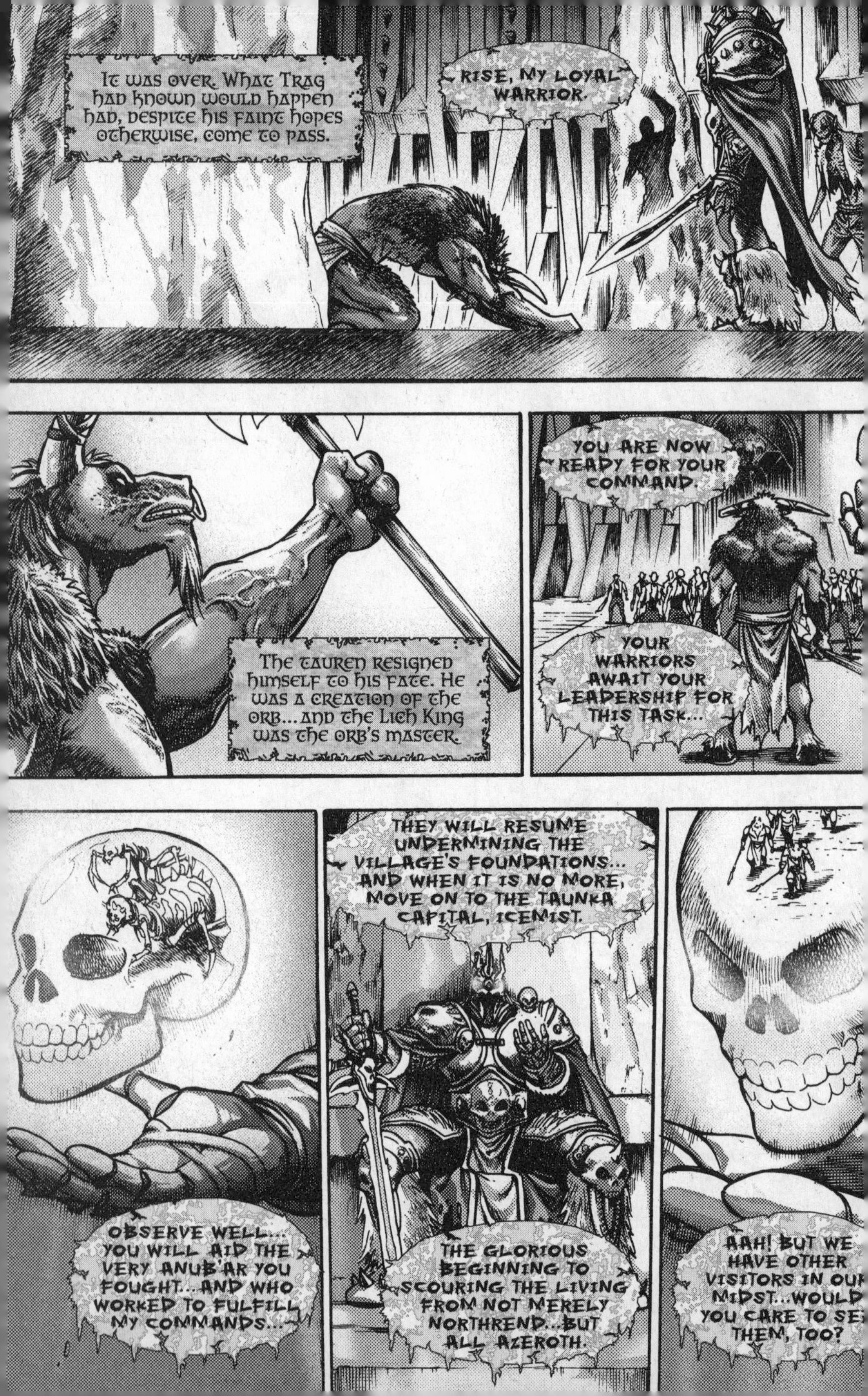
It was over. What Trag had known would happen had, despite his faint hopes otherwise, come to pass.
RISE, MY LOYAL WARRIOR.
The tauren resigned himself to his fate. He was a creation of the orb... and the Lich King was the orb's master.
YOU ARE NOW READY FOR YOUR COMMAND.
YOUR WARRIORS AWAIT YOUR LEADERSHIP FOR THIS TASK...
OBSERVE WELL... YOU WILL AID THE VERY ANUB'AR YOU FOUGHT...AND WHO WORKED TO FULFILL MY COMMANDS...
THEY WILL RESUME UNDERMINING THE VILLAGE'S FOUNDATIONS... AND WHEN IT IS NO MORE, MOVE ON TO THE TAUNKA CAPITAL, ICEMIST.
THE GLORIOUS BEGINNING TO SCOURING THE LIVING FROM NOT MERELY NORTHREND...BUT ALL AZEROTH.
AAH! BUT WE HAVE OTHER VISITORS IN OUR MIDST...WOULD YOU CARE TO SEE THEM, TOO?

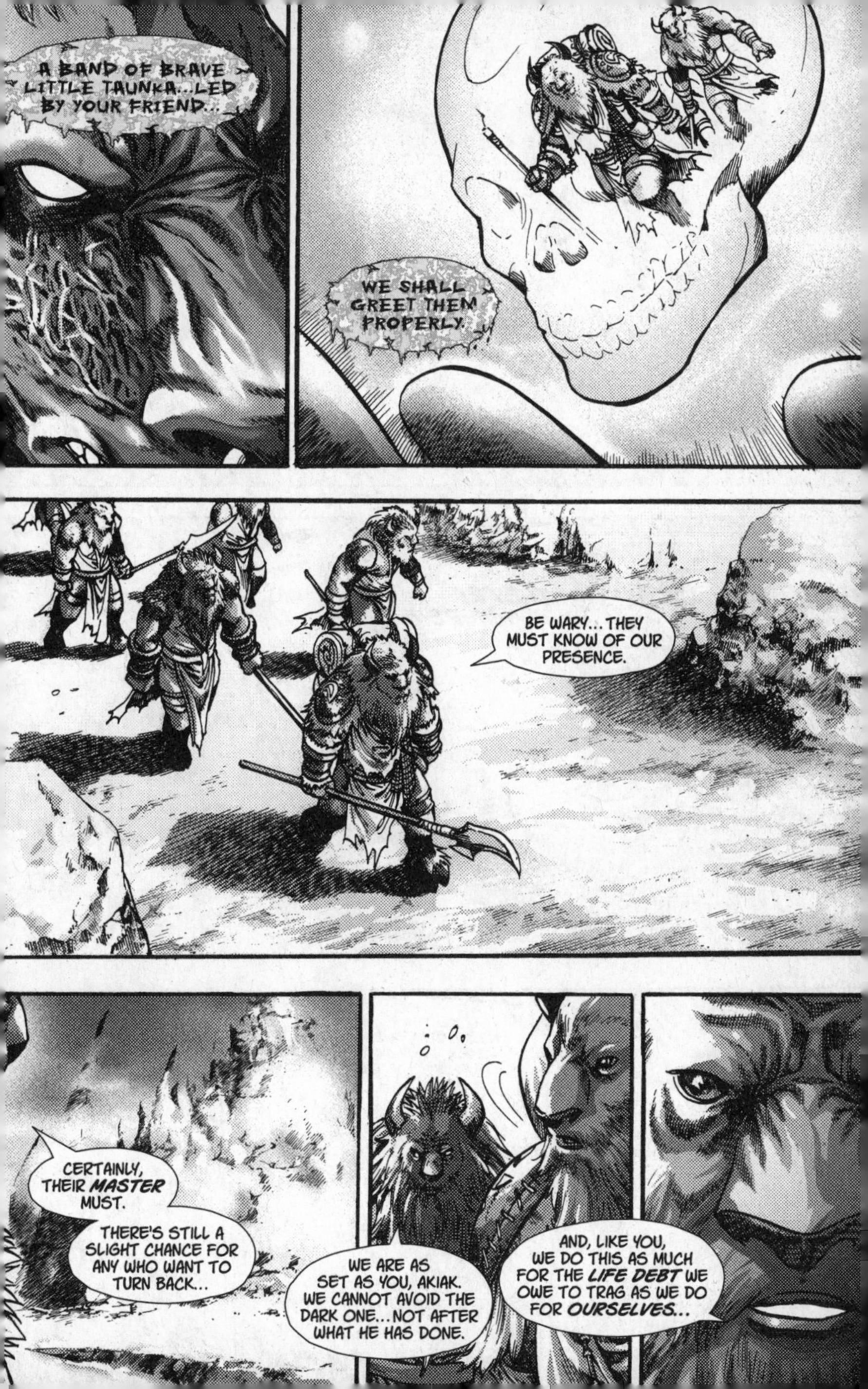
A BAND OF BRAVE LITTLE TAUNKA...LED BY YOUR FRIEND...
WE SHALL GREET THEM PROPERLY.
BE WARY... THEY MUST KNOW OF OUR PRESENCE.
CERTAINLY, THEIR *MASTER* MUST.
THERE'S STILL A SLIGHT CHANCE FOR ANY WHO WANT TO TURN BACK...
WE ARE AS SET AS YOU, AKIAK. WE CANNOT AVOID THE DARK ONE...NOT AFTER WHAT HE HAS DONE.
AND, LIKE YOU, WE DO THIS AS MUCH FOR THE *LIFE DEBT* WE OWE TO TRAG AS WE DO FOR *OURSELVES...*

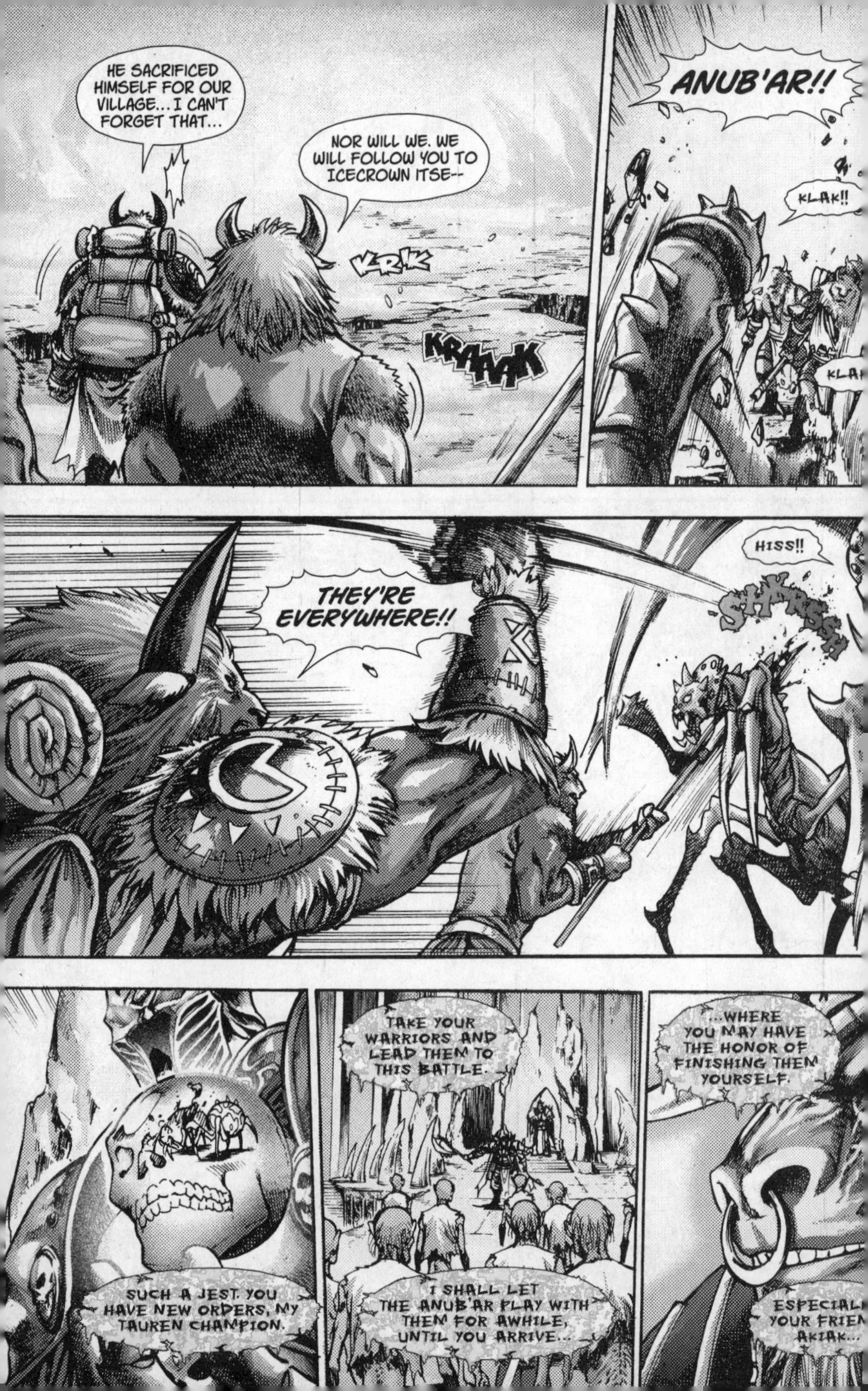
HE SACRIFICED HIMSELF FOR OUR VILLAGE... I CAN'T FORGET THAT...
NOR WILL WE. WE WILL FOLLOW YOU TO ICECROWN ITSE--
KRIK
KRAAAAK
ANUB'AR!!
KLAK!!
THEY'RE EVERYWHERE!!
HISS!!
SHKRSSH
SUCH A JEST. YOU HAVE NEW ORDERS, MY TAUREN CHAMPION.
TAKE YOUR WARRIORS AND LEAD THEM TO THIS BATTLE.
I SHALL LET THE ANUB'AR PLAY WITH THEM FOR AWHILE, UNTIL YOU ARRIVE...
...WHERE YOU MAY HAVE THE HONOR OF FINISHING THEM YOURSELF.

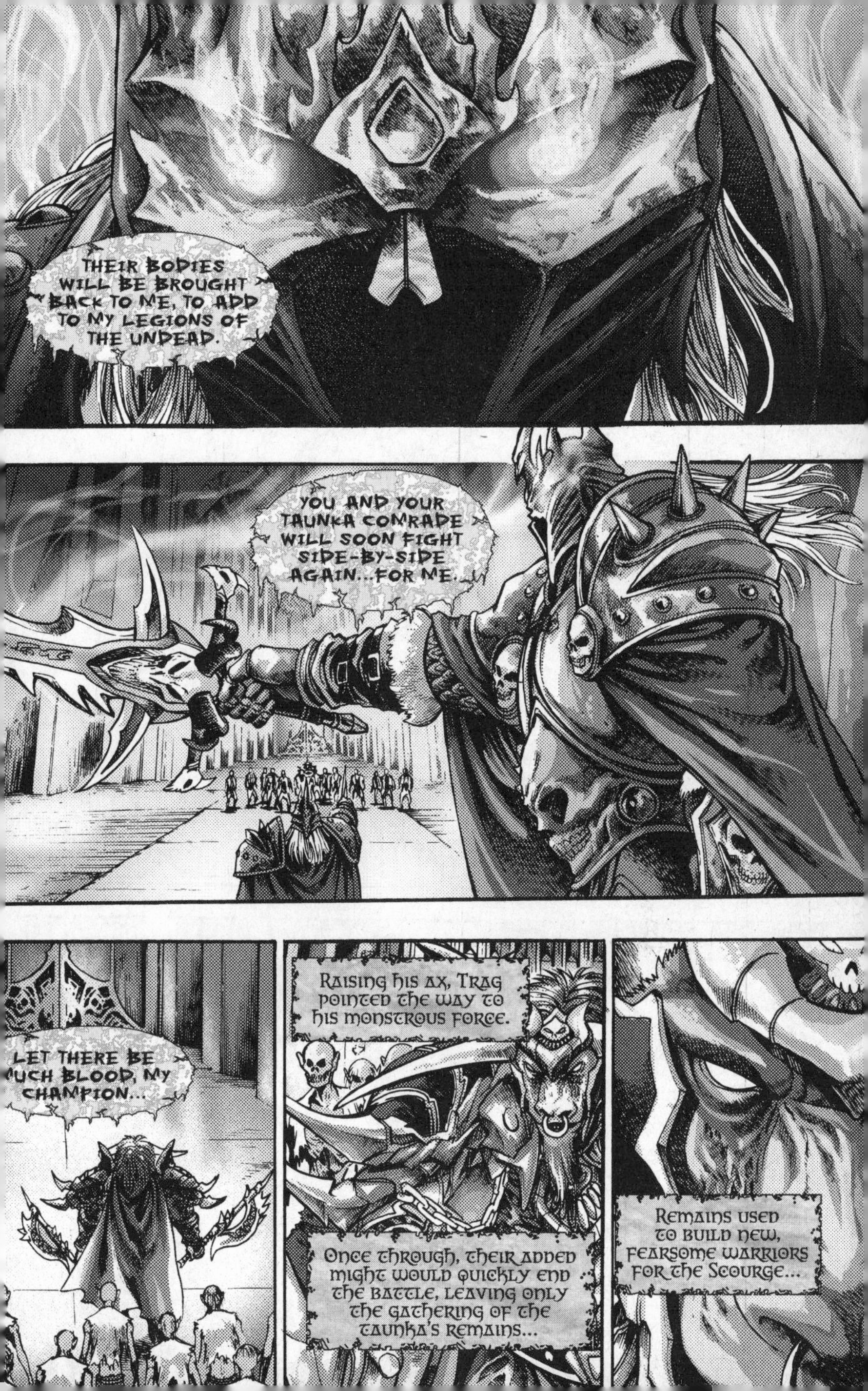
THEIR BODIES WILL BE BROUGHT BACK TO ME, TO ADD TO MY LEGIONS OF THE UNDEAD.
YOU AND YOUR TAUNKA COMRADE WILL SOON FIGHT SIDE-BY-SIDE AGAIN...FOR ME.
LET THERE BE MUCH BLOOD, MY CHAMPION...
Raising his ax, Trag pointed the way to his monstrous force.
Once through, their added might would quickly end the battle, leaving only the gathering of the taunka's remains...
Remains used to build new, fearsome warriors for the Scourge...

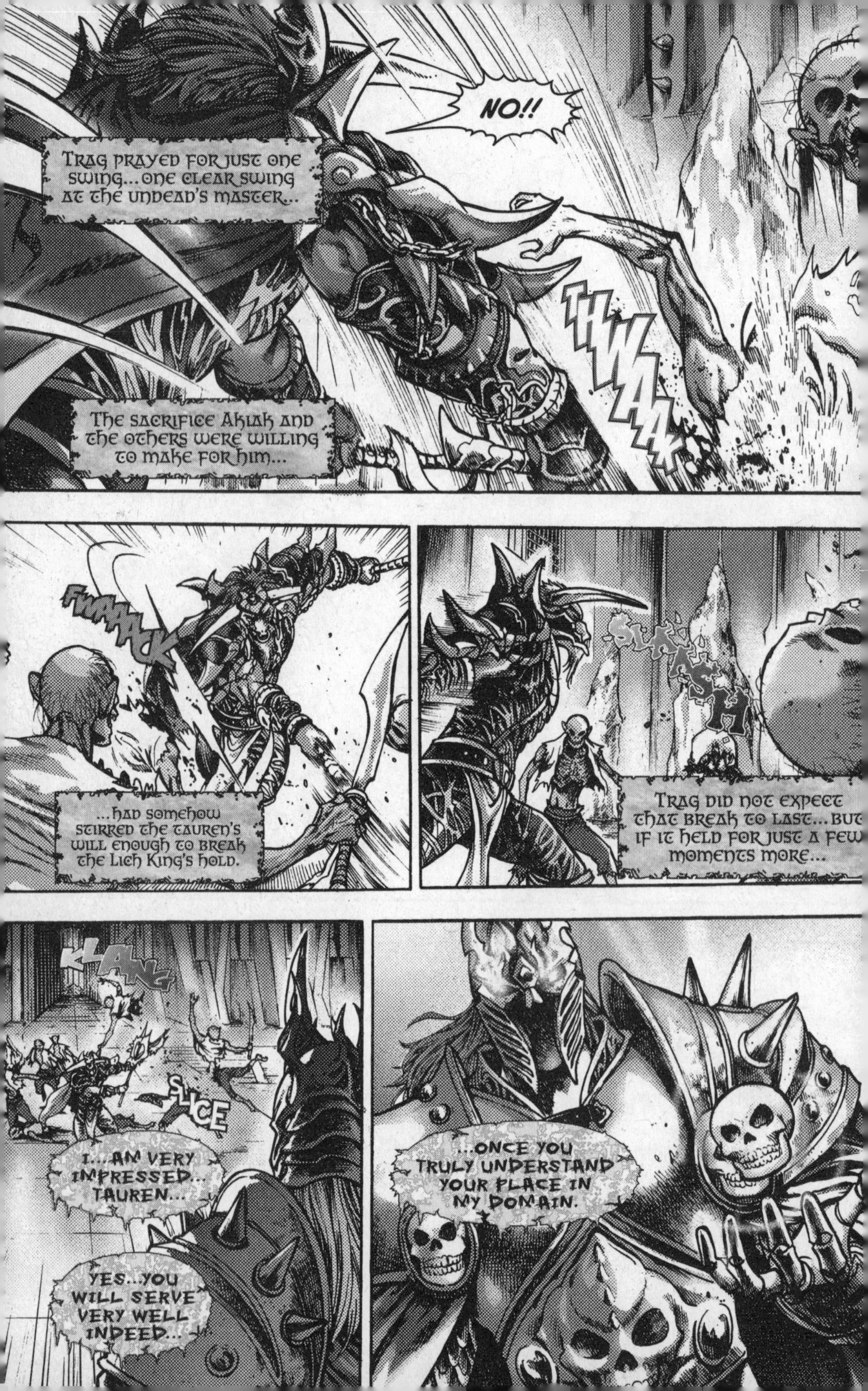
NO!!
Trag prayed for just one swing...one clear swing at the undead's master...
THWAAAK
The sacrifice Akiak and the others were willing to make for him...
FWAAACK
...had somehow stirred the tauren's will enough to break the Lich King's hold.
SLAAASH
Trag did not expect that break to last...but if it held for just a few moments more...
KLANG
SLICE
I...AM VERY IMPRESSED...TAUREN...
YES...YOU WILL SERVE VERY WELL INDEED...
...ONCE YOU TRULY UNDERSTAND YOUR PLACE IN MY DOMAIN.

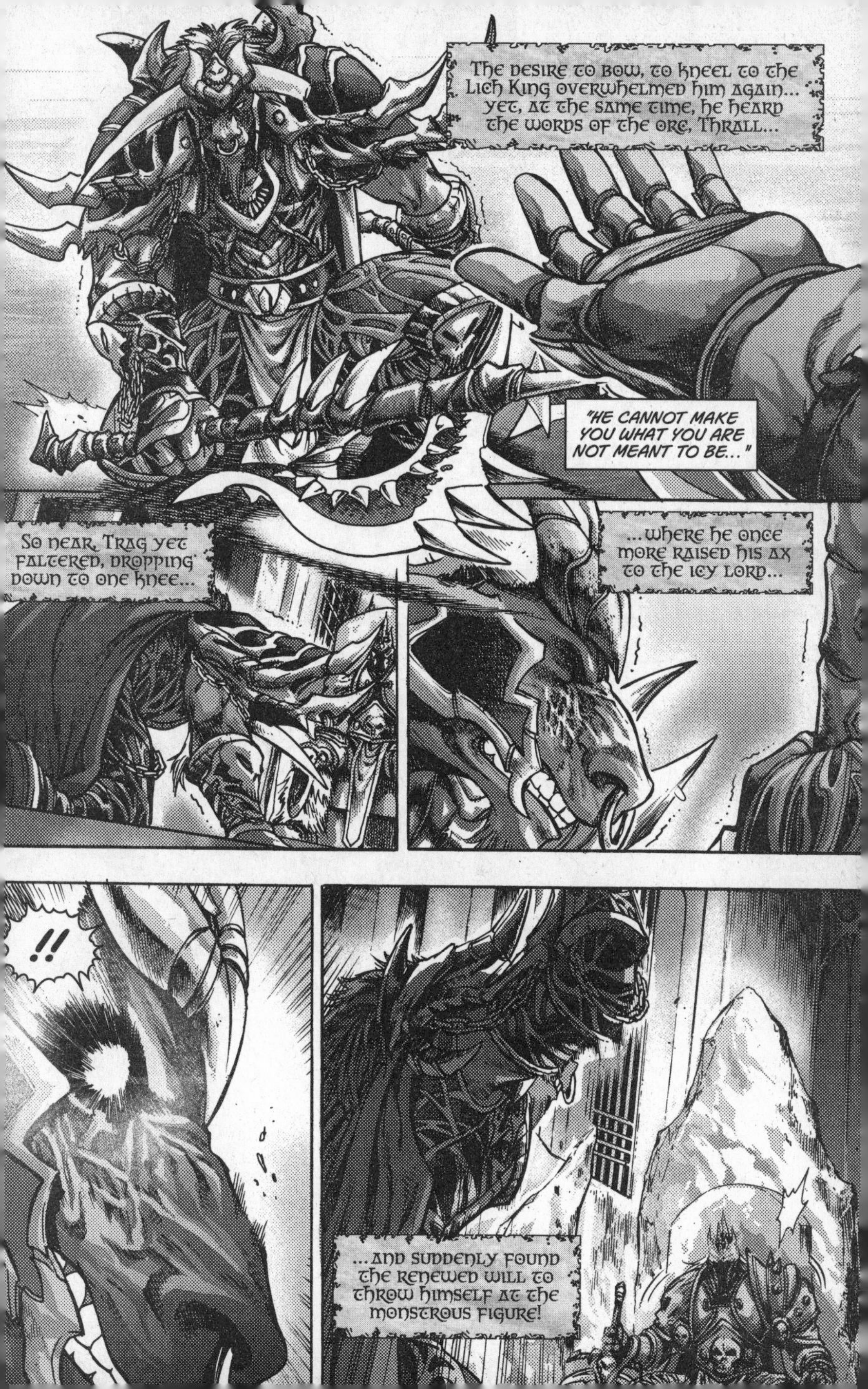
The desire to bow, to kneel to the Lich King overwhelmed him again... yet, at the same time, he heard the words of the orc, Thrall...
"HE CANNOT MAKE YOU WHAT YOU ARE NOT MEANT TO BE..."
So near, Trag yet faltered, dropping down to one knee...
...where he once more raised his ax to the icy lord...
!!
...and suddenly found the renewed will to throw himself at the monstrous figure!

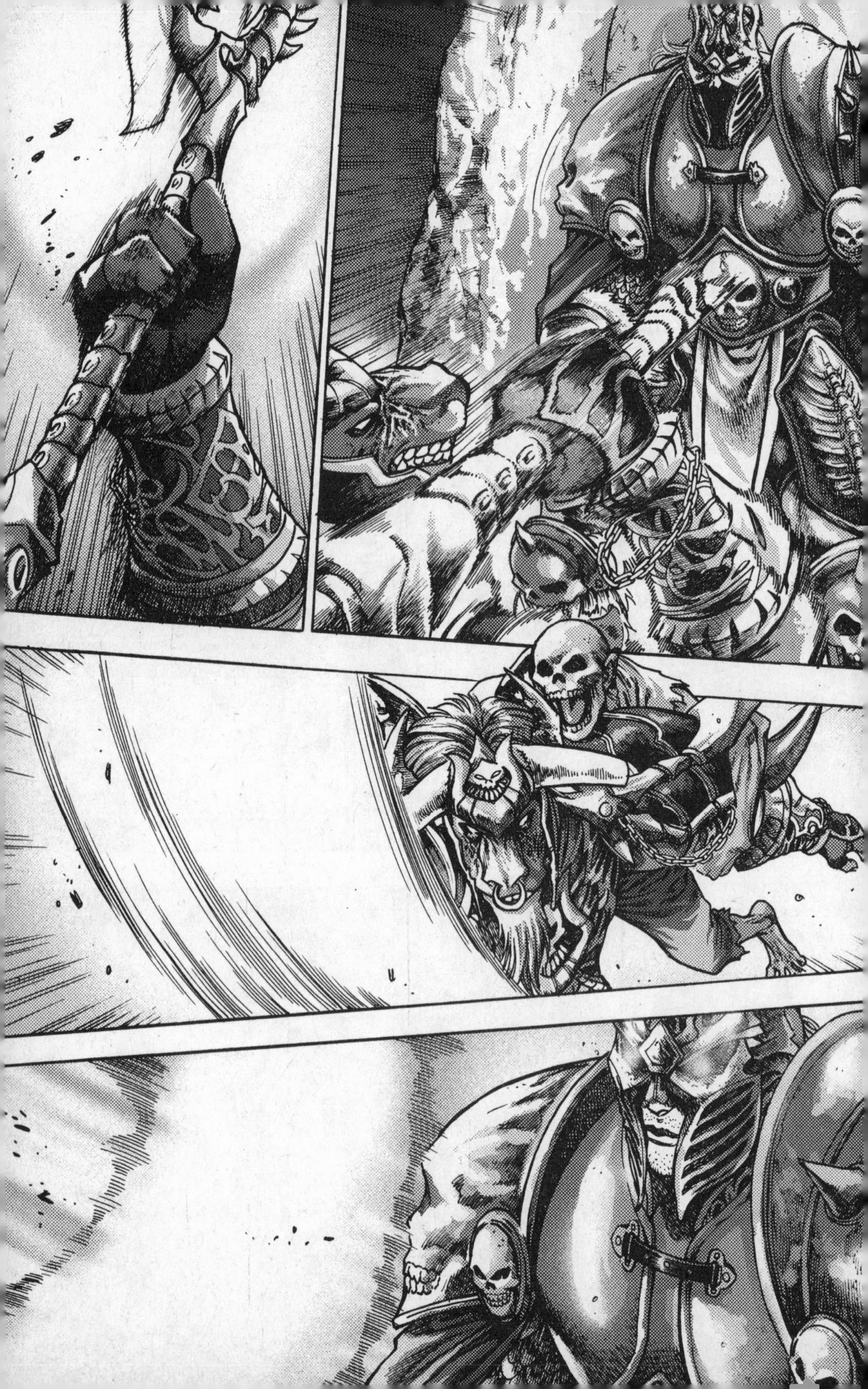

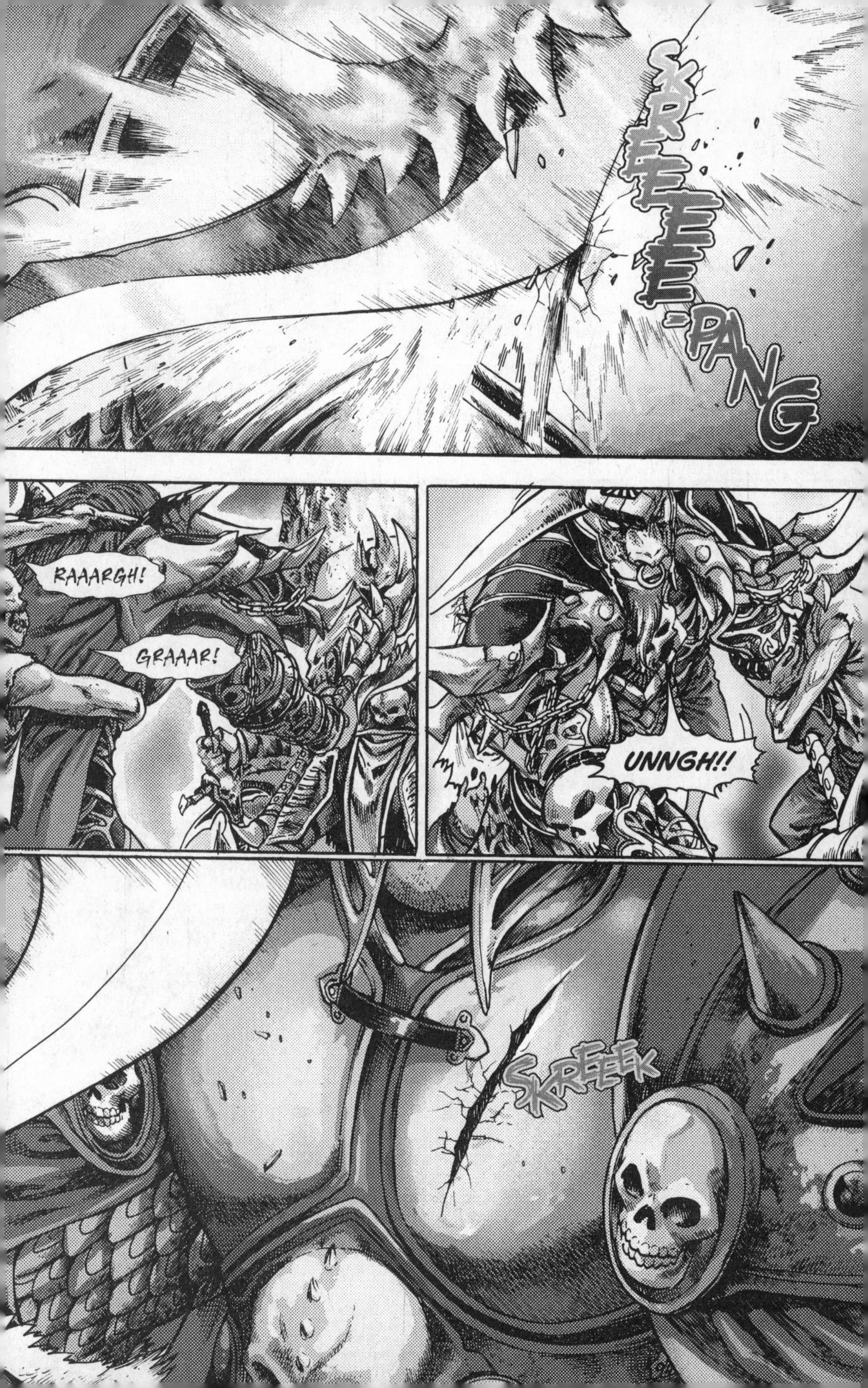
SKREEEEE-PANG
RAAARGH!
GRAAAR!
UNNGH!!
SKREEEK

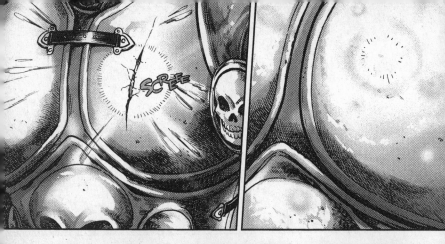

SCREEE
YOU...HAVE DARED...STRIKE ME...
BUT TRAG WAS DISTRACTED FROM THE LICH KING'S IRE AS SOMETHING JABBED AGAINST HIS SIDE...
THE BONE FRAGMENT FROM GALAKROND...

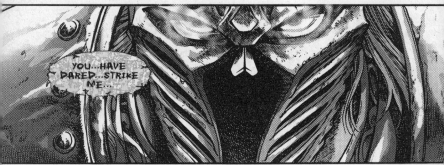

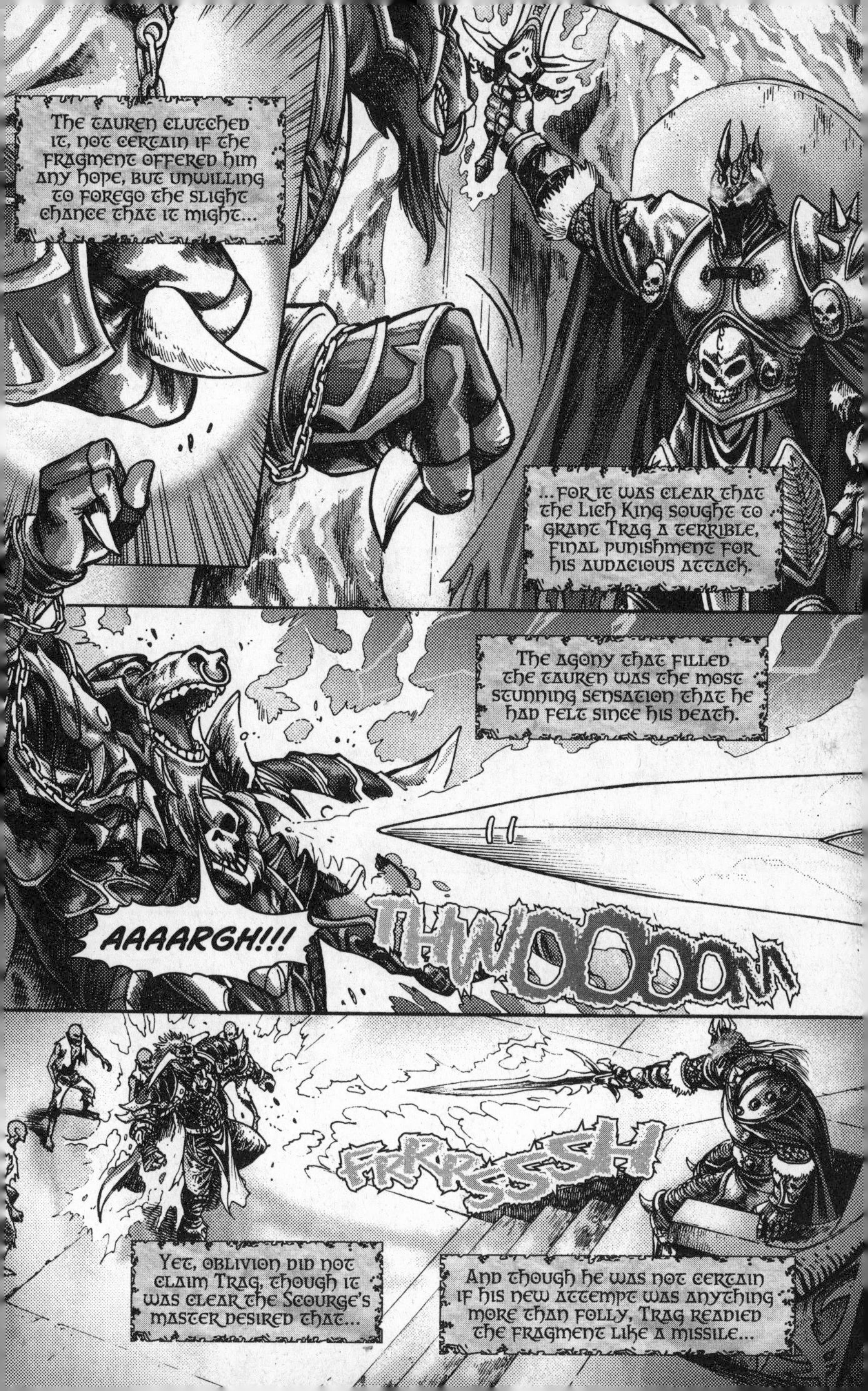
The tauren clutched it, not certain if the fragment offered him any hope, but unwilling to forego the slight chance that it might...
...for it was clear that the Lich King sought to grant Trag a terrible, final punishment for his audacious attack.
The agony that filled the tauren was the most stunning sensation that he had felt since his death.
AAAARGH!!!
THWOOOOM
FRRRSSSH
Yet, oblivion did not claim Trag, though it was clear the Scourge's master desired that...
And though he was not certain if his new attempt was anything more than folly, Trag readied the fragment like a missile...

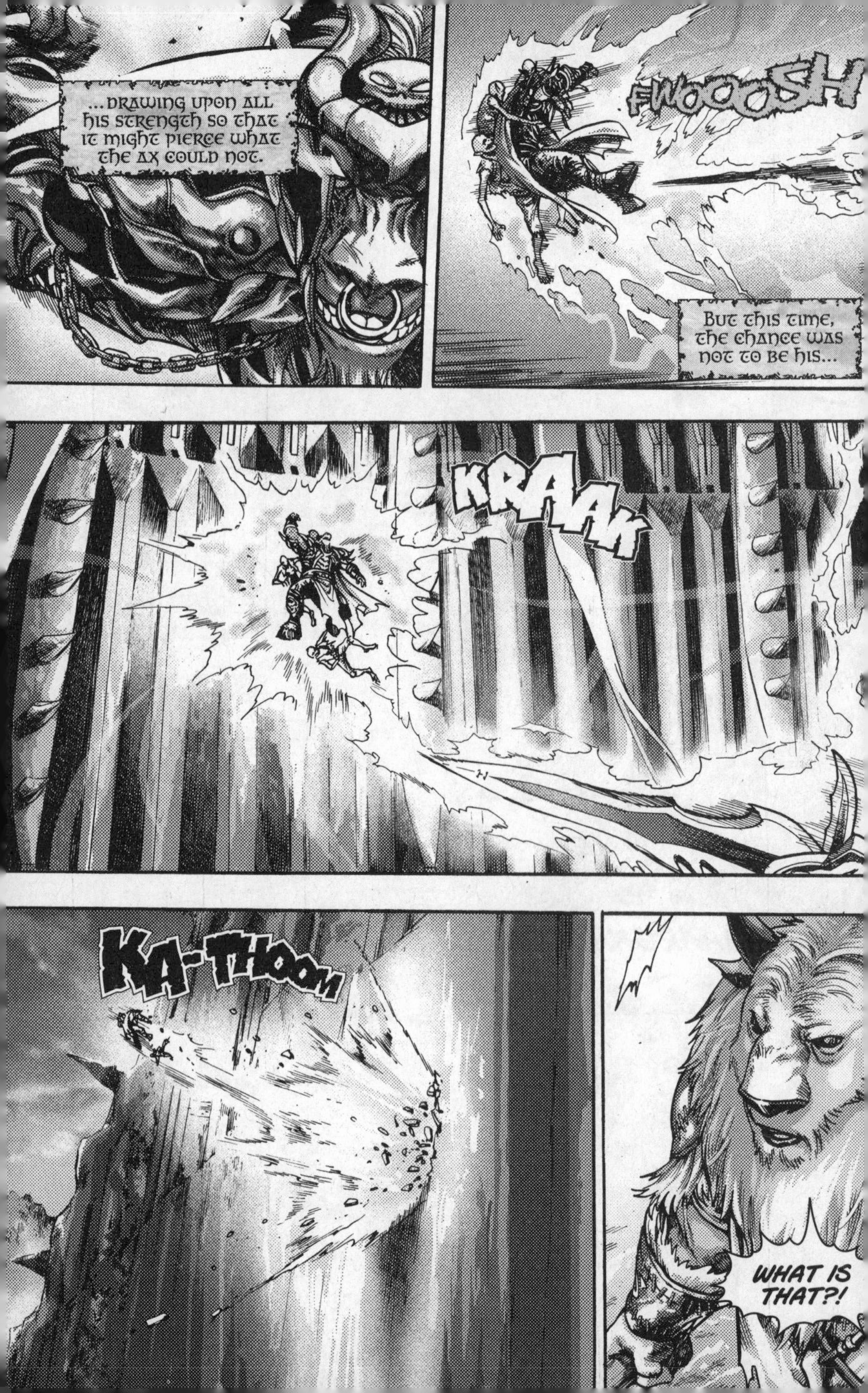
...DRAWING UPON ALL HIS STRENGTH SO THAT IT MIGHT PIERCE WHAT THE AX COULD NOT.
FWOOOSH
BUT THIS TIME, THE CHANCE WAS NOT TO BE HIS...
KRAAK
KA-THOOM
WHAT IS THAT?!

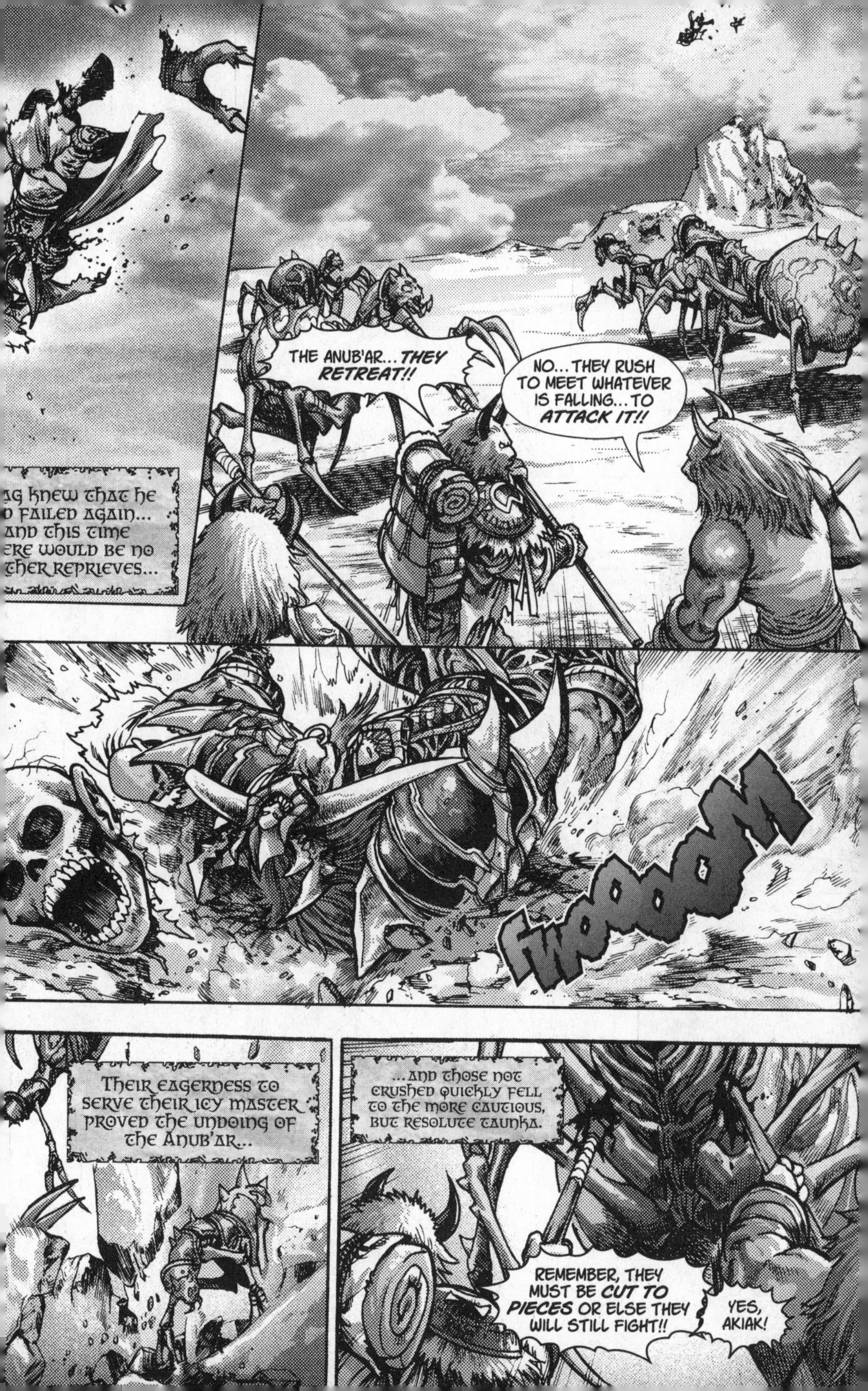
ag knew that he o failed again... and this time ere would be no ther reprieves...
THE ANUB'AR... *THEY RETREAT!!*
NO... THEY RUSH TO MEET WHATEVER IS FALLING... TO *ATTACK IT!!*
FWOOOOOM
Their eagerness to serve their icy master proved the undoing of the Anub'ar...
...and those not crushed quickly fell to the more cautious, but resolute taunka.
REMEMBER, THEY MUST BE *CUT TO PIECES* OR ELSE THEY WILL STILL FIGHT!!
YES, AKIAK!

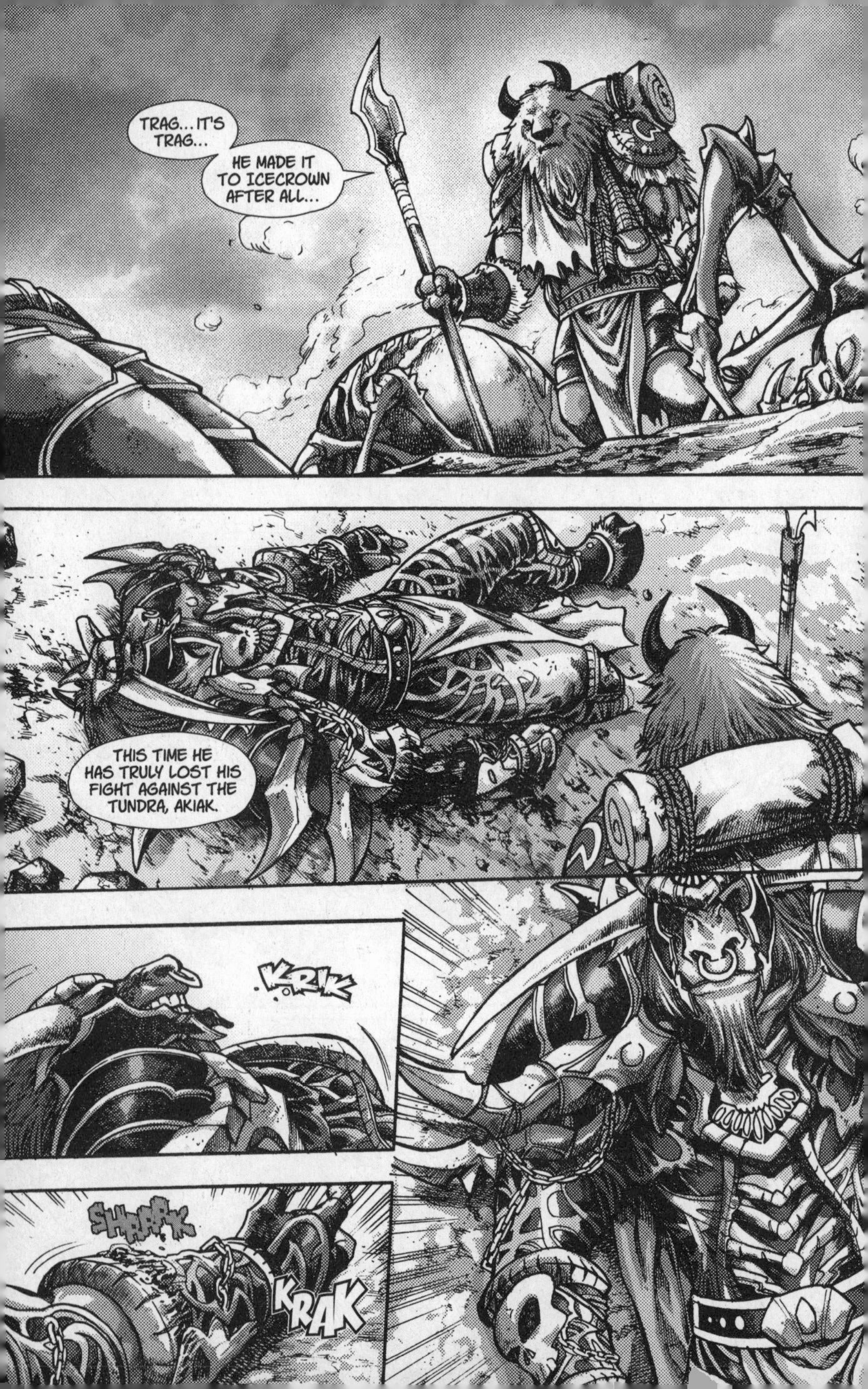
TRAG... IT'S TRAG...
HE MADE IT TO ICECROWN AFTER ALL...
THIS TIME HE HAS TRULY LOST HIS FIGHT AGAINST THE TUNDRA, AKIAK.
KRIK
SHRRRK
KRAK

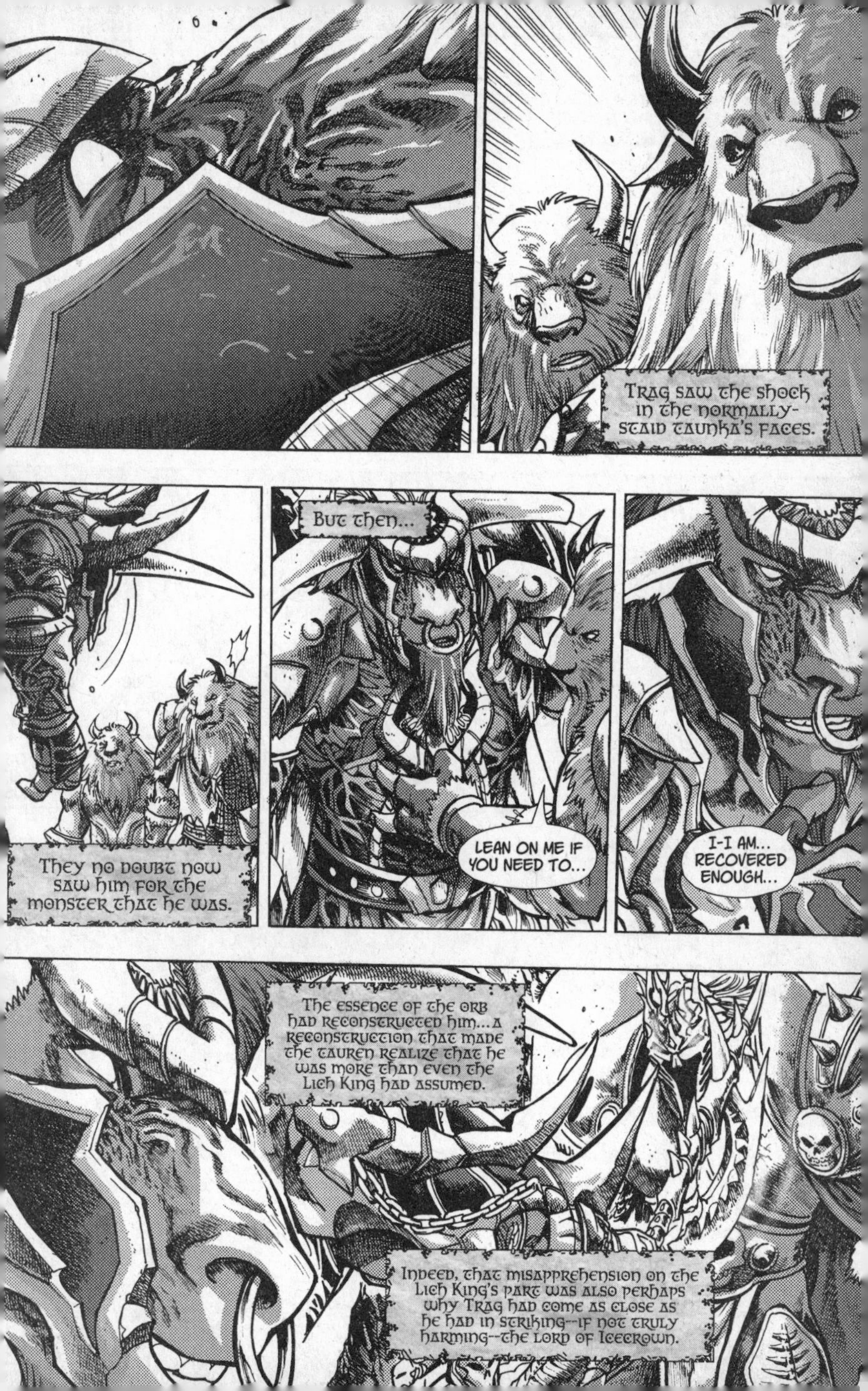

Trag saw the shock in the normally-staid taunka's faces.
They no doubt now saw him for the monster that he was.
But then...
LEAN ON ME IF YOU NEED TO...
I-I AM... RECOVERED ENOUGH...
The essence of the orb had reconstructed him... a reconstruction that made the tauren realize that he was more than even the Lich King had assumed.
Indeed, that misapprehension on the Lich King's part was also perhaps why Trag had come as close as he had in striking--if not truly harming--the Lord of Icecrown.

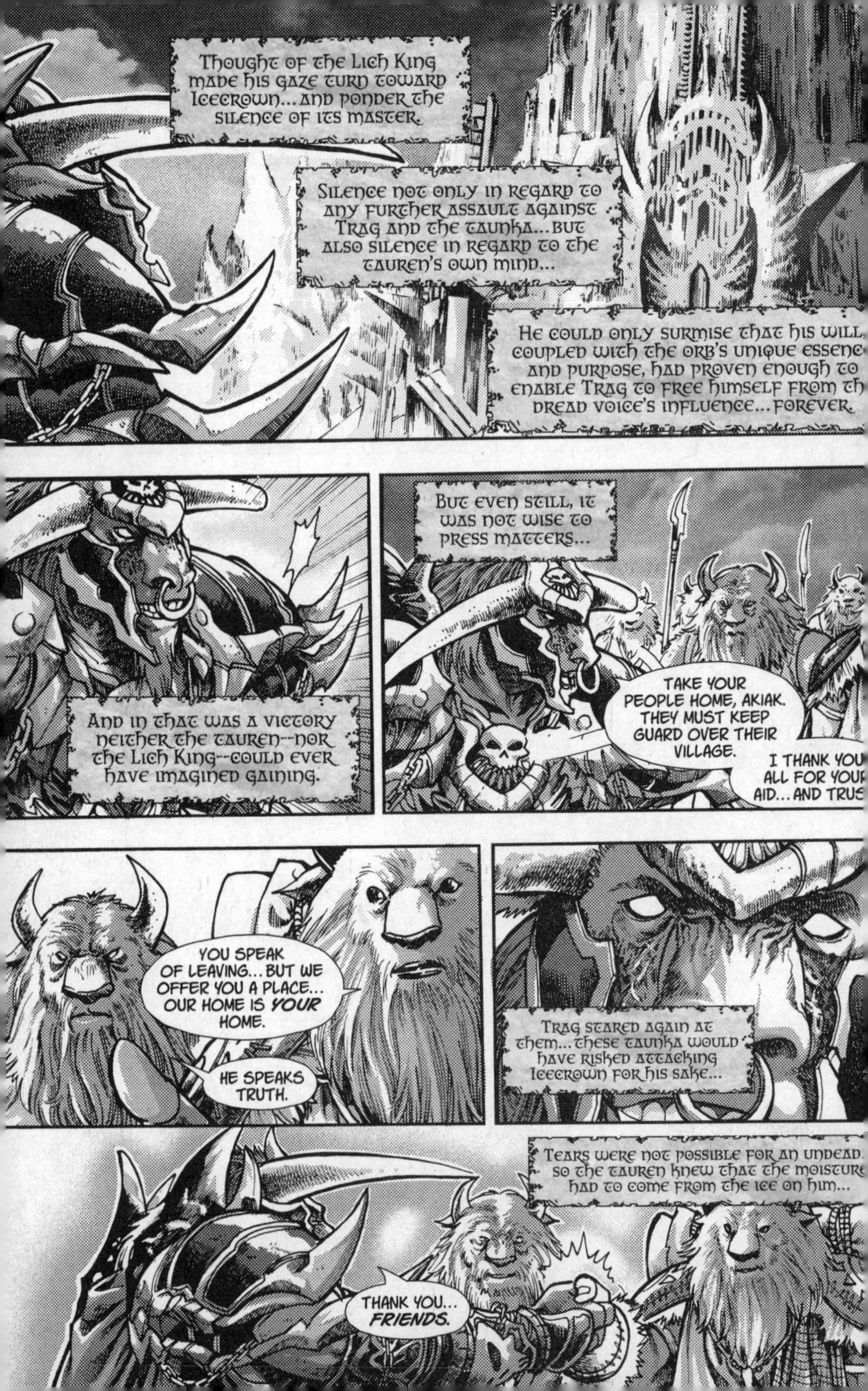
Thought of the Lich King made his gaze turn toward Icecrown... and ponder the silence of its master.
Silence not only in regard to any further assault against Trag and the taunka... but also silence in regard to the tauren's own mind...
He could only surmise that his will, coupled with the orb's unique essenc and purpose, had proven enough to enable Trag to free himself from th dread voice's influence... forever.
And in that was a victory neither the tauren--nor the Lich King--could ever have imagined gaining.
But even still, it was not wise to press matters...
TAKE YOUR PEOPLE HOME, AKIAK. THEY MUST KEEP GUARD OVER THEIR VILLAGE.
I THANK YOU ALL FOR YOUR AID... AND TRUS
YOU SPEAK OF LEAVING... BUT WE OFFER YOU A PLACE... OUR HOME IS *YOUR* HOME.
HE SPEAKS TRUTH.
Trag stared again at them... these taunka would have risked attacking Icecrown for his sake...
Tears were not possible for an undead, so the tauren knew that the moisture had to come from the ice on him...
THANK YOU... *FRIENDS.*

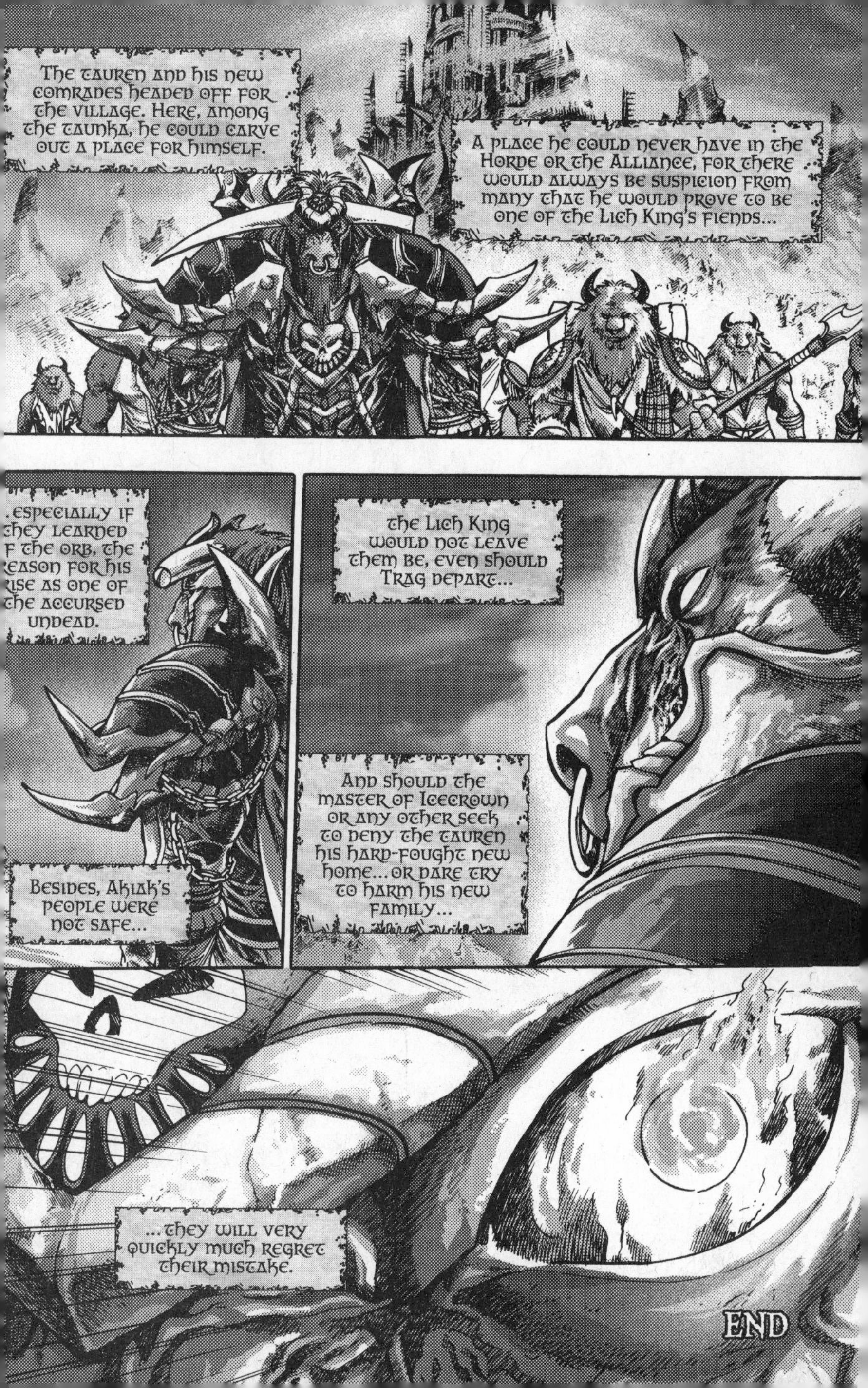
The tauren and his new comrades headed off for the village. Here, among the taunka, he could carve out a place for himself.
A place he could never have in the Horde or the Alliance, for there would always be suspicion from many that he would prove to be one of the Lich King's fiends...
. especially if hey learned f the orb, the eason for his ise as one of the accursed undead.
Besides, Akiak's people were not safe...
The Lich King would not leave them be, even should Trag depart...
And should the master of Icecrown or any other seek to deny the tauren his hard-fought new home... or dare try to harm his new family...
...they will very quickly much regret their mistake.
END

WARCRAFT
LEGENDS
VOLUME FOUR

BLOODSAIL
BUCCANEER

WRITTEN BY DAN JOLLEY

PENCILS BY FERNANDO HEINZ FURUKAWA
INKS BY GABRIEL LUQUE
TONES BY ARIEL IACCI, GONZALO DUARTE
& WALLY GOMEZ

Letterer: Michael Paolilli

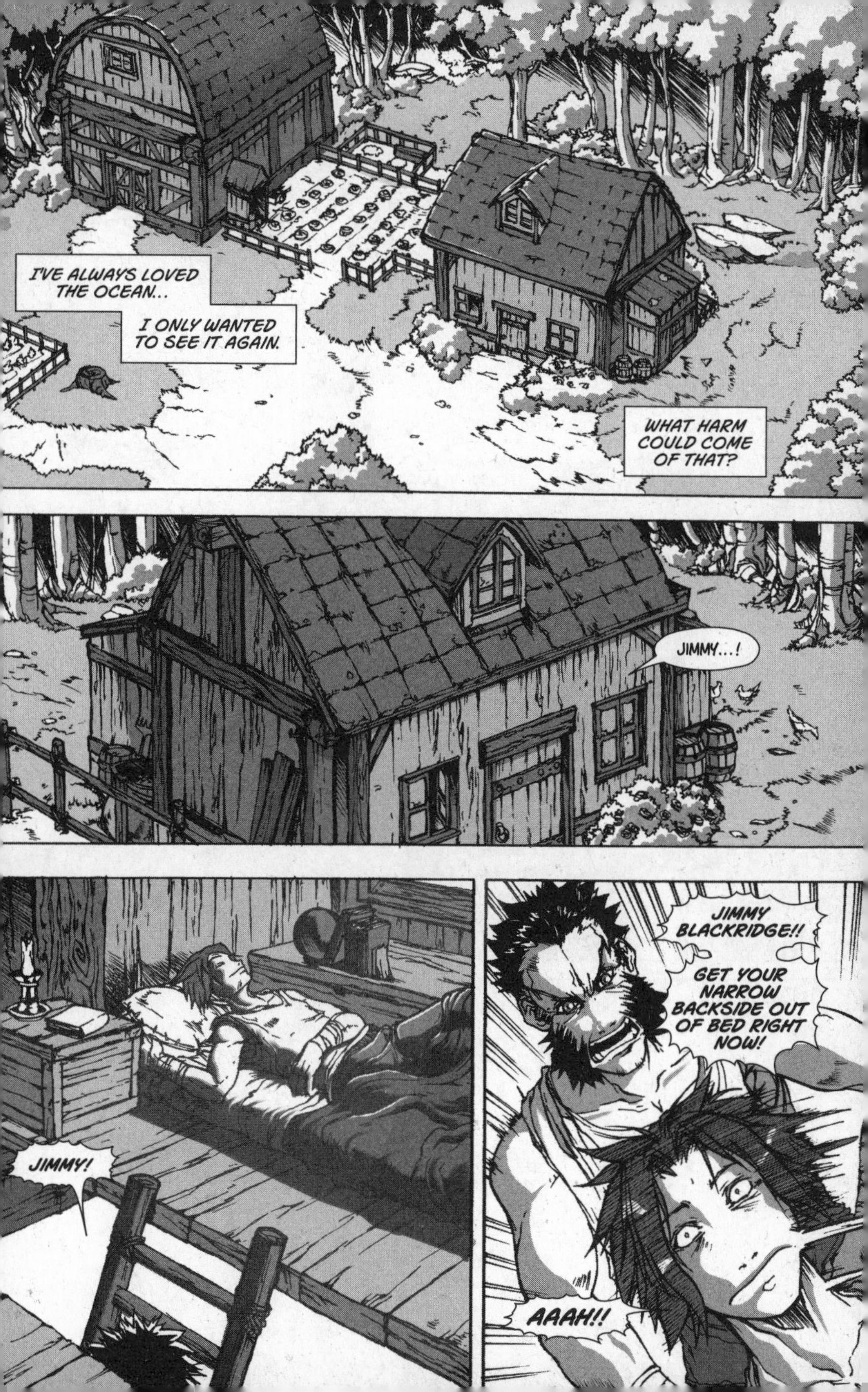
I'VE ALWAYS LOVED THE OCEAN...
I ONLY WANTED TO SEE IT AGAIN.
WHAT HARM COULD COME OF THAT?
JIMMY...!
JIMMY!
JIMMY BLACKRIDGE!!
GET YOUR NARROW BACKSIDE OUT OF BED RIGHT NOW!
AAAH!!

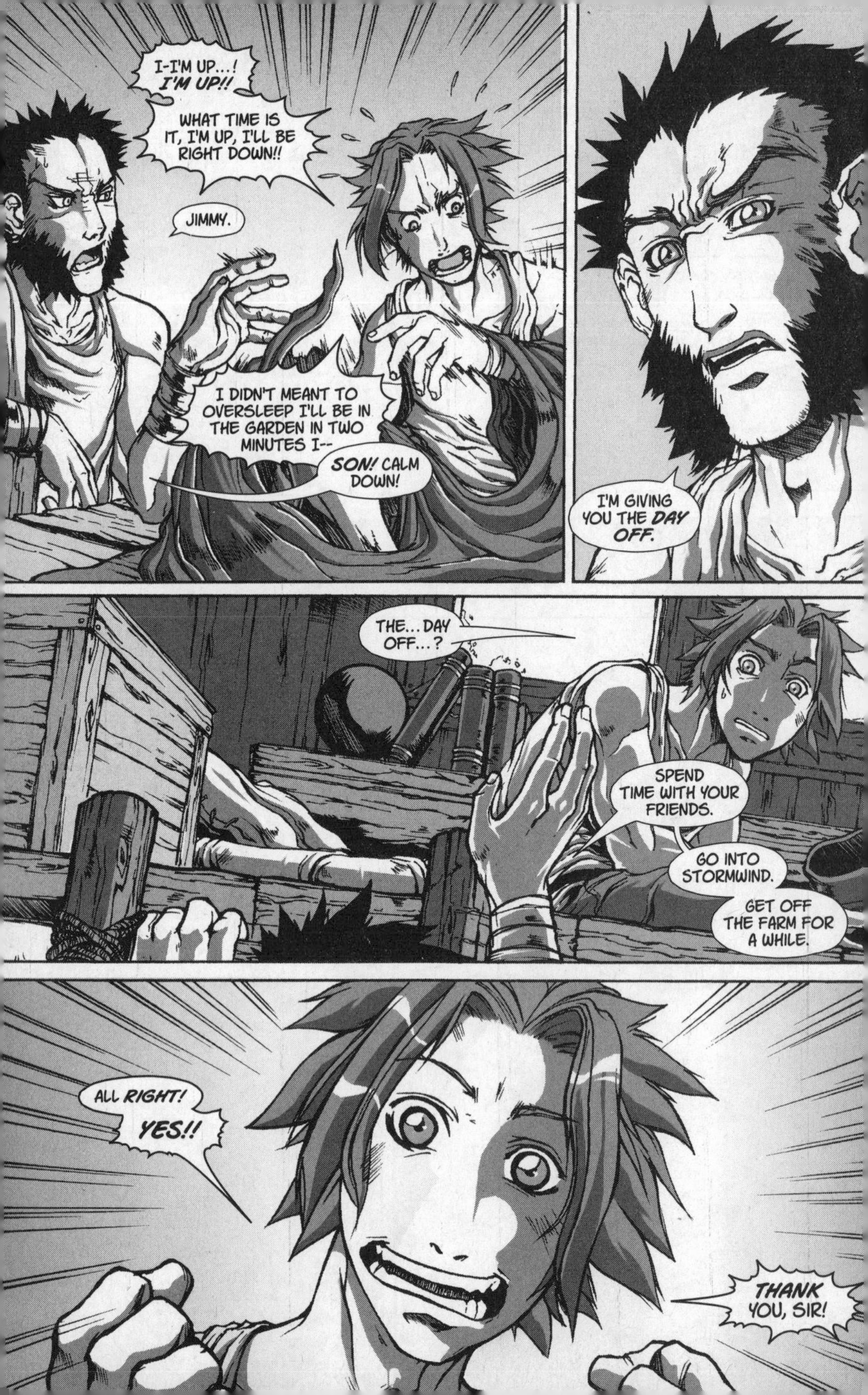
I-I'M UP...! *I'M UP!!*
WHAT TIME IS IT, I'M UP, I'LL BE RIGHT DOWN!!
JIMMY.
I DIDN'T MEANT TO OVERSLEEP I'LL BE IN THE GARDEN IN TWO MINUTES I--
SON! CALM DOWN!
I'M GIVING YOU THE *DAY OFF.*
THE... DAY OFF...?
SPEND TIME WITH YOUR FRIENDS.
GO INTO STORMWIND.
GET OFF THE FARM FOR A WHILE.
ALL *RIGHT!*
YES!!
THANK YOU, SIR!

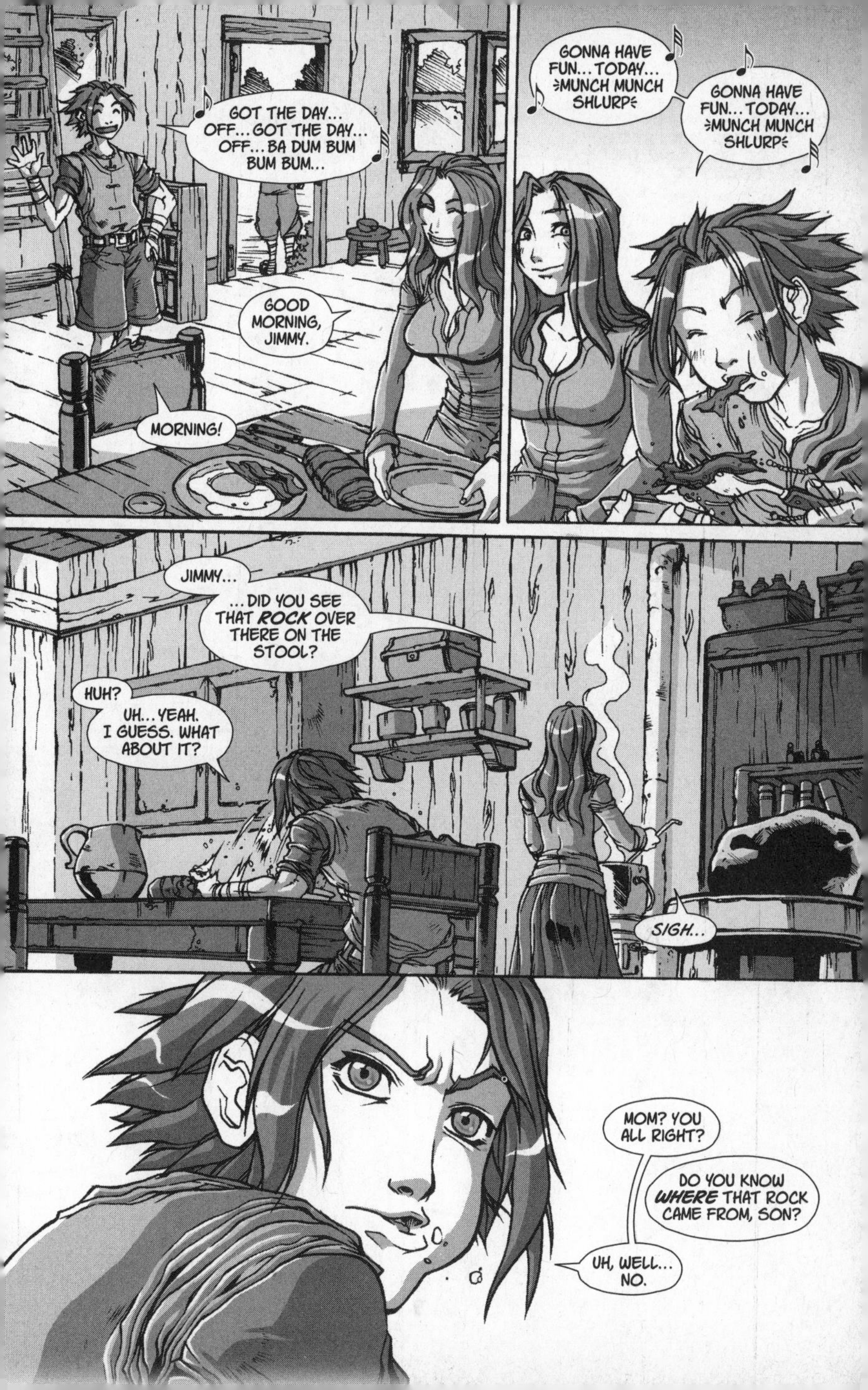
GOT THE DAY... OFF... GOT THE DAY... OFF... BA DUM BUM BUM BUM...
GOOD MORNING, JIMMY.
MORNING!
GONNA HAVE FUN... TODAY... MUNCH MUNCH SHLURP
GONNA HAVE FUN... TODAY... MUNCH MUNCH SHLURP
JIMMY...
...DID YOU SEE THAT ROCK OVER THERE ON THE STOOL?
HUH?
UH... YEAH. I GUESS. WHAT ABOUT IT?
SIGH...
MOM? YOU ALL RIGHT?
DO YOU KNOW WHERE THAT ROCK CAME FROM, SON?
UH, WELL... NO.

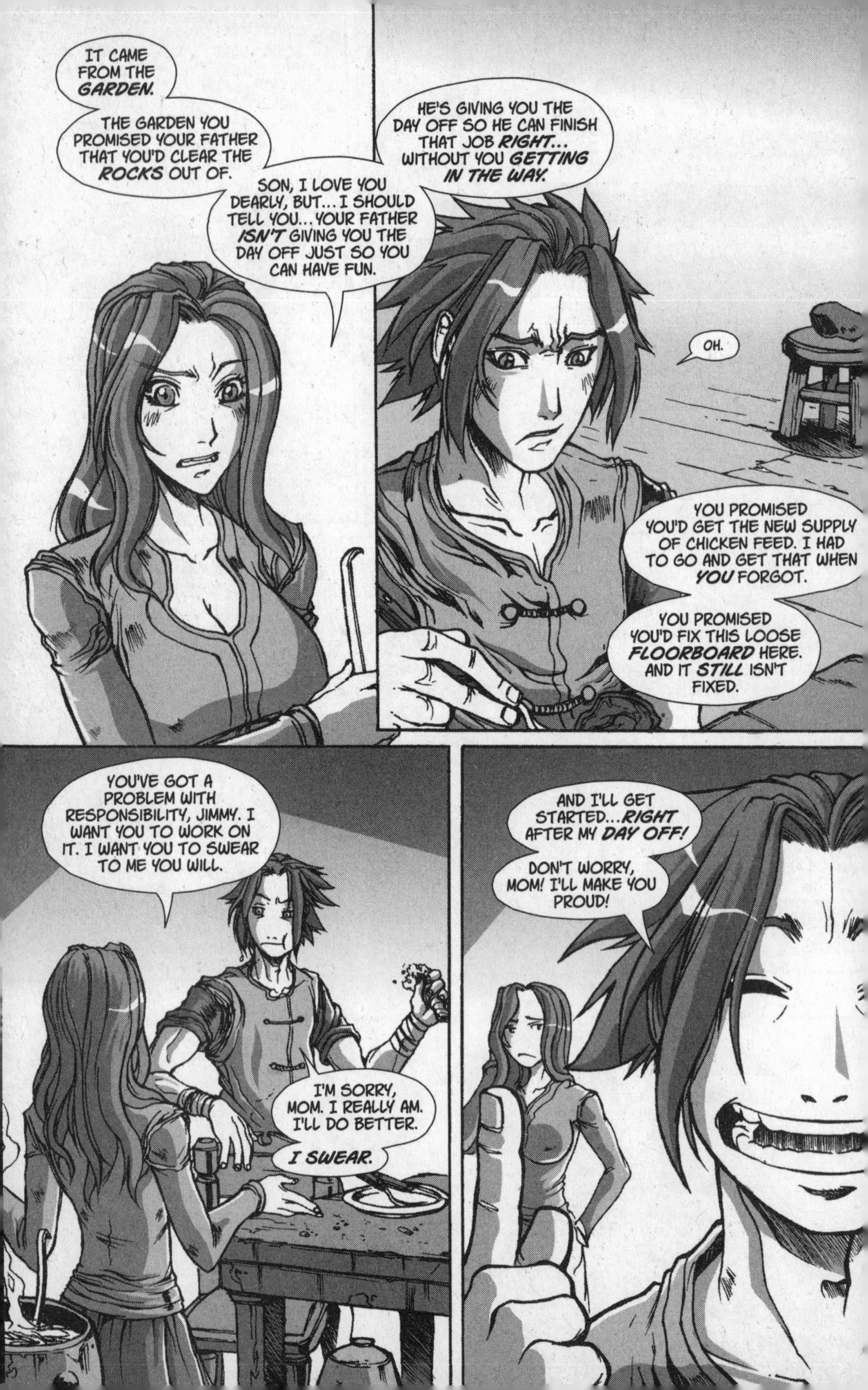
IT CAME FROM THE GARDEN.
THE GARDEN YOU PROMISED YOUR FATHER THAT YOU'D CLEAR THE ROCKS OUT OF.
SON, I LOVE YOU DEARLY, BUT... I SHOULD TELL YOU... YOUR FATHER ISN'T GIVING YOU THE DAY OFF JUST SO YOU CAN HAVE FUN.
HE'S GIVING YOU THE DAY OFF SO HE CAN FINISH THAT JOB RIGHT... WITHOUT YOU GETTING IN THE WAY.
OH.
YOU PROMISED YOU'D GET THE NEW SUPPLY OF CHICKEN FEED. I HAD TO GO AND GET THAT WHEN YOU FORGOT.
YOU PROMISED YOU'D FIX THIS LOOSE FLOORBOARD HERE. AND IT STILL ISN'T FIXED.
YOU'VE GOT A PROBLEM WITH RESPONSIBILITY, JIMMY. I WANT YOU TO WORK ON IT. I WANT YOU TO SWEAR TO ME YOU WILL.
I'M SORRY, MOM. I REALLY AM. I'LL DO BETTER.
I SWEAR.
AND I'LL GET STARTED... RIGHT AFTER MY DAY OFF!
DON'T WORRY, MOM! I'LL MAKE YOU PROUD!

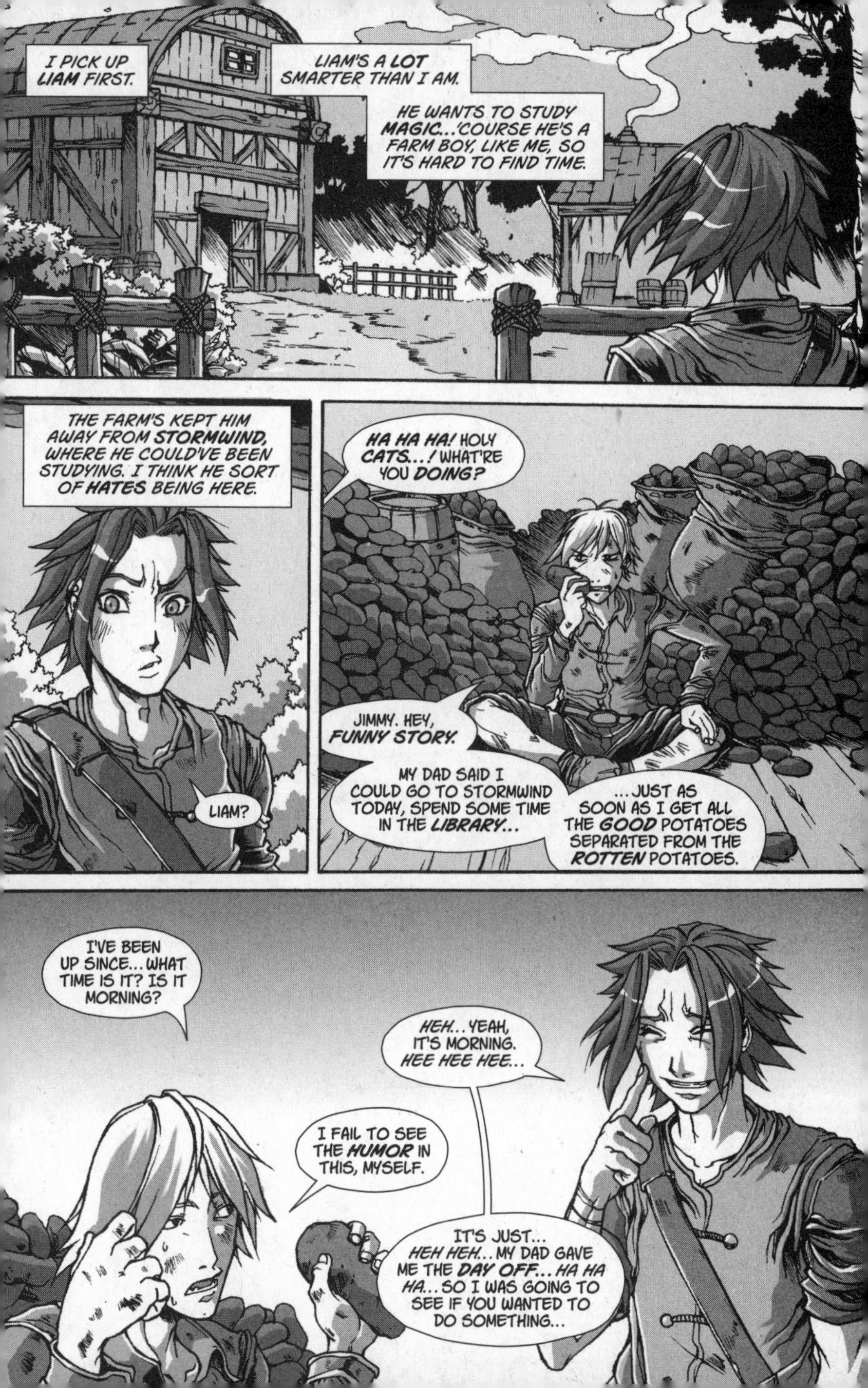
I PICK UP LIAM FIRST.
LIAM'S A LOT SMARTER THAN I AM.
HE WANTS TO STUDY MAGIC...'COURSE HE'S A FARM BOY, LIKE ME, SO IT'S HARD TO FIND TIME.
THE FARM'S KEPT HIM AWAY FROM STORMWIND, WHERE HE COULD'VE BEEN STUDYING. I THINK HE SORT OF HATES BEING HERE.
LIAM?
HA HA HA! HOLY CATS...! WHAT'RE YOU DOING?
JIMMY. HEY, FUNNY STORY.
MY DAD SAID I COULD GO TO STORMWIND TODAY, SPEND SOME TIME IN THE LIBRARY...
...JUST AS SOON AS I GET ALL THE GOOD POTATOES SEPARATED FROM THE ROTTEN POTATOES.
I'VE BEEN UP SINCE... WHAT TIME IS IT? IS IT MORNING?
HEH... YEAH, IT'S MORNING. HEE HEE HEE...
I FAIL TO SEE THE HUMOR IN THIS, MYSELF.
IT'S JUST... HEH HEH... MY DAD GAVE ME THE DAY OFF... HA HA HA... SO I WAS GOING TO SEE IF YOU WANTED TO DO SOMETHING...

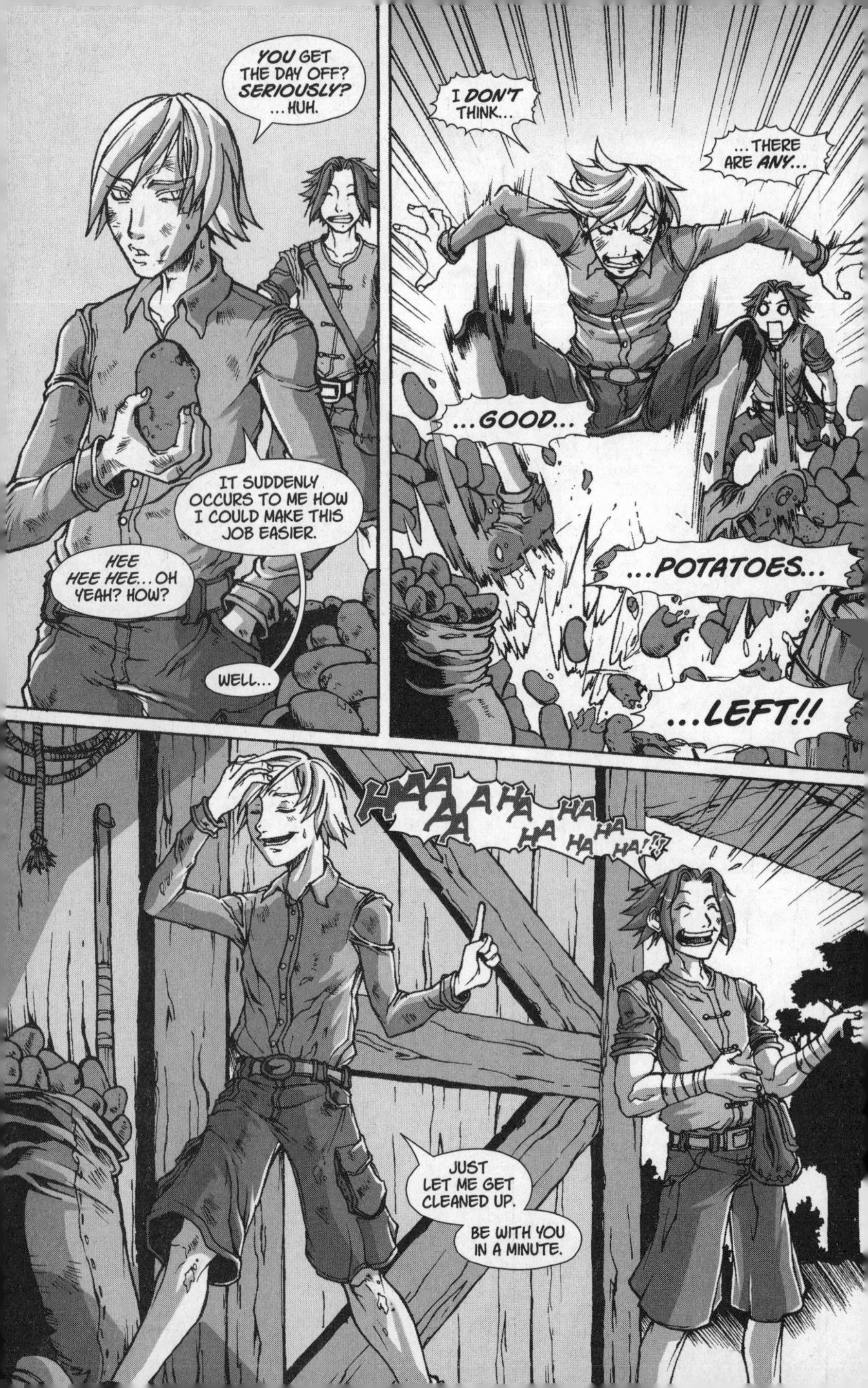
YOU GET THE DAY OFF? SERIOUSLY? ...HUH.
IT SUDDENLY OCCURS TO ME HOW I COULD MAKE THIS JOB EASIER.
HEE HEE HEE... OH YEAH? HOW?
WELL...
I DON'T THINK...
...THERE ARE ANY...
...GOOD...
...POTATOES...
...LEFT!!
HAAAAA HA HA HA HA HA HA!!!
JUST LET ME GET CLEANED UP.
BE WITH YOU IN A MINUTE.

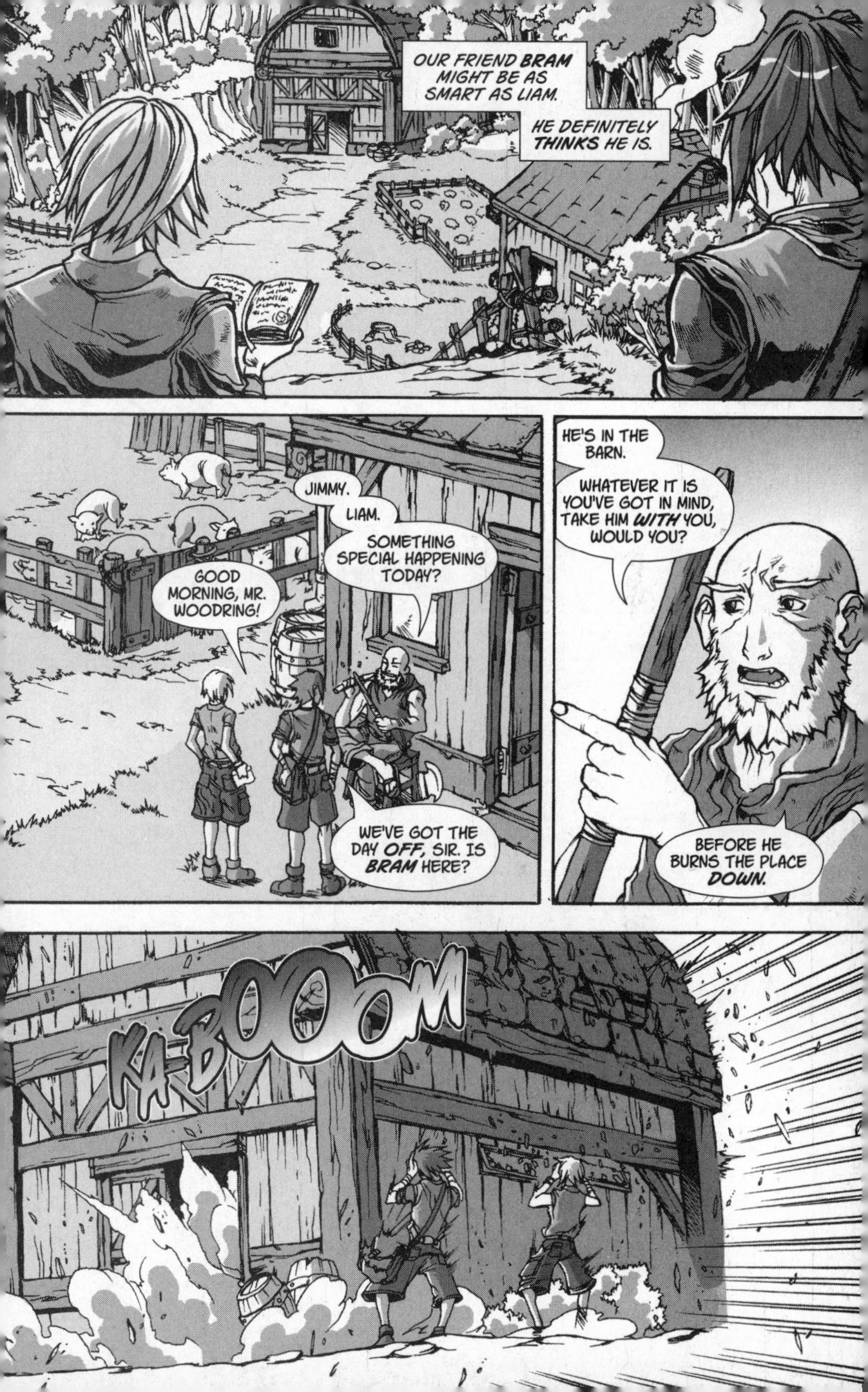
OUR FRIEND BRAM MIGHT BE AS SMART AS LIAM.
HE DEFINITELY THINKS HE IS.
GOOD MORNING, MR. WOODRING!
JIMMY.
LIAM.
SOMETHING SPECIAL HAPPENING TODAY?
WE'VE GOT THE DAY OFF, SIR. IS BRAM HERE?
HE'S IN THE BARN.
WHATEVER IT IS YOU'VE GOT IN MIND, TAKE HIM WITH YOU, WOULD YOU?
BEFORE HE BURNS THE PLACE DOWN.
KA-BOOOOM

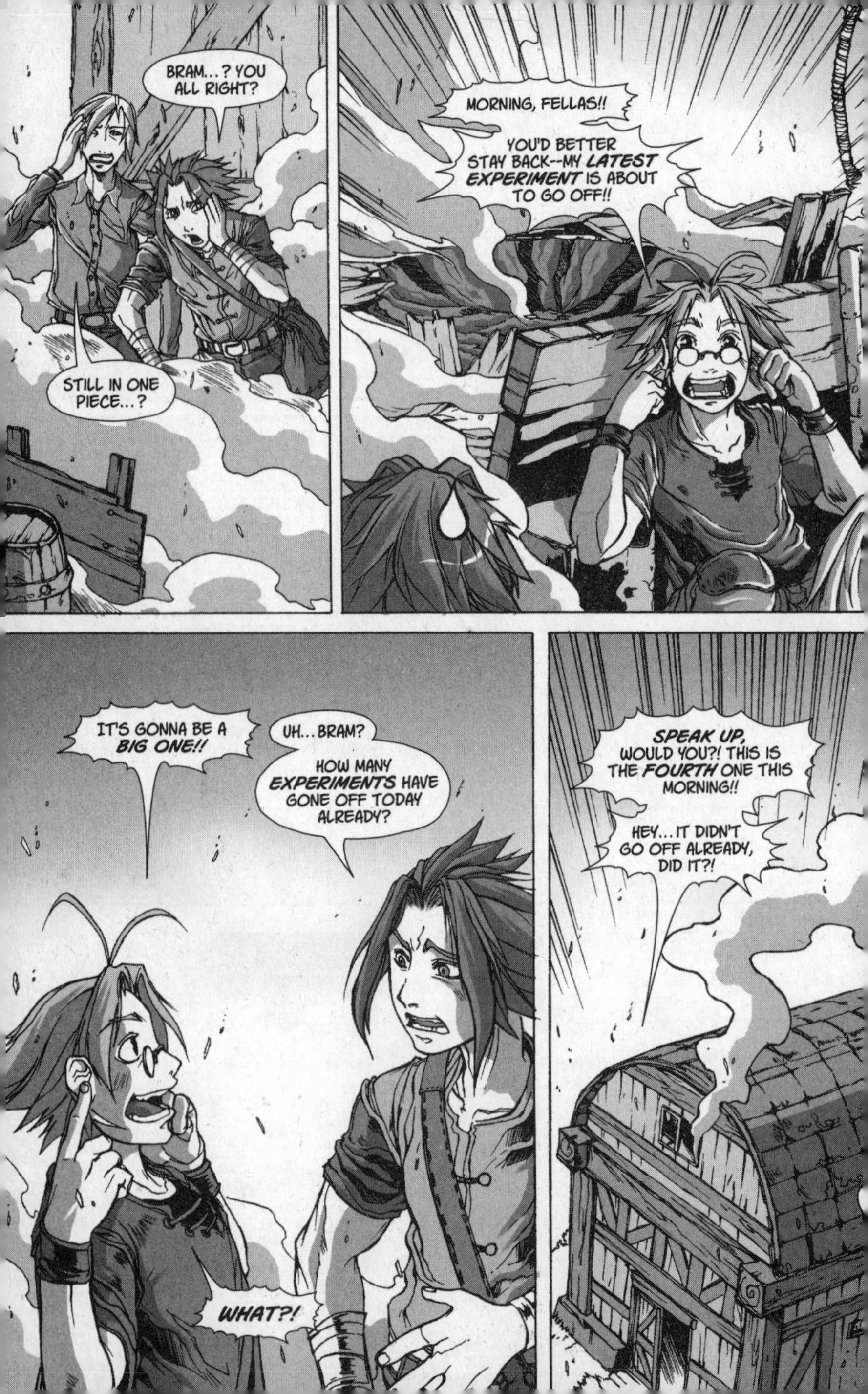
BRAM...? YOU ALL RIGHT?
STILL IN ONE PIECE...?
MORNING, FELLAS!!
YOU'D BETTER STAY BACK--MY LATEST EXPERIMENT IS ABOUT TO GO OFF!!
IT'S GONNA BE A BIG ONE!!
UH...BRAM?
HOW MANY EXPERIMENTS HAVE GONE OFF TODAY ALREADY?
WHAT?!
SPEAK UP, WOULD YOU?! THIS IS THE FOURTH ONE THIS MORNING!!
HEY...IT DIDN'T GO OFF ALREADY, DID IT?!

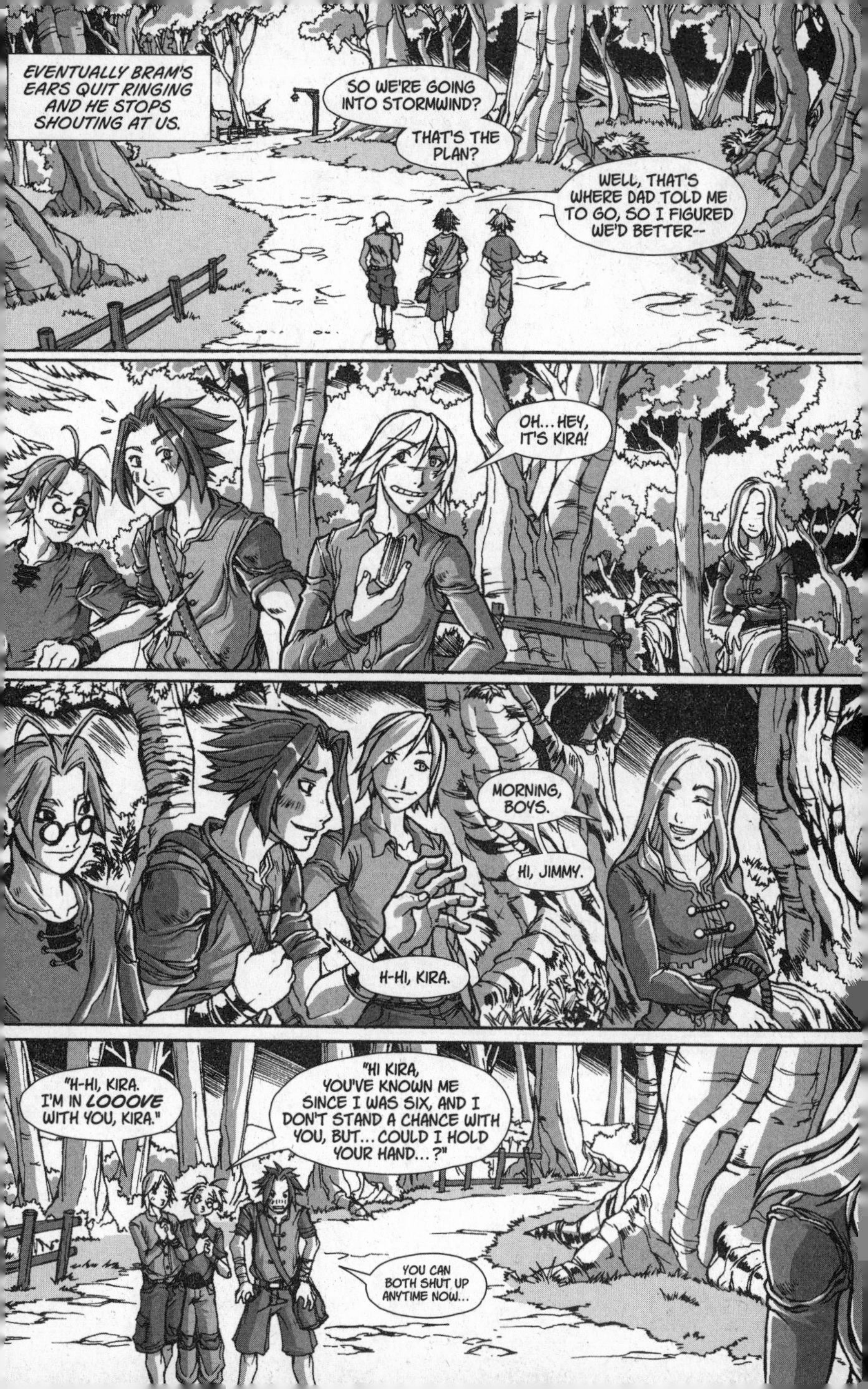
EVENTUALLY BRAM'S EARS QUIT RINGING AND HE STOPS SHOUTING AT US.
SO WE'RE GOING INTO STORMWIND?
THAT'S THE PLAN?
WELL, THAT'S WHERE DAD TOLD ME TO GO, SO I FIGURED WE'D BETTER--
OH... HEY, IT'S KIRA!
MORNING, BOYS.
HI, JIMMY.
H-HI, KIRA.
"H-HI, KIRA. I'M IN *LOOOVE* WITH YOU, KIRA."
"HI KIRA, YOU'VE KNOWN ME SINCE I WAS SIX, AND I DON'T STAND A CHANCE WITH YOU, BUT... COULD I HOLD YOUR HAND...?"
YOU CAN BOTH SHUT UP ANYTIME NOW...

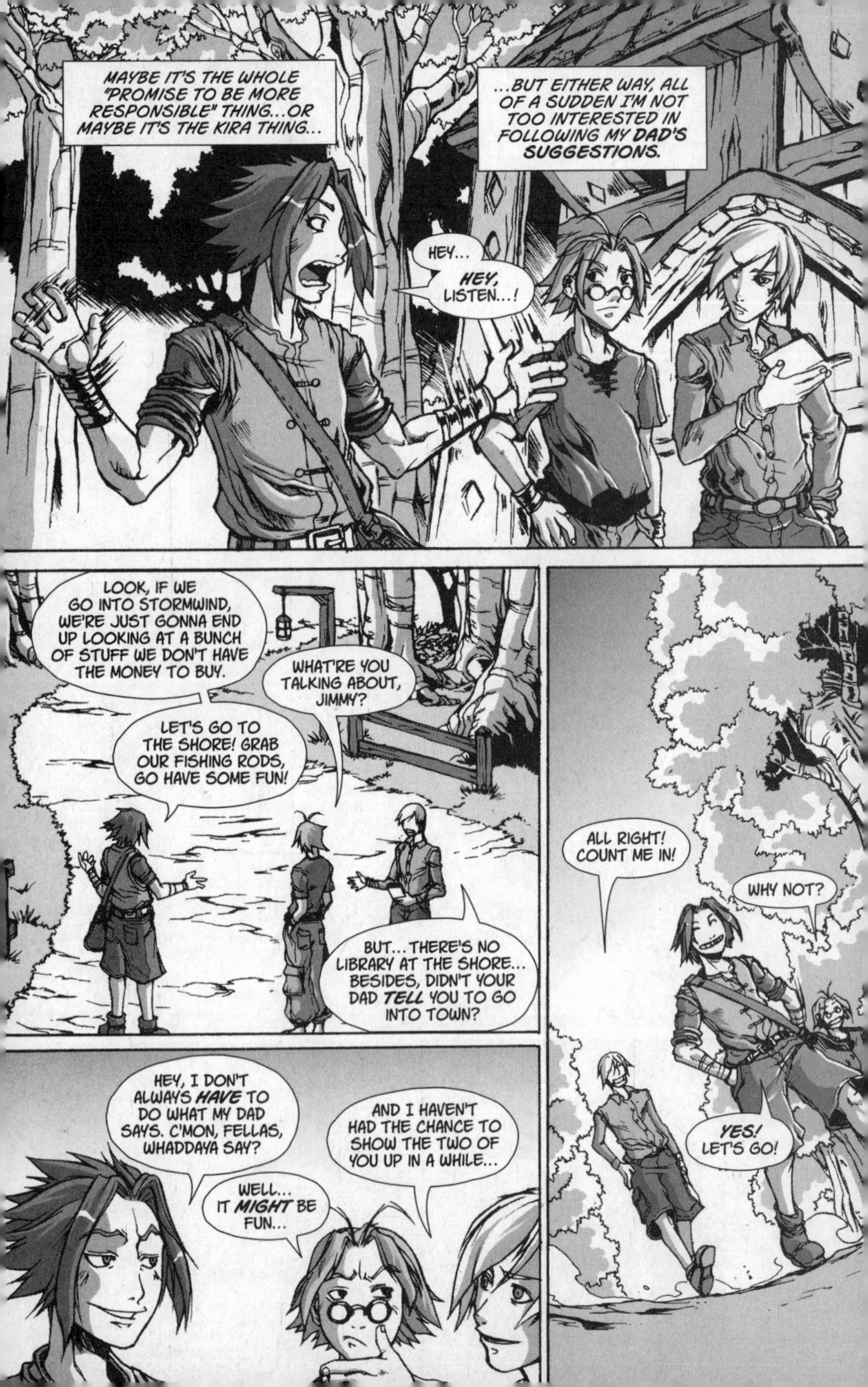
MAYBE IT'S THE WHOLE "PROMISE TO BE MORE RESPONSIBLE" THING...OR MAYBE IT'S THE KIRA THING...
...BUT EITHER WAY, ALL OF A SUDDEN I'M NOT TOO INTERESTED IN FOLLOWING MY DAD'S SUGGESTIONS.
HEY... HEY, LISTEN...!
LOOK, IF WE GO INTO STORMWIND, WE'RE JUST GONNA END UP LOOKING AT A BUNCH OF STUFF WE DON'T HAVE THE MONEY TO BUY.
WHAT'RE YOU TALKING ABOUT, JIMMY?
LET'S GO TO THE SHORE! GRAB OUR FISHING RODS, GO HAVE SOME FUN!
BUT... THERE'S NO LIBRARY AT THE SHORE... BESIDES, DIDN'T YOUR DAD TELL YOU TO GO INTO TOWN?
HEY, I DON'T ALWAYS HAVE TO DO WHAT MY DAD SAYS. C'MON, FELLAS, WHADDAYA SAY?
AND I HAVEN'T HAD THE CHANCE TO SHOW THE TWO OF YOU UP IN A WHILE...
WELL... IT MIGHT BE FUN...
ALL RIGHT! COUNT ME IN!
WHY NOT?
YES! LET'S GO!

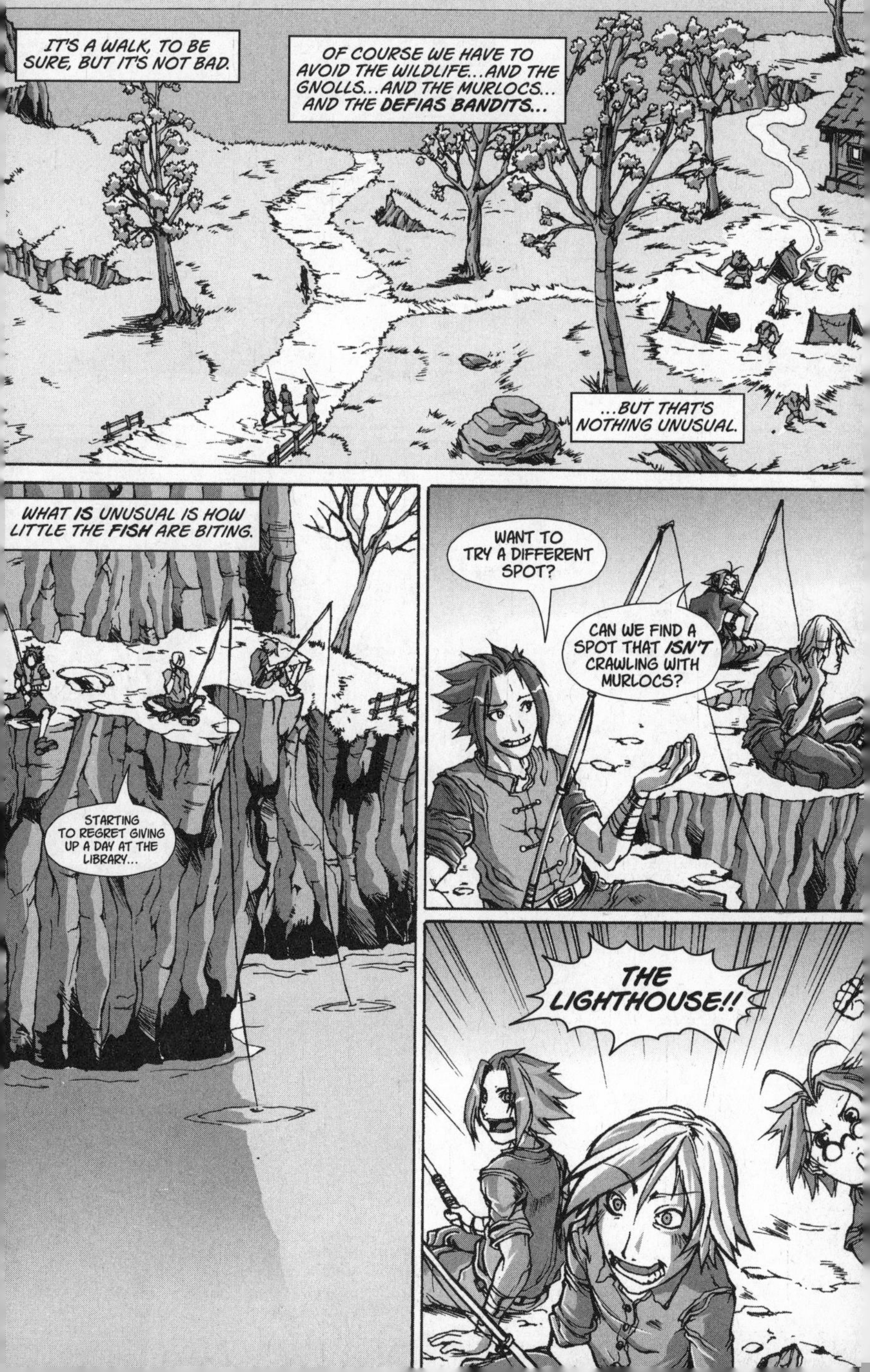
IT'S A WALK, TO BE SURE, BUT IT'S NOT BAD.
OF COURSE WE HAVE TO AVOID THE WILDLIFE...AND THE GNOLLS...AND THE MURLOCS... AND THE DEFIAS BANDITS...
...BUT THAT'S NOTHING UNUSUAL.
WHAT IS UNUSUAL IS HOW LITTLE THE FISH ARE BITING.
STARTING TO REGRET GIVING UP A DAY AT THE LIBRARY...
WANT TO TRY A DIFFERENT SPOT?
CAN WE FIND A SPOT THAT ISN'T CRAWLING WITH MURLOCS?
THE LIGHTHOUSE!!

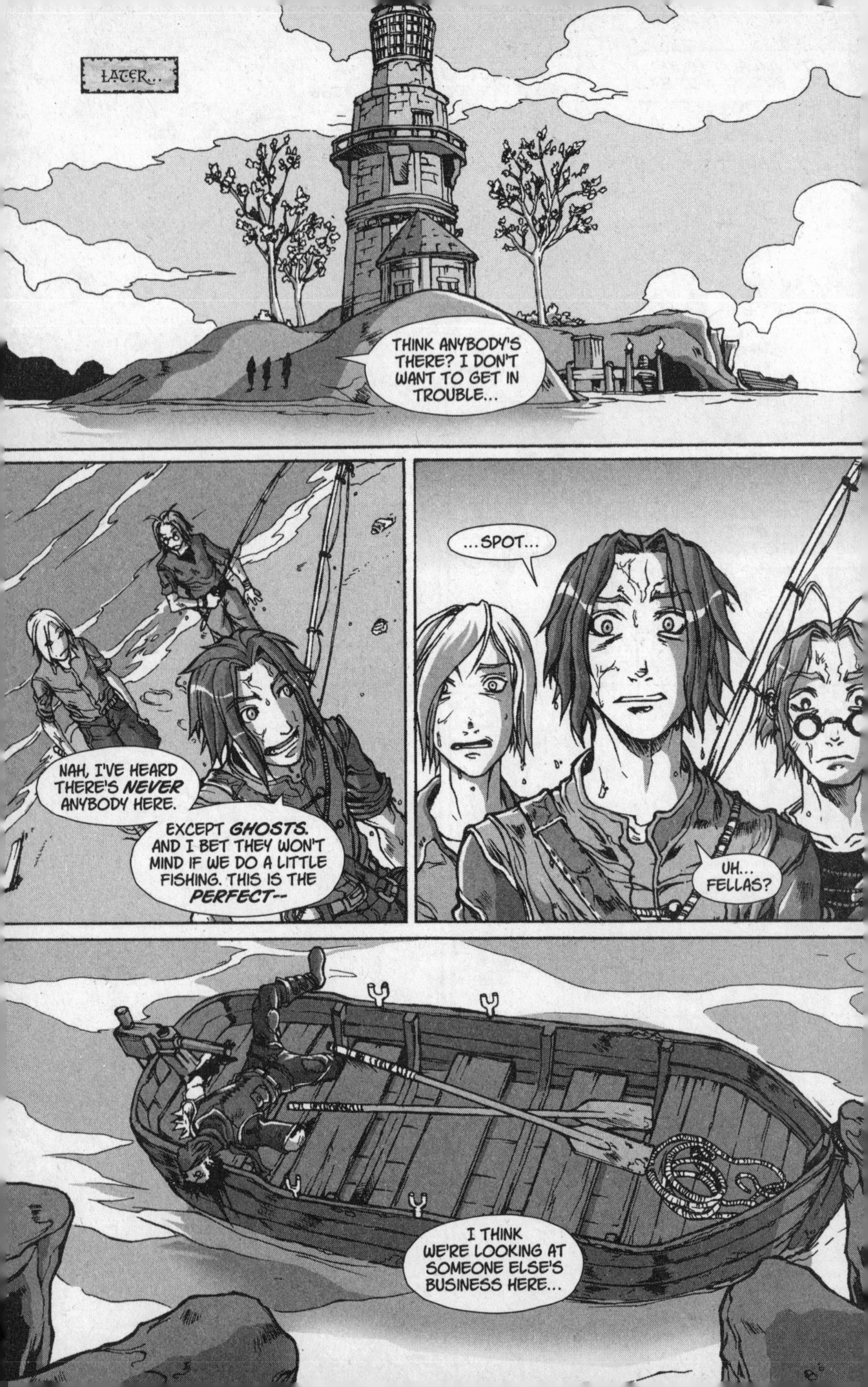
LATER...
THINK ANYBODY'S THERE? I DON'T WANT TO GET IN TROUBLE...
NAH, I'VE HEARD THERE'S NEVER ANYBODY HERE.
EXCEPT GHOSTS. AND I BET THEY WON'T MIND IF WE DO A LITTLE FISHING. THIS IS THE PERFECT--
...SPOT...
UH... FELLAS?
I THINK WE'RE LOOKING AT SOMEONE ELSE'S BUSINESS HERE...

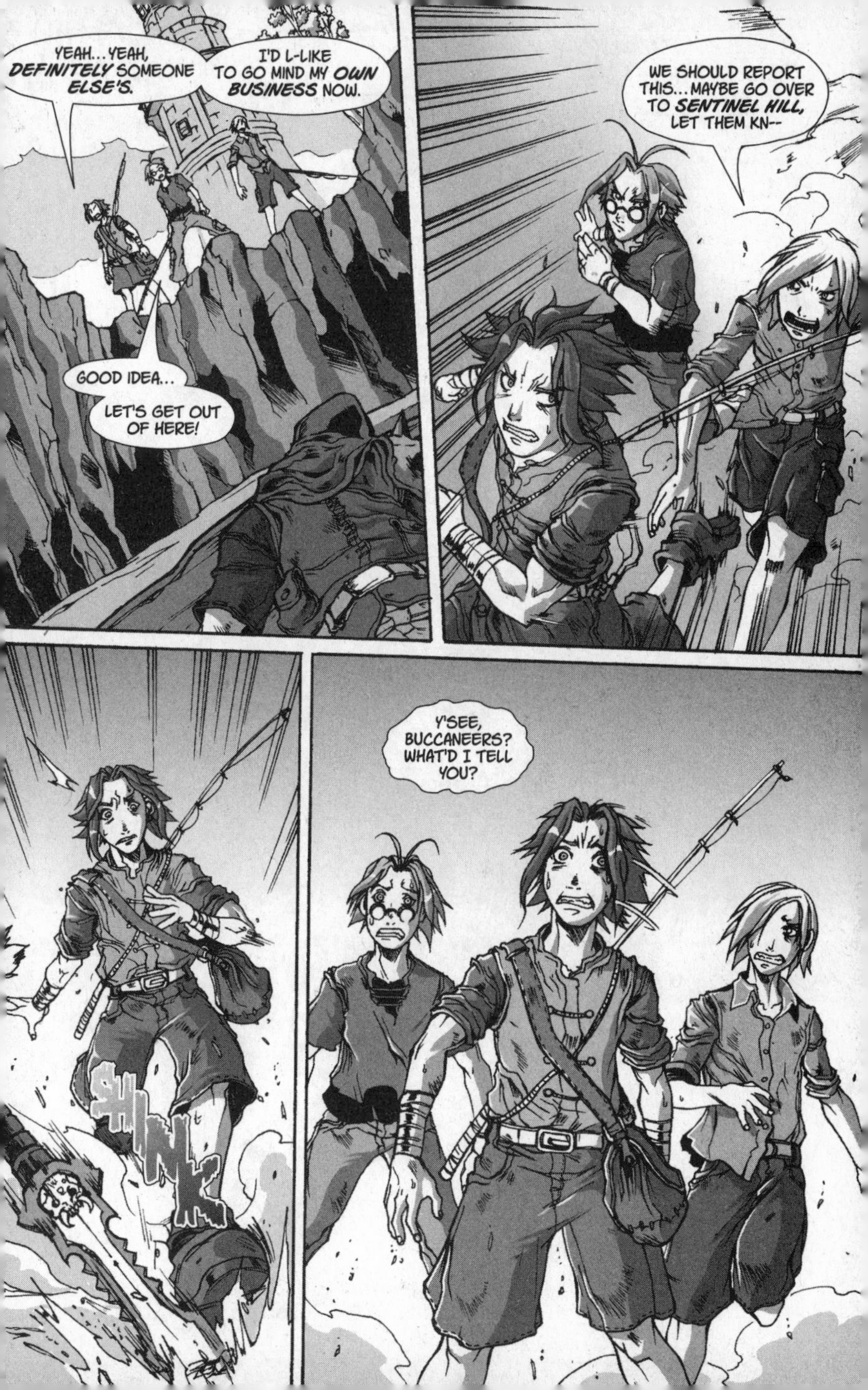
YEAH... YEAH, DEFINITELY SOMEONE ELSE'S.
I'D L-LIKE TO GO MIND MY OWN BUSINESS NOW.
GOOD IDEA...
LET'S GET OUT OF HERE!
WE SHOULD REPORT THIS... MAYBE GO OVER TO SENTINEL HILL, LET THEM KN--
SHINK
Y'SEE, BUCCANEERS? WHAT'D I TELL YOU?

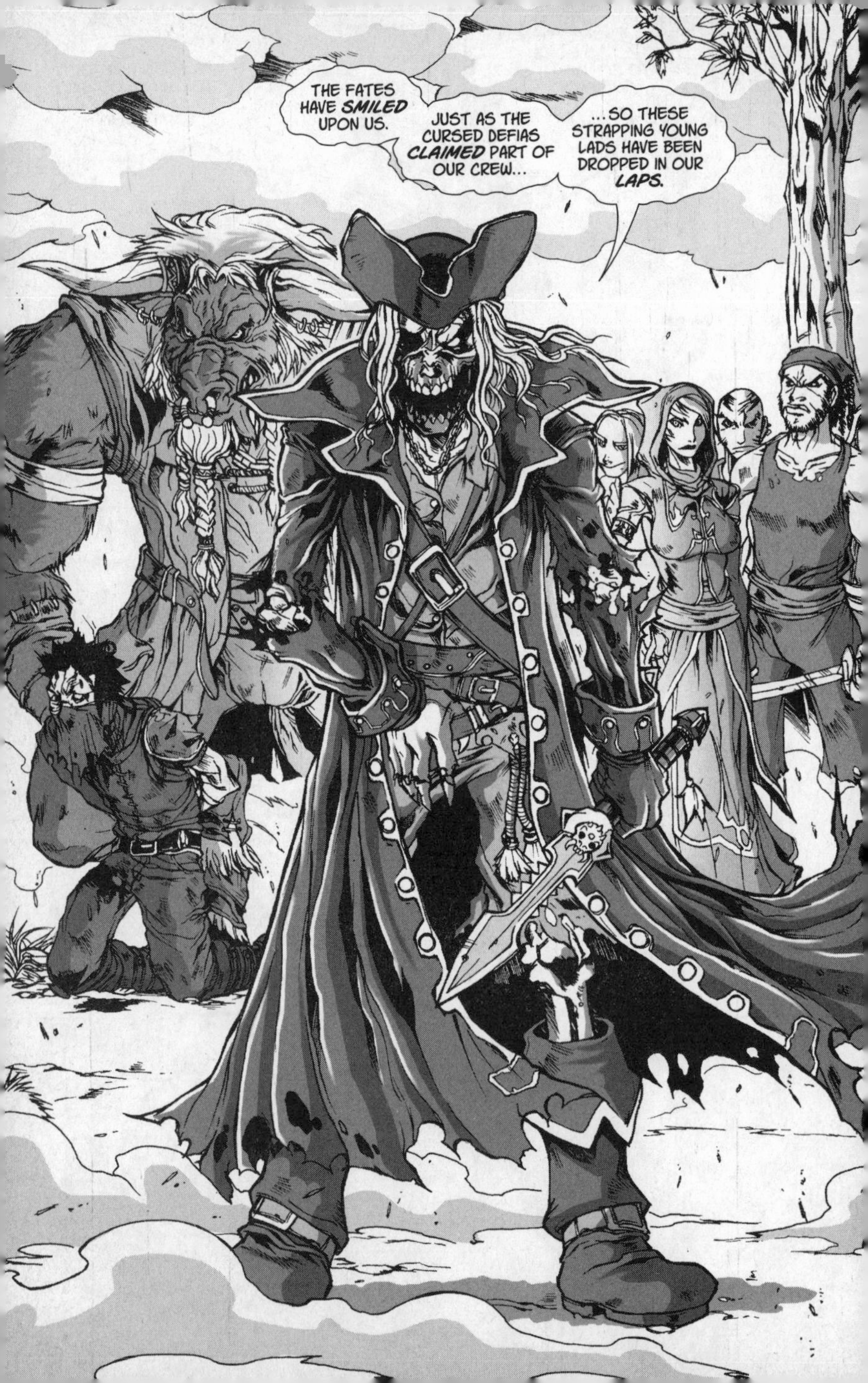
THE FATES HAVE SMILED UPON US.
JUST AS THE CURSED DEFIAS CLAIMED PART OF OUR CREW...
...SO THESE STRAPPING YOUNG LADS HAVE BEEN DROPPED IN OUR LAPS.

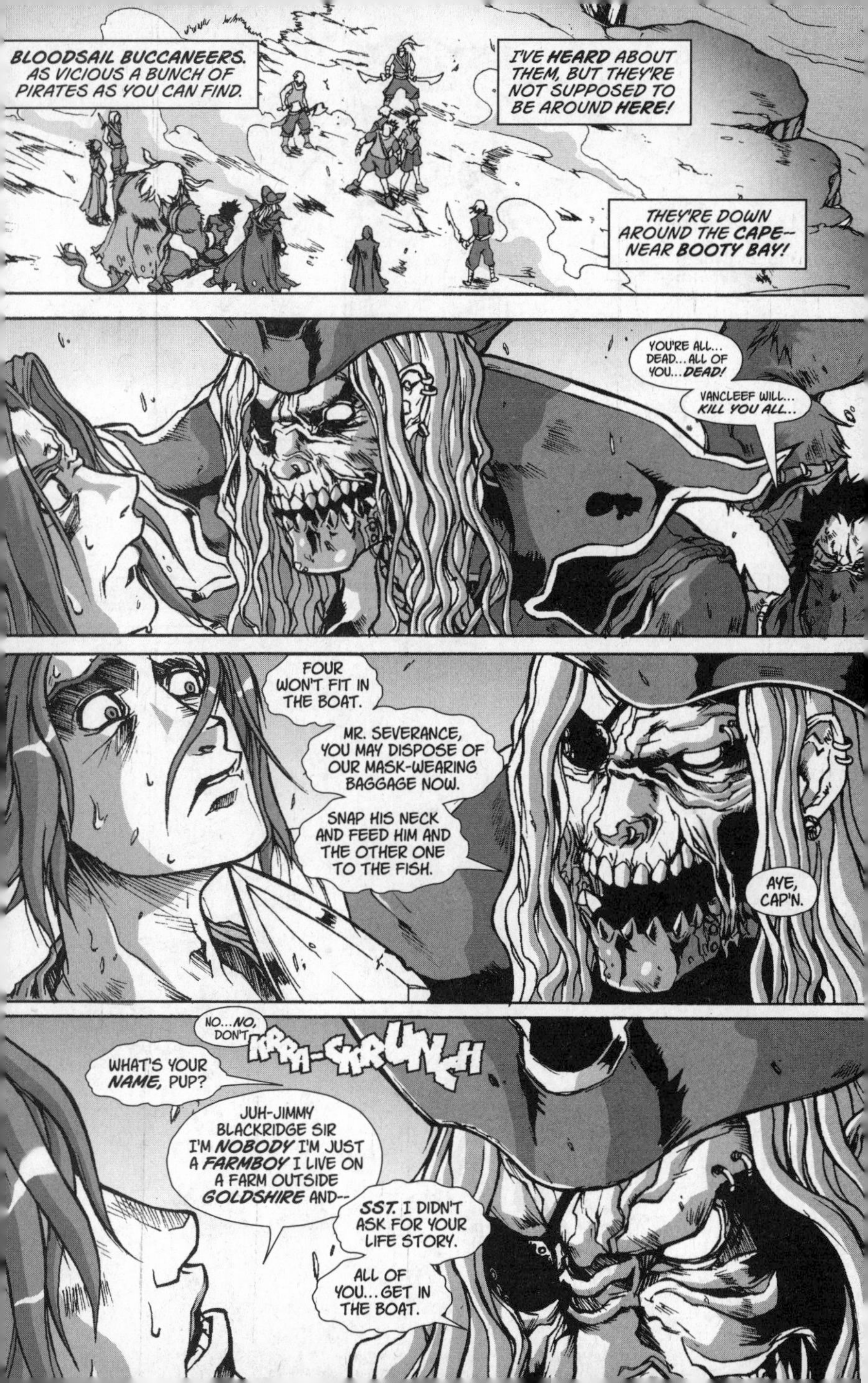
BLOODSAIL BUCCANEERS. AS VICIOUS A BUNCH OF PIRATES AS YOU CAN FIND.
I'VE HEARD ABOUT THEM, BUT THEY'RE NOT SUPPOSED TO BE AROUND HERE!
THEY'RE DOWN AROUND THE CAPE-- NEAR BOOTY BAY!
YOU'RE ALL... DEAD... ALL OF YOU... DEAD!
VANCLEEF WILL... KILL YOU ALL...
FOUR WON'T FIT IN THE BOAT.
MR. SEVERANCE, YOU MAY DISPOSE OF OUR MASK-WEARING BAGGAGE NOW.
SNAP HIS NECK AND FEED HIM AND THE OTHER ONE TO THE FISH.
AYE, CAP'N.
NO... NO, DON'T
KRRA-SKRUNCH
WHAT'S YOUR NAME, PUP?
JUH-JIMMY BLACKRIDGE SIR I'M NOBODY I'M JUST A FARMBOY I LIVE ON A FARM OUTSIDE GOLDSHIRE AND--
SST. I DIDN'T ASK FOR YOUR LIFE STORY.
ALL OF YOU... GET IN THE BOAT.

TAKE A GOOD LOOK, PUPS. 'TIS THE *GARROTE*... FINEST VESSEL EVER TO SAIL THE GREAT SEA.

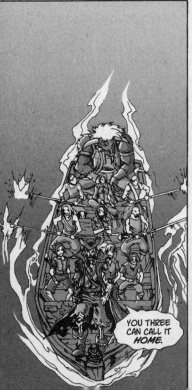

YOU THREE CAN CALL IT *HOME.*

HA HA HA HA!!

NOT *SCARED* ARE YOU?

UP YOU GO, PUPS! AND GET A MOVE ON, OR YOU'LL FEEL MY *BLADE!*

HA! I THINK THIS ONE'S WET HIS PANTS!

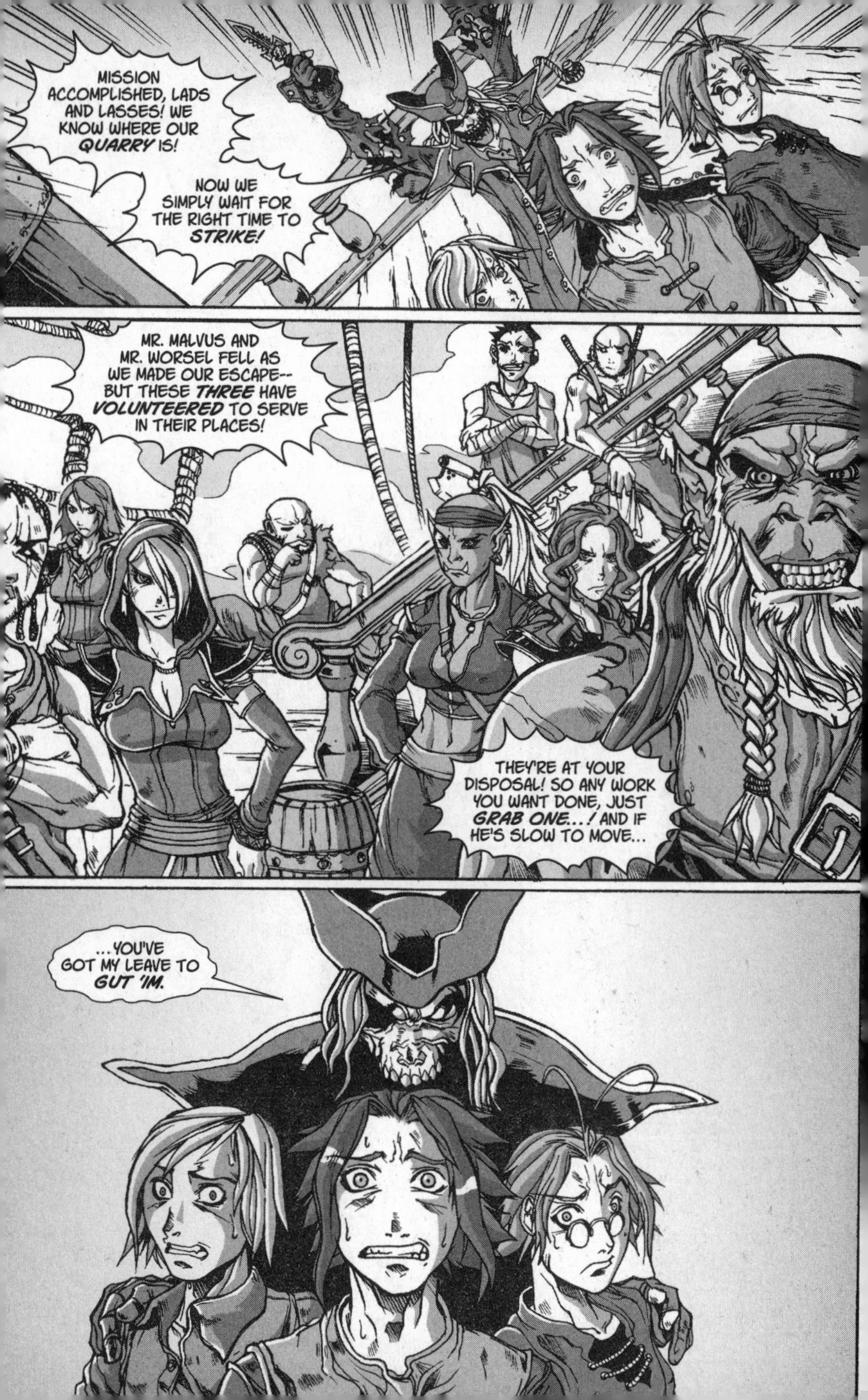
MISSION ACCOMPLISHED, LADS AND LASSES! WE KNOW WHERE OUR QUARRY IS!
NOW WE SIMPLY WAIT FOR THE RIGHT TIME TO STRIKE!
MR. MALVUS AND MR. WORSEL FELL AS WE MADE OUR ESCAPE-- BUT THESE THREE HAVE VOLUNTEERED TO SERVE IN THEIR PLACES!
THEY'RE AT YOUR DISPOSAL! SO ANY WORK YOU WANT DONE, JUST GRAB ONE...! AND IF HE'S SLOW TO MOVE...
...YOU'VE GOT MY LEAVE TO GUT 'IM.

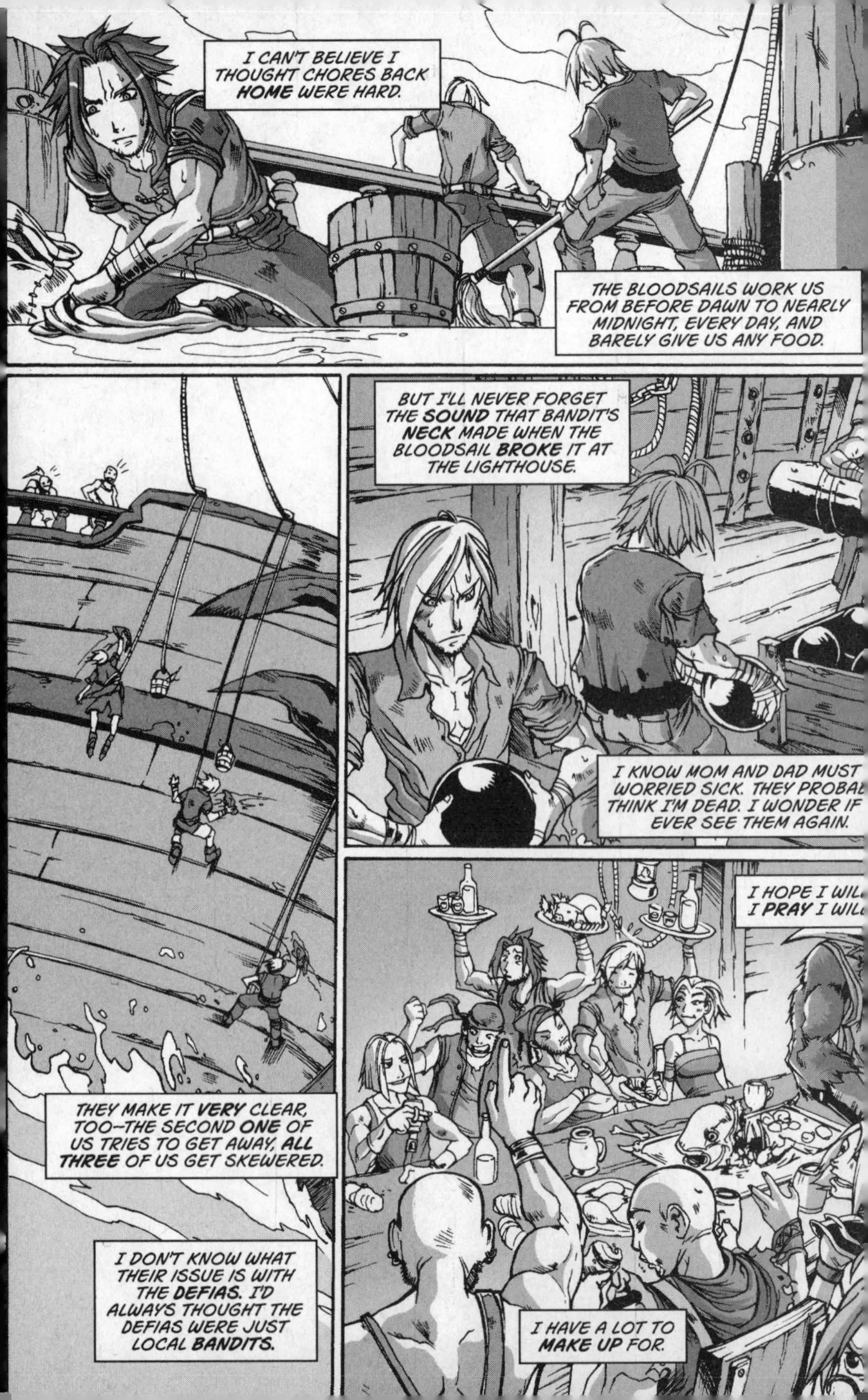
I CAN'T BELIEVE I THOUGHT CHORES BACK HOME WERE HARD.
THE BLOODSAILS WORK US FROM BEFORE DAWN TO NEARLY MIDNIGHT, EVERY DAY, AND BARELY GIVE US ANY FOOD.
THEY MAKE IT VERY CLEAR, TOO--THE SECOND ONE OF US TRIES TO GET AWAY, ALL THREE OF US GET SKEWERED.
I DON'T KNOW WHAT THEIR ISSUE IS WITH THE DEFIAS. I'D ALWAYS THOUGHT THE DEFIAS WERE JUST LOCAL BANDITS.
BUT I'LL NEVER FORGET THE SOUND THAT BANDIT'S NECK MADE WHEN THE BLOODSAIL BROKE IT AT THE LIGHTHOUSE.
I KNOW MOM AND DAD MUST WORRIED SICK. THEY PROBA THINK I'M DEAD. I WONDER IF EVER SEE THEM AGAIN.
I HOPE I WIL I PRAY I WIL
I HAVE A LOT TO MAKE UP FOR.

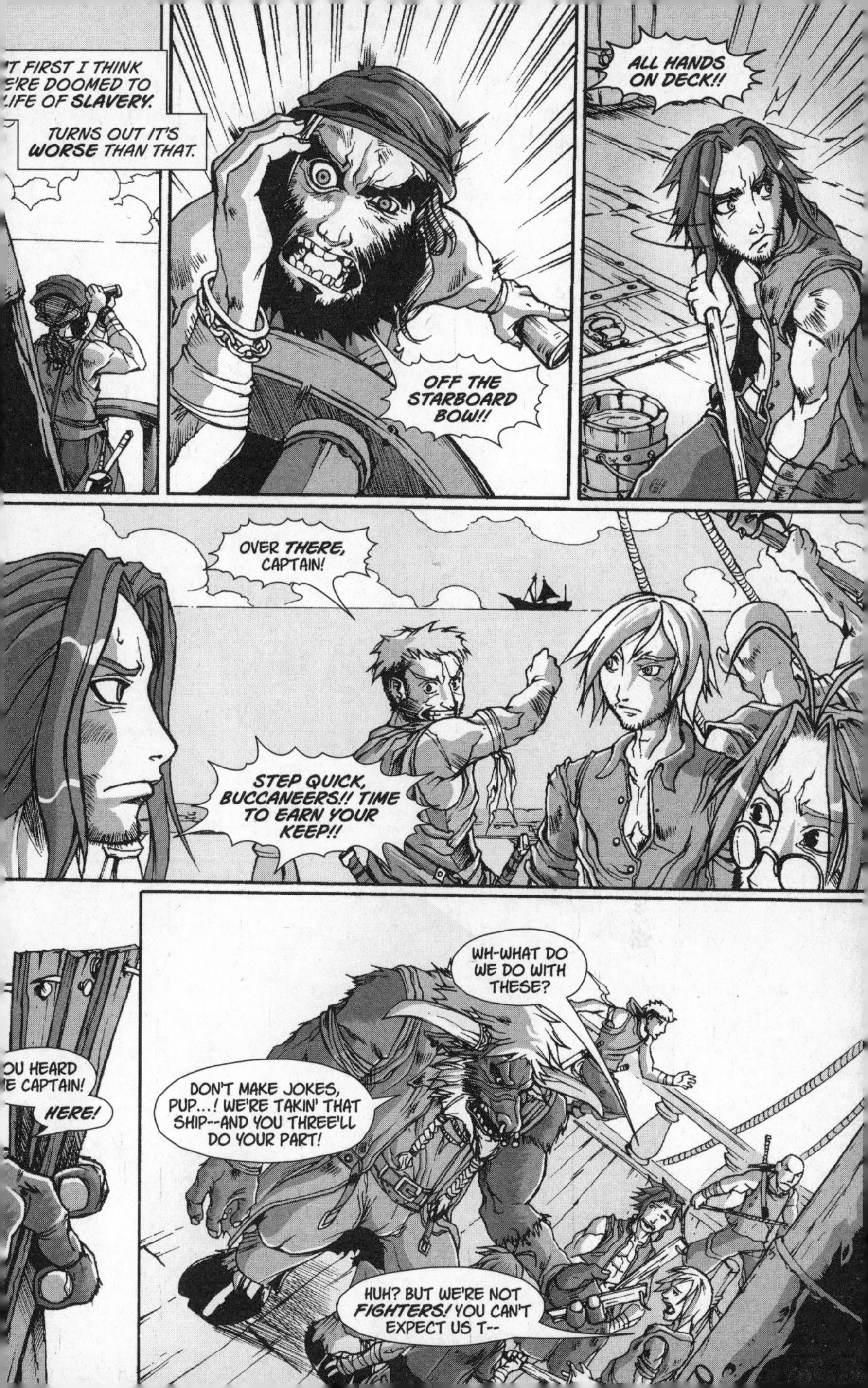

T FIRST I THINK
E'RE DOOMED TO
LIFE OF **SLAVERY.**
TURNS OUT IT'S **WORSE** THAN THAT.
OFF THE STARBOARD BOW!!
ALL HANDS ON DECK!!
OVER *THERE,* CAPTAIN!
STEP QUICK, BUCCANEERS!! TIME TO EARN YOUR KEEP!!
OU HEARD
E CAPTAIN!
HERE!
WH-WHAT DO WE DO WITH THESE?
DON'T MAKE JOKES, PUP...! WE'RE TAKIN' THAT SHIP--AND YOU THREE'LL DO YOUR PART!
HUH? BUT WE'RE NOT *FIGHTERS!* YOU CAN'T EXPECT US T--

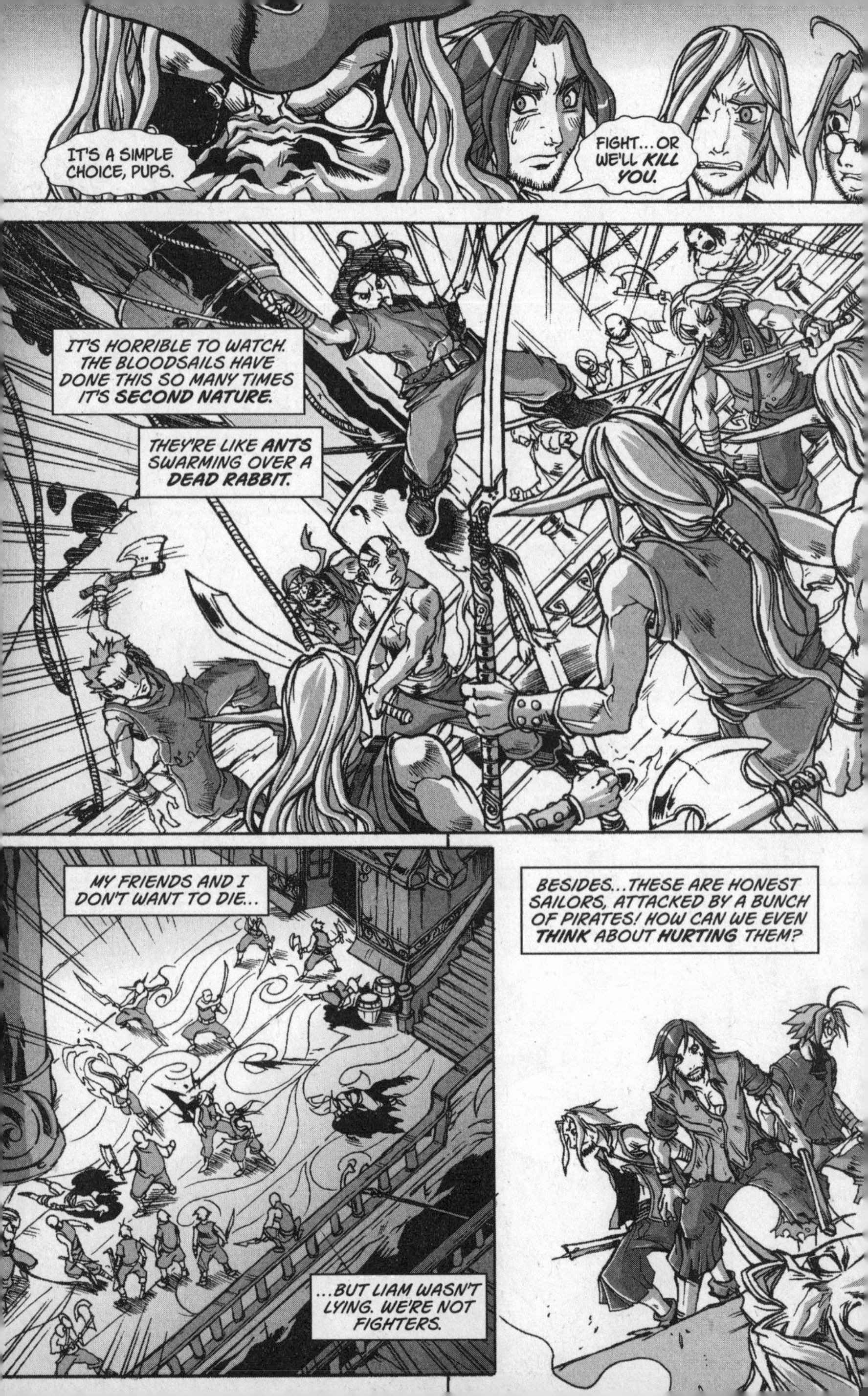

IT'S A SIMPLE CHOICE, PUPS.
FIGHT... OR WE'LL KILL YOU.
IT'S HORRIBLE TO WATCH. THE BLOODSAILS HAVE DONE THIS SO MANY TIMES IT'S SECOND NATURE.
THEY'RE LIKE ANTS SWARMING OVER A DEAD RABBIT.
MY FRIENDS AND I DON'T WANT TO DIE...
...BUT LIAM WASN'T LYING. WE'RE NOT FIGHTERS.
BESIDES...THESE ARE HONEST SAILORS, ATTACKED BY A BUNCH OF PIRATES! HOW CAN WE EVEN THINK ABOUT HURTING THEM?

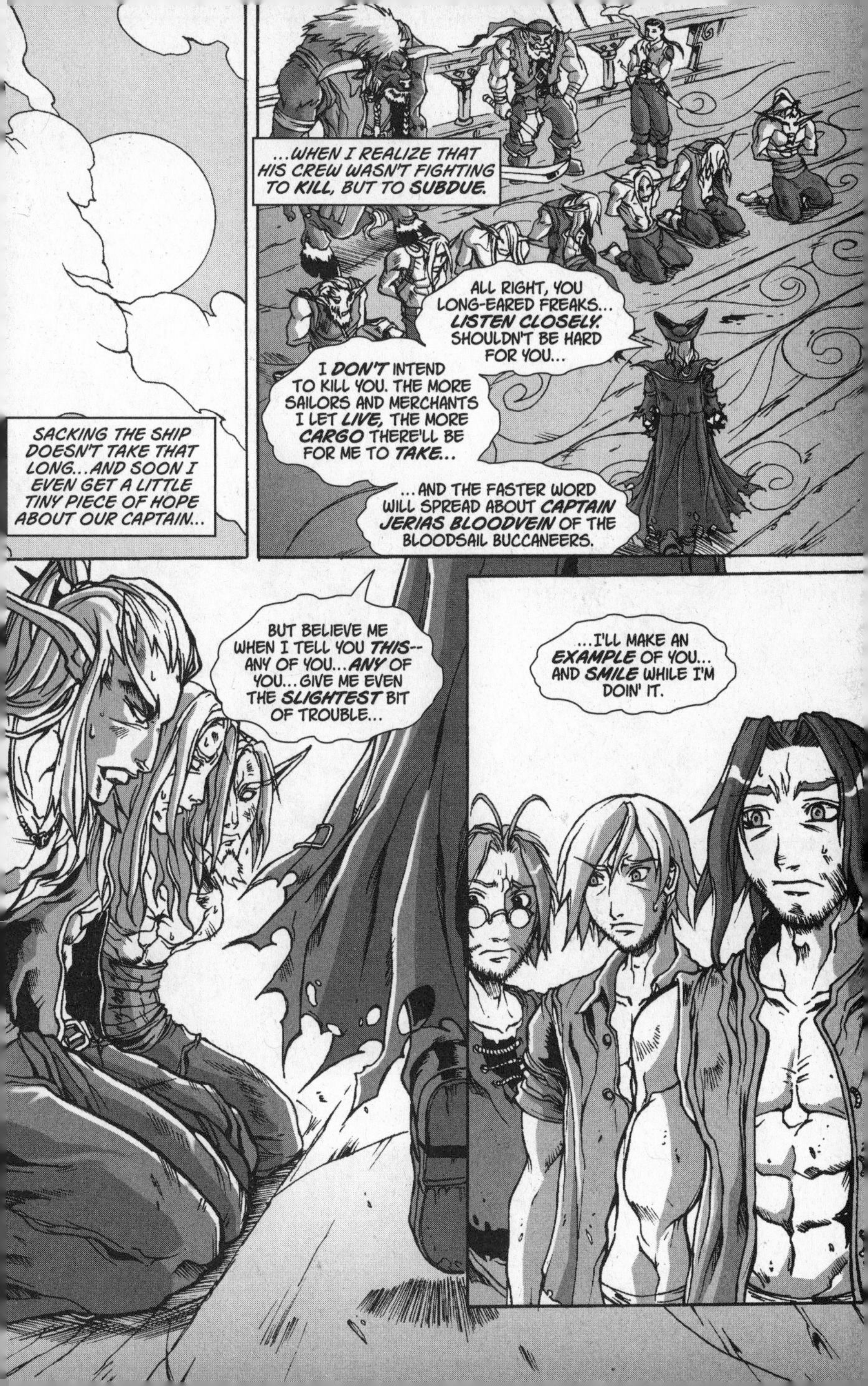
SACKING THE SHIP DOESN'T TAKE THAT LONG...AND SOON I EVEN GET A LITTLE TINY PIECE OF HOPE ABOUT OUR CAPTAIN...
...WHEN I REALIZE THAT HIS CREW WASN'T FIGHTING TO KILL, BUT TO SUBDUE.
ALL RIGHT, YOU LONG-EARED FREAKS... LISTEN CLOSELY. SHOULDN'T BE HARD FOR YOU...
I DON'T INTEND TO KILL YOU. THE MORE SAILORS AND MERCHANTS I LET LIVE, THE MORE CARGO THERE'LL BE FOR ME TO TAKE...
...AND THE FASTER WORD WILL SPREAD ABOUT CAPTAIN JERIAS BLOODVEIN OF THE BLOODSAIL BUCCANEERS.
BUT BELIEVE ME WHEN I TELL YOU THIS-- ANY OF YOU...ANY OF YOU...GIVE ME EVEN THE SLIGHTEST BIT OF TROUBLE...
...I'LL MAKE AN EXAMPLE OF YOU... AND SMILE WHILE I'M DOIN' IT.

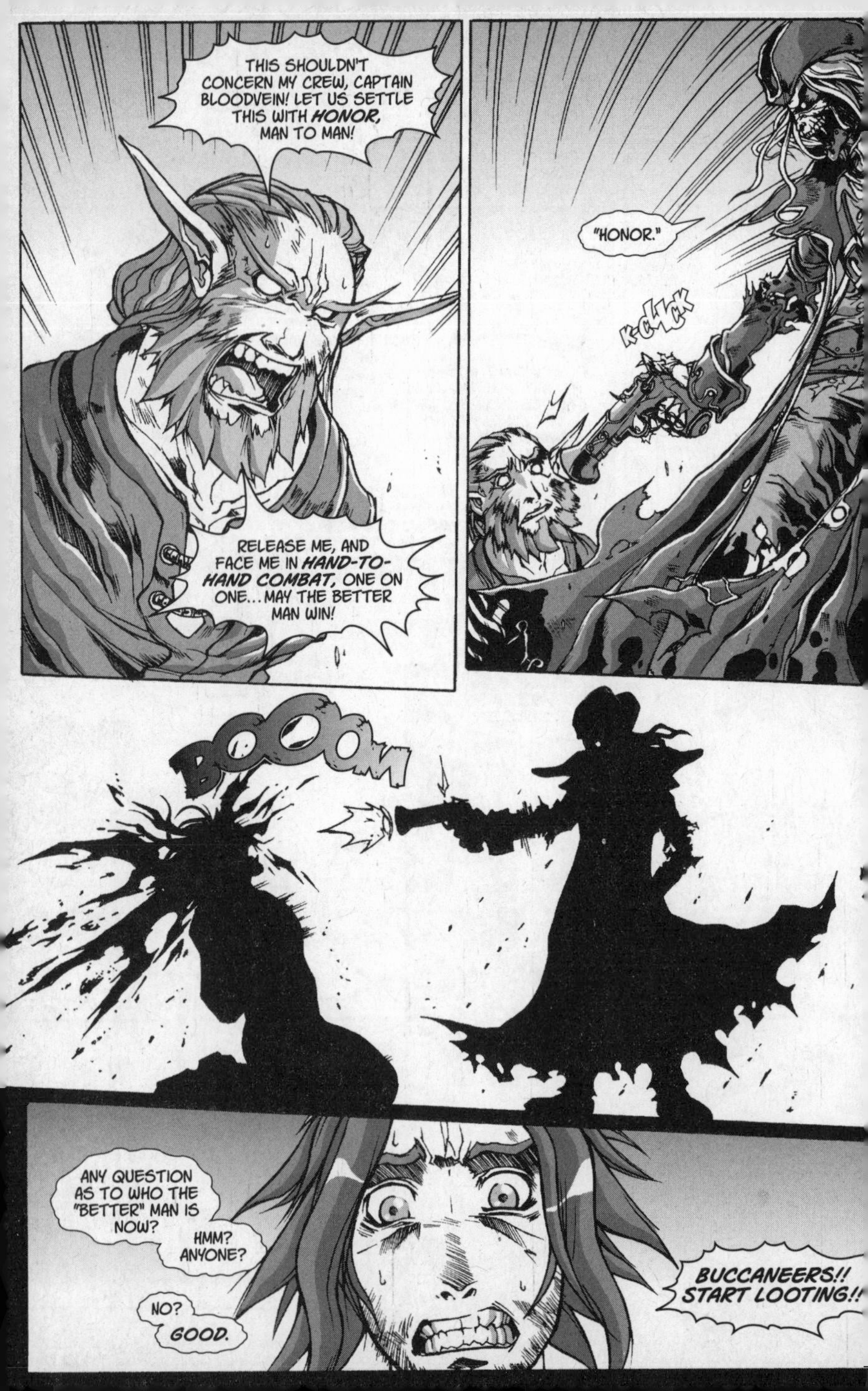
THIS SHOULDN'T CONCERN MY CREW, CAPTAIN BLOODVEIN! LET US SETTLE THIS WITH *HONOR,* MAN TO MAN!
RELEASE ME, AND FACE ME IN *HAND-TO-HAND COMBAT,* ONE ON ONE... MAY THE BETTER MAN WIN!
"HONOR."
K-CLIICK
BOOOOM
ANY QUESTION AS TO WHO THE "BETTER" MAN IS NOW?
HMM? ANYONE?
NO?
GOOD.
BUCCANEERS!! START LOOTING!!

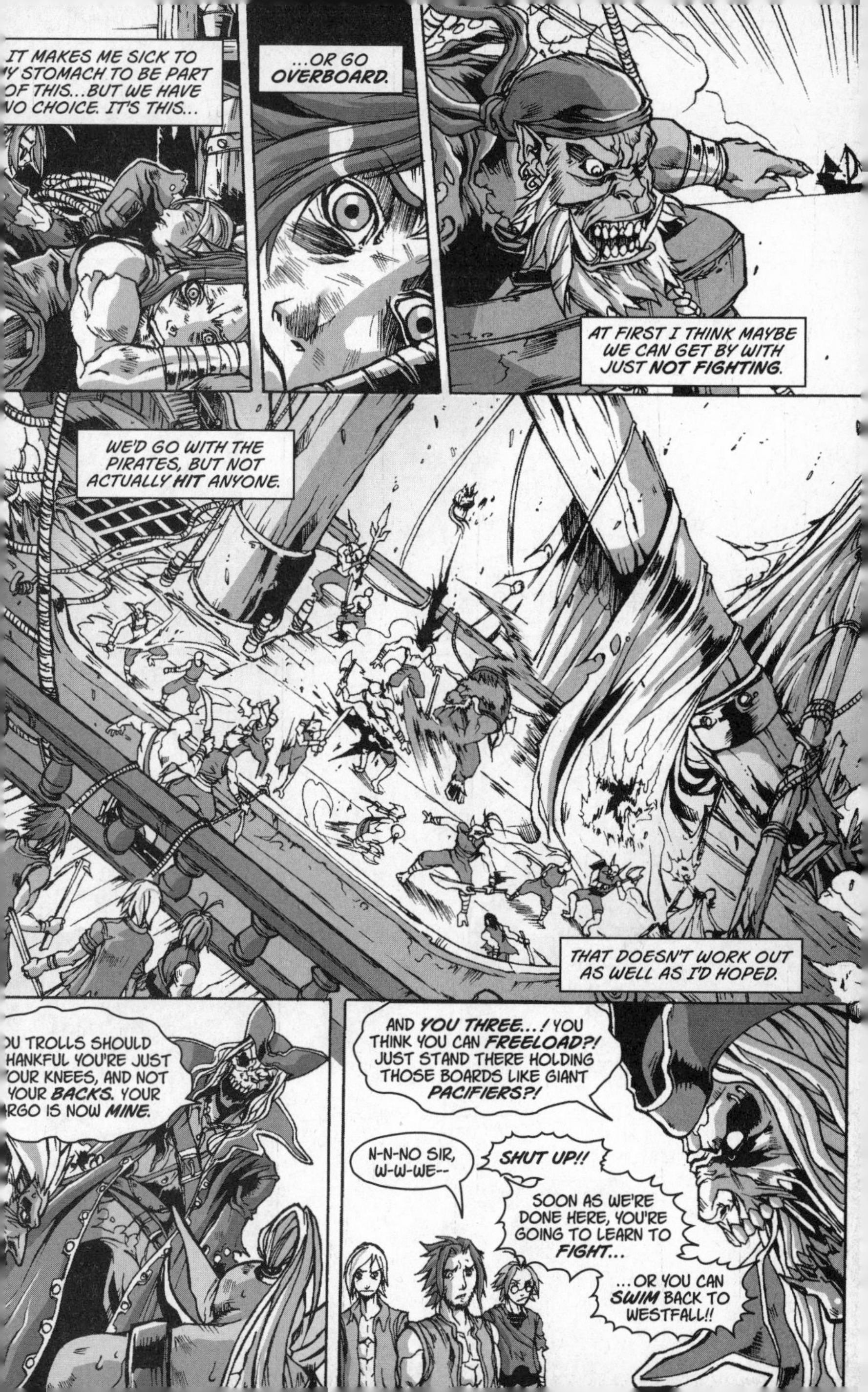
IT MAKES ME SICK TO MY STOMACH TO BE PART OF THIS...BUT WE HAVE NO CHOICE. IT'S THIS...
...OR GO OVERBOARD.
AT FIRST I THINK MAYBE WE CAN GET BY WITH JUST NOT FIGHTING.
WE'D GO WITH THE PIRATES, BUT NOT ACTUALLY HIT ANYONE.
THAT DOESN'T WORK OUT AS WELL AS I'D HOPED.
OU TROLLS SHOULD HANKFUL YOU'RE JUST OUR KNEES, AND NOT YOUR BACKS. YOUR ARGO IS NOW MINE.
AND YOU THREE...! YOU THINK YOU CAN FREELOAD?! JUST STAND THERE HOLDING THOSE BOARDS LIKE GIANT PACIFIERS?!
N-N-NO SIR, W-W-WE--
SHUT UP!!
SOON AS WE'RE DONE HERE, YOU'RE GOING TO LEARN TO FIGHT...
...OR YOU CAN SWIM BACK TO WESTFALL!!

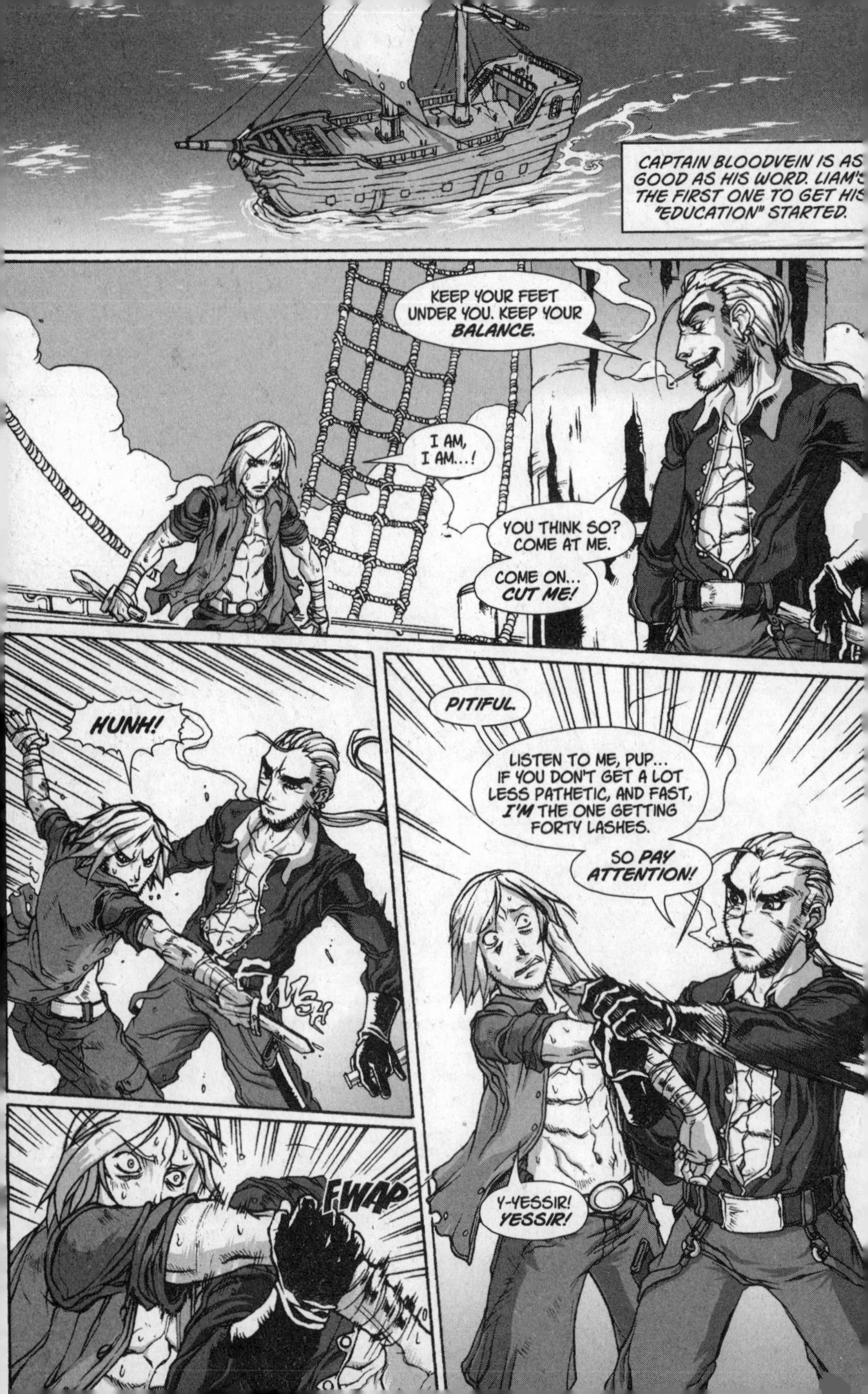
CAPTAIN BLOODVEIN IS AS GOOD AS HIS WORD. LIAM'S THE FIRST ONE TO GET HIS "EDUCATION" STARTED.
KEEP YOUR FEET UNDER YOU. KEEP YOUR BALANCE.
I AM, I AM...!
YOU THINK SO? COME AT ME.
COME ON... CUT ME!
HUNH!
FWAP
PITIFUL.
LISTEN TO ME, PUP... IF YOU DON'T GET A LOT LESS PATHETIC, AND FAST, I'M THE ONE GETTING FORTY LASHES.
SO PAY ATTENTION!
Y-YESSIR! YESSIR!

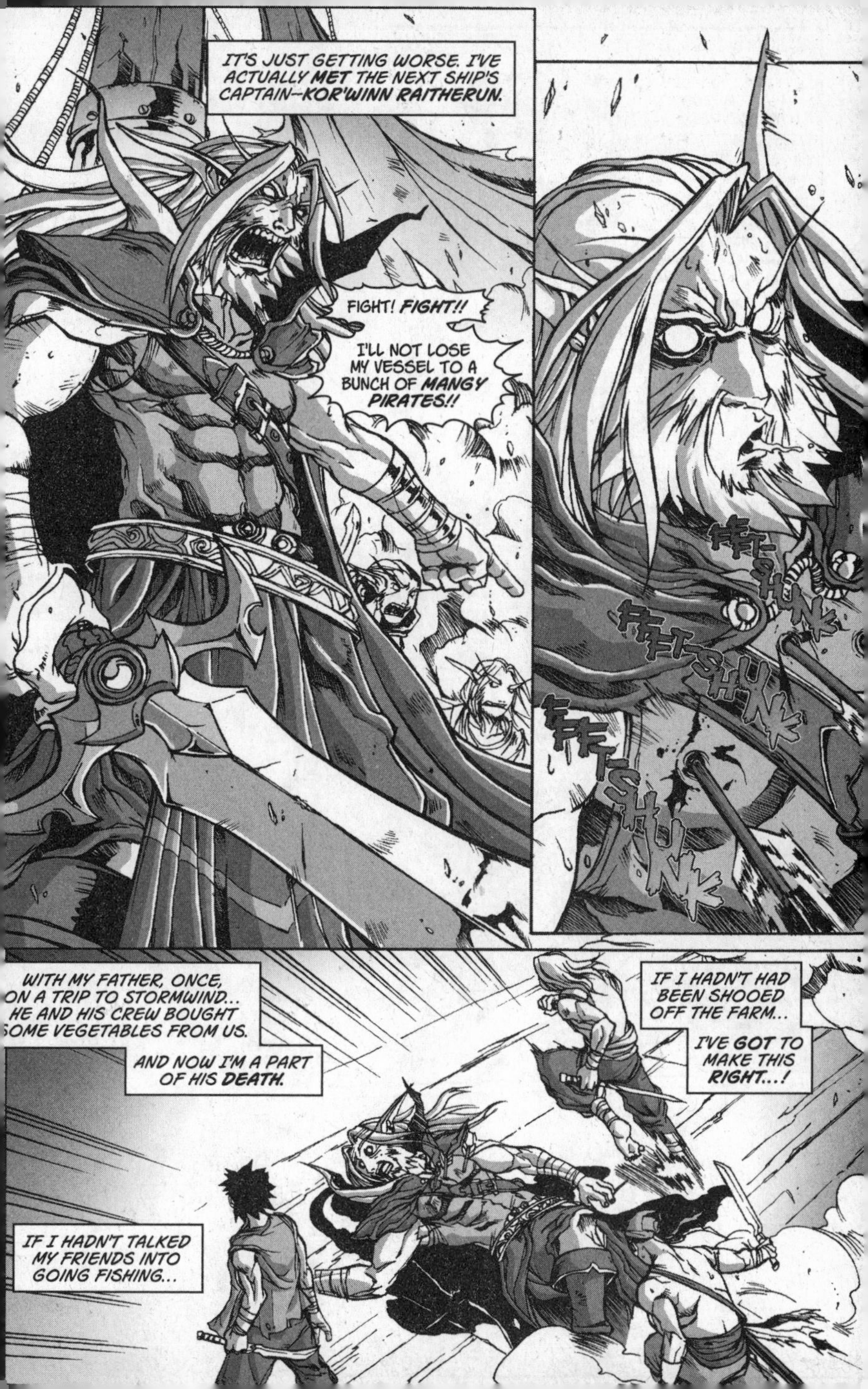
IT'S JUST GETTING WORSE. I'VE ACTUALLY MET THE NEXT SHIP'S CAPTAIN--KOR'WINN RAITHERUN.
FIGHT! FIGHT!!
I'LL NOT LOSE MY VESSEL TO A BUNCH OF MANGY PIRATES!!
FFT-SHUNK
FFFT-SHUNK
FFFT-SHUNK
WITH MY FATHER, ONCE, ON A TRIP TO STORMWIND... HE AND HIS CREW BOUGHT SOME VEGETABLES FROM US.
AND NOW I'M A PART OF HIS DEATH.
IF I HADN'T HAD BEEN SHOOED OFF THE FARM...
I'VE GOT TO MAKE THIS RIGHT...!
IF I HADN'T TALKED MY FRIENDS INTO GOING FISHING...

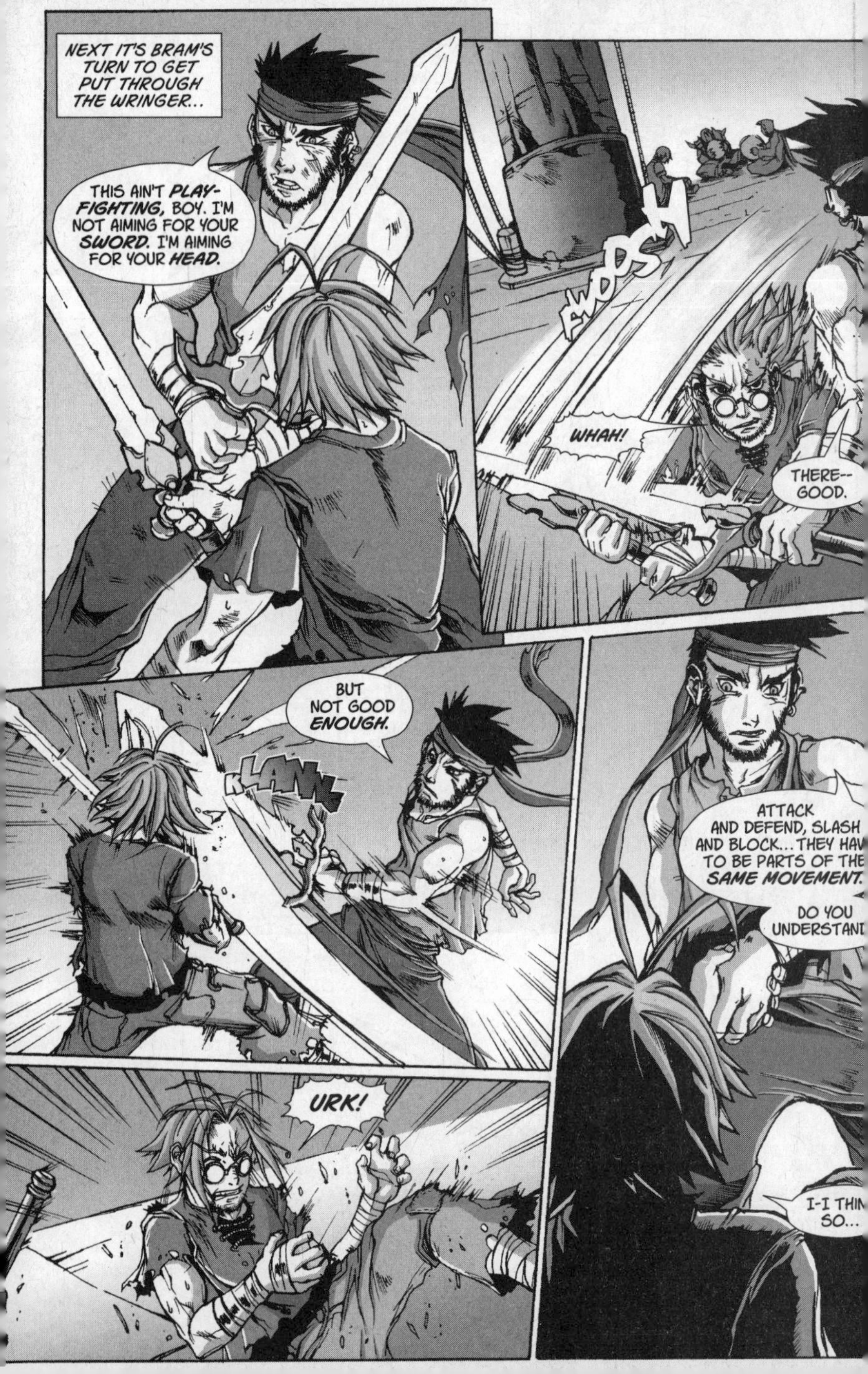
NEXT IT'S BRAM'S TURN TO GET PUT THROUGH THE WRINGER...
THIS AIN'T PLAY-FIGHTING, BOY. I'M NOT AIMING FOR YOUR SWORD. I'M AIMING FOR YOUR HEAD.
FWOOSH
WHAH!
THERE-- GOOD.
BUT NOT GOOD ENOUGH.
KLANK
ATTACK AND DEFEND, SLASH AND BLOCK... THEY HAV TO BE PARTS OF THE SAME MOVEMENT.
DO YOU UNDERSTAN
URK!
I-I THIN SO...

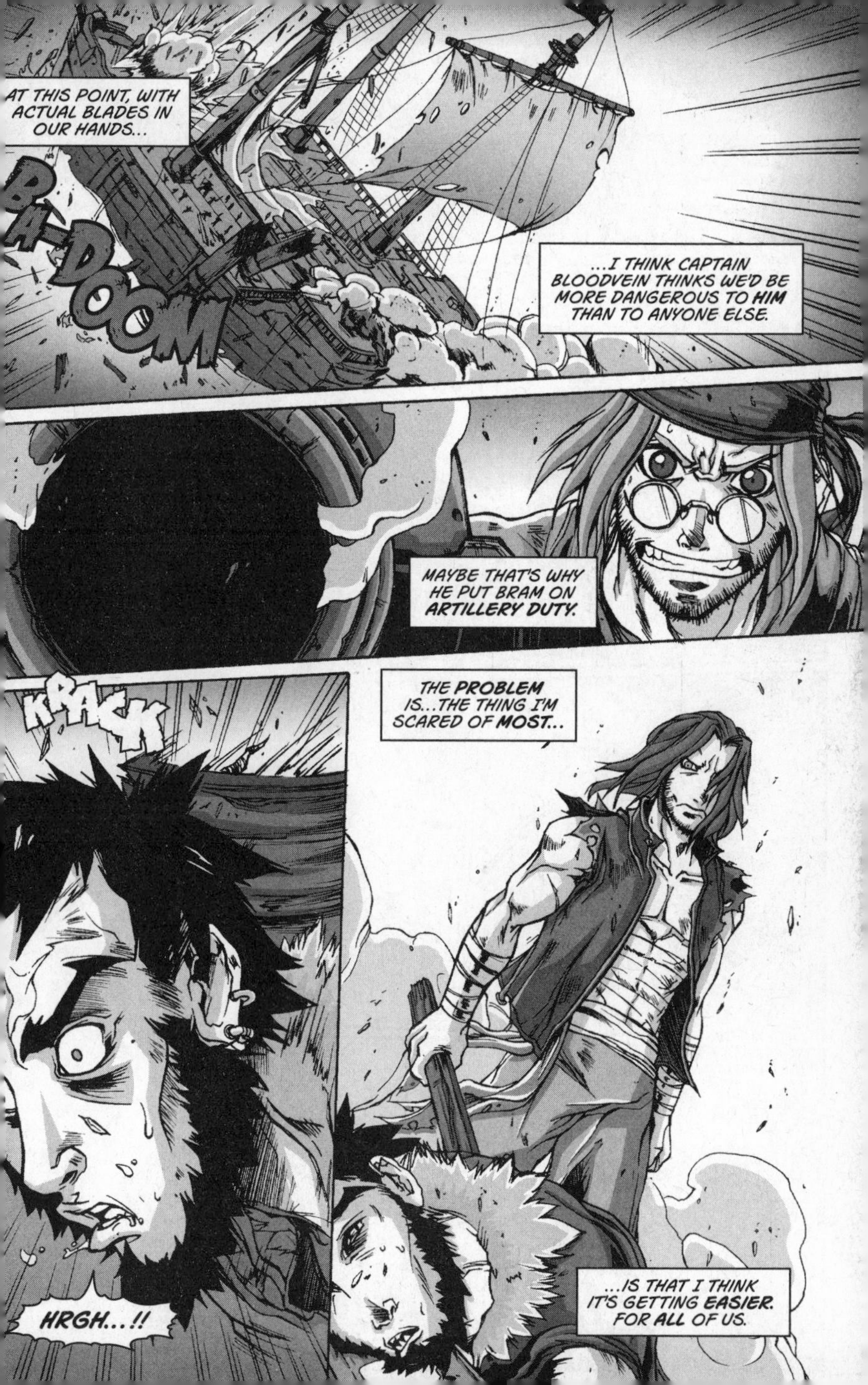
AT THIS POINT, WITH ACTUAL BLADES IN OUR HANDS...
BA-DOOM
...I THINK CAPTAIN BLOODVEIN THINKS WE'D BE MORE DANGEROUS TO **HIM** THAN TO ANYONE ELSE.
MAYBE THAT'S WHY HE PUT BRAM ON **ARTILLERY DUTY**.
KRACK
THE **PROBLEM** IS...THE THING I'M SCARED OF **MOST**...
HRGH...!!
...IS THAT I THINK IT'S GETTING **EASIER**. FOR **ALL** OF US.

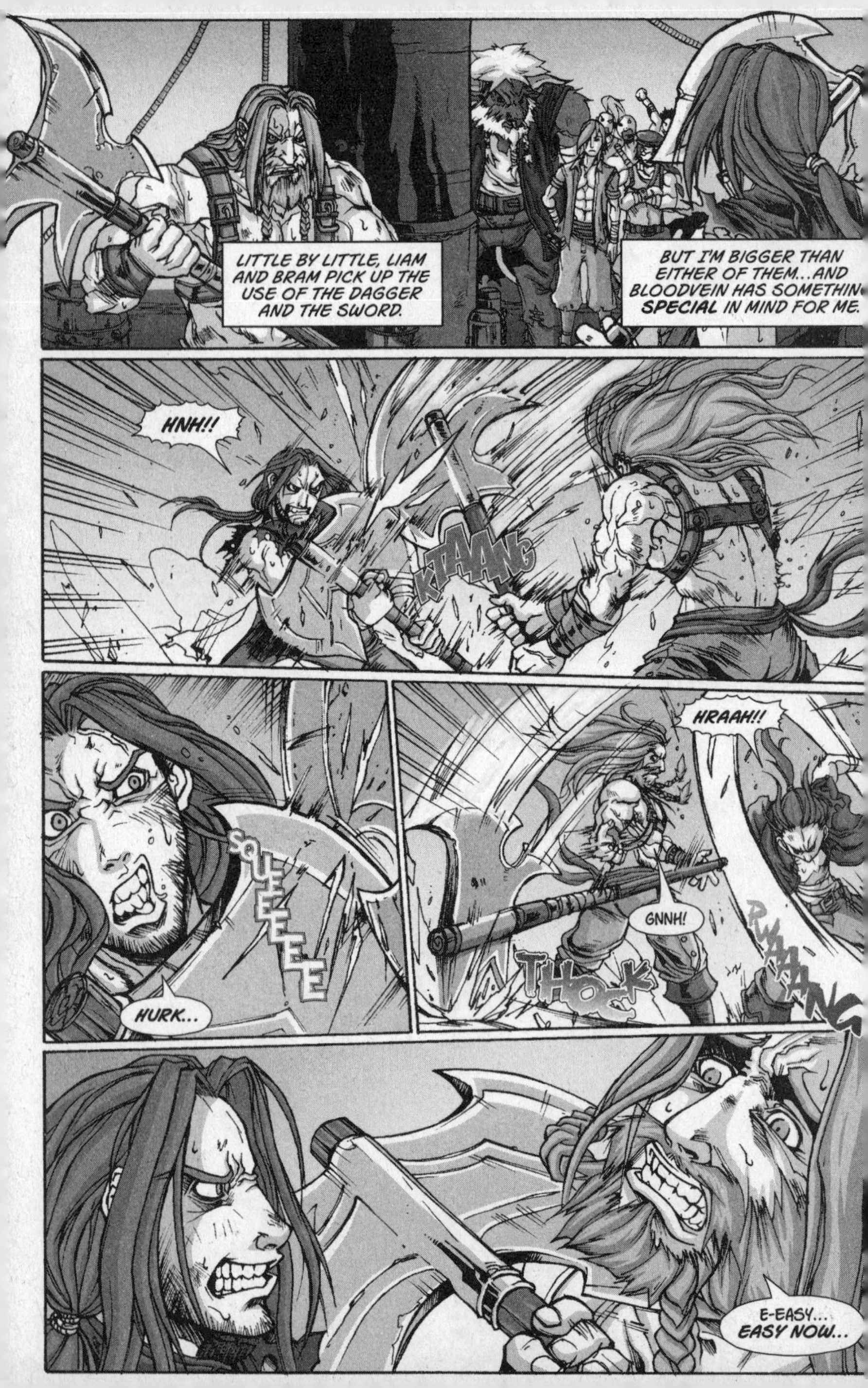
LITTLE BY LITTLE, LIAM AND BRAM PICK UP THE USE OF THE DAGGER AND THE SWORD.
BUT I'M BIGGER THAN EITHER OF THEM...AND BLOODVEIN HAS SOMETHIN SPECIAL IN MIND FOR ME.
HNH!!
KTAANG
SQUEEEEEE
HURK...
HRAAH!!
GNNH!
THOK
RWAAANG
E-EASY... EASY NOW...

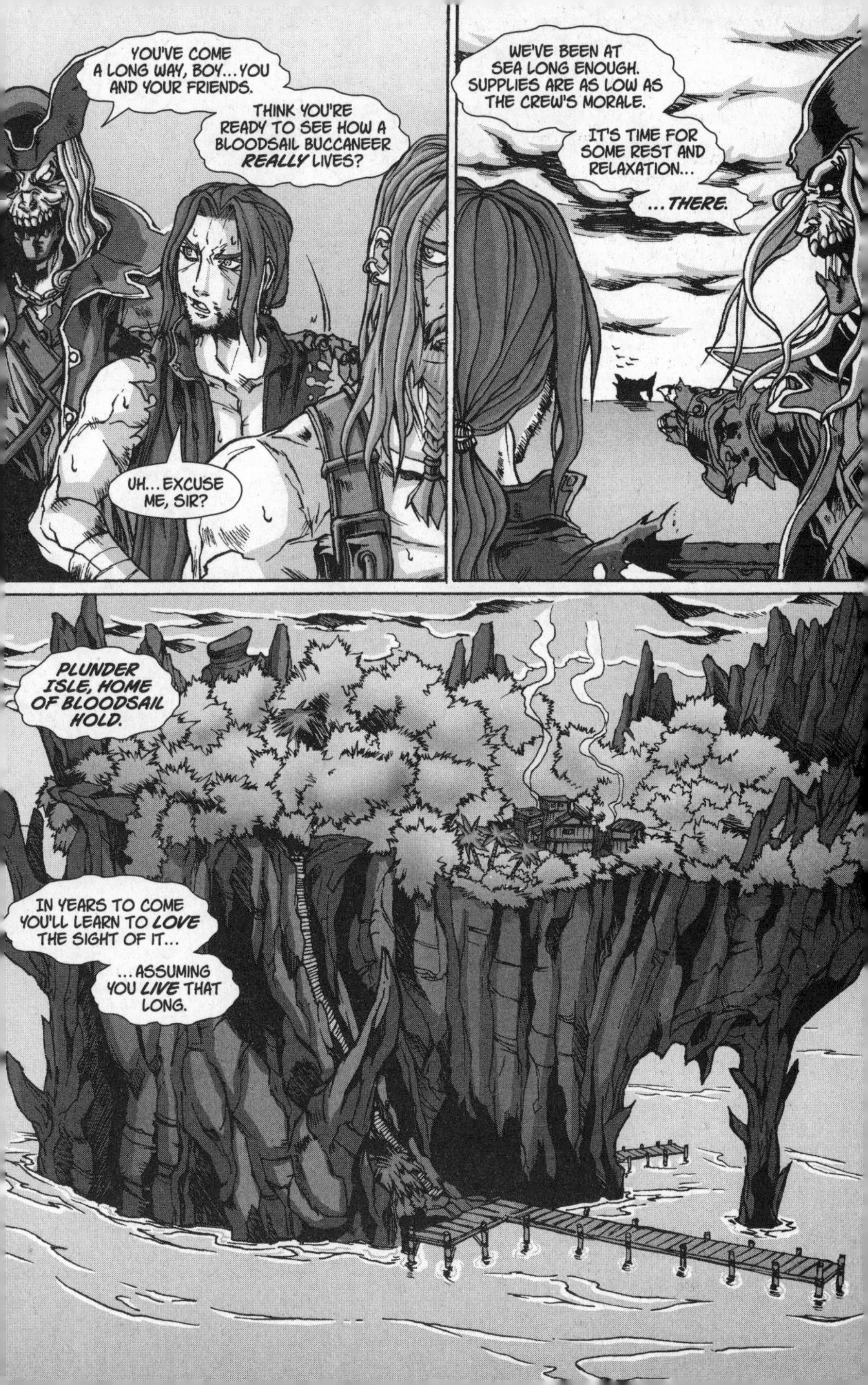
YOU'VE COME A LONG WAY, BOY...YOU AND YOUR FRIENDS.
THINK YOU'RE READY TO SEE HOW A BLOODSAIL BUCCANEER *REALLY* LIVES?
UH...EXCUSE ME, SIR?
WE'VE BEEN AT SEA LONG ENOUGH. SUPPLIES ARE AS LOW AS THE CREW'S MORALE.
IT'S TIME FOR SOME REST AND RELAXATION...
...*THERE*.
PLUNDER ISLE, HOME OF BLOODSAIL HOLD.
IN YEARS TO COME YOU'LL LEARN TO *LOVE* THE SIGHT OF IT...
...ASSUMING YOU *LIVE* THAT LONG.

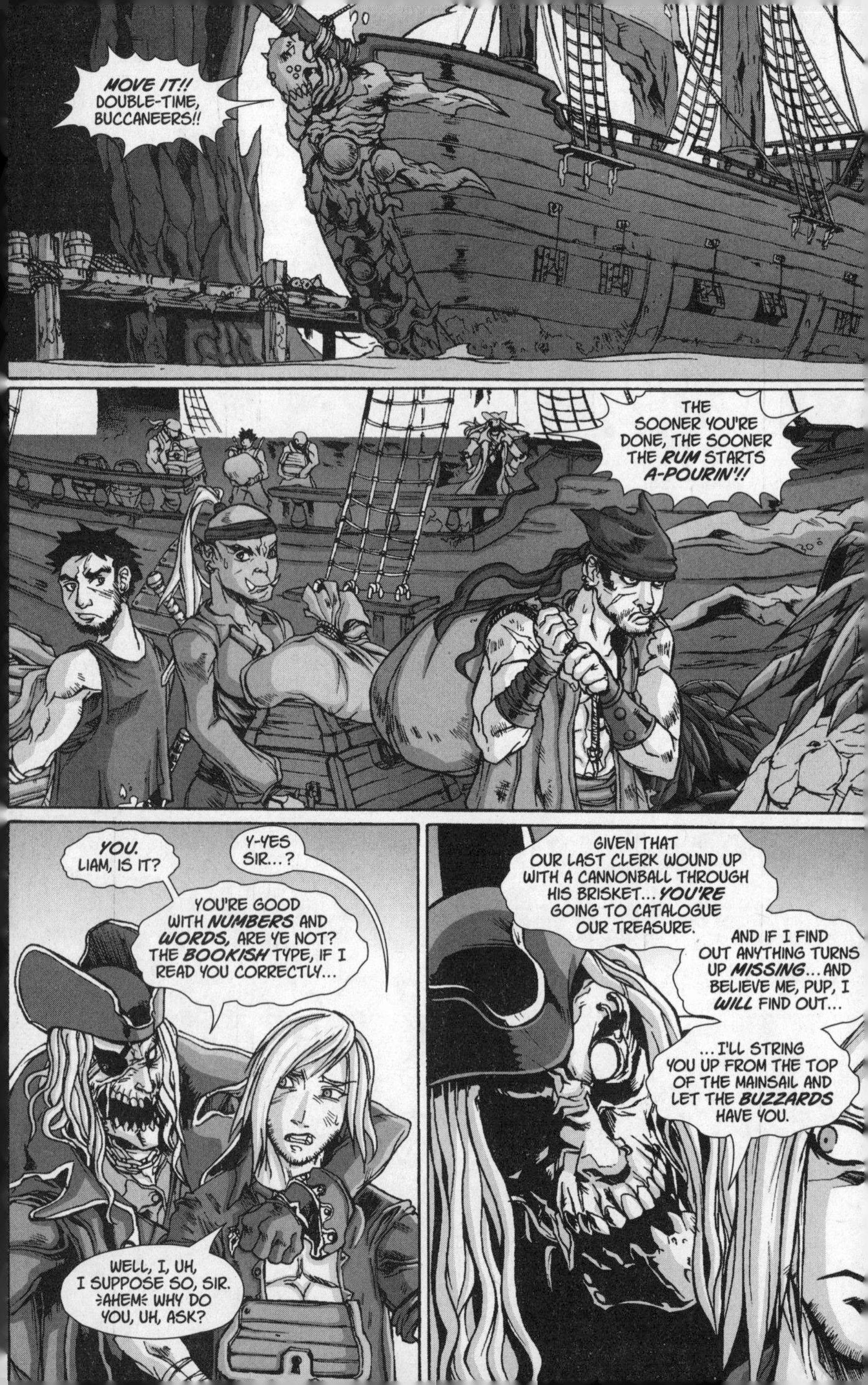
MOVE IT!! DOUBLE-TIME, BUCCANEERS!!
THE SOONER YOU'RE DONE, THE SOONER THE RUM STARTS A-POURIN'!!
YOU. LIAM, IS IT?
Y-YES SIR...?
YOU'RE GOOD WITH NUMBERS AND WORDS, ARE YE NOT? THE BOOKISH TYPE, IF I READ YOU CORRECTLY...
WELL, I, UH, I SUPPOSE SO, SIR. ≶AHEM≶ WHY DO YOU, UH, ASK?
GIVEN THAT OUR LAST CLERK WOUND UP WITH A CANNONBALL THROUGH HIS BRISKET... YOU'RE GOING TO CATALOGUE OUR TREASURE.
AND IF I FIND OUT ANYTHING TURNS UP MISSING... AND BELIEVE ME, PUP, I WILL FIND OUT...
...I'LL STRING YOU UP FROM THE TOP OF THE MAINSAIL AND LET THE BUZZARDS HAVE YOU.

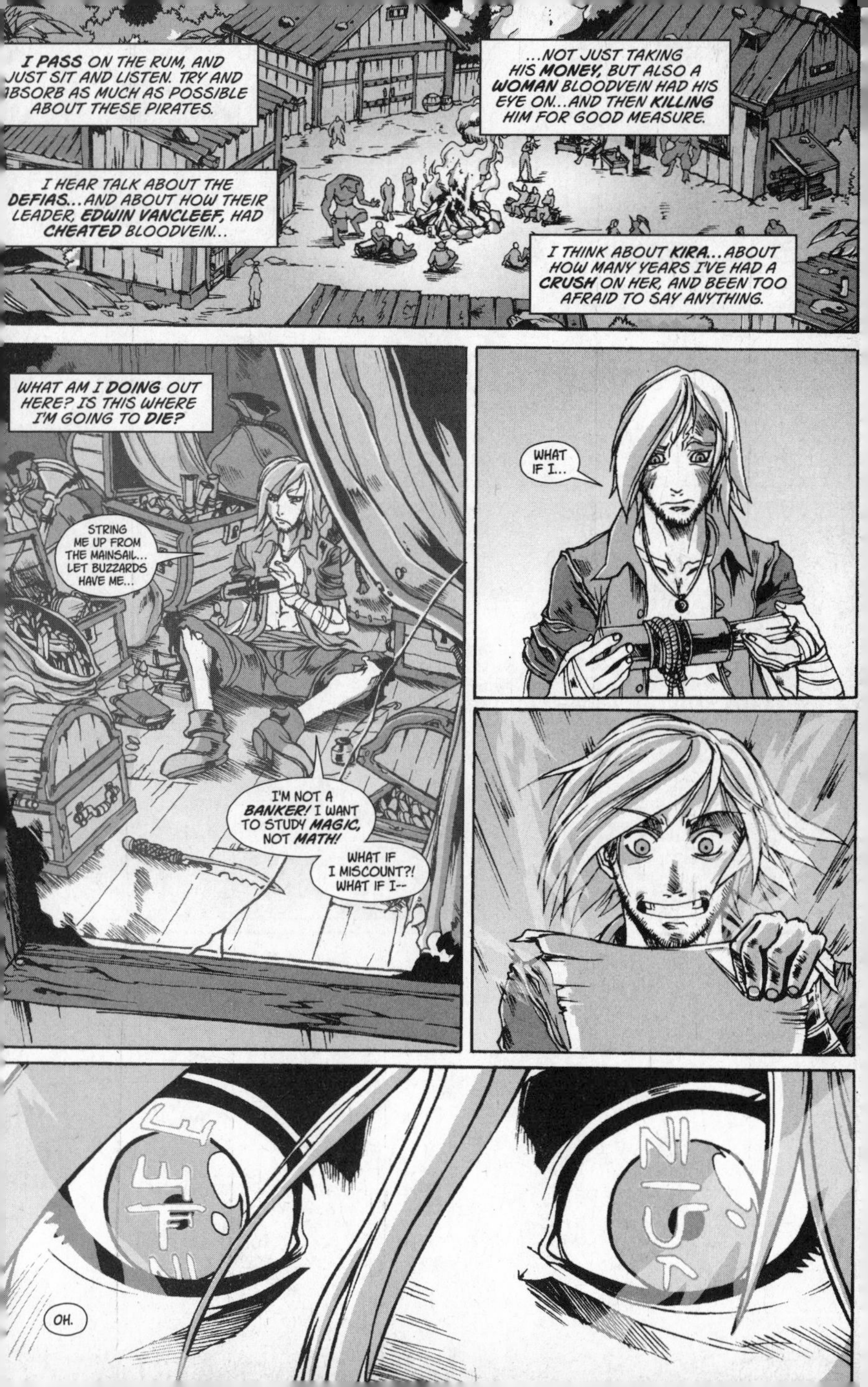
I PASS ON THE RUM, AND JUST SIT AND LISTEN. TRY AND ABSORB AS MUCH AS POSSIBLE ABOUT THESE PIRATES.
I HEAR TALK ABOUT THE DEFIAS... AND ABOUT HOW THEIR LEADER, EDWIN VANCLEEF, HAD CHEATED BLOODVEIN...
...NOT JUST TAKING HIS MONEY, BUT ALSO A WOMAN BLOODVEIN HAD HIS EYE ON... AND THEN KILLING HIM FOR GOOD MEASURE.
I THINK ABOUT KIRA... ABOUT HOW MANY YEARS I'VE HAD A CRUSH ON HER, AND BEEN TOO AFRAID TO SAY ANYTHING.
WHAT AM I DOING OUT HERE? IS THIS WHERE I'M GOING TO DIE?
STRING ME UP FROM THE MAINSAIL... LET BUZZARDS HAVE ME...
I'M NOT A BANKER! I WANT TO STUDY MAGIC, NOT MATH!
WHAT IF I MISCOUNT?! WHAT IF I--
WHAT IF I...
OH.

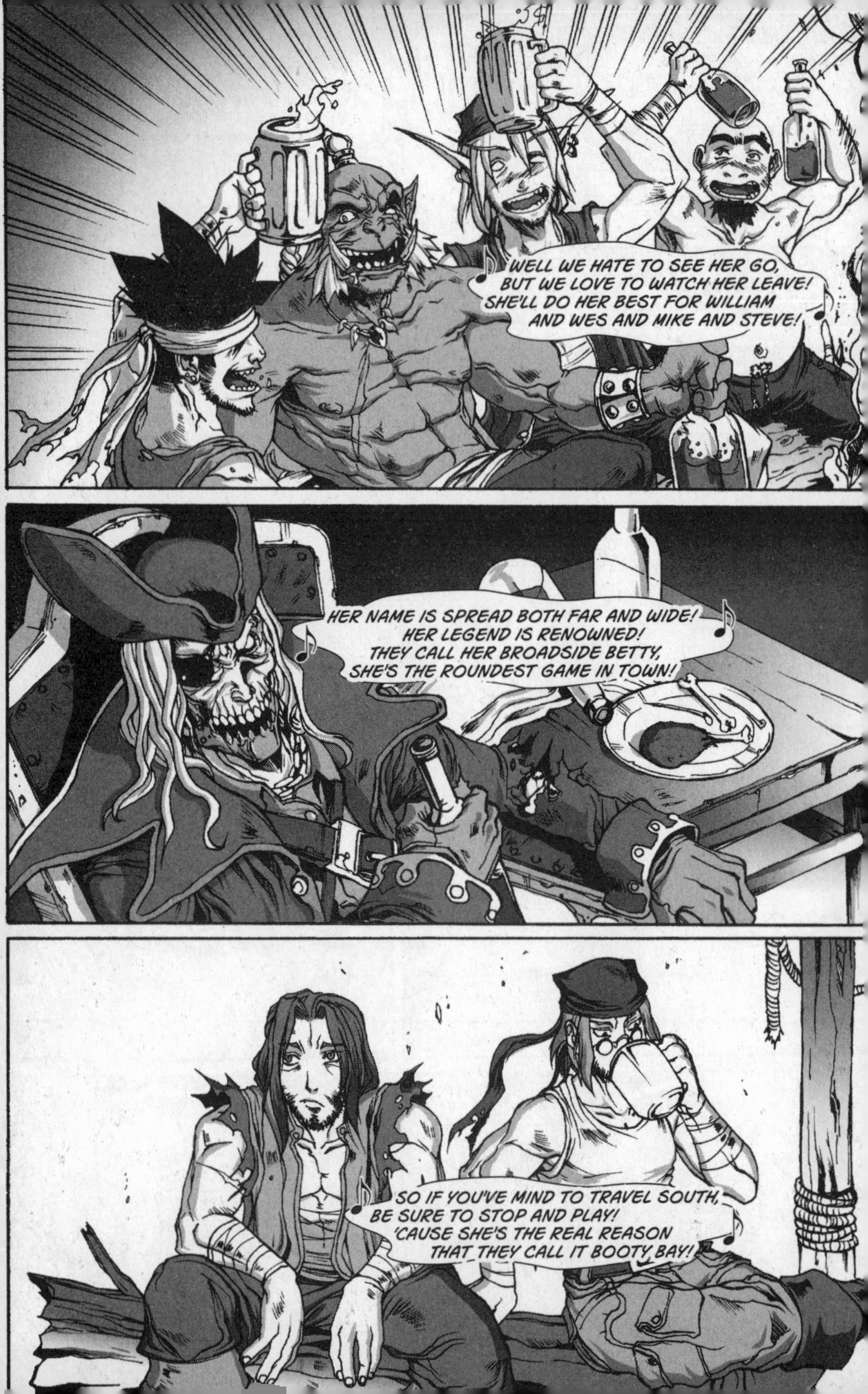
WELL WE HATE TO SEE HER GO, BUT WE LOVE TO WATCH HER LEAVE! SHE'LL DO HER BEST FOR WILLIAM AND WES AND MIKE AND STEVE!
HER NAME IS SPREAD BOTH FAR AND WIDE! HER LEGEND IS RENOWNED! THEY CALL HER BROADSIDE BETTY, SHE'S THE ROUNDEST GAME IN TOWN!
SO IF YOU'VE MIND TO TRAVEL SOUTH, BE SURE TO STOP AND PLAY! 'CAUSE SHE'S THE REAL REASON THAT THEY CALL IT BOOTY BAY!

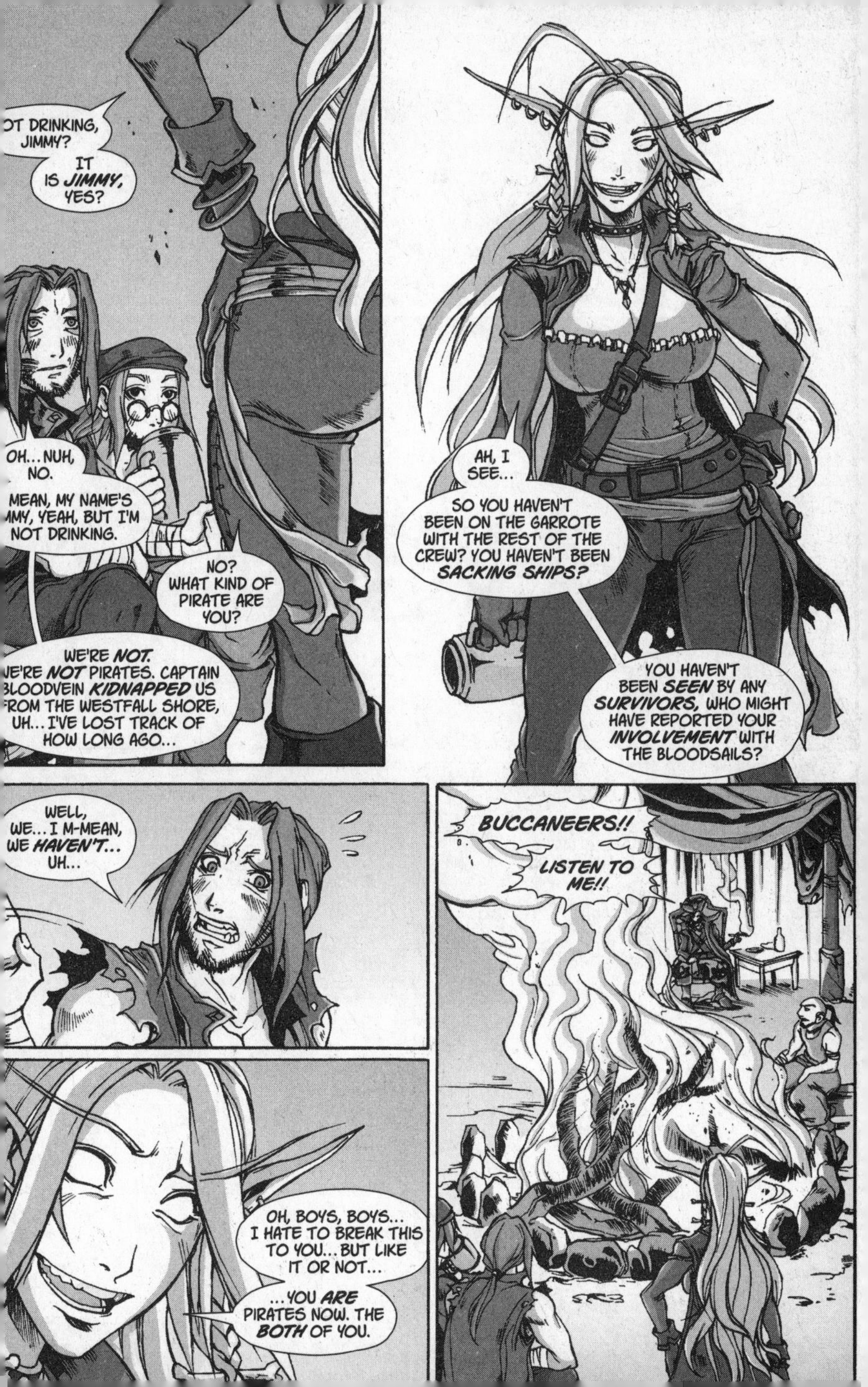

OT DRINKING, JIMMY?
IT IS JIMMY, YES?
OH... NUH, NO.
MEAN, MY NAME'S MMY, YEAH, BUT I'M NOT DRINKING.
NO? WHAT KIND OF PIRATE ARE YOU?
WE'RE NOT. JE'RE NOT PIRATES. CAPTAIN BLOODVEIN KIDNAPPED US FROM THE WESTFALL SHORE, UH... I'VE LOST TRACK OF HOW LONG AGO...
AH, I SEE...
SO YOU HAVEN'T BEEN ON THE GARROTE WITH THE REST OF THE CREW? YOU HAVEN'T BEEN SACKING SHIPS?
YOU HAVEN'T BEEN SEEN BY ANY SURVIVORS, WHO MIGHT HAVE REPORTED YOUR INVOLVEMENT WITH THE BLOODSAILS?
WELL, WE... I M-MEAN, WE HAVEN'T... UH...
OH, BOYS, BOYS... I HATE TO BREAK THIS TO YOU... BUT LIKE IT OR NOT...
...YOU ARE PIRATES NOW. THE BOTH OF YOU.
BUCCANEERS!!
LISTEN TO ME!!

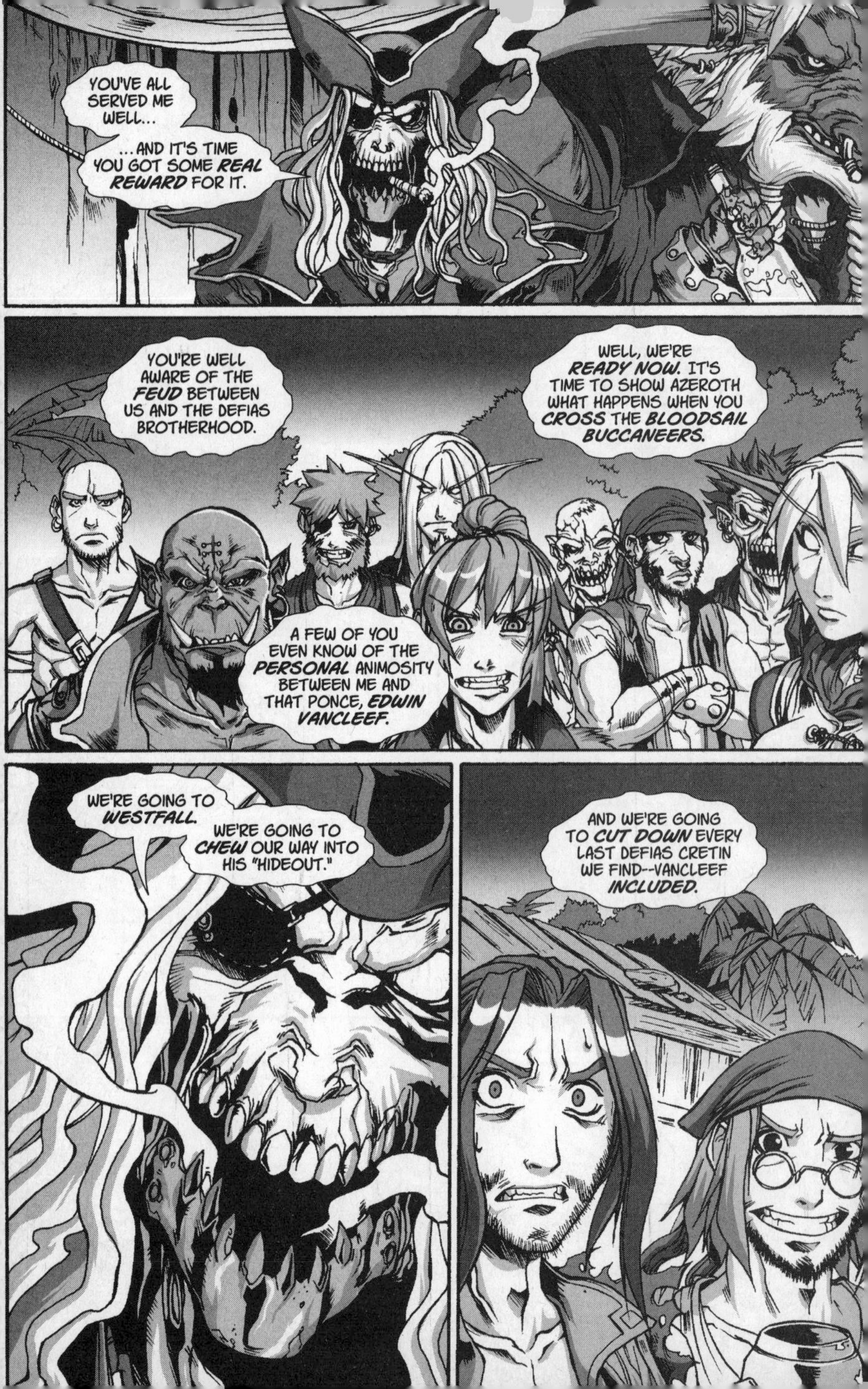
YOU'VE ALL SERVED ME WELL...
...AND IT'S TIME YOU GOT SOME REAL REWARD FOR IT.
YOU'RE WELL AWARE OF THE FEUD BETWEEN US AND THE DEFIAS BROTHERHOOD.
A FEW OF YOU EVEN KNOW OF THE PERSONAL ANIMOSITY BETWEEN ME AND THAT PONCE, EDWIN VANCLEEF.
WELL, WE'RE READY NOW. IT'S TIME TO SHOW AZEROTH WHAT HAPPENS WHEN YOU CROSS THE BLOODSAIL BUCCANEERS.
WE'RE GOING TO WESTFALL.
WE'RE GOING TO CHEW OUR WAY INTO HIS "HIDEOUT."
AND WE'RE GOING TO CUT DOWN EVERY LAST DEFIAS CRETIN WE FIND--VANCLEEF INCLUDED.

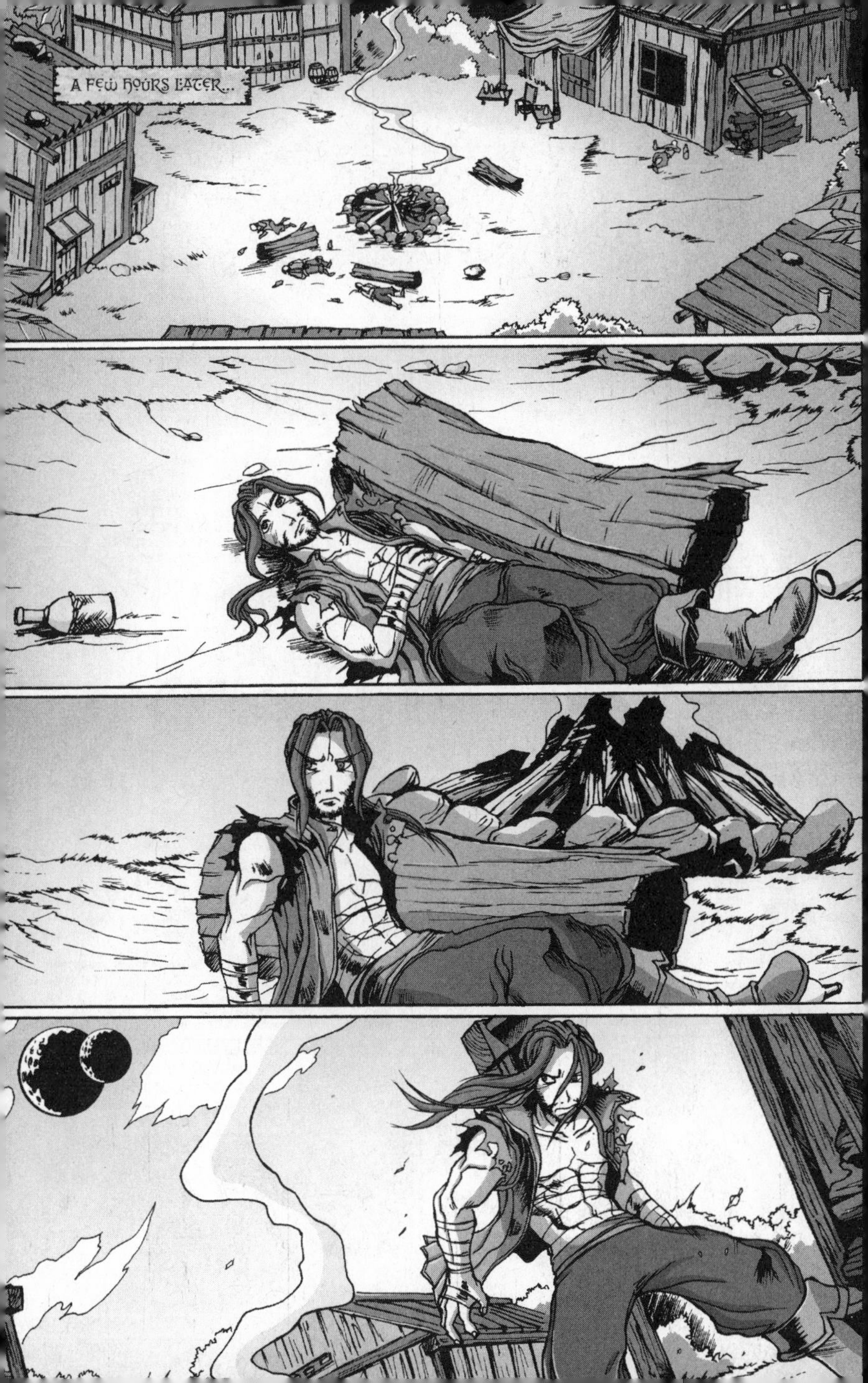
A FEW HOURS LATER...

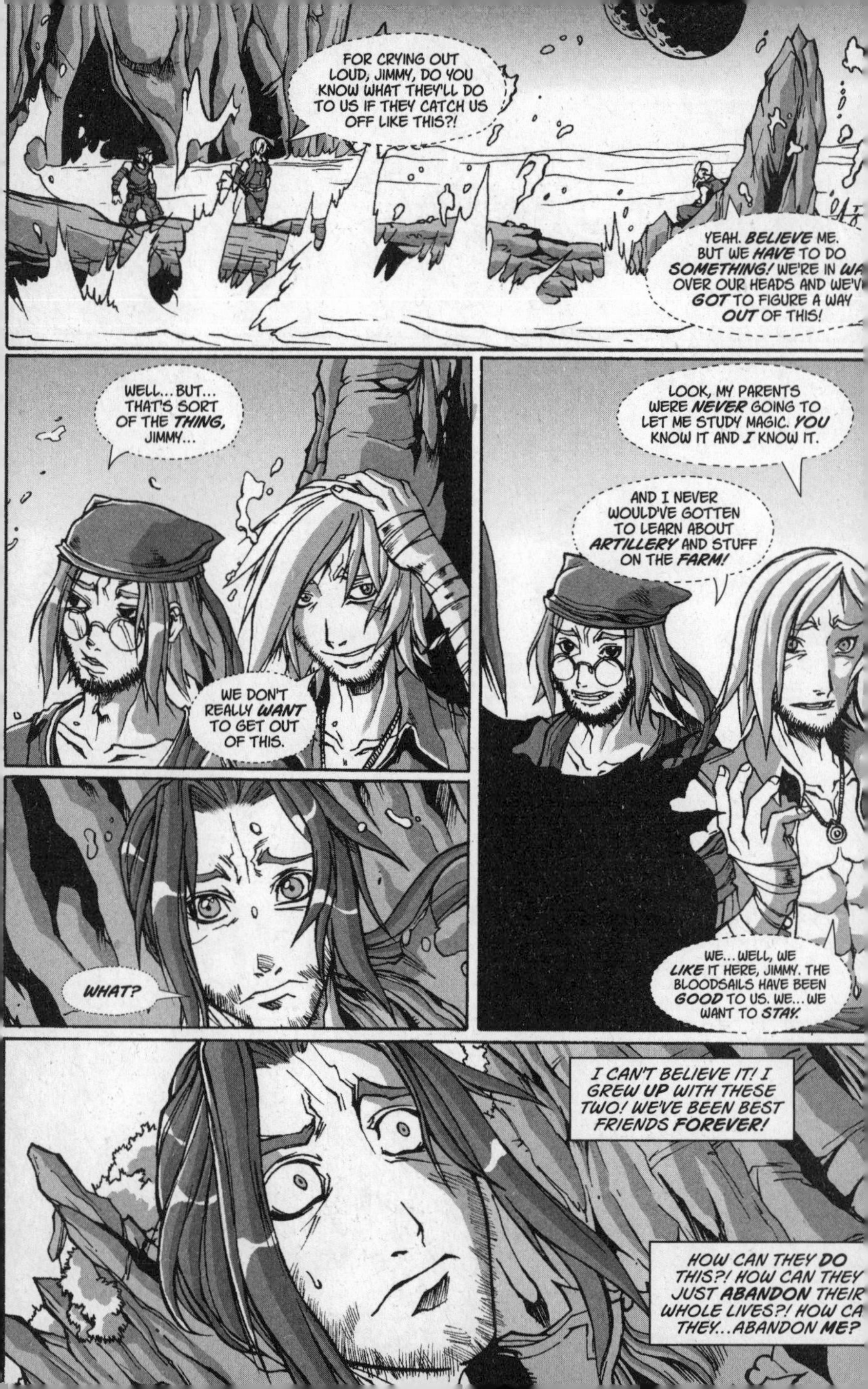
FOR CRYING OUT LOUD, JIMMY, DO YOU KNOW WHAT THEY'LL DO TO US IF THEY CATCH US OFF LIKE THIS?!
YEAH. BELIEVE ME. BUT WE HAVE TO DO SOMETHING! WE'RE IN WA OVER OUR HEADS AND WE'V GOT TO FIGURE A WAY OUT OF THIS!
WELL... BUT... THAT'S SORT OF THE THING, JIMMY...
WE DON'T REALLY WANT TO GET OUT OF THIS.
WHAT?
LOOK, MY PARENTS WERE NEVER GOING TO LET ME STUDY MAGIC. YOU KNOW IT AND I KNOW IT.
AND I NEVER WOULD'VE GOTTEN TO LEARN ABOUT ARTILLERY AND STUFF ON THE FARM!
WE... WELL, WE LIKE IT HERE, JIMMY. THE BLOODSAILS HAVE BEEN GOOD TO US. WE... WE WANT TO STAY.
I CAN'T BELIEVE IT! I GREW UP WITH THESE TWO! WE'VE BEEN BEST FRIENDS FOREVER!
HOW CAN THEY DO THIS?! HOW CAN THEY JUST ABANDON THEIR WHOLE LIVES?! HOW CA THEY... ABANDON ME?

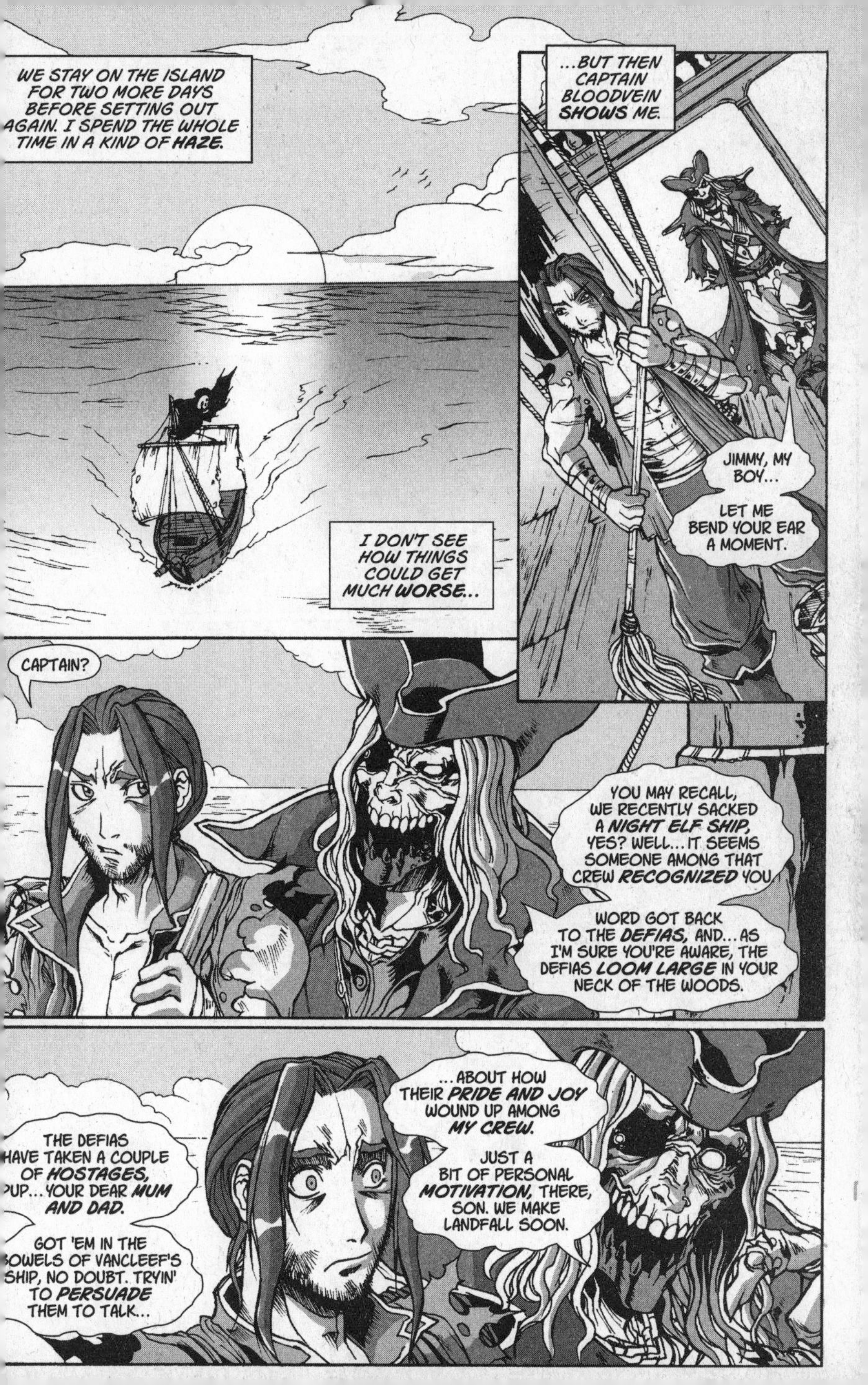
WE STAY ON THE ISLAND FOR TWO MORE DAYS BEFORE SETTING OUT AGAIN. I SPEND THE WHOLE TIME IN A KIND OF HAZE.
I DON'T SEE HOW THINGS COULD GET MUCH WORSE...
...BUT THEN CAPTAIN BLOODVEIN SHOWS ME.
JIMMY, MY BOY...
LET ME BEND YOUR EAR A MOMENT.
CAPTAIN?
YOU MAY RECALL, WE RECENTLY SACKED A NIGHT ELF SHIP, YES? WELL... IT SEEMS SOMEONE AMONG THAT CREW RECOGNIZED YOU.
WORD GOT BACK TO THE DEFIAS, AND... AS I'M SURE YOU'RE AWARE, THE DEFIAS LOOM LARGE IN YOUR NECK OF THE WOODS.
THE DEFIAS HAVE TAKEN A COUPLE OF HOSTAGES, PUP... YOUR DEAR MUM AND DAD.
GOT 'EM IN THE BOWELS OF VANCLEEF'S SHIP, NO DOUBT. TRYIN' TO PERSUADE THEM TO TALK...
...ABOUT HOW THEIR PRIDE AND JOY WOUND UP AMONG MY CREW.
JUST A BIT OF PERSONAL MOTIVATION, THERE, SON. WE MAKE LANDFALL SOON.

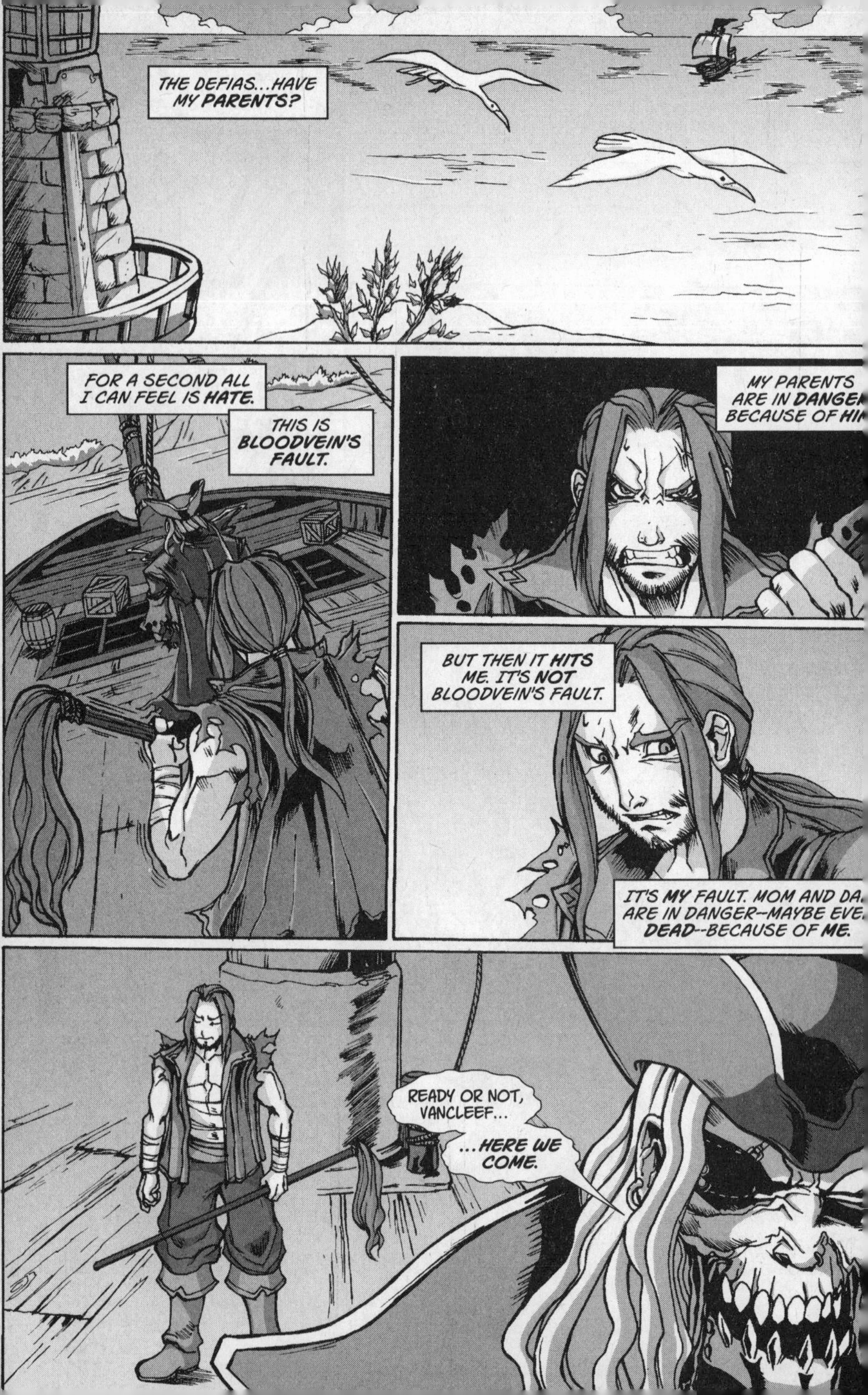
THE DEFIAS...HAVE MY **PARENTS?**
FOR A SECOND ALL I CAN FEEL IS **HATE.**
THIS IS **BLOODVEIN'S FAULT.**
MY PARENTS ARE IN **DANGE**
BECAUSE OF **HI**
BUT THEN IT **HITS** ME. IT'S **NOT** BLOODVEIN'S FAULT.
IT'S **MY** FAULT. MOM AND DA
ARE IN DANGER--MAYBE EVE
DEAD--BECAUSE OF **ME.**
READY OR NOT, VANCLEEF...
...**HERE WE COME.**

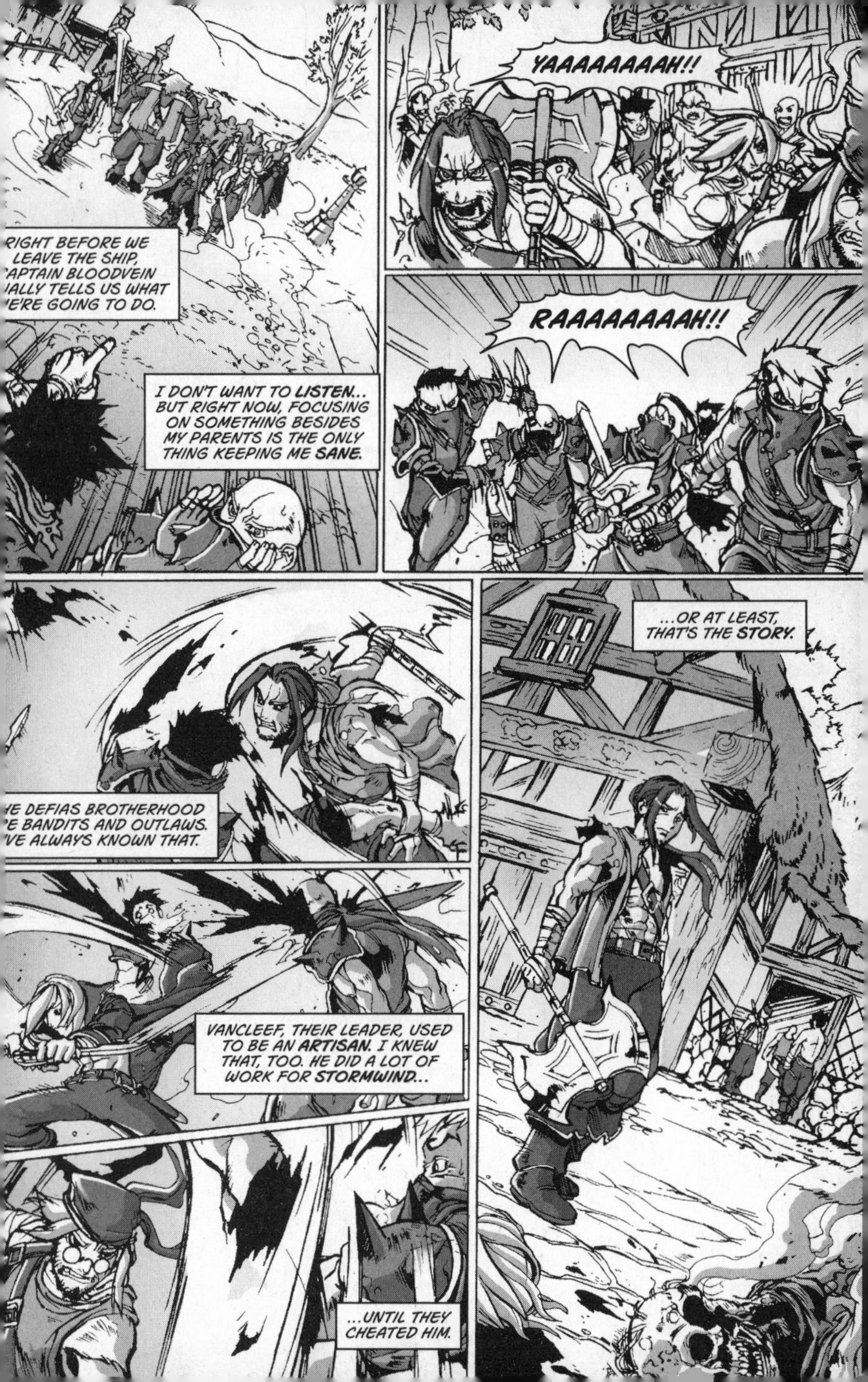
RIGHT BEFORE WE LEAVE THE SHIP, APTAIN BLOODVEIN IALLY TELLS US WHAT E'RE GOING TO DO.
YAAAAAAAAH!!
I DON'T WANT TO **LISTEN**... BUT RIGHT NOW, FOCUSING ON SOMETHING BESIDES MY PARENTS IS THE ONLY THING KEEPING ME **SANE**.
RAAAAAAAAH!!
HE DEFIAS BROTHERHOOD E BANDITS AND OUTLAWS. VE ALWAYS KNOWN THAT.
VANCLEEF, THEIR LEADER, USED TO BE AN **ARTISAN**. I KNEW THAT, TOO. HE DID A LOT OF WORK FOR **STORMWIND**...
...UNTIL THEY CHEATED HIM.
...OR AT LEAST, THAT'S THE **STORY**.

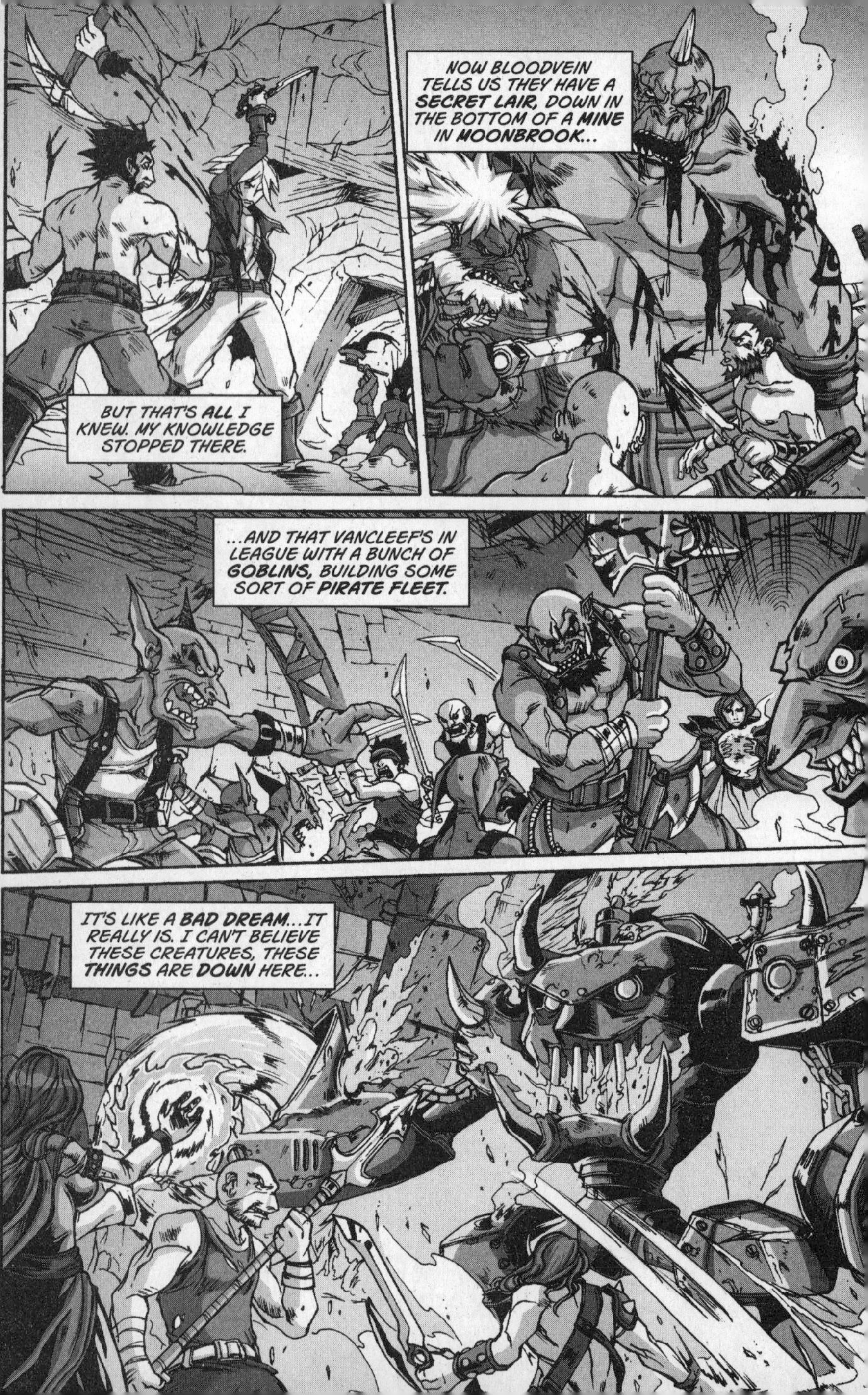
BUT THAT'S ALL I KNEW. MY KNOWLEDGE STOPPED THERE.
NOW BLOODVEIN TELLS US THEY HAVE A SECRET LAIR, DOWN IN THE BOTTOM OF A MINE IN MOONBROOK...
...AND THAT VANCLEEF'S IN LEAGUE WITH A BUNCH OF GOBLINS, BUILDING SOME SORT OF PIRATE FLEET.
IT'S LIKE A BAD DREAM...IT REALLY IS. I CAN'T BELIEVE THESE CREATURES, THESE THINGS ARE DOWN HERE...

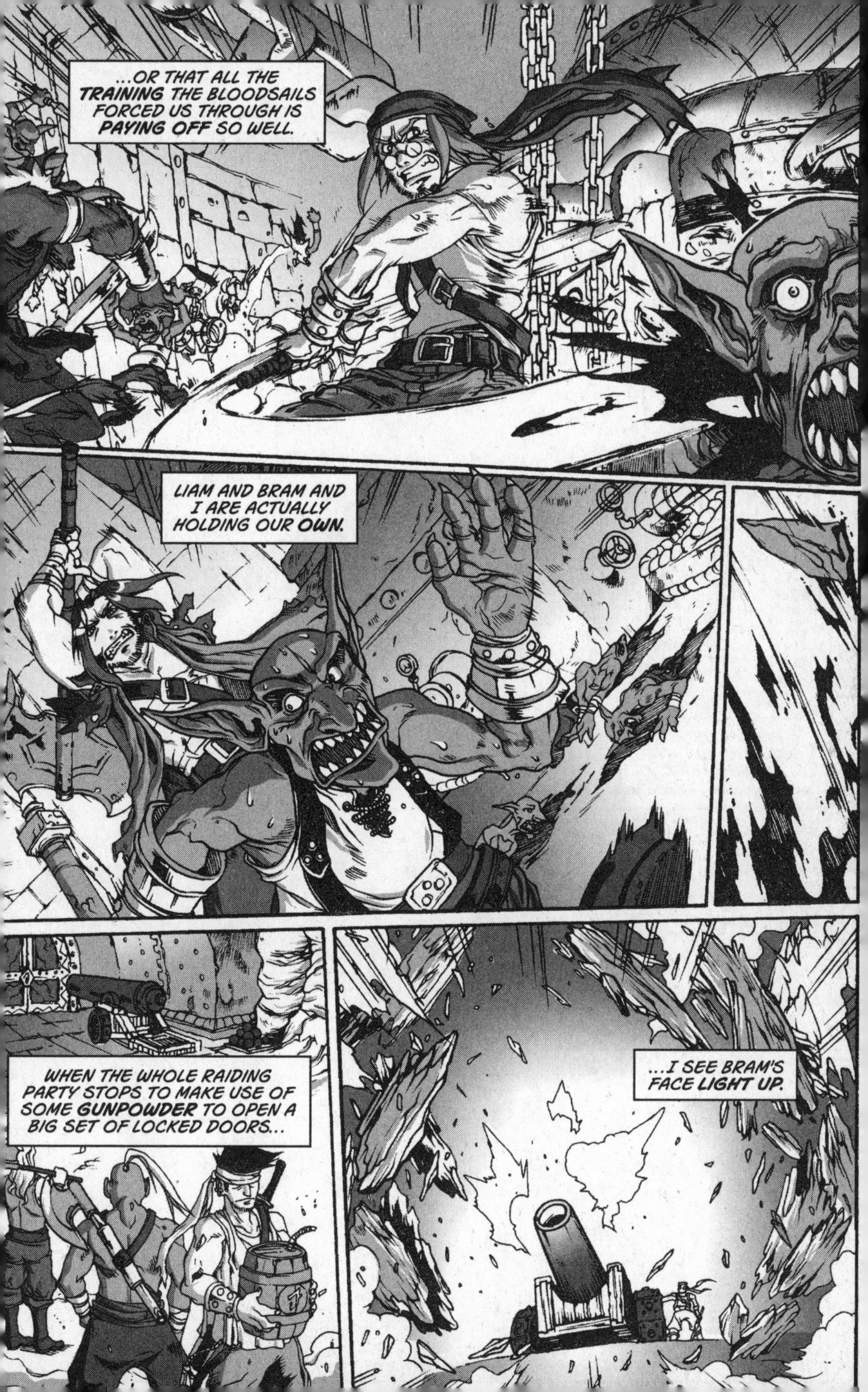
...OR THAT ALL THE TRAINING THE BLOODSAILS FORCED US THROUGH IS PAYING OFF SO WELL.
LIAM AND BRAM AND I ARE ACTUALLY HOLDING OUR OWN.
WHEN THE WHOLE RAIDING PARTY STOPS TO MAKE USE OF SOME GUNPOWDER TO OPEN A BIG SET OF LOCKED DOORS...
...I SEE BRAM'S FACE LIGHT UP.

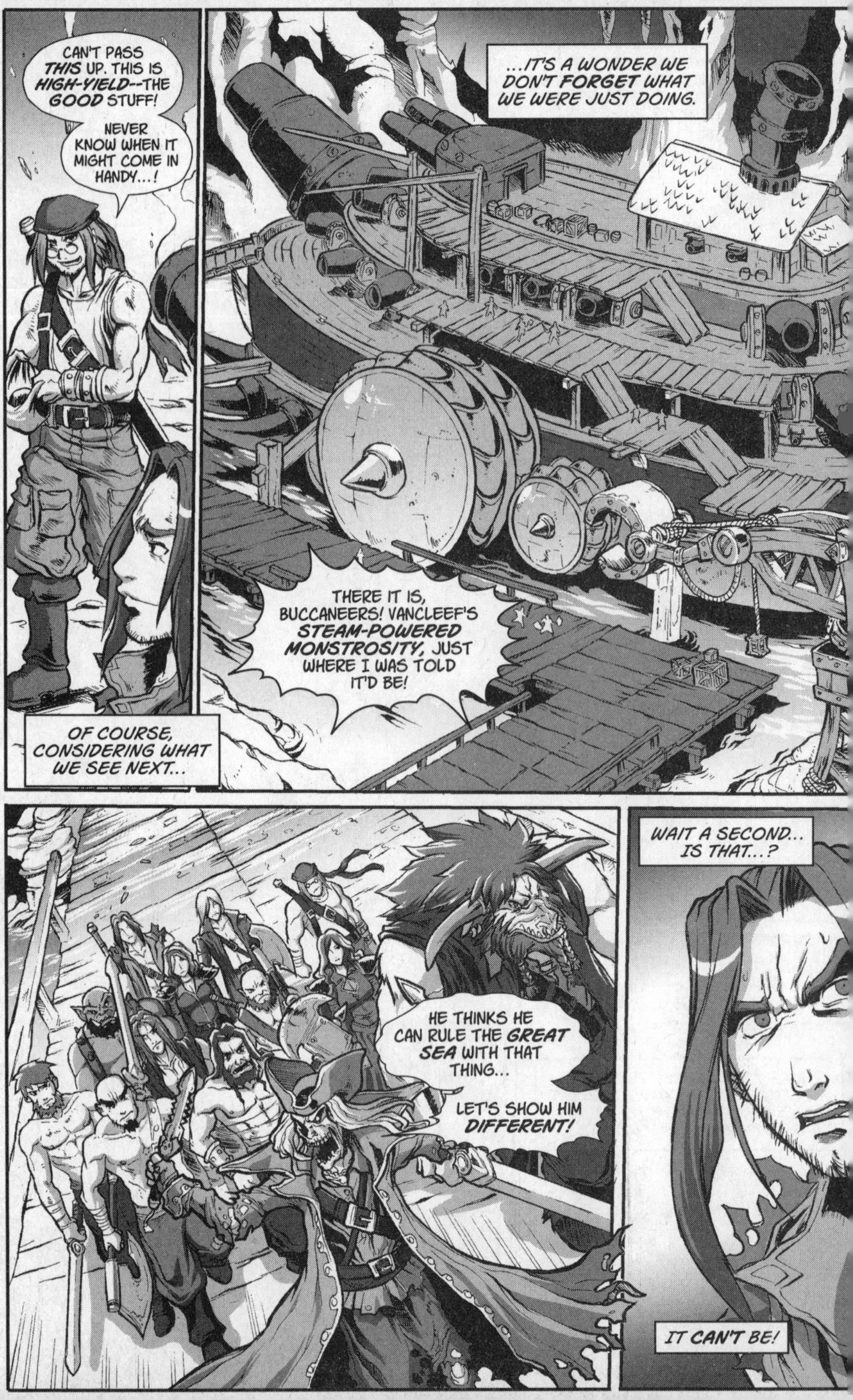

CAN'T PASS THIS UP. THIS IS HIGH-YIELD--THE GOOD STUFF!
NEVER KNOW WHEN IT MIGHT COME IN HANDY...!
OF COURSE, CONSIDERING WHAT WE SEE NEXT...
...IT'S A WONDER WE DON'T FORGET WHAT WE WERE JUST DOING.
THERE IT IS, BUCCANEERS! VANCLEEF'S STEAM-POWERED MONSTROSITY, JUST WHERE I WAS TOLD IT'D BE!
HE THINKS HE CAN RULE THE GREAT SEA WITH THAT THING...
LET'S SHOW HIM DIFFERENT!
WAIT A SECOND... IS THAT...?
IT CAN'T BE!

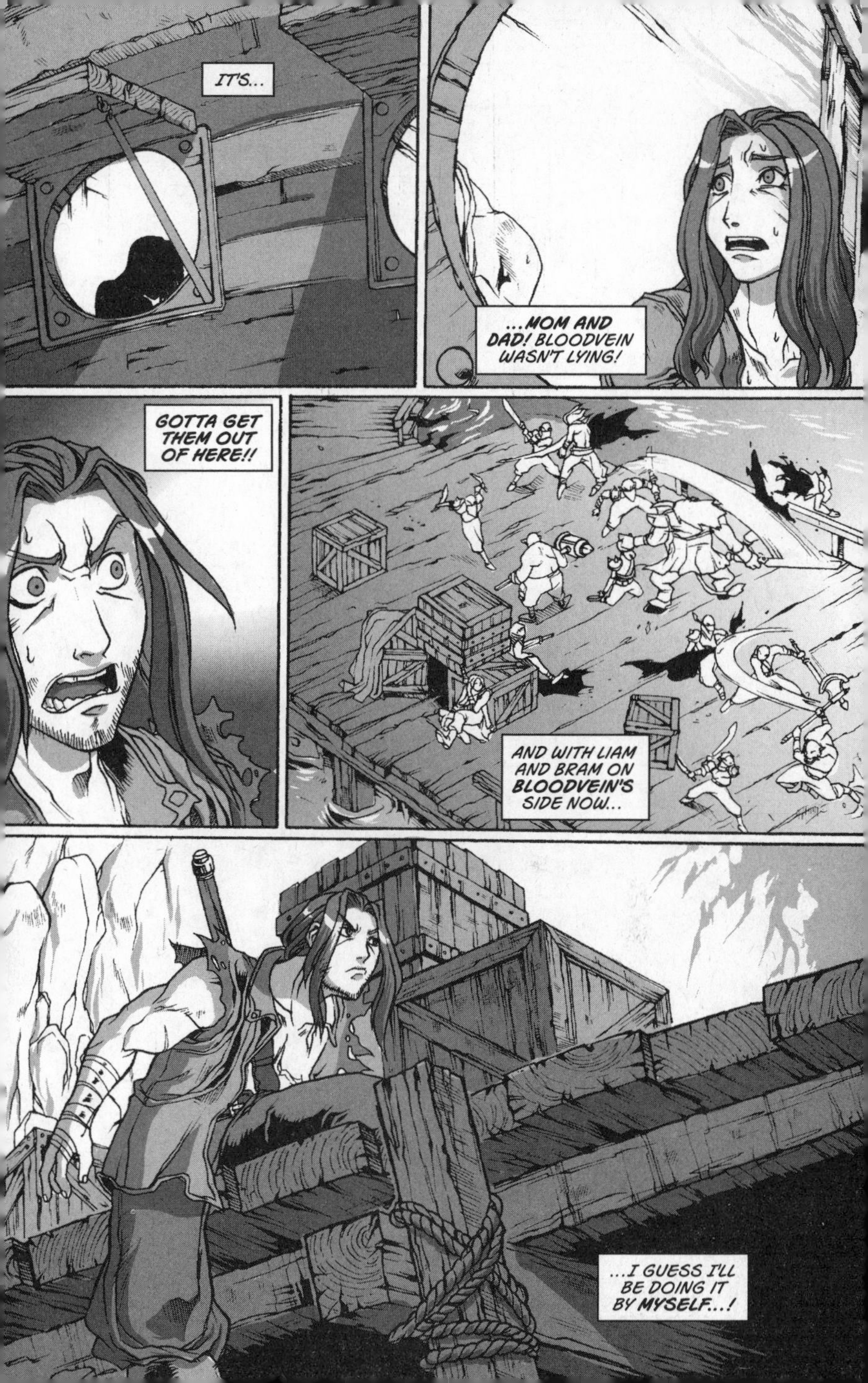
IT'S...
...MOM AND DAD! BLOODVEIN WASN'T LYING!
GOTTA GET THEM OUT OF HERE!!
AND WITH LIAM AND BRAM ON BLOODVEIN'S SIDE NOW...
...I GUESS I'LL BE DOING IT BY MYSELF...!

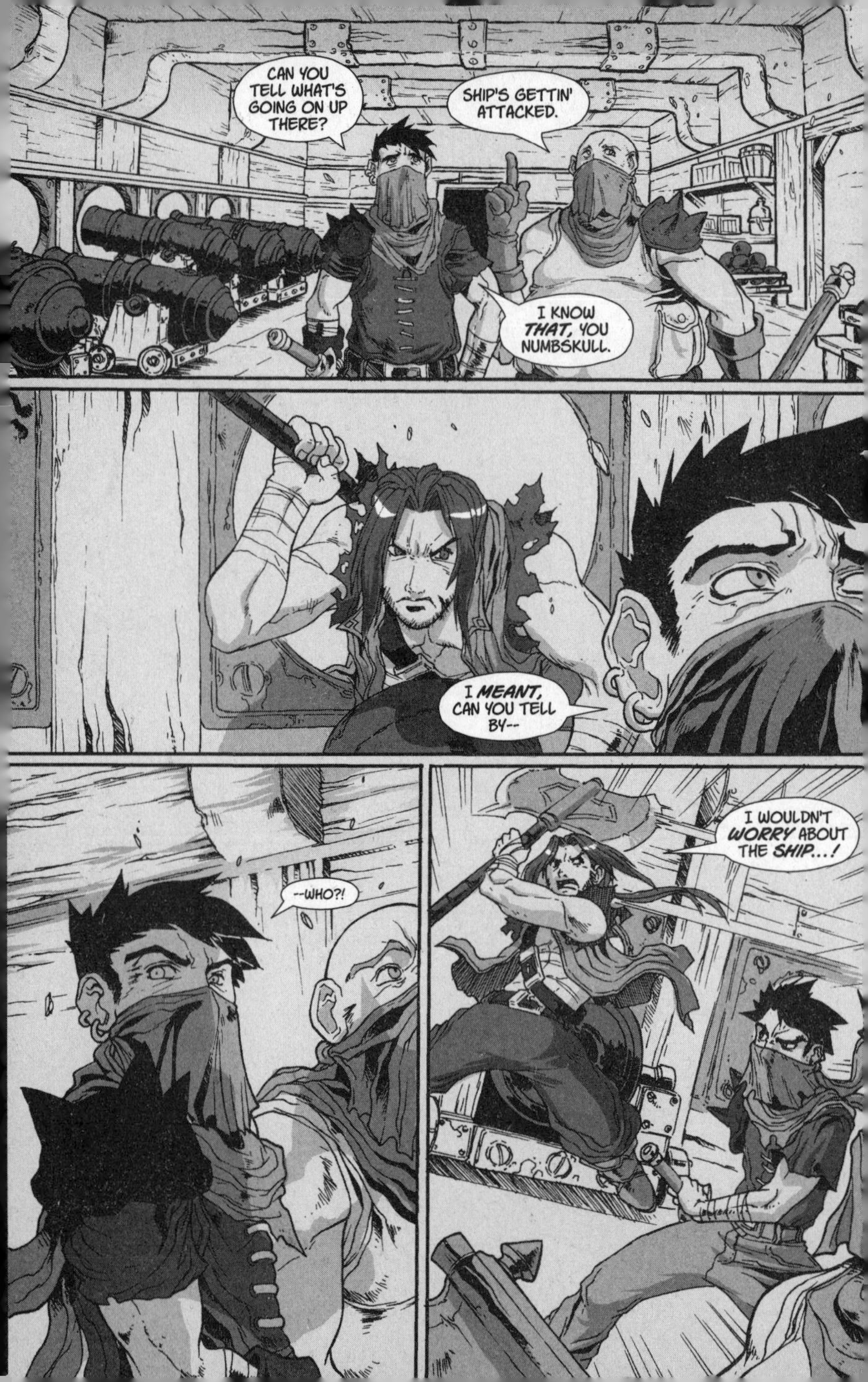
CAN YOU TELL WHAT'S GOING ON UP THERE?
SHIP'S GETTIN' ATTACKED.
I KNOW *THAT,* YOU NUMBSKULL.
I *MEANT,* CAN YOU TELL BY--
--WHO?!
I WOULDN'T *WORRY* ABOUT THE *SHIP...!*

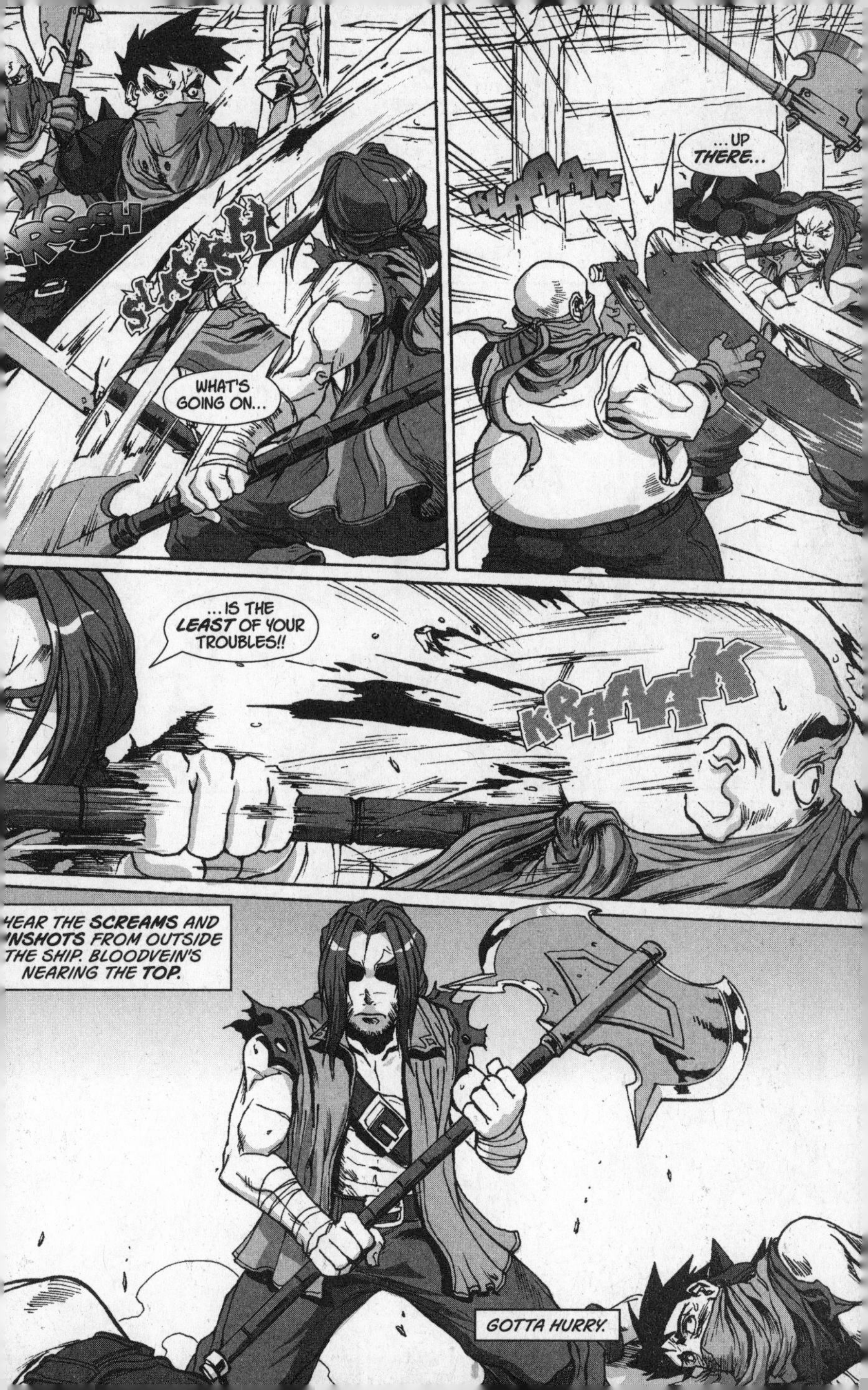

KRSSH
SLAASH
WHAT'S GOING ON...
KLAAANK
...UP THERE...
...IS THE LEAST OF YOUR TROUBLES!!
KRAAAK
HEAR THE SCREAMS AND NSHOTS FROM OUTSIDE THE SHIP. BLOODVEIN'S NEARING THE TOP.
GOTTA HURRY.

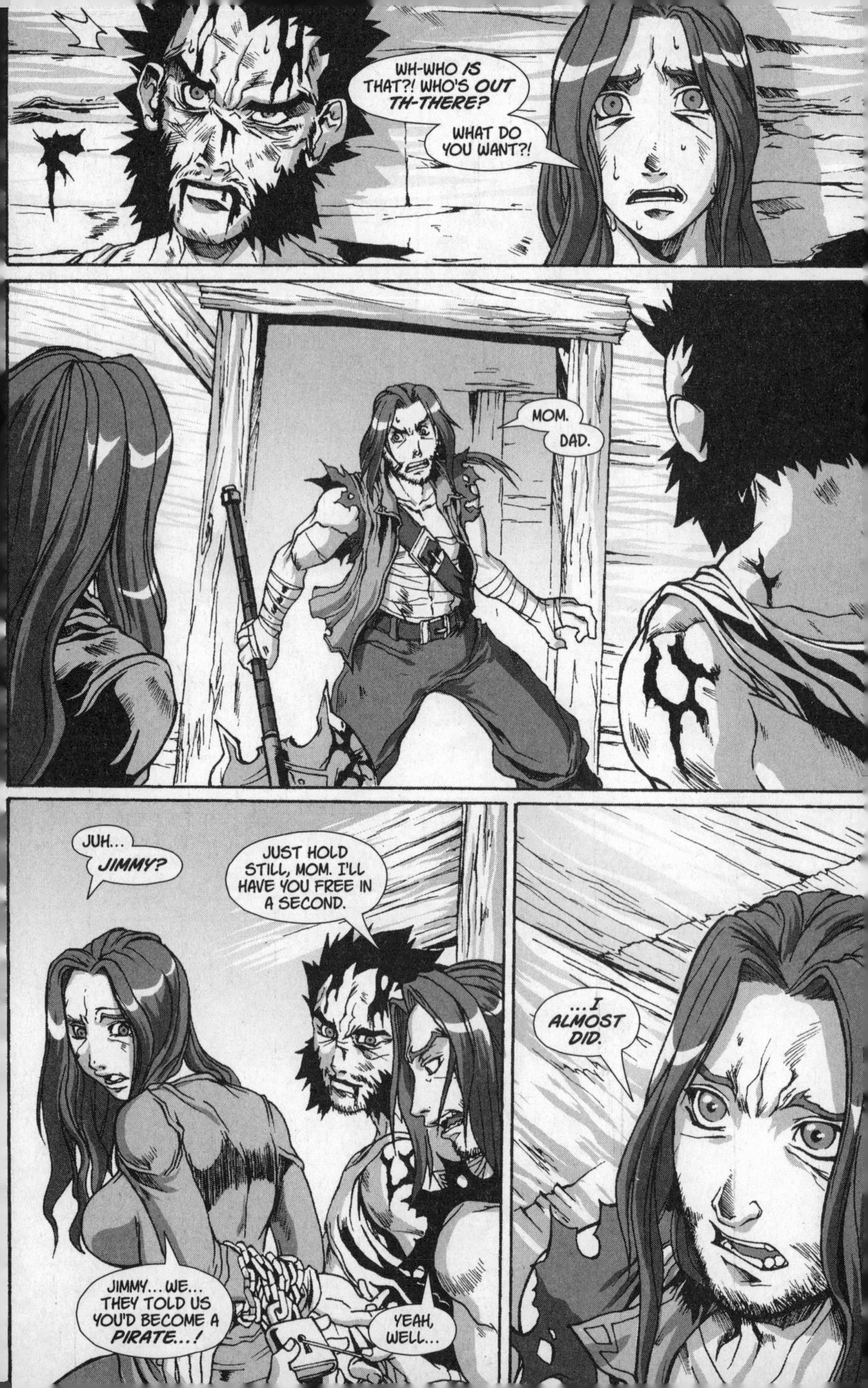
WH-WHO *IS* THAT?! WHO'S *OUT TH-THERE?*
WHAT DO YOU WANT?!
MOM.
DAD.
JUH... *JIMMY?*
JUST HOLD STILL, MOM. I'LL HAVE YOU FREE IN A SECOND.
JIMMY... WE... THEY TOLD US YOU'D BECOME A *PIRATE...!*
YEAH, WELL...
...*I ALMOST DID.*

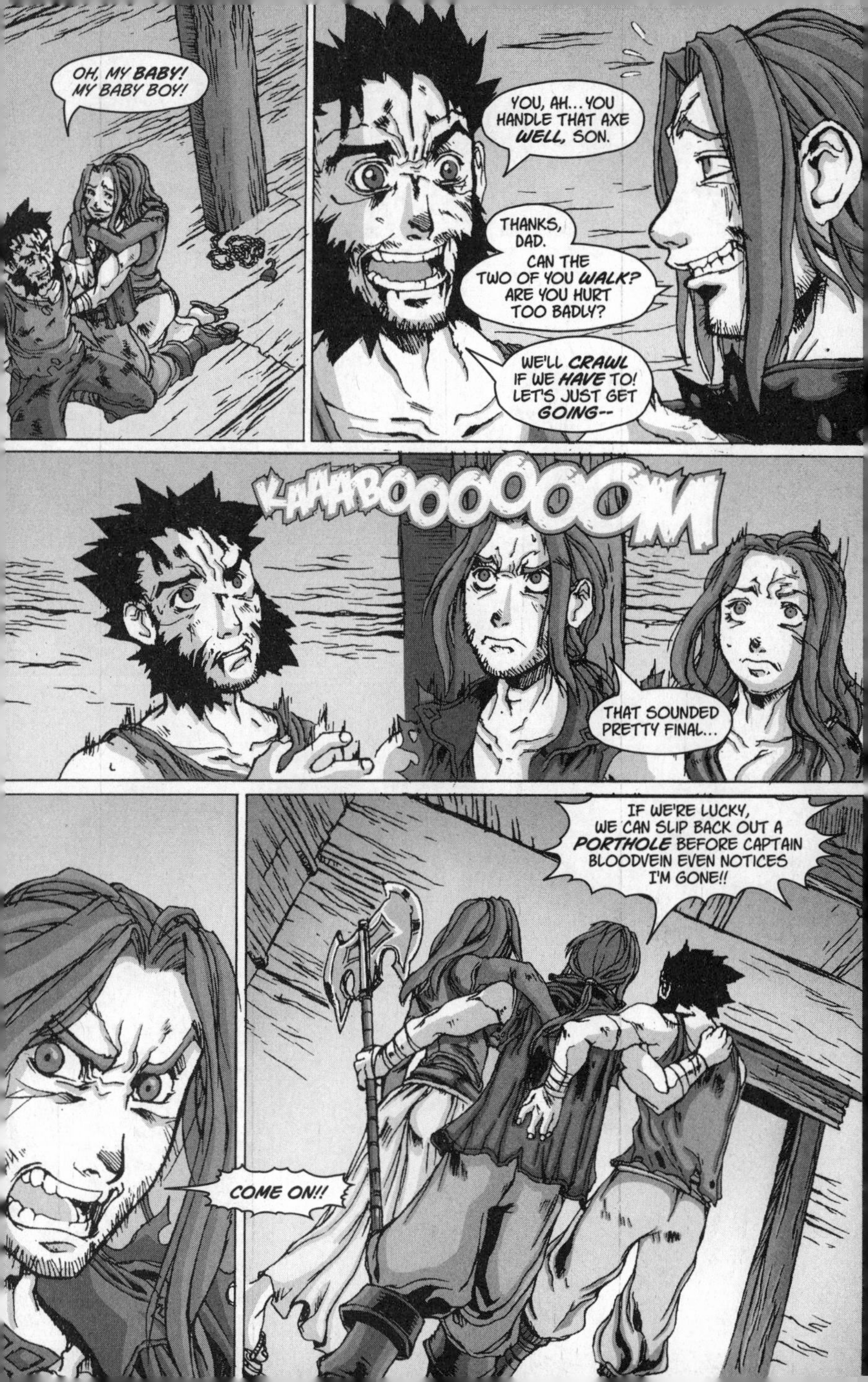
OH, MY BABY! MY BABY BOY!
YOU, AH... YOU HANDLE THAT AXE WELL, SON.
THANKS, DAD.
CAN THE TWO OF YOU WALK? ARE YOU HURT TOO BADLY?
WE'LL CRAWL IF WE HAVE TO! LET'S JUST GET GOING--
KAAABOOOOOOOM
THAT SOUNDED PRETTY FINAL...
COME ON!!
IF WE'RE LUCKY, WE CAN SLIP BACK OUT A PORTHOLE BEFORE CAPTAIN BLOODVEIN EVEN NOTICES I'M GONE!!

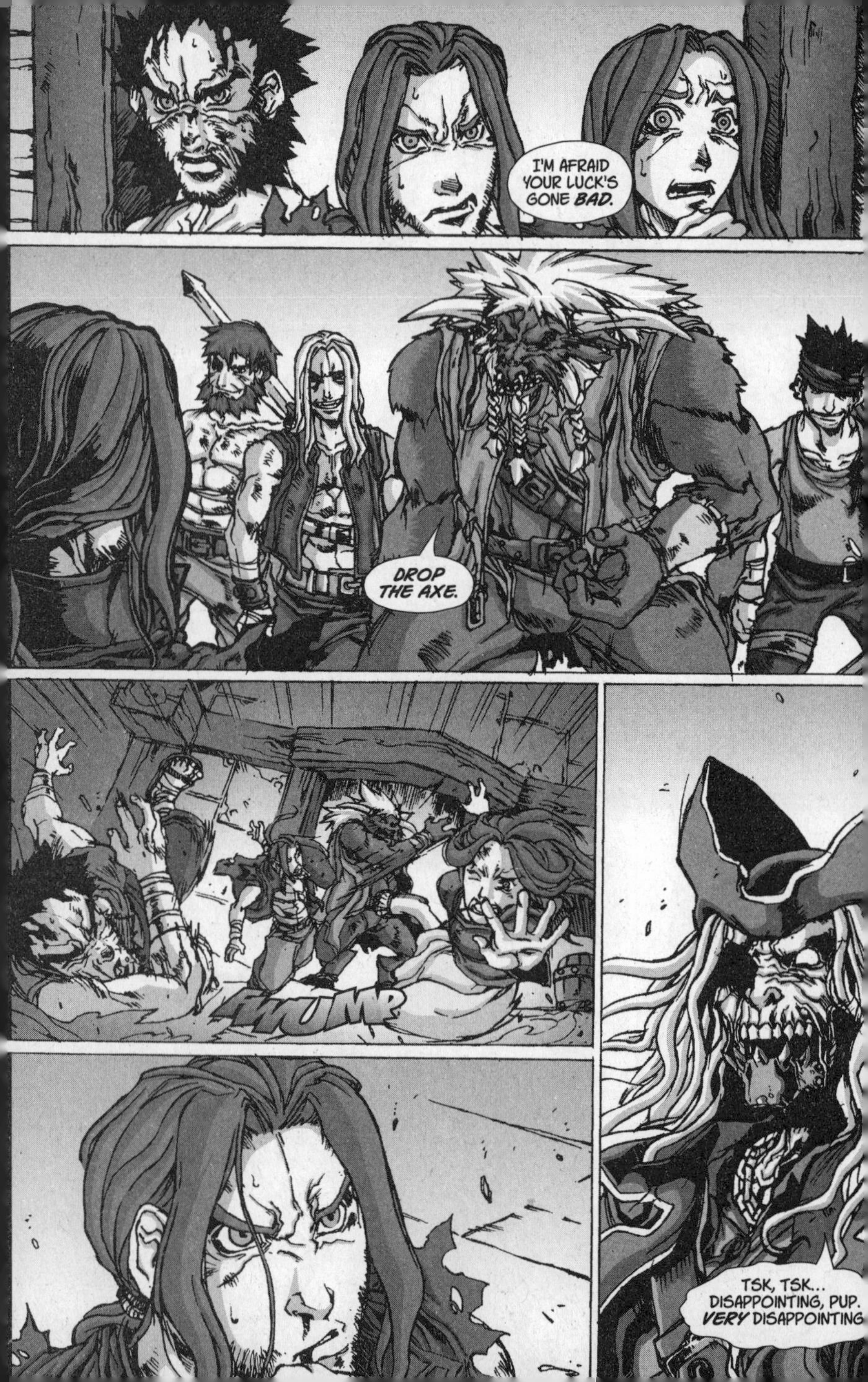
I'M AFRAID YOUR LUCK'S GONE BAD.
DROP THE AXE.
TSK, TSK... DISAPPOINTING, PUP. VERY DISAPPOINTING

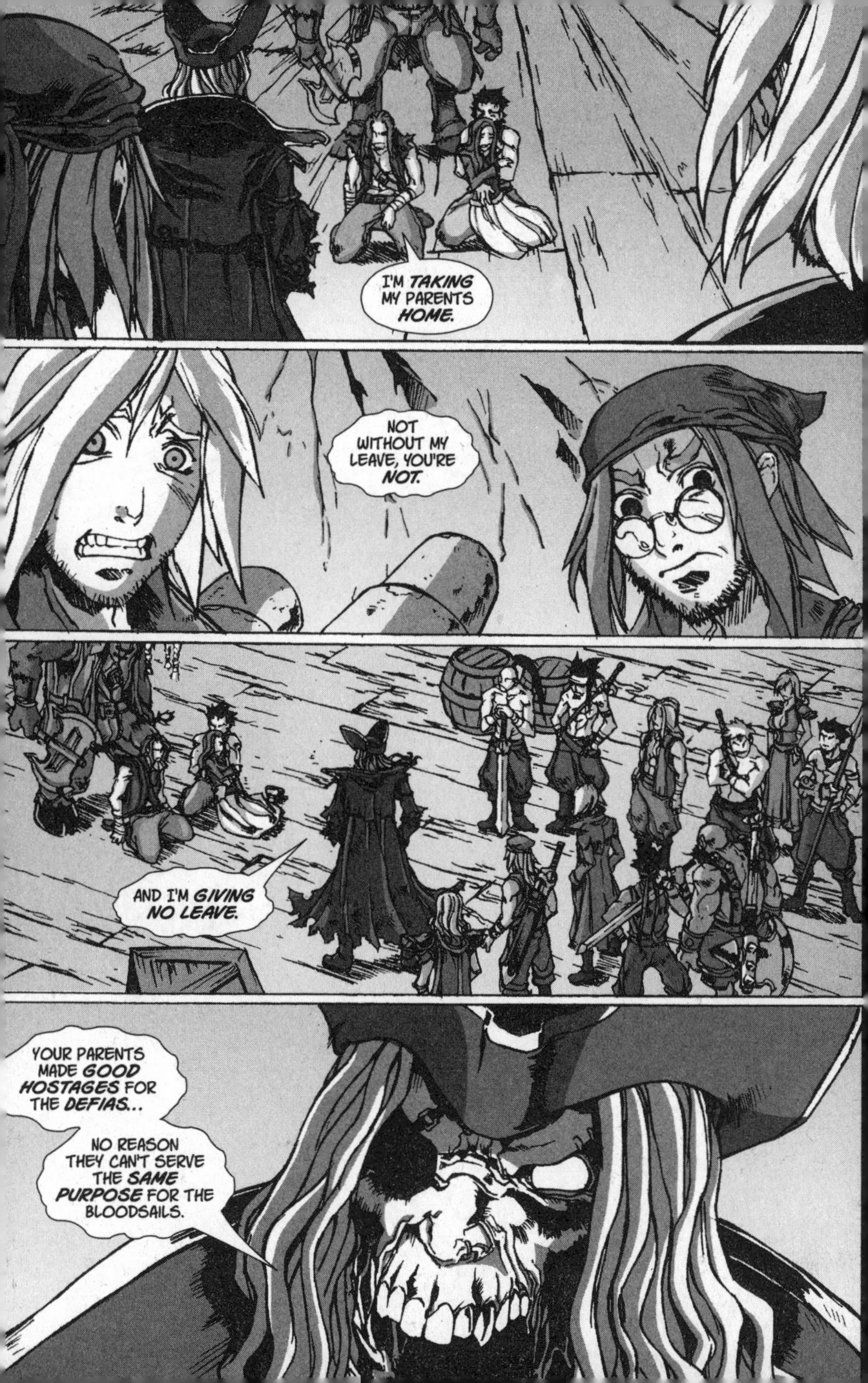

I'M *TAKING* MY PARENTS *HOME.*
NOT WITHOUT MY LEAVE, YOU'RE *NOT.*
AND I'M *GIVING NO LEAVE.*
YOUR PARENTS MADE *GOOD HOSTAGES* FOR THE *DEFIAS...*
NO REASON THEY CAN'T SERVE THE *SAME PURPOSE* FOR THE BLOODSAILS.

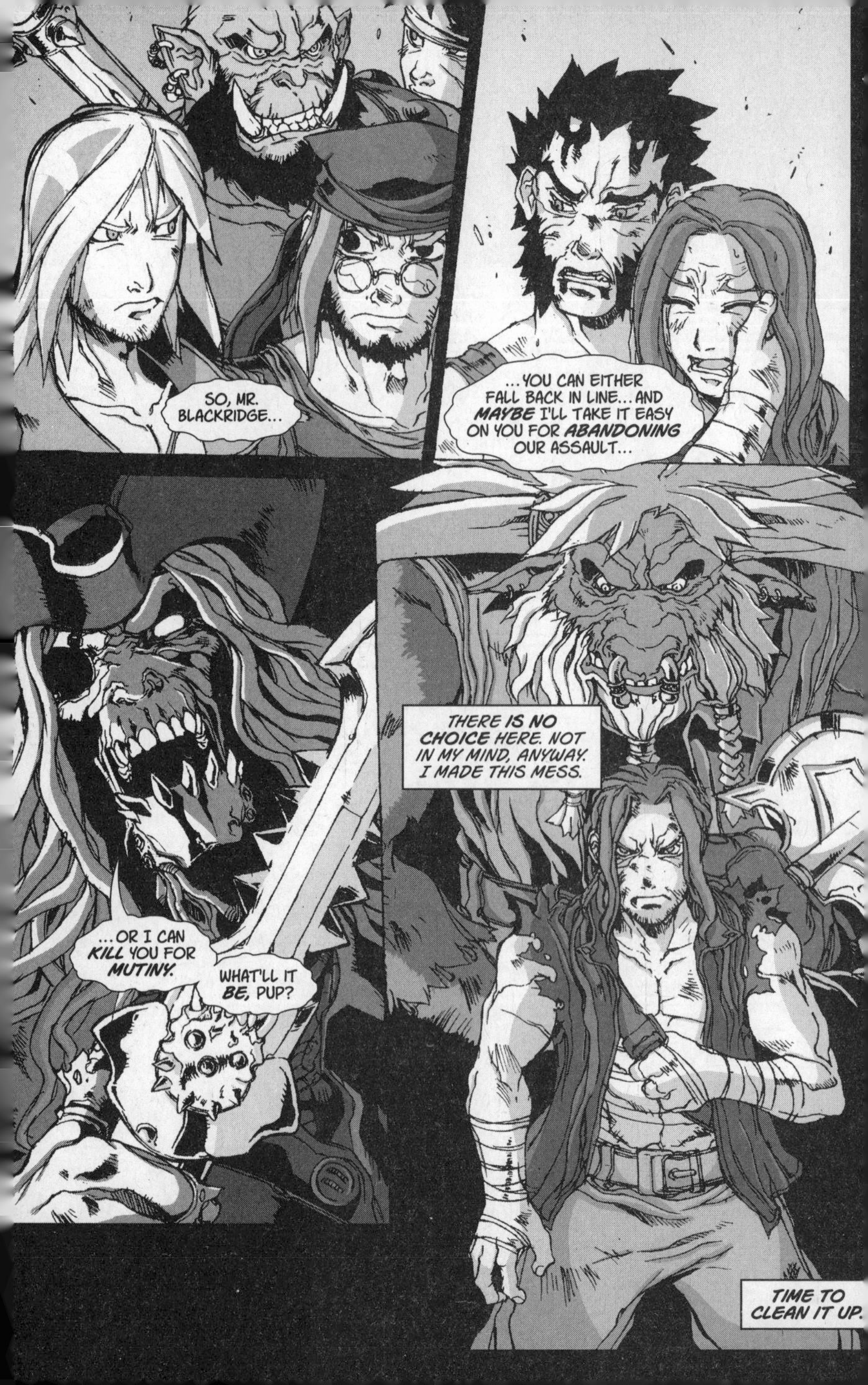
SO, MR. BLACKRIDGE...
...YOU CAN EITHER FALL BACK IN LINE...AND MAYBE I'LL TAKE IT EASY ON YOU FOR ABANDONING OUR ASSAULT...
...OR I CAN KILL YOU FOR MUTINY.
WHAT'LL IT BE, PUP?
THERE IS NO CHOICE HERE. NOT IN MY MIND, ANYWAY. I MADE THIS MESS.
TIME TO CLEAN IT UP.

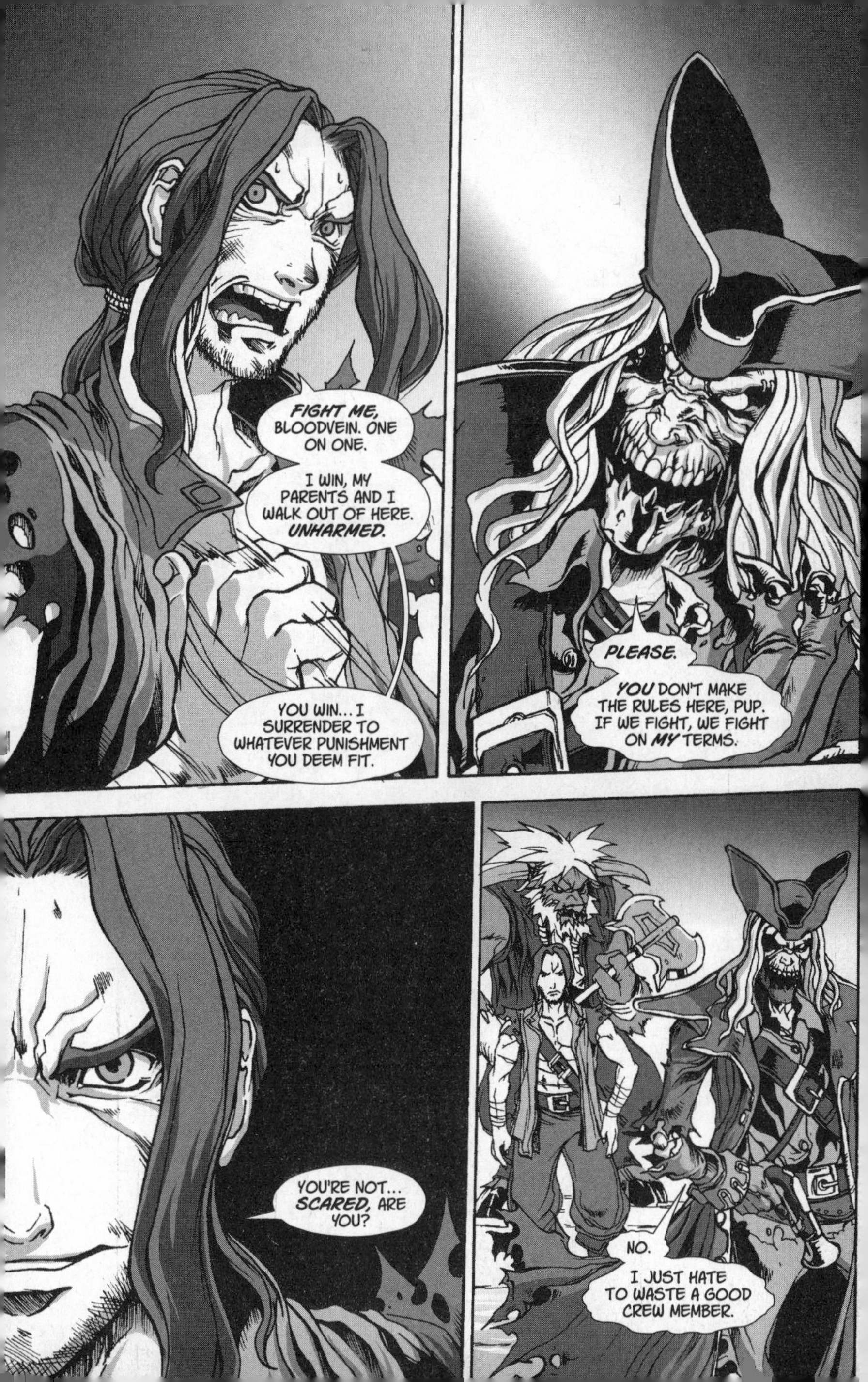

FIGHT ME, BLOODVEIN. ONE ON ONE.
I WIN, MY PARENTS AND I WALK OUT OF HERE. UNHARMED.
YOU WIN... I SURRENDER TO WHATEVER PUNISHMENT YOU DEEM FIT.
PLEASE.
YOU DON'T MAKE THE RULES HERE, PUP. IF WE FIGHT, WE FIGHT ON MY TERMS.
YOU'RE NOT... SCARED, ARE YOU?
NO.
I JUST HATE TO WASTE A GOOD CREW MEMBER.

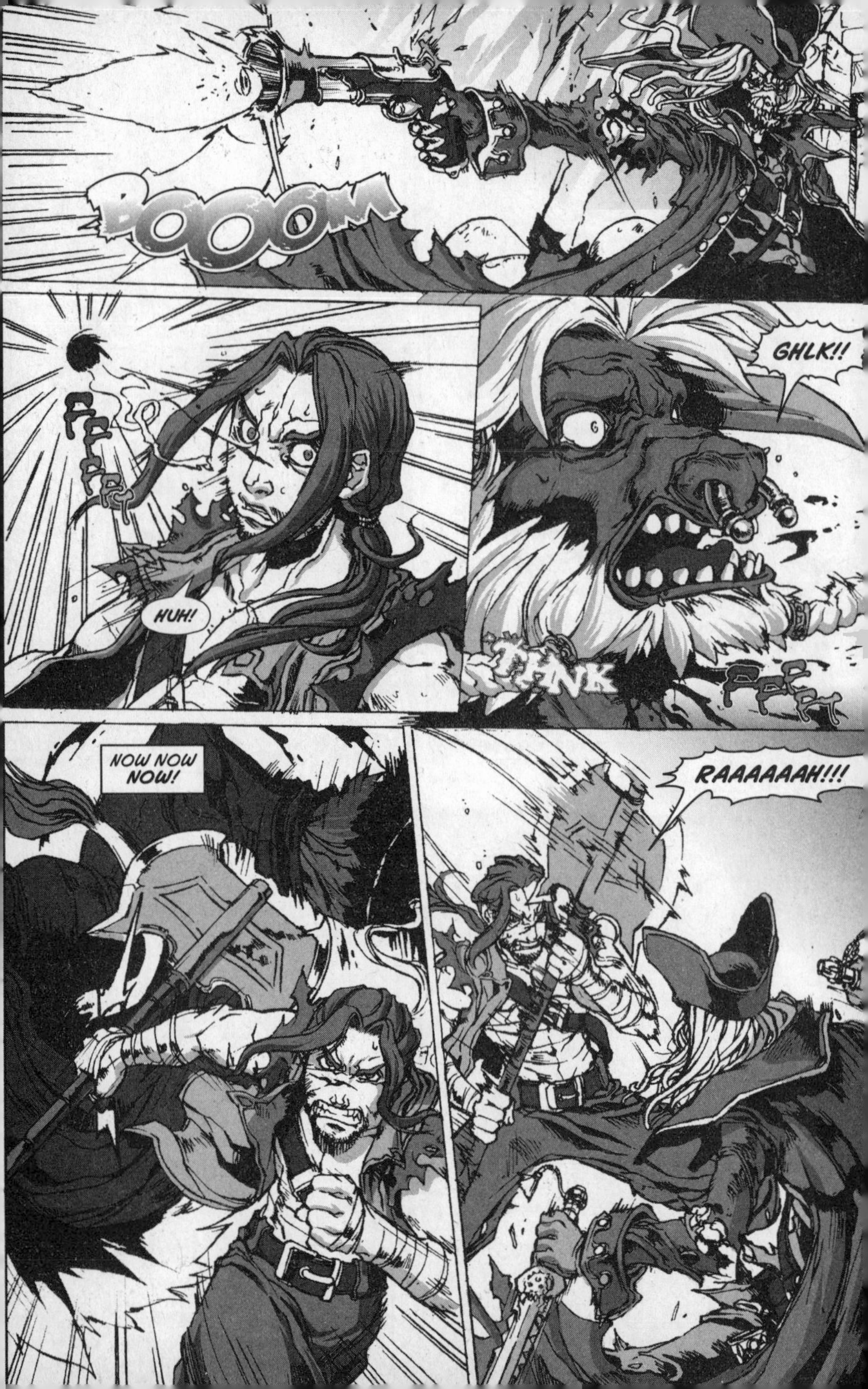
BOOOM
HUH!
GHLK!!
THNK
NOW NOW NOW!
RAAAAAAH!!!

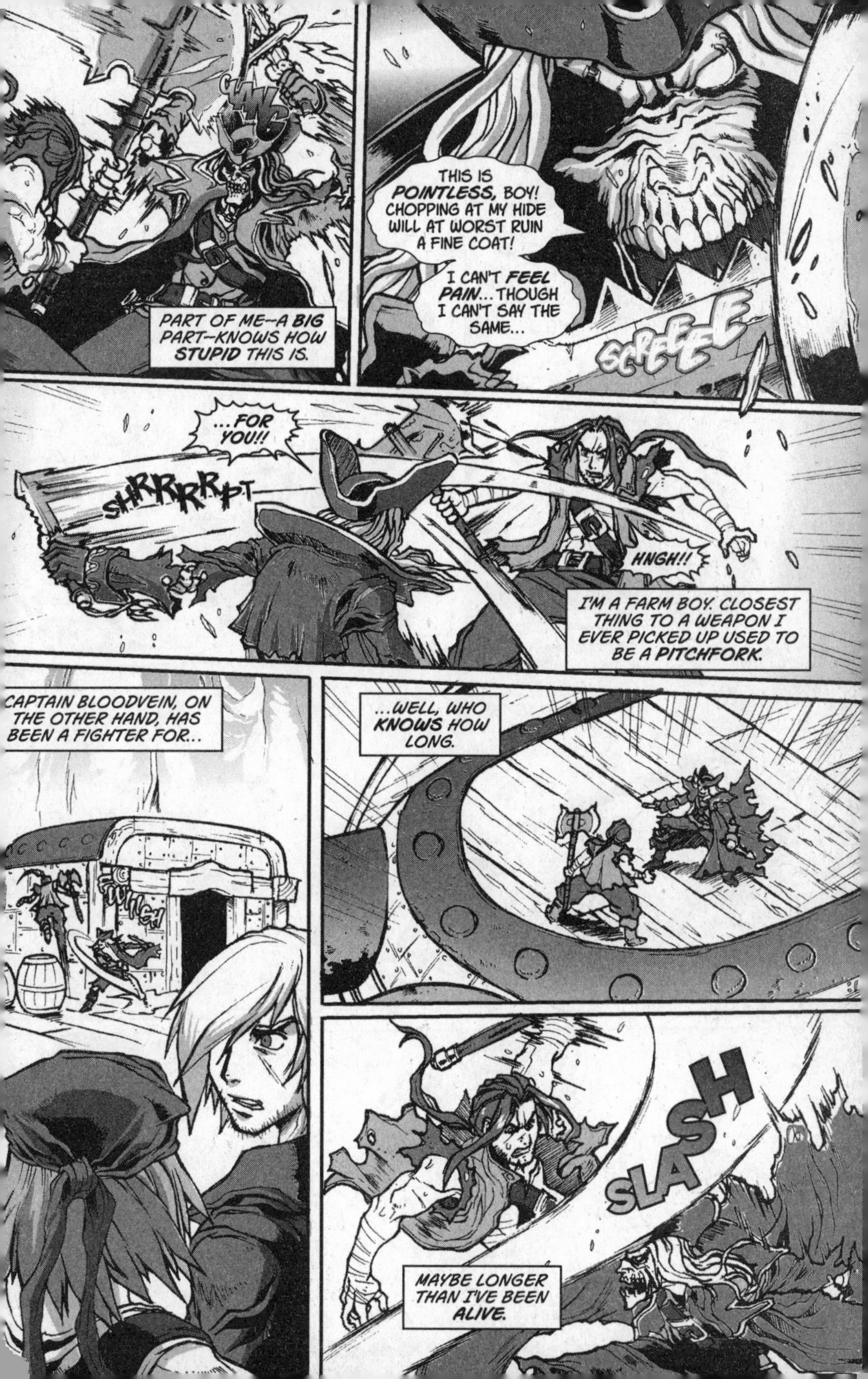
PART OF ME--A BIG PART--KNOWS HOW STUPID THIS IS.
THIS IS POINTLESS, BOY! CHOPPING AT MY HIDE WILL AT WORST RUIN A FINE COAT!
I CAN'T FEEL PAIN... THOUGH I CAN'T SAY THE SAME...
SCREEEEE
...FOR YOU!!
SHRRRRPT
HNGH!!
I'M A FARM BOY. CLOSEST THING TO A WEAPON I EVER PICKED UP USED TO BE A PITCHFORK.
CAPTAIN BLOODVEIN, ON THE OTHER HAND, HAS BEEN A FIGHTER FOR...
...WELL, WHO KNOWS HOW LONG.
SLASH
MAYBE LONGER THAN I'VE BEEN ALIVE.

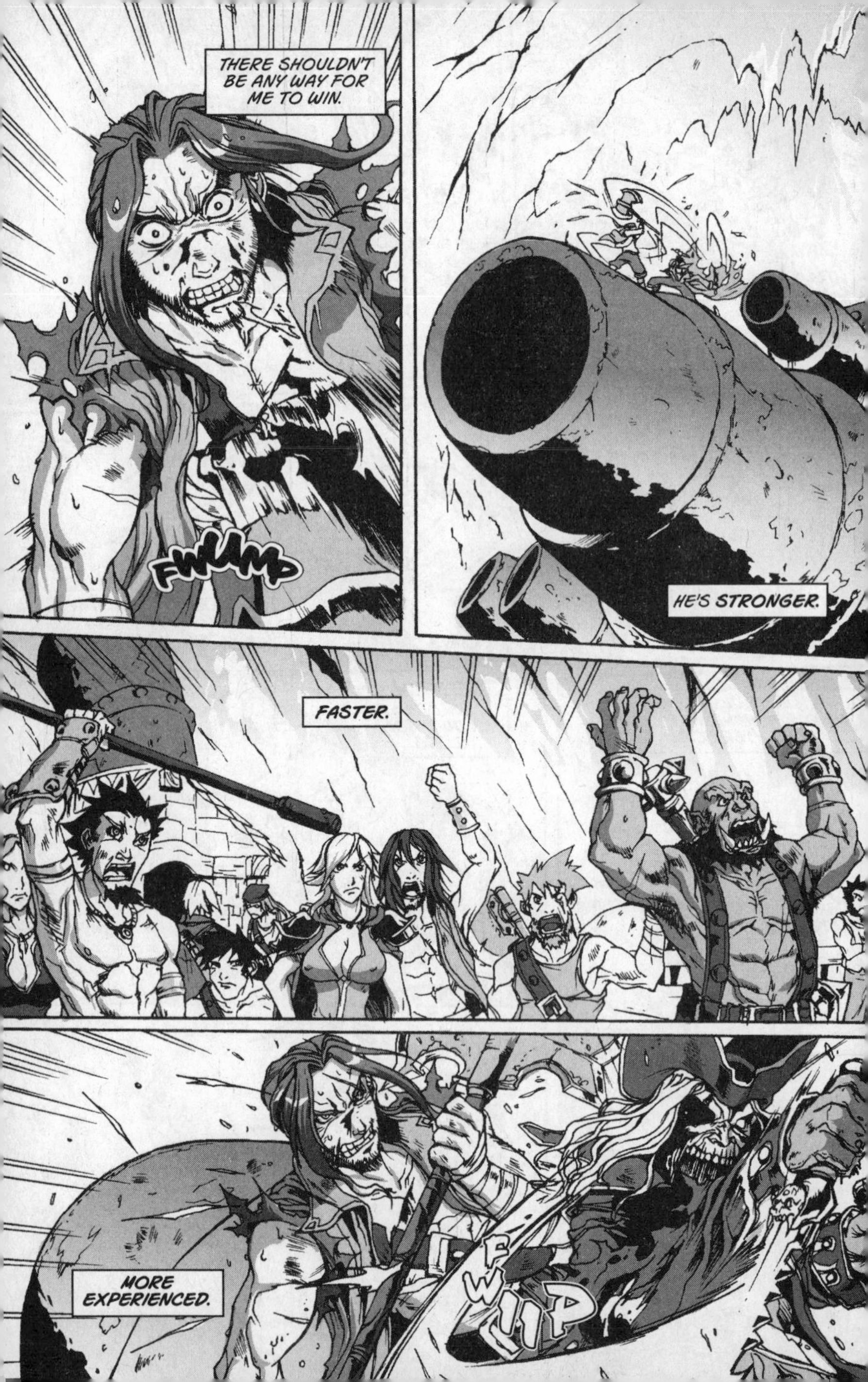
THERE SHOULDN'T BE ANY WAY FOR ME TO WIN.
FWUMP
HE'S STRONGER.
FASTER.
MORE EXPERIENCED.
FWIIP

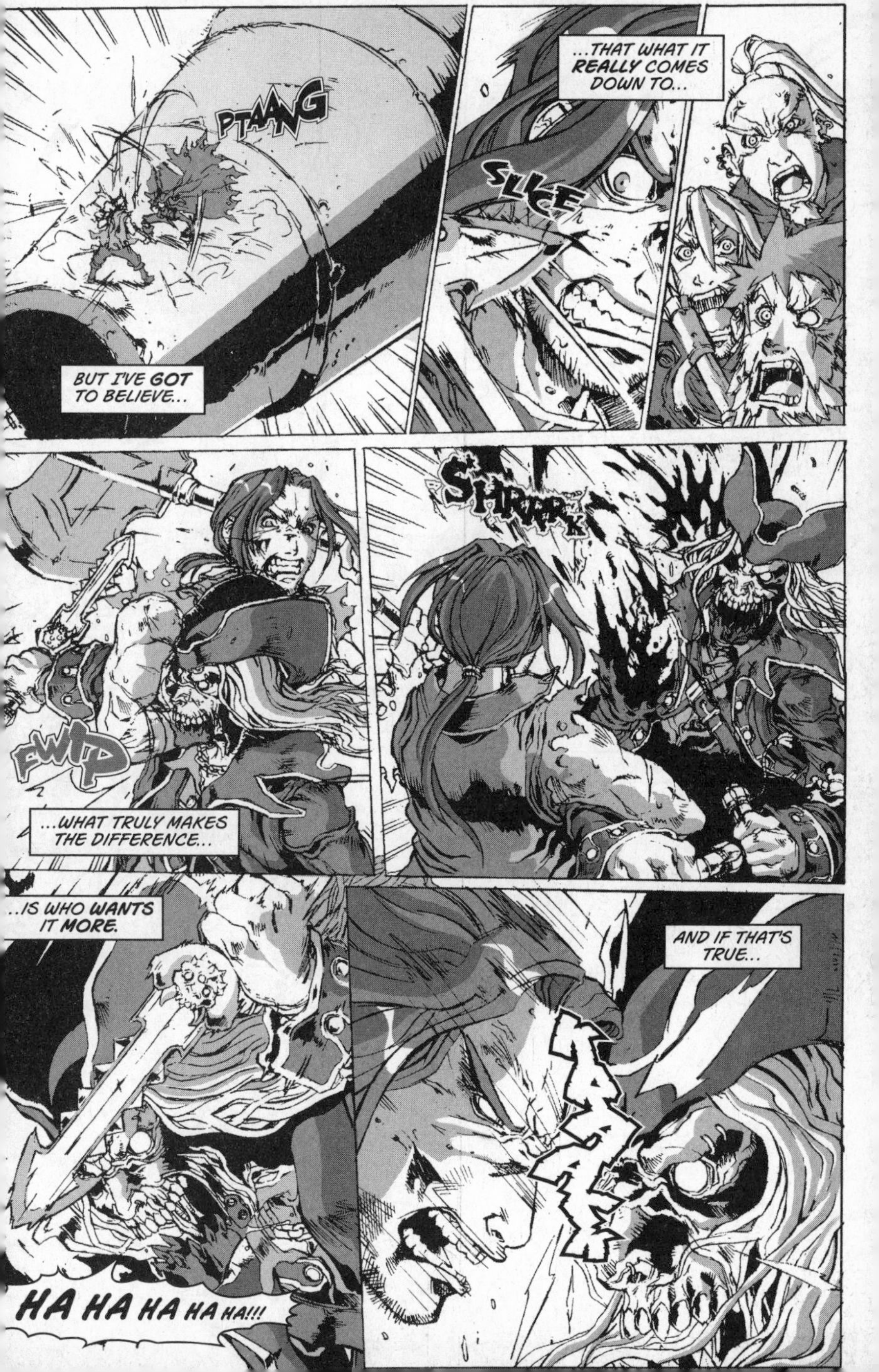
PTAANG
BUT I'VE GOT TO BELIEVE...
SLICE
...THAT WHAT IT REALLY COMES DOWN TO...
...WHAT TRULY MAKES THE DIFFERENCE...
FWIP
SHRAAK
...IS WHO WANTS IT MORE.
HA HA HA HA HA!!!
AND IF THAT'S TRUE...

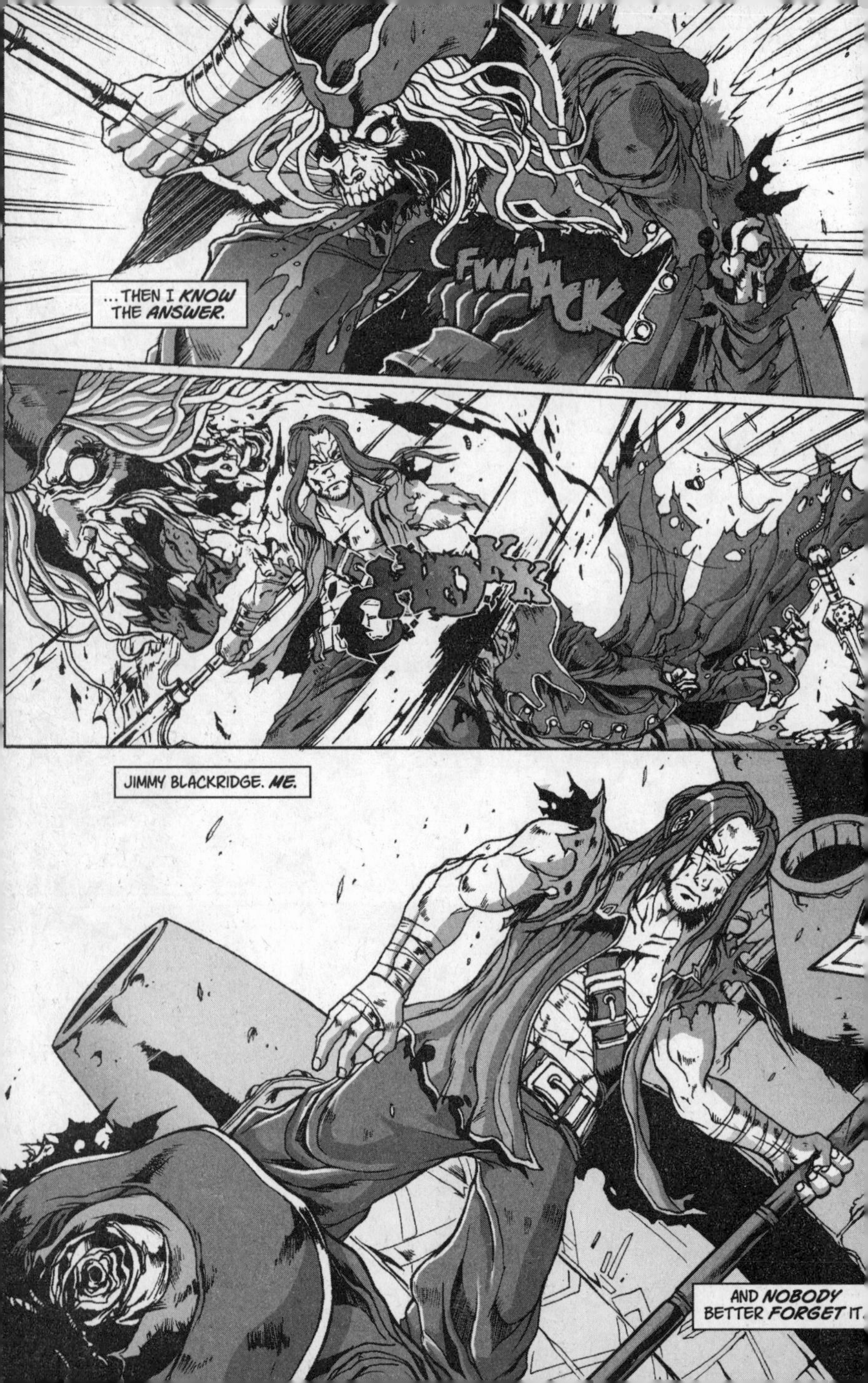
...THEN I *KNOW* THE *ANSWER.*
FWAAACK
JIMMY BLACKRIDGE. *ME.*
AND *NOBODY* BETTER *FORGET* IT.

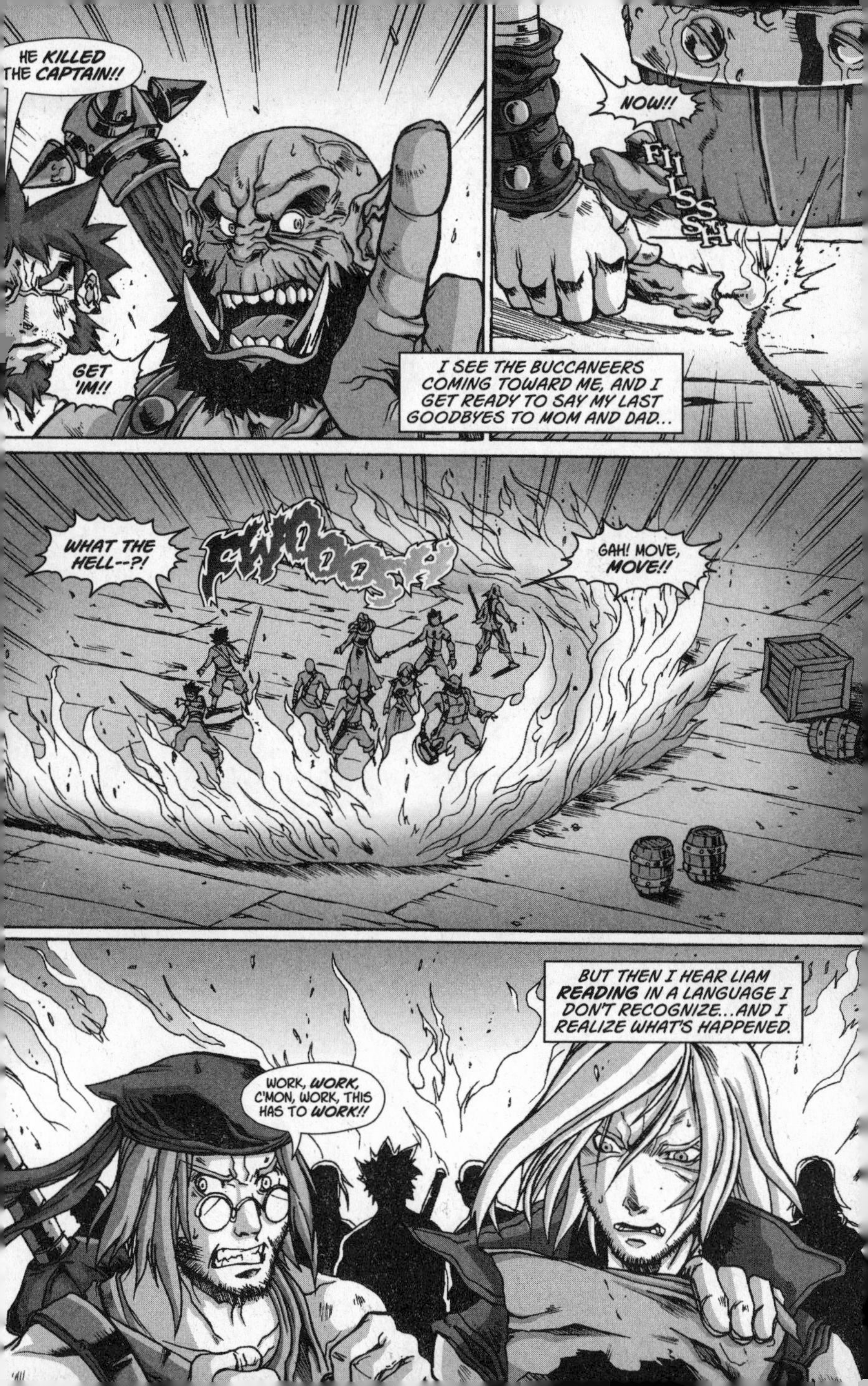
HE KILLED THE CAPTAIN!!
GET 'IM!!
NOW!!
FHISSSH
I SEE THE BUCCANEERS COMING TOWARD ME, AND I GET READY TO SAY MY LAST GOODBYES TO MOM AND DAD...
WHAT THE HELL--?!
FWOOSH
GAH! MOVE, MOVE!!
BUT THEN I HEAR LIAM READING IN A LANGUAGE I DON'T RECOGNIZE...AND I REALIZE WHAT'S HAPPENED.
WORK, WORK, C'MON, WORK, THIS HAS TO WORK!!

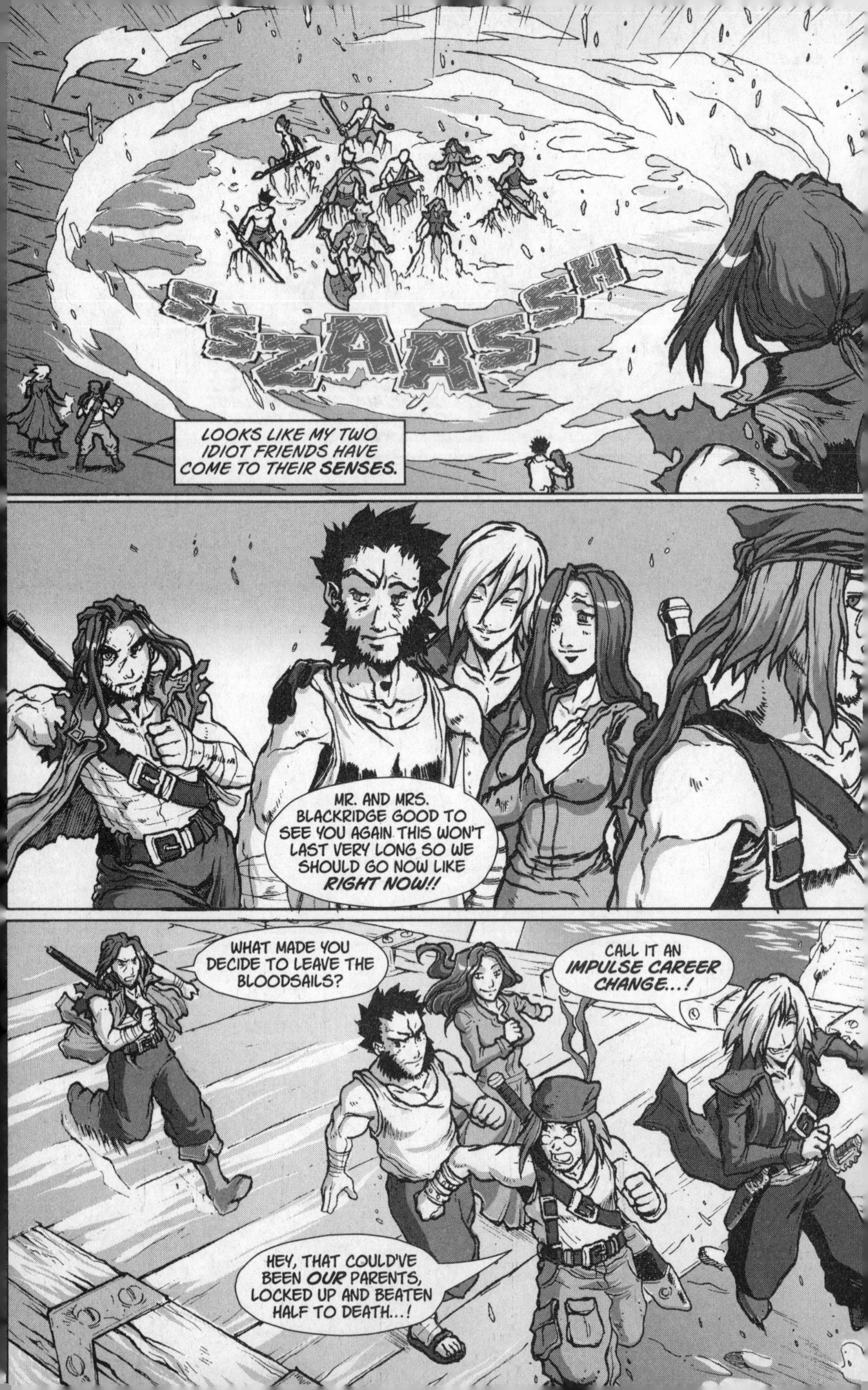
SSZAASSH
LOOKS LIKE MY TWO IDIOT FRIENDS HAVE COME TO THEIR SENSES.
MR. AND MRS. BLACKRIDGE GOOD TO SEE YOU AGAIN. THIS WON'T LAST VERY LONG SO WE SHOULD GO NOW LIKE RIGHT NOW!!
WHAT MADE YOU DECIDE TO LEAVE THE BLOODSAILS?
CALL IT AN IMPULSE CAREER CHANGE...!
HEY, THAT COULD'VE BEEN OUR PARENTS, LOCKED UP AND BEATEN HALF TO DEATH...!

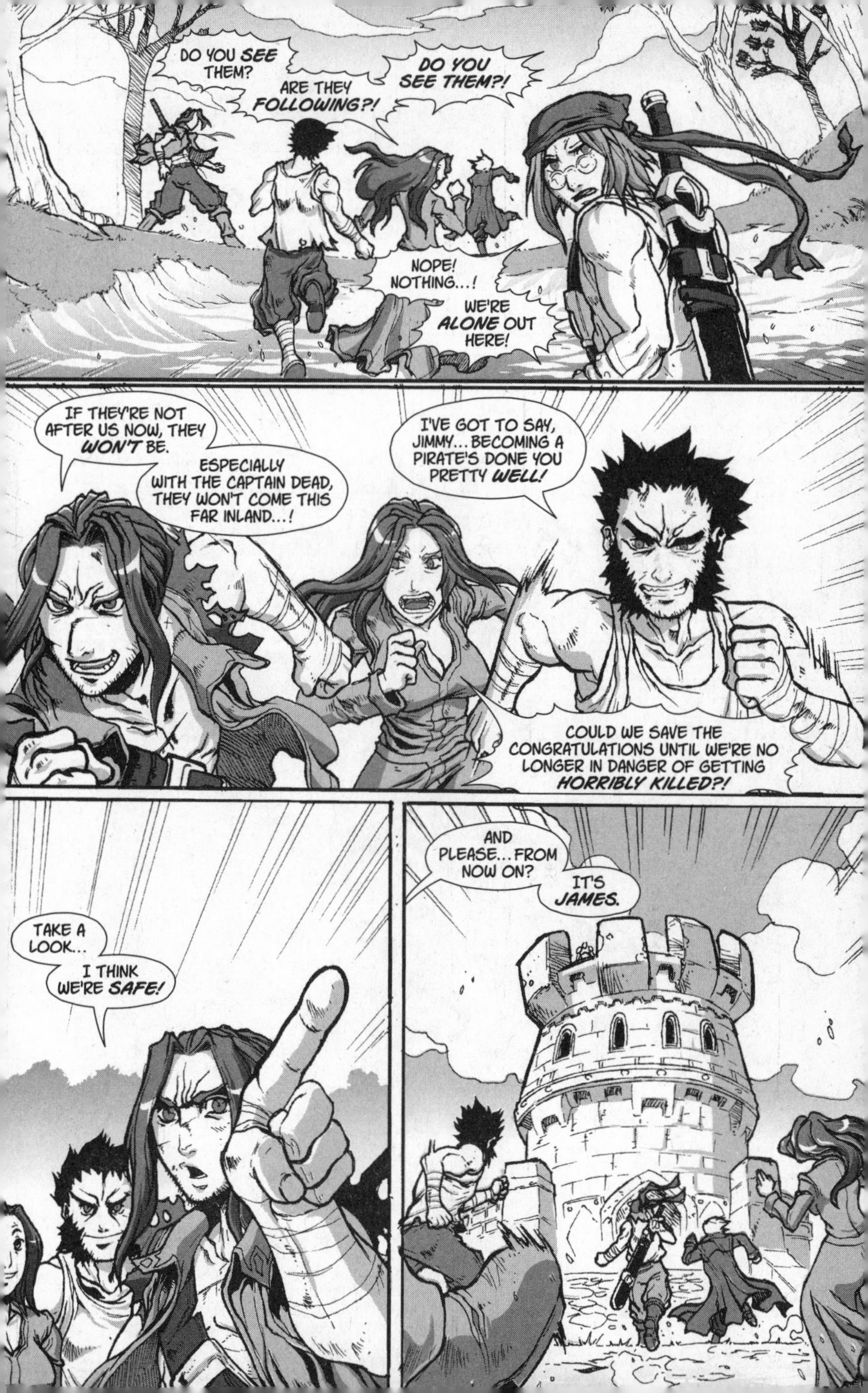
DO YOU SEE THEM?
ARE THEY FOLLOWING?!
DO YOU SEE THEM?!
NOPE! NOTHING...!
WE'RE ALONE OUT HERE!
IF THEY'RE NOT AFTER US NOW, THEY WON'T BE.
ESPECIALLY WITH THE CAPTAIN DEAD, THEY WON'T COME THIS FAR INLAND...!
I'VE GOT TO SAY, JIMMY... BECOMING A PIRATE'S DONE YOU PRETTY WELL!
COULD WE SAVE THE CONGRATULATIONS UNTIL WE'RE NO LONGER IN DANGER OF GETTING HORRIBLY KILLED?!
TAKE A LOOK...
I THINK WE'RE SAFE!
AND PLEASE... FROM NOW ON?
IT'S JAMES.

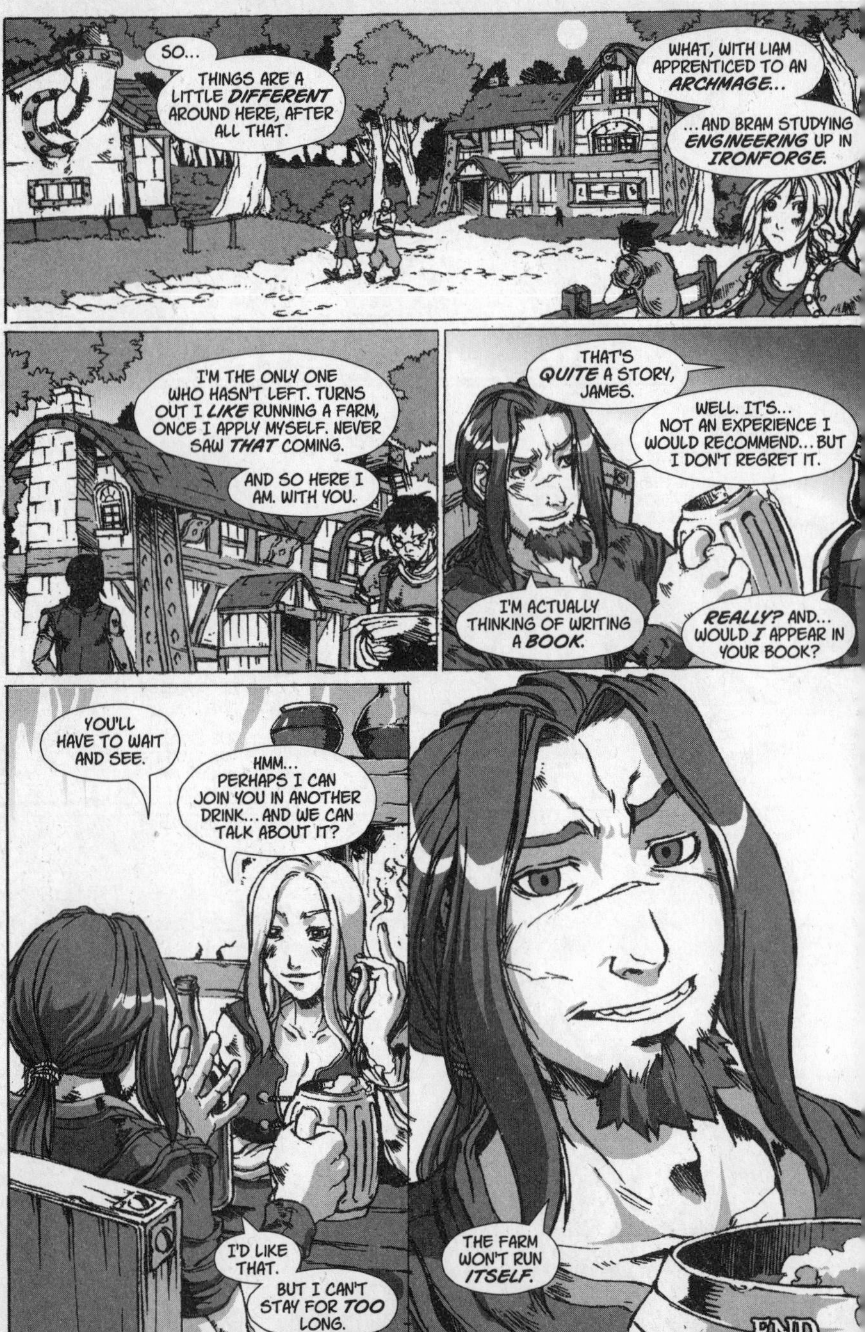
SO...
THINGS ARE A LITTLE DIFFERENT AROUND HERE, AFTER ALL THAT.
WHAT, WITH LIAM APPRENTICED TO AN ARCHMAGE...
...AND BRAM STUDYING ENGINEERING UP IN IRONFORGE.
I'M THE ONLY ONE WHO HASN'T LEFT. TURNS OUT I LIKE RUNNING A FARM, ONCE I APPLY MYSELF. NEVER SAW THAT COMING.
AND SO HERE I AM. WITH YOU.
THAT'S QUITE A STORY, JAMES.
WELL. IT'S... NOT AN EXPERIENCE I WOULD RECOMMEND... BUT I DON'T REGRET IT.
I'M ACTUALLY THINKING OF WRITING A BOOK.
REALLY? AND... WOULD I APPEAR IN YOUR BOOK?
YOU'LL HAVE TO WAIT AND SEE.
HMM... PERHAPS I CAN JOIN YOU IN ANOTHER DRINK... AND WE CAN TALK ABOUT IT?
I'D LIKE THAT.
BUT I CAN'T STAY FOR TOO LONG.
THE FARM WON'T RUN ITSELF.
END

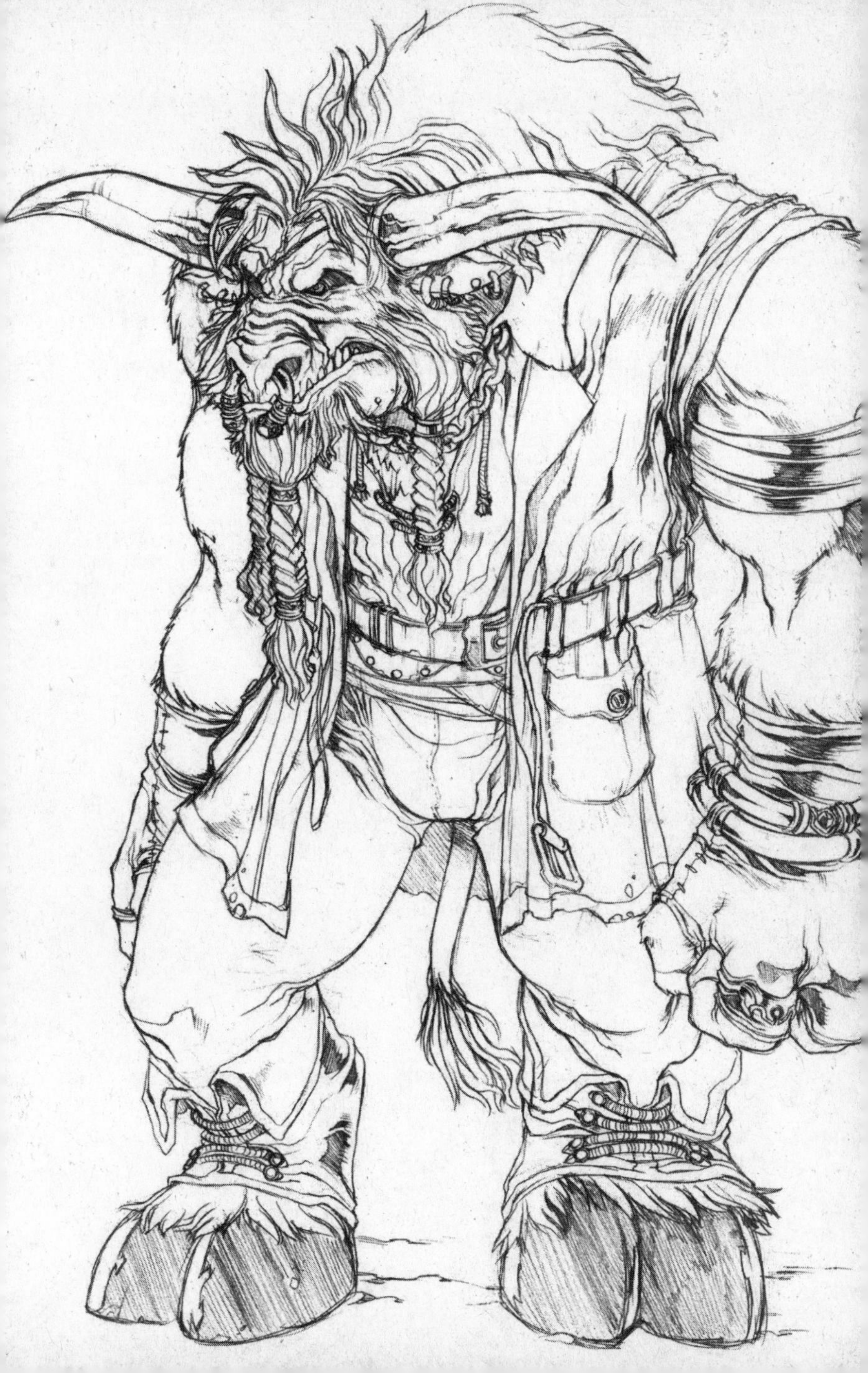

WARCRAFT

LEGENDS
VOLUME FOUR

BLOOD RUNS
THICKER

WRITTEN BY TIM BEEDLE

PENCILS & TONES BY RYO KAWAKAMI
INKS BY FERNANDO MELEK

LETTERER: MICHAEL PAOLILLI

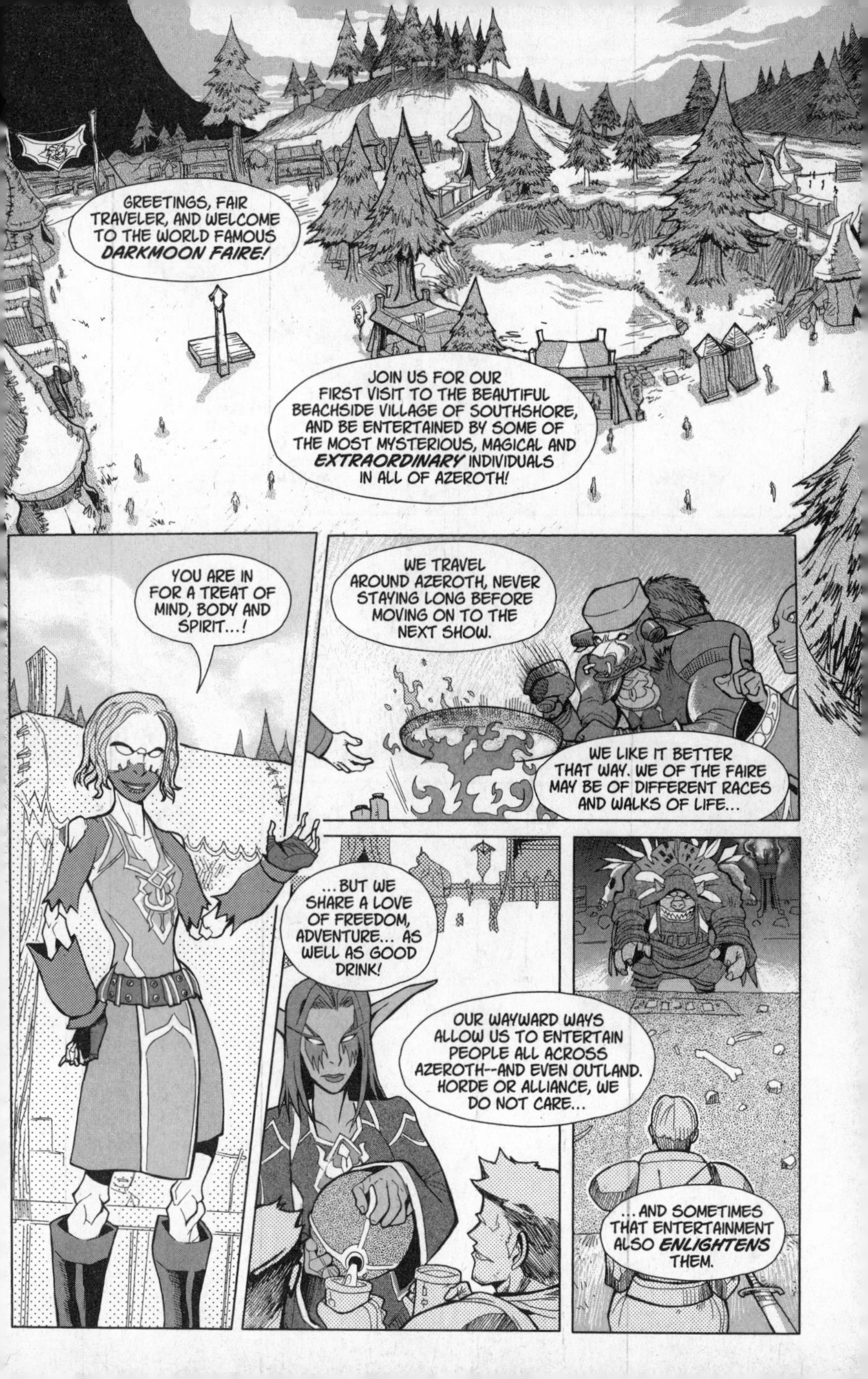
GREETINGS, FAIR TRAVELER, AND WELCOME TO THE WORLD FAMOUS *DARKMOON FAIRE!*
JOIN US FOR OUR FIRST VISIT TO THE BEAUTIFUL BEACHSIDE VILLAGE OF SOUTHSHORE, AND BE ENTERTAINED BY SOME OF THE MOST MYSTERIOUS, MAGICAL AND *EXTRAORDINARY* INDIVIDUALS IN ALL OF AZEROTH!
YOU ARE IN FOR A TREAT OF MIND, BODY AND SPIRIT...!
WE TRAVEL AROUND AZEROTH, NEVER STAYING LONG BEFORE MOVING ON TO THE NEXT SHOW.
WE LIKE IT BETTER THAT WAY. WE OF THE FAIRE MAY BE OF DIFFERENT RACES AND WALKS OF LIFE...
...BUT WE SHARE A LOVE OF FREEDOM, ADVENTURE... AS WELL AS GOOD DRINK!
OUR WAYWARD WAYS ALLOW US TO ENTERTAIN PEOPLE ALL ACROSS AZEROTH--AND EVEN OUTLAND. HORDE OR ALLIANCE, WE DO NOT CARE...
...AND SOMETIMES THAT ENTERTAINMENT ALSO *ENLIGHTENS* THEM.

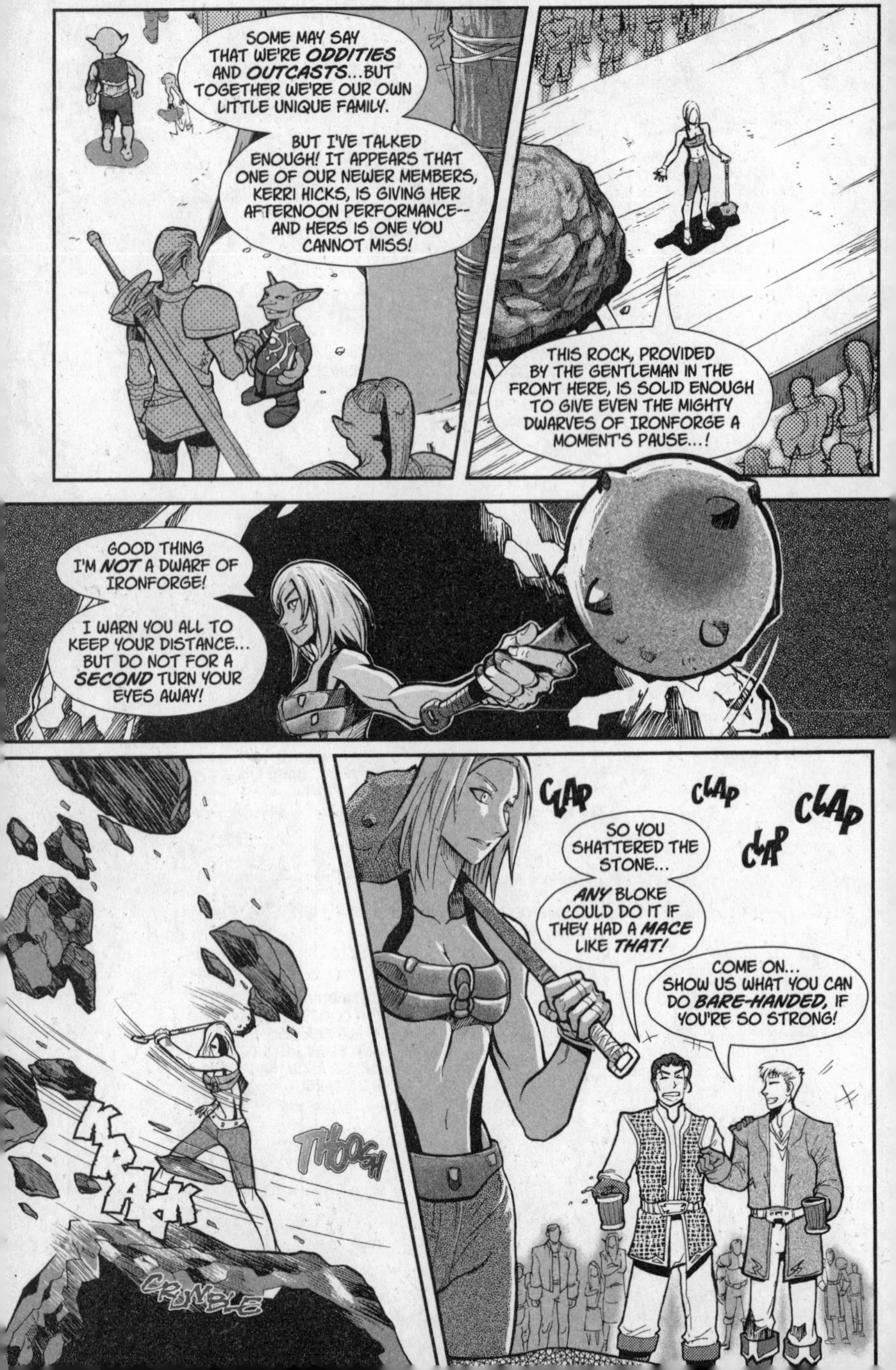
SOME MAY SAY THAT WE'RE ODDITIES AND OUTCASTS...BUT TOGETHER WE'RE OUR OWN LITTLE UNIQUE FAMILY.
BUT I'VE TALKED ENOUGH! IT APPEARS THAT ONE OF OUR NEWER MEMBERS, KERRI HICKS, IS GIVING HER AFTERNOON PERFORMANCE-- AND HERS IS ONE YOU CANNOT MISS!
THIS ROCK, PROVIDED BY THE GENTLEMAN IN THE FRONT HERE, IS SOLID ENOUGH TO GIVE EVEN THE MIGHTY DWARVES OF IRONFORGE A MOMENT'S PAUSE...!
GOOD THING I'M NOT A DWARF OF IRONFORGE!
I WARN YOU ALL TO KEEP YOUR DISTANCE... BUT DO NOT FOR A SECOND TURN YOUR EYES AWAY!
KRACK
THOOSH
CRUMBLE
CLAP
CLAP
CLAP
CLAP
SO YOU SHATTERED THE STONE...
ANY BLOKE COULD DO IT IF THEY HAD A MACE LIKE THAT!
COME ON... SHOW US WHAT YOU CAN DO BARE-HANDED, IF YOU'RE SO STRONG!

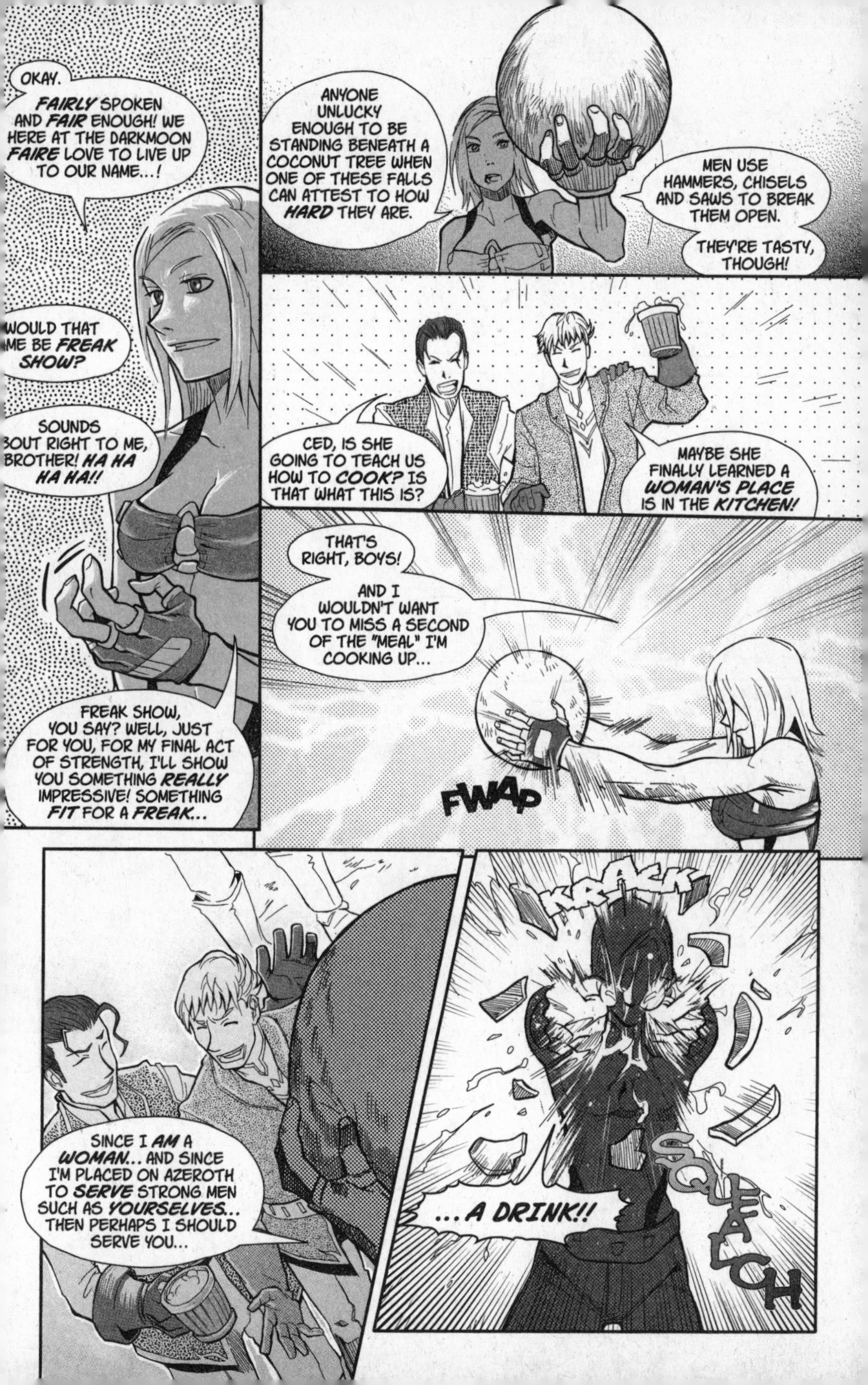
OKAY.
FAIRLY SPOKEN AND FAIR ENOUGH! WE HERE AT THE DARKMOON FAIRE LOVE TO LIVE UP TO OUR NAME...!
WOULD THAT ME BE FREAK SHOW?
SOUNDS BOUT RIGHT TO ME, BROTHER! HA HA HA HA!!
FREAK SHOW, YOU SAY? WELL, JUST FOR YOU, FOR MY FINAL ACT OF STRENGTH, I'LL SHOW YOU SOMETHING REALLY IMPRESSIVE! SOMETHING FIT FOR A FREAK...
ANYONE UNLUCKY ENOUGH TO BE STANDING BENEATH A COCONUT TREE WHEN ONE OF THESE FALLS CAN ATTEST TO HOW HARD THEY ARE.
MEN USE HAMMERS, CHISELS AND SAWS TO BREAK THEM OPEN.
THEY'RE TASTY, THOUGH!
CED, IS SHE GOING TO TEACH US HOW TO COOK? IS THAT WHAT THIS IS?
MAYBE SHE FINALLY LEARNED A WOMAN'S PLACE IS IN THE KITCHEN!
THAT'S RIGHT, BOYS!
AND I WOULDN'T WANT YOU TO MISS A SECOND OF THE "MEAL" I'M COOKING UP...
FWAP
SINCE I AM A WOMAN... AND SINCE I'M PLACED ON AZEROTH TO SERVE STRONG MEN SUCH AS YOURSELVES... THEN PERHAPS I SHOULD SERVE YOU...
KRACK
...A DRINK!!
SQUELCH

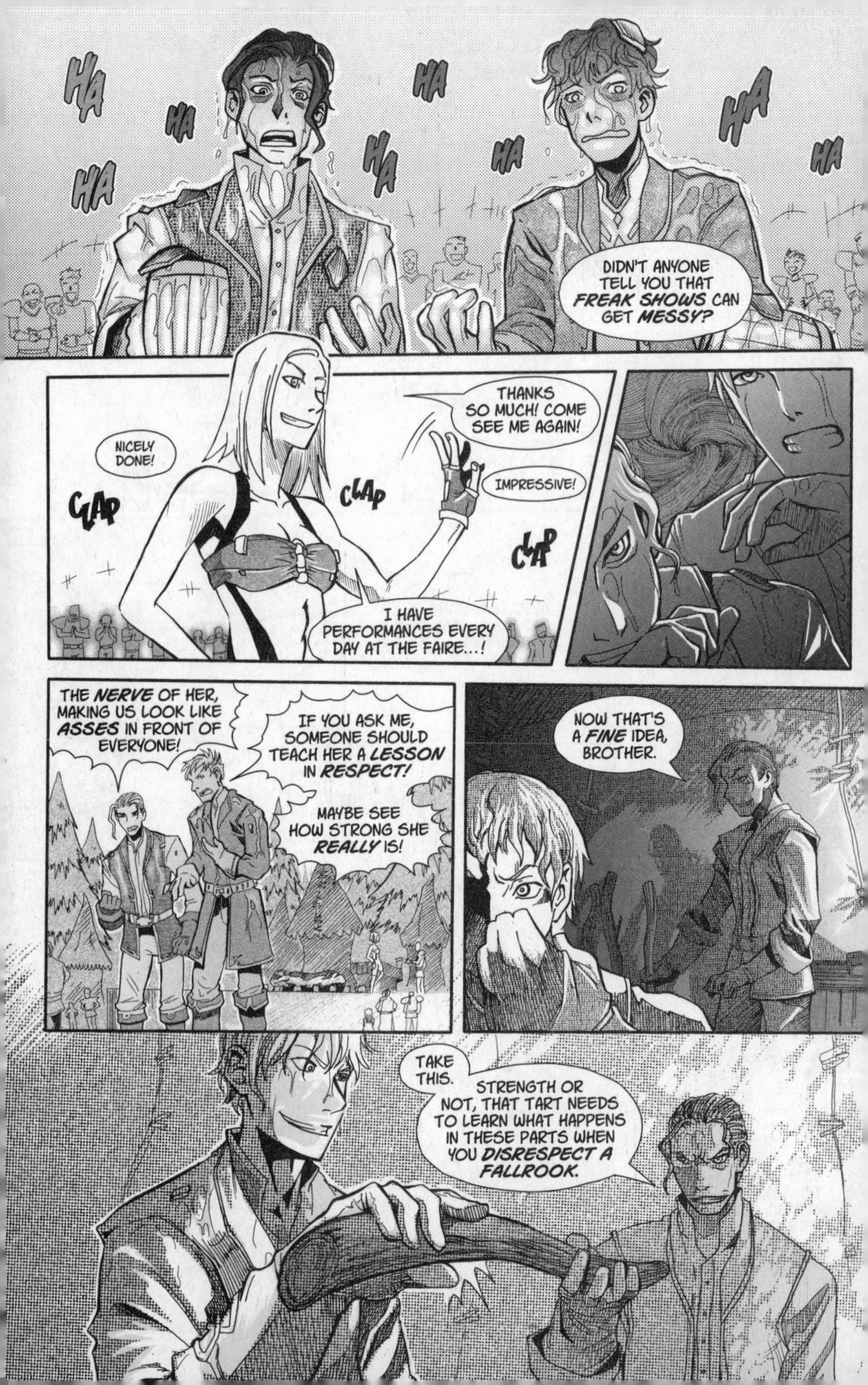
HA HA HA HA HA HA HA HA HA
DIDN'T ANYONE TELL YOU THAT FREAK SHOWS CAN GET MESSY?
NICELY DONE!
THANKS SO MUCH! COME SEE ME AGAIN!
CLAP
CLAP
IMPRESSIVE!
CLAP
I HAVE PERFORMANCES EVERY DAY AT THE FAIRE...!
THE NERVE OF HER, MAKING US LOOK LIKE ASSES IN FRONT OF EVERYONE!
IF YOU ASK ME, SOMEONE SHOULD TEACH HER A LESSON IN RESPECT!
MAYBE SEE HOW STRONG SHE REALLY IS!
NOW THAT'S A FINE IDEA, BROTHER.
TAKE THIS.
STRENGTH OR NOT, THAT TART NEEDS TO LEARN WHAT HAPPENS IN THESE PARTS WHEN YOU DISRESPECT A FALLROOK.

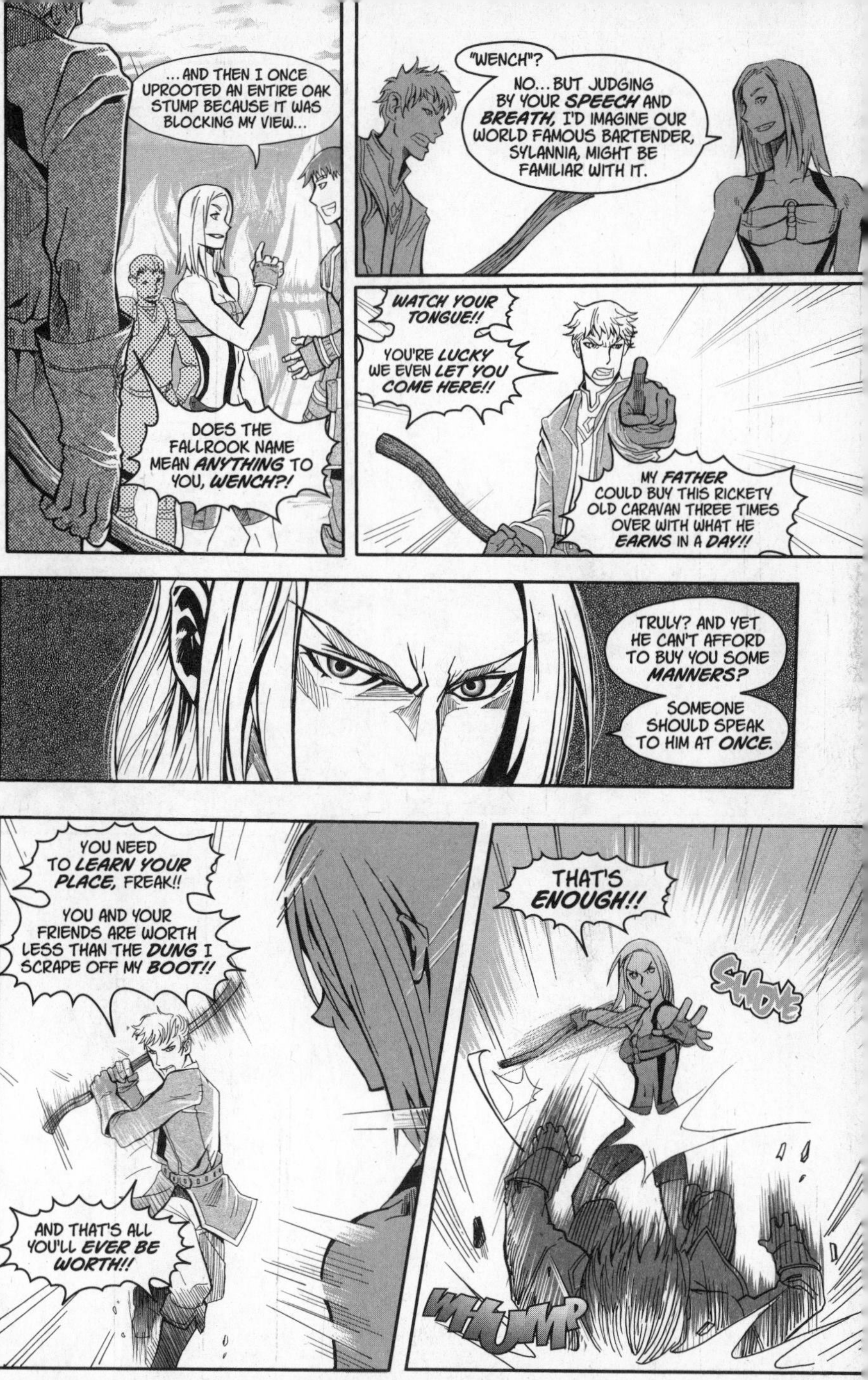
...AND THEN I ONCE UPROOTED AN ENTIRE OAK STUMP BECAUSE IT WAS BLOCKING MY VIEW...
DOES THE FALLROOK NAME MEAN ANYTHING TO YOU, WENCH?!
"WENCH"?
NO... BUT JUDGING BY YOUR SPEECH AND BREATH, I'D IMAGINE OUR WORLD FAMOUS BARTENDER, SYLANNIA, MIGHT BE FAMILIAR WITH IT.
WATCH YOUR TONGUE!!
YOU'RE LUCKY WE EVEN LET YOU COME HERE!!
MY FATHER COULD BUY THIS RICKETY OLD CARAVAN THREE TIMES OVER WITH WHAT HE EARNS IN A DAY!!
TRULY? AND YET HE CAN'T AFFORD TO BUY YOU SOME MANNERS?
SOMEONE SHOULD SPEAK TO HIM AT ONCE.
YOU NEED TO LEARN YOUR PLACE, FREAK!!
YOU AND YOUR FRIENDS ARE WORTH LESS THAN THE DUNG I SCRAPE OFF MY BOOT!!
AND THAT'S ALL YOU'LL EVER BE WORTH!!
THAT'S ENOUGH!!!
SHOVE
WHUMP

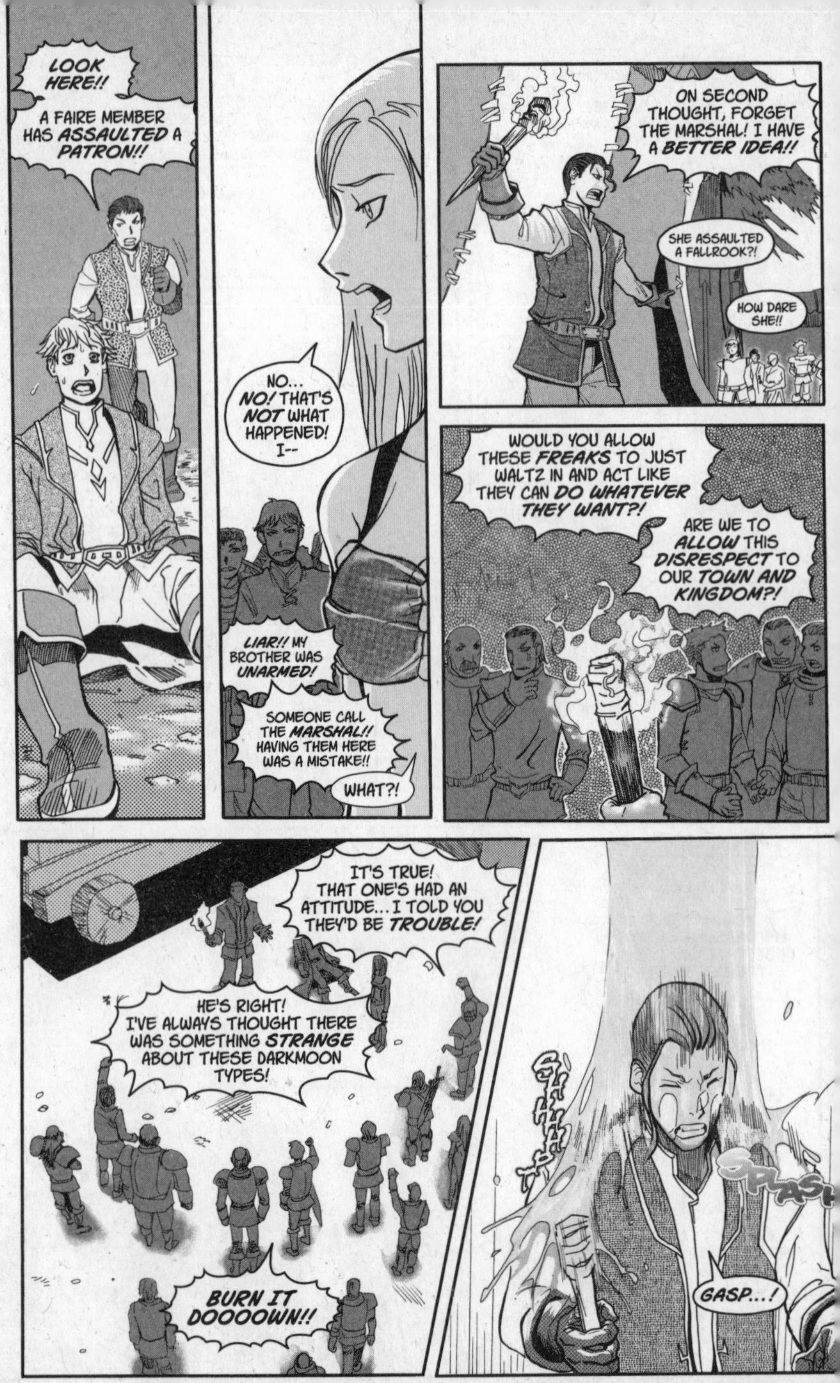
LOOK HERE!!
A FAIRE MEMBER HAS ASSAULTED A PATRON!!
NO... NO! THAT'S NOT WHAT HAPPENED! I--
LIAR!! MY BROTHER WAS UNARMED!
SOMEONE CALL THE MARSHAL!! HAVING THEM HERE WAS A MISTAKE!!
WHAT?!
ON SECOND THOUGHT, FORGET THE MARSHAL! I HAVE A BETTER IDEA!!
SHE ASSAULTED A FALLROOK?!
HOW DARE SHE!!
WOULD YOU ALLOW THESE FREAKS TO JUST WALTZ IN AND ACT LIKE THEY CAN DO WHATEVER THEY WANT?!
ARE WE TO ALLOW THIS DISRESPECT TO OUR TOWN AND KINGDOM?!
IT'S TRUE! THAT ONE'S HAD AN ATTITUDE... I TOLD YOU THEY'D BE TROUBLE!
HE'S RIGHT! I'VE ALWAYS THOUGHT THERE WAS SOMETHING STRANGE ABOUT THESE DARKMOON TYPES!
BURN IT DOOOOWN!!
GASP...!

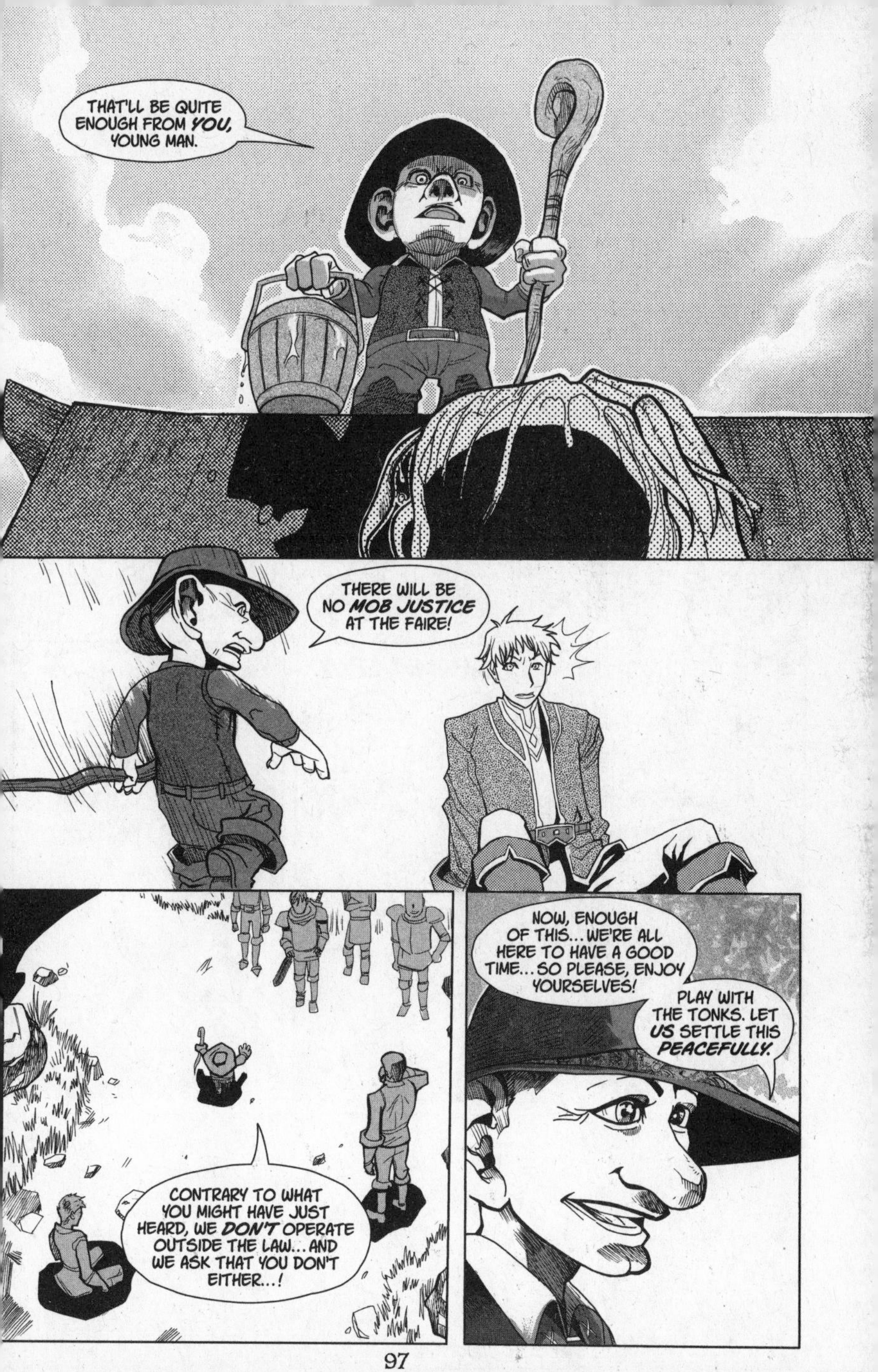
THAT'LL BE QUITE ENOUGH FROM *YOU,* YOUNG MAN.
THERE WILL BE NO *MOB JUSTICE* AT THE FAIRE!
CONTRARY TO WHAT YOU MIGHT HAVE JUST HEARD, WE *DON'T* OPERATE OUTSIDE THE LAW... AND WE ASK THAT YOU DON'T EITHER...!
NOW, ENOUGH OF THIS... WE'RE ALL HERE TO HAVE A GOOD TIME... SO PLEASE, ENJOY YOURSELVES!
PLAY WITH THE TONKS. LET *US* SETTLE THIS *PEACEFULLY.*

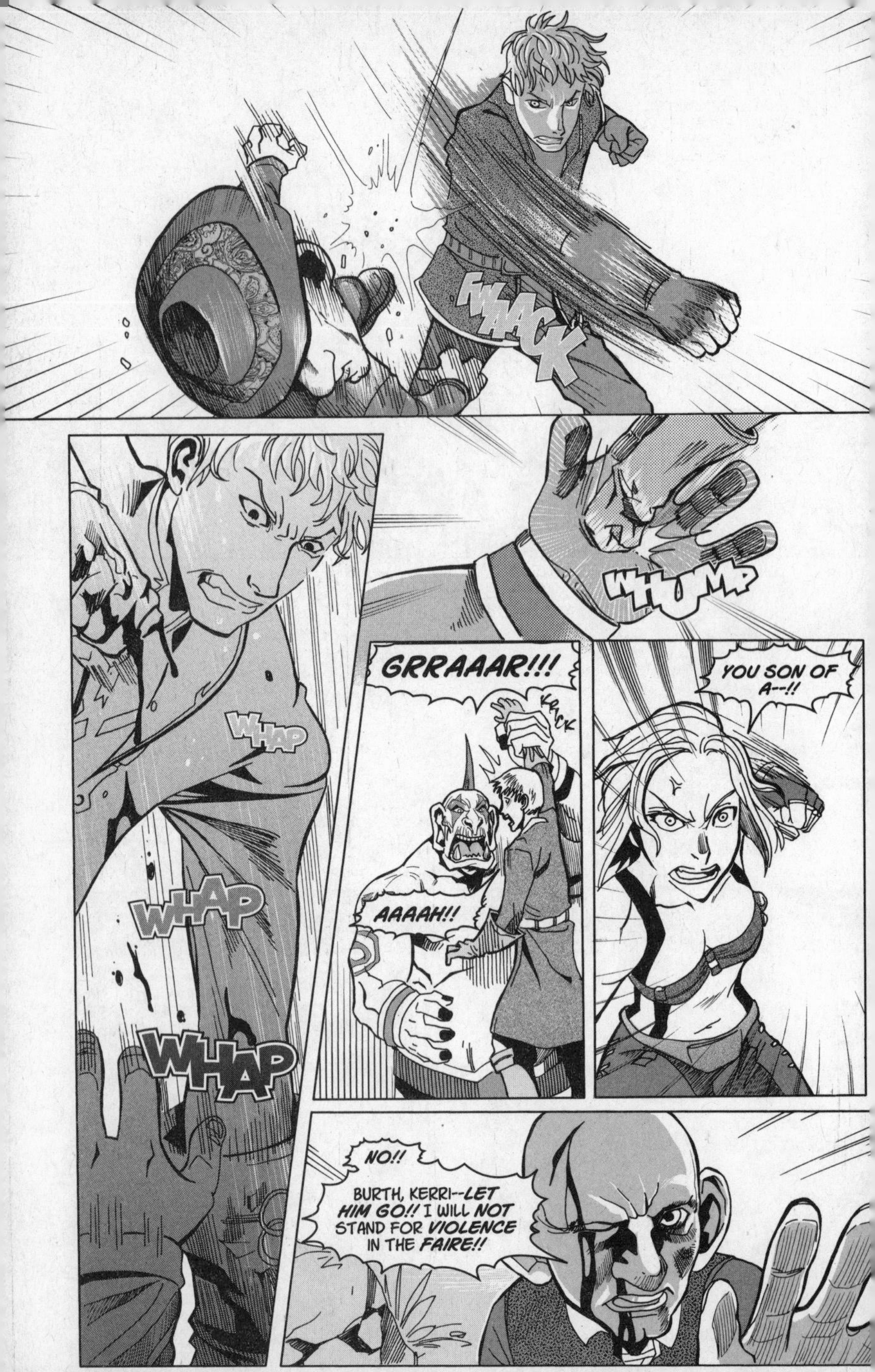
FWAACK
WHAP
WHAP
WHAP
WHUMP
GRRAAAR!!!
KRACK
AAAAH!!
YOU SON OF A--!!
NO!!
BURTH, KERRI--*LET HIM GO!!* I WILL *NOT* STAND FOR *VIOLENCE* IN THE *FAIRE!!*

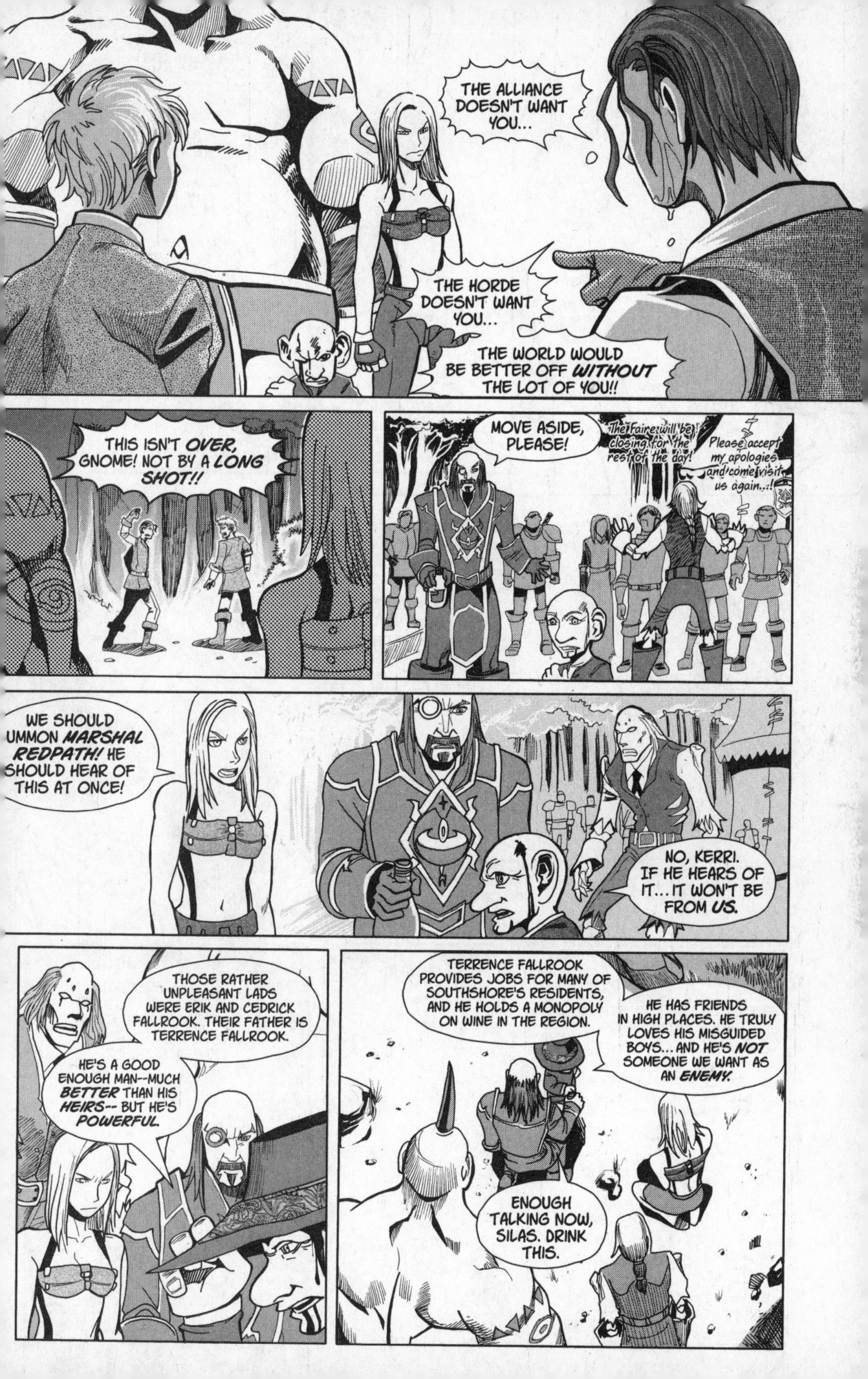
THE ALLIANCE DOESN'T WANT YOU...
THE HORDE DOESN'T WANT YOU...
THE WORLD WOULD BE BETTER OFF *WITHOUT* THE LOT OF YOU!!
THIS ISN'T *OVER,* GNOME! NOT BY A *LONG SHOT!!*
MOVE ASIDE, PLEASE!
The Faire will be closing for the rest of the day!
Please accept my apologies and come visit us again...!
WE SHOULD UMMON *MARSHAL REDPATH!* HE SHOULD HEAR OF THIS AT ONCE!
NO, KERRI. IF HE HEARS OF IT... IT WON'T BE FROM *US.*
THOSE RATHER UNPLEASANT LADS WERE ERIK AND CEDRICK FALLROOK. THEIR FATHER IS TERRENCE FALLROOK.
HE'S A GOOD ENOUGH MAN--MUCH *BETTER* THAN HIS *HEIRS*-- BUT HE'S *POWERFUL.*
TERRENCE FALLROOK PROVIDES JOBS FOR MANY OF SOUTHSHORE'S RESIDENTS, AND HE HOLDS A MONOPOLY ON WINE IN THE REGION.
HE HAS FRIENDS IN HIGH PLACES. HE TRULY LOVES HIS MISGUIDED BOYS... AND HE'S *NOT* SOMEONE WE WANT AS AN *ENEMY.*
ENOUGH TALKING NOW, SILAS. DRINK THIS.

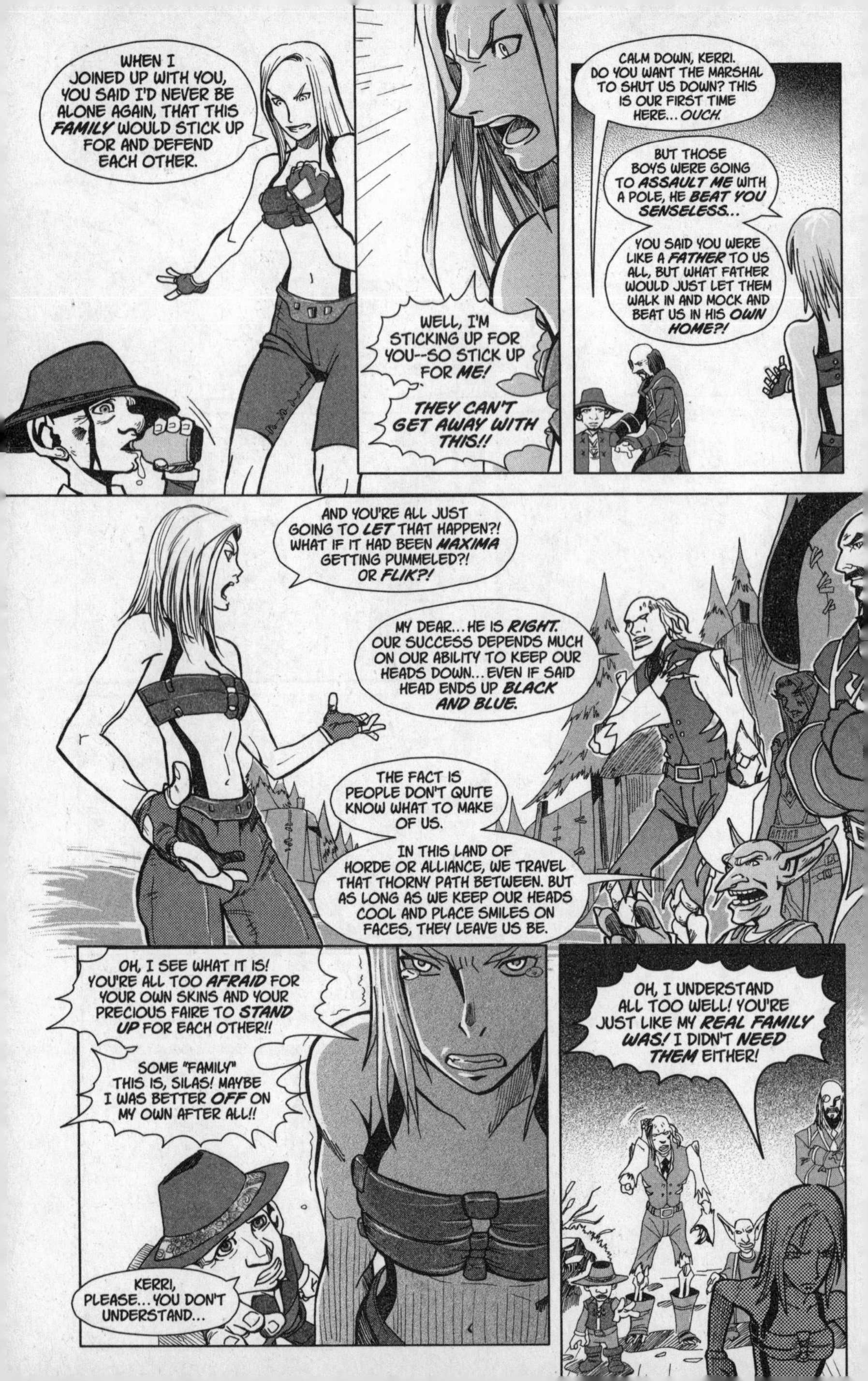
WHEN I JOINED UP WITH YOU, YOU SAID I'D NEVER BE ALONE AGAIN, THAT THIS FAMILY WOULD STICK UP FOR AND DEFEND EACH OTHER.
WELL, I'M STICKING UP FOR YOU--SO STICK UP FOR ME!
THEY CAN'T GET AWAY WITH THIS!!
CALM DOWN, KERRI. DO YOU WANT THE MARSHAL TO SHUT US DOWN? THIS IS OUR FIRST TIME HERE... OUCH.
BUT THOSE BOYS WERE GOING TO ASSAULT ME WITH A POLE, HE BEAT YOU SENSELESS...
YOU SAID YOU WERE LIKE A FATHER TO US ALL, BUT WHAT FATHER WOULD JUST LET THEM WALK IN AND MOCK AND BEAT US IN HIS OWN HOME?!
AND YOU'RE ALL JUST GOING TO LET THAT HAPPEN?! WHAT IF IT HAD BEEN MAXIMA GETTING PUMMELED?! OR FLIK?!
MY DEAR... HE IS RIGHT. OUR SUCCESS DEPENDS MUCH ON OUR ABILITY TO KEEP OUR HEADS DOWN... EVEN IF SAID HEAD ENDS UP BLACK AND BLUE.
THE FACT IS PEOPLE DON'T QUITE KNOW WHAT TO MAKE OF US.
IN THIS LAND OF HORDE OR ALLIANCE, WE TRAVEL THAT THORNY PATH BETWEEN. BUT AS LONG AS WE KEEP OUR HEADS COOL AND PLACE SMILES ON FACES, THEY LEAVE US BE.
OH, I SEE WHAT IT IS! YOU'RE ALL TOO AFRAID FOR YOUR OWN SKINS AND YOUR PRECIOUS FAIRE TO STAND UP FOR EACH OTHER!!
SOME "FAMILY" THIS IS, SILAS! MAYBE I WAS BETTER OFF ON MY OWN AFTER ALL!!
KERRI, PLEASE... YOU DON'T UNDERSTAND...
OH, I UNDERSTAND ALL TOO WELL! YOU'RE JUST LIKE MY REAL FAMILY WAS! I DIDN'T NEED THEM EITHER!

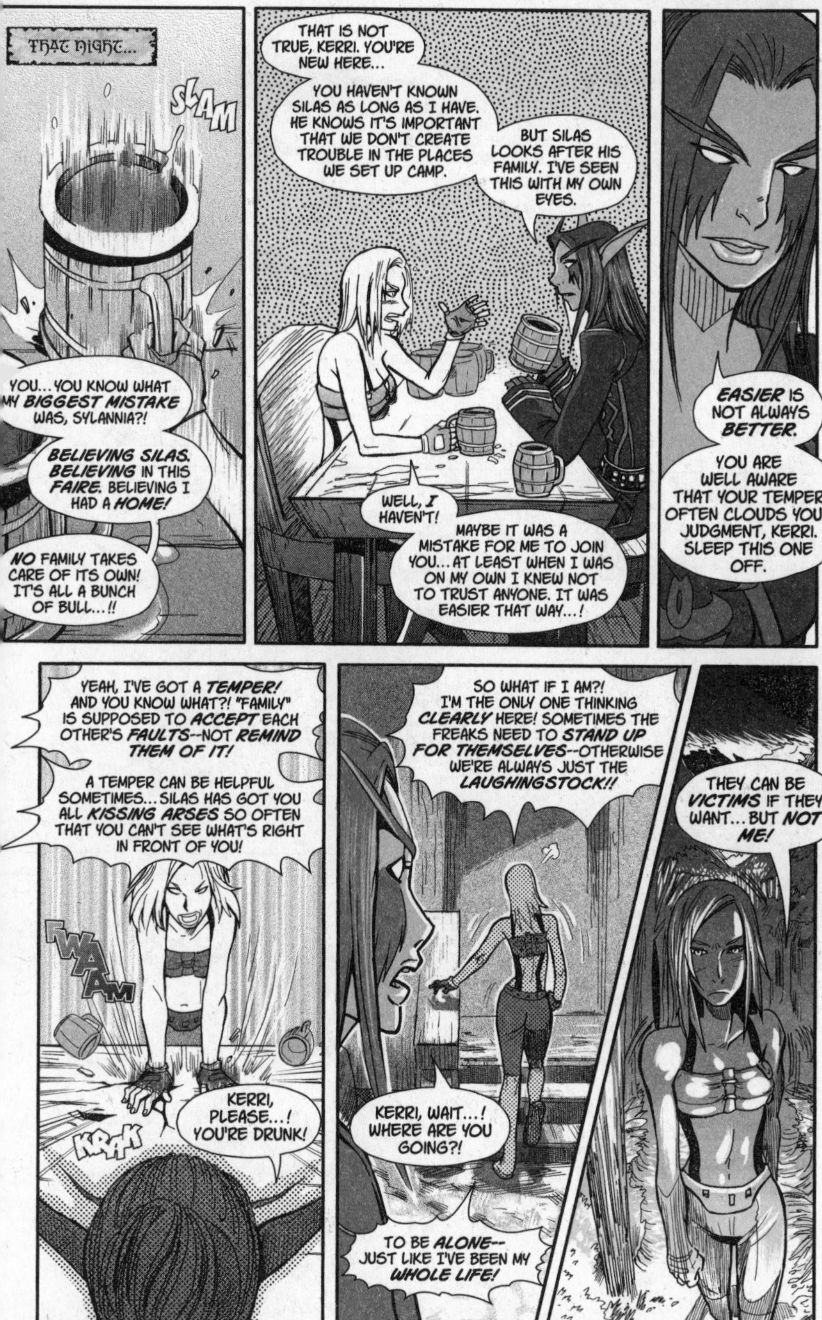
THAT NIGHT...
SLAM
YOU... YOU KNOW WHAT MY BIGGEST MISTAKE WAS, SYLANNIA?!
BELIEVING SILAS. BELIEVING IN THIS FAIRE. BELIEVING I HAD A HOME!
NO FAMILY TAKES CARE OF ITS OWN! IT'S ALL A BUNCH OF BULL...!!
THAT IS NOT TRUE, KERRI. YOU'RE NEW HERE...
YOU HAVEN'T KNOWN SILAS AS LONG AS I HAVE. HE KNOWS IT'S IMPORTANT THAT WE DON'T CREATE TROUBLE IN THE PLACES WE SET UP CAMP.
BUT SILAS LOOKS AFTER HIS FAMILY. I'VE SEEN THIS WITH MY OWN EYES.
WELL, I HAVEN'T!
MAYBE IT WAS A MISTAKE FOR ME TO JOIN YOU... AT LEAST WHEN I WAS ON MY OWN I KNEW NOT TO TRUST ANYONE. IT WAS EASIER THAT WAY...!
EASIER IS NOT ALWAYS BETTER.
YOU ARE WELL AWARE THAT YOUR TEMPER OFTEN CLOUDS YOUR JUDGMENT, KERRI. SLEEP THIS ONE OFF.
YEAH, I'VE GOT A TEMPER! AND YOU KNOW WHAT?! "FAMILY" IS SUPPOSED TO ACCEPT EACH OTHER'S FAULTS--NOT REMIND THEM OF IT!
A TEMPER CAN BE HELPFUL SOMETIMES... SILAS HAS GOT YOU ALL KISSING ARSES SO OFTEN THAT YOU CAN'T SEE WHAT'S RIGHT IN FRONT OF YOU!
FWAAM
KRAK
KERRI, PLEASE...! YOU'RE DRUNK!
SO WHAT IF I AM?! I'M THE ONLY ONE THINKING CLEARLY HERE! SOMETIMES THE FREAKS NEED TO STAND UP FOR THEMSELVES--OTHERWISE WE'RE ALWAYS JUST THE LAUGHINGSTOCK!!
KERRI, WAIT...! WHERE ARE YOU GOING?!
TO BE ALONE--JUST LIKE I'VE BEEN MY WHOLE LIFE!
THEY CAN BE VICTIMS IF THEY WANT... BUT NOT ME!

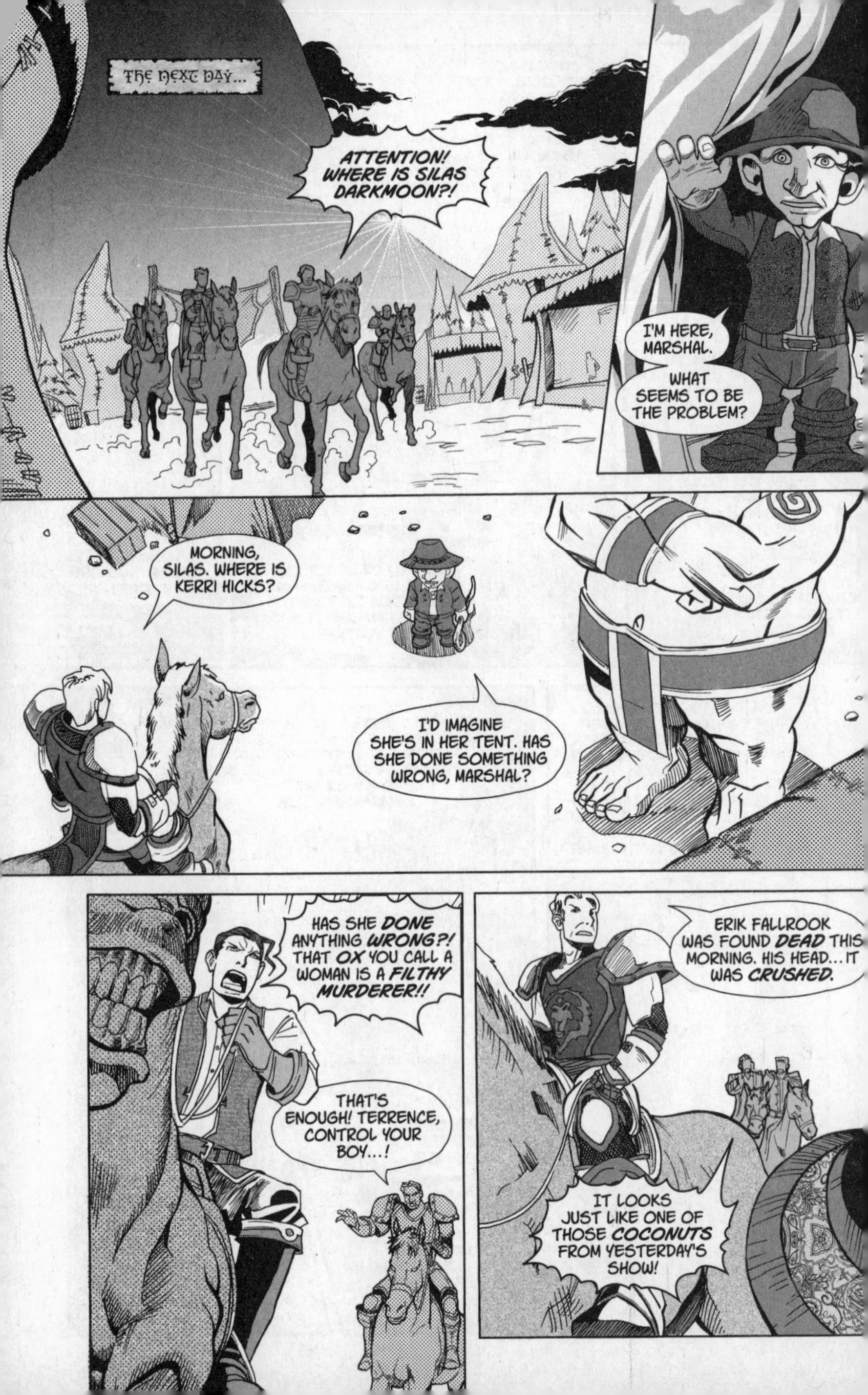
THE NEXT DAY...
ATTENTION! WHERE IS SILAS DARKMOON?!
I'M HERE, MARSHAL.
WHAT SEEMS TO BE THE PROBLEM?
MORNING, SILAS. WHERE IS KERRI HICKS?
I'D IMAGINE SHE'S IN HER TENT. HAS SHE DONE SOMETHING WRONG, MARSHAL?
HAS SHE *DONE* ANYTHING *WRONG*?! THAT *OX* YOU CALL A WOMAN IS A *FILTHY MURDERER!!*
THAT'S ENOUGH! TERRENCE, CONTROL YOUR BOY...!
ERIK FALLROOK WAS FOUND *DEAD* THIS MORNING. HIS HEAD... IT WAS *CRUSHED.*
IT LOOKS JUST LIKE ONE OF THOSE *COCONUTS* FROM YESTERDAY'S SHOW!

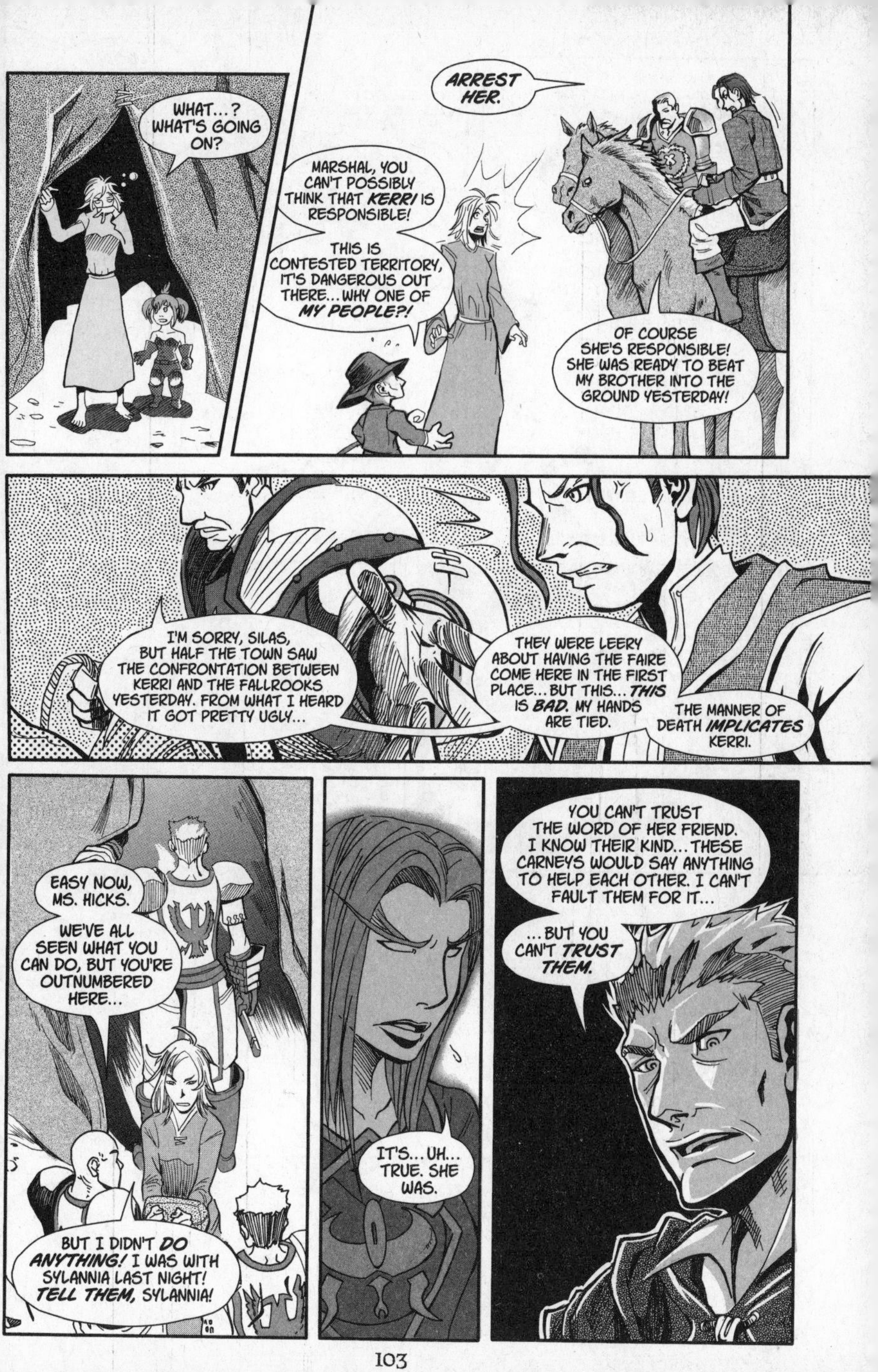
WHAT...? WHAT'S GOING ON?
ARREST HER.
MARSHAL, YOU CAN'T POSSIBLY THINK THAT KERRI IS RESPONSIBLE!
THIS IS CONTESTED TERRITORY, IT'S DANGEROUS OUT THERE... WHY ONE OF MY PEOPLE?!
OF COURSE SHE'S RESPONSIBLE! SHE WAS READY TO BEAT MY BROTHER INTO THE GROUND YESTERDAY!
I'M SORRY, SILAS, BUT HALF THE TOWN SAW THE CONFRONTATION BETWEEN KERRI AND THE FALLROOKS YESTERDAY. FROM WHAT I HEARD IT GOT PRETTY UGLY...
THEY WERE LEERY ABOUT HAVING THE FAIRE COME HERE IN THE FIRST PLACE... BUT THIS... THIS IS BAD. MY HANDS ARE TIED.
THE MANNER OF DEATH IMPLICATES KERRI.
EASY NOW, MS. HICKS.
WE'VE ALL SEEN WHAT YOU CAN DO, BUT YOU'RE OUTNUMBERED HERE...
BUT I DIDN'T DO ANYTHING! I WAS WITH SYLANNIA LAST NIGHT! TELL THEM, SYLANNIA!
IT'S... UH... TRUE. SHE WAS.
YOU CAN'T TRUST THE WORD OF HER FRIEND. I KNOW THEIR KIND... THESE CARNEYS WOULD SAY ANYTHING TO HELP EACH OTHER. I CAN'T FAULT THEM FOR IT...
... BUT YOU CAN'T TRUST THEM.

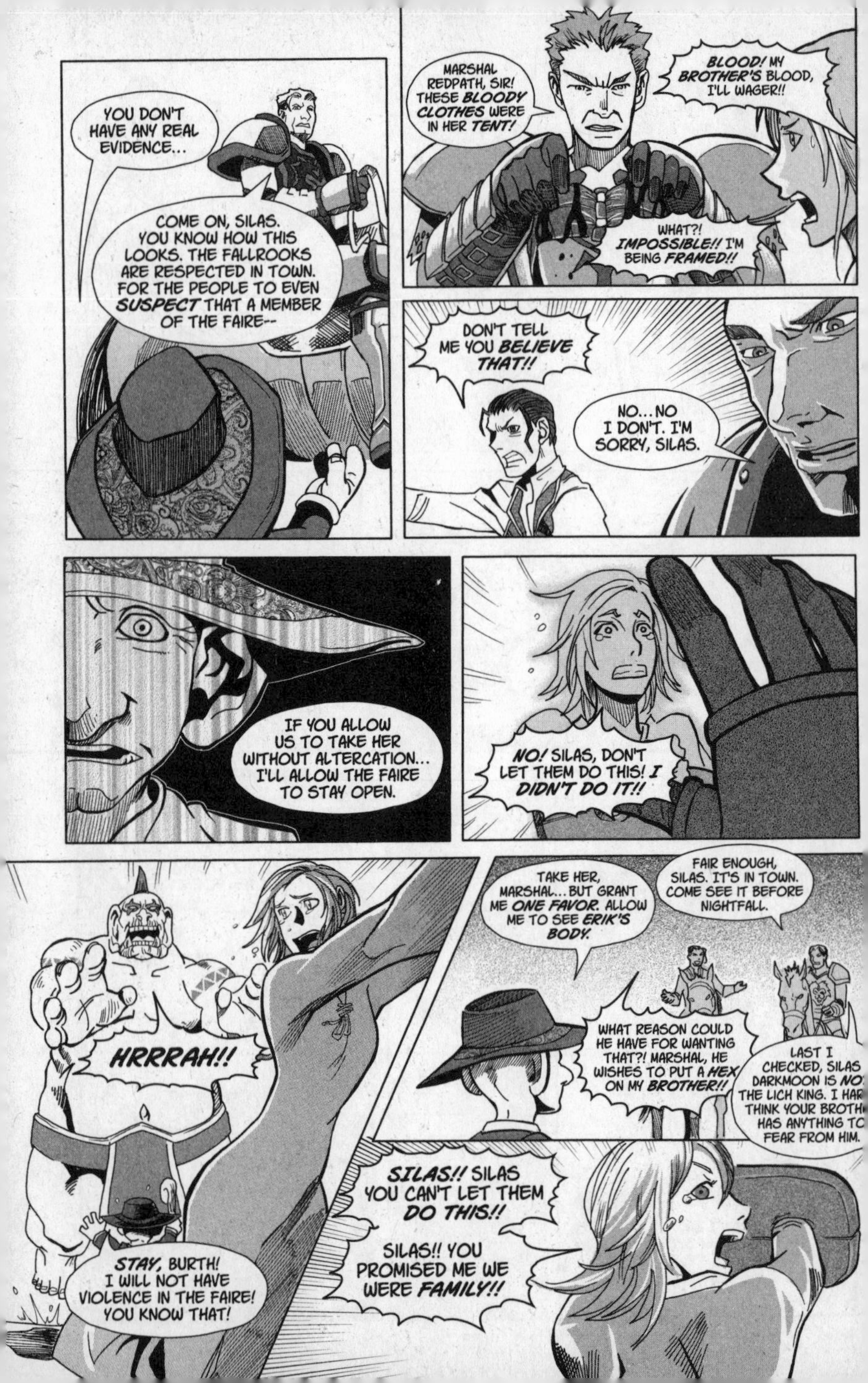
YOU DON'T HAVE ANY REAL EVIDENCE...
COME ON, SILAS. YOU KNOW HOW THIS LOOKS. THE FALLROOKS ARE RESPECTED IN TOWN. FOR THE PEOPLE TO EVEN SUSPECT THAT A MEMBER OF THE FAIRE--
MARSHAL REDPATH, SIR! THESE BLOODY CLOTHES WERE IN HER TENT!
BLOOD! MY BROTHER'S BLOOD, I'LL WAGER!!
WHAT?! IMPOSSIBLE!! I'M BEING FRAMED!!
DON'T TELL ME YOU BELIEVE THAT!!
NO...NO I DON'T. I'M SORRY, SILAS.
IF YOU ALLOW US TO TAKE HER WITHOUT ALTERCATION... I'LL ALLOW THE FAIRE TO STAY OPEN.
NO! SILAS, DON'T LET THEM DO THIS! I DIDN'T DO IT!!
HRRRAH!!
STAY, BURTH! I WILL NOT HAVE VIOLENCE IN THE FAIRE! YOU KNOW THAT!
TAKE HER, MARSHAL... BUT GRANT ME ONE FAVOR. ALLOW ME TO SEE ERIK'S BODY.
FAIR ENOUGH, SILAS. IT'S IN TOWN. COME SEE IT BEFORE NIGHTFALL.
WHAT REASON COULD HE HAVE FOR WANTING THAT?! MARSHAL, HE WISHES TO PUT A HEX ON MY BROTHER!!
LAST I CHECKED, SILAS DARKMOON IS NO THE LICH KING. I HAR THINK YOUR BROTH HAS ANYTHING TO FEAR FROM HIM.
SILAS!! SILAS YOU CAN'T LET THEM DO THIS!!
SILAS!! YOU PROMISED ME WE WERE FAMILY!!

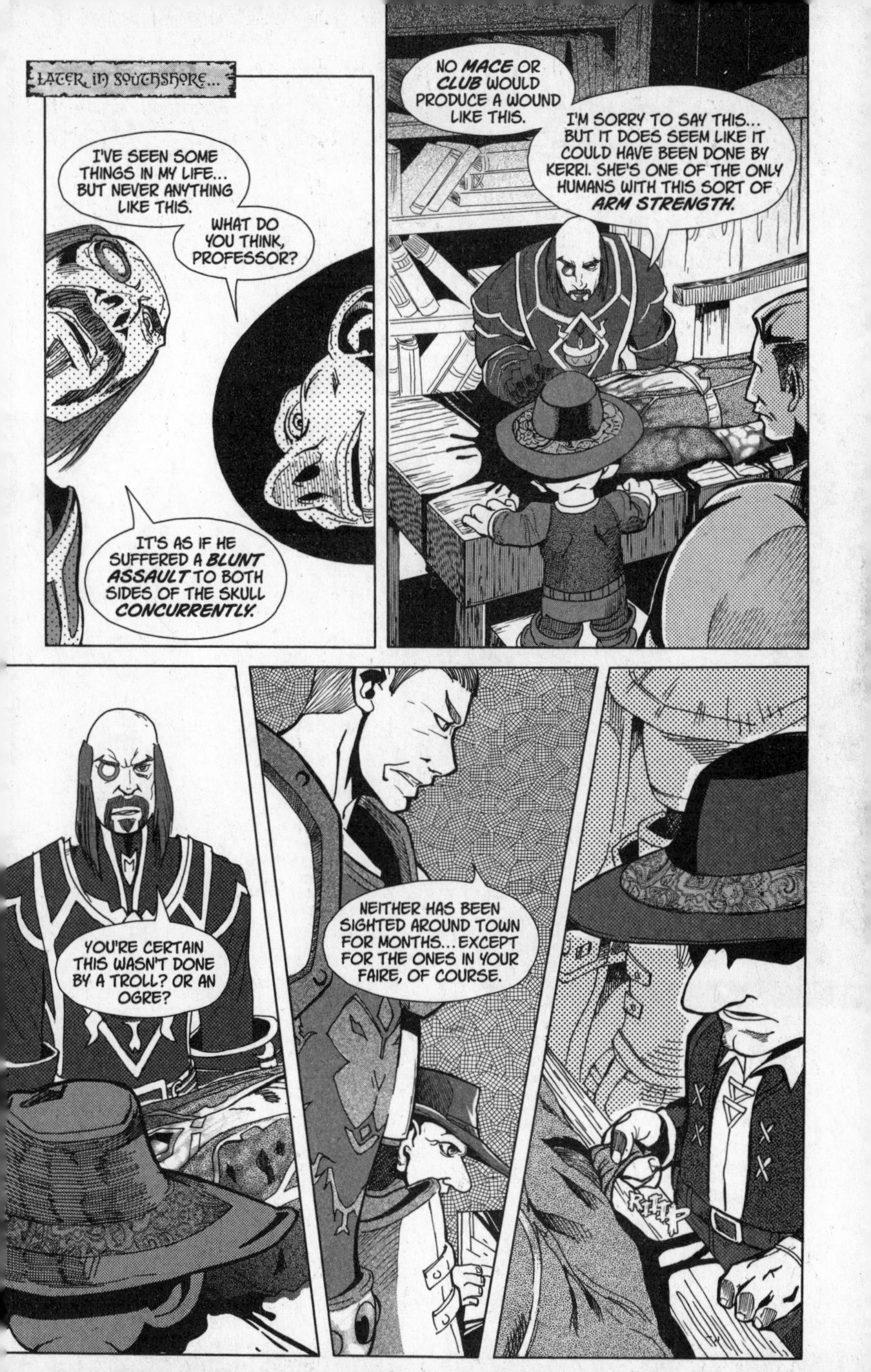
LATER, IN SOUTHSHORE...
I'VE SEEN SOME THINGS IN MY LIFE... BUT NEVER ANYTHING LIKE THIS.
WHAT DO YOU THINK, PROFESSOR?
IT'S AS IF HE SUFFERED A *BLUNT ASSAULT* TO BOTH SIDES OF THE SKULL *CONCURRENTLY.*
NO *MACE* OR *CLUB* WOULD PRODUCE A WOUND LIKE THIS.
I'M SORRY TO SAY THIS... BUT IT DOES SEEM LIKE IT COULD HAVE BEEN DONE BY KERRI. SHE'S ONE OF THE ONLY HUMANS WITH THIS SORT OF *ARM STRENGTH.*
YOU'RE CERTAIN THIS WASN'T DONE BY A TROLL? OR AN OGRE?
NEITHER HAS BEEN SIGHTED AROUND TOWN FOR MONTHS... EXCEPT FOR THE ONES IN YOUR FAIRE, OF COURSE.

THIS...
THIS CAN'T BE
HAPPENING...

I DIDN'T
DO THIS...

THIS IS A
SETUP.

RAAAAR!! I DIDN'T
DO THIS!! LET ME
OUUUUUUUUUT!!

THAT MOMENT AT
DARKMOON FAIRE...

WELL, IT TRULY
ISN'T MUCH TO WORK
WITH...BUT TOUCHING
THE LITTLE BIT OF
BLOOD THAT'S ON THIS
CLOTH SHOULD ALLOW
ME SOME GLIMPSE...

EMOTIONAL
TRAUMA USUALLY
LEAVES A
RESONANCE...SO
WE SHALL SEE.

IF THIS WORKS...
AND THAT'S A BIG
IF...I SHOULD GET A
GLIMPSE AT ERIK'S
LAST THOUGHTS.

THERE'S NO "IF"
ABOUT IT, SAYGE. IT HAS
TO WORK. YOU'RE OUR
CLAIRVOYANT AND ONE OF
THE BEST I'VE SEEN. I HAVE
ALL THE FAITH IN THE WORLD
IN YOUR ABILITIES.

TO BE HONEST, SILAS,
YOU MAY NOT LIKE WHAT YOU
SEE. KERRI'S TEMPER IS ONE
FOR THE RECORD BOOKS...AND
LAST EVE SHE WAS A BURNING
CAULDRON OF IT.

DON'T EVEN
SUGGEST THAT
UNTIL YOU HAVE SOME
REAL FACTS...!!

FORGIVE ME,
SILAS...LET'S
BEGIN, SHALL WE?

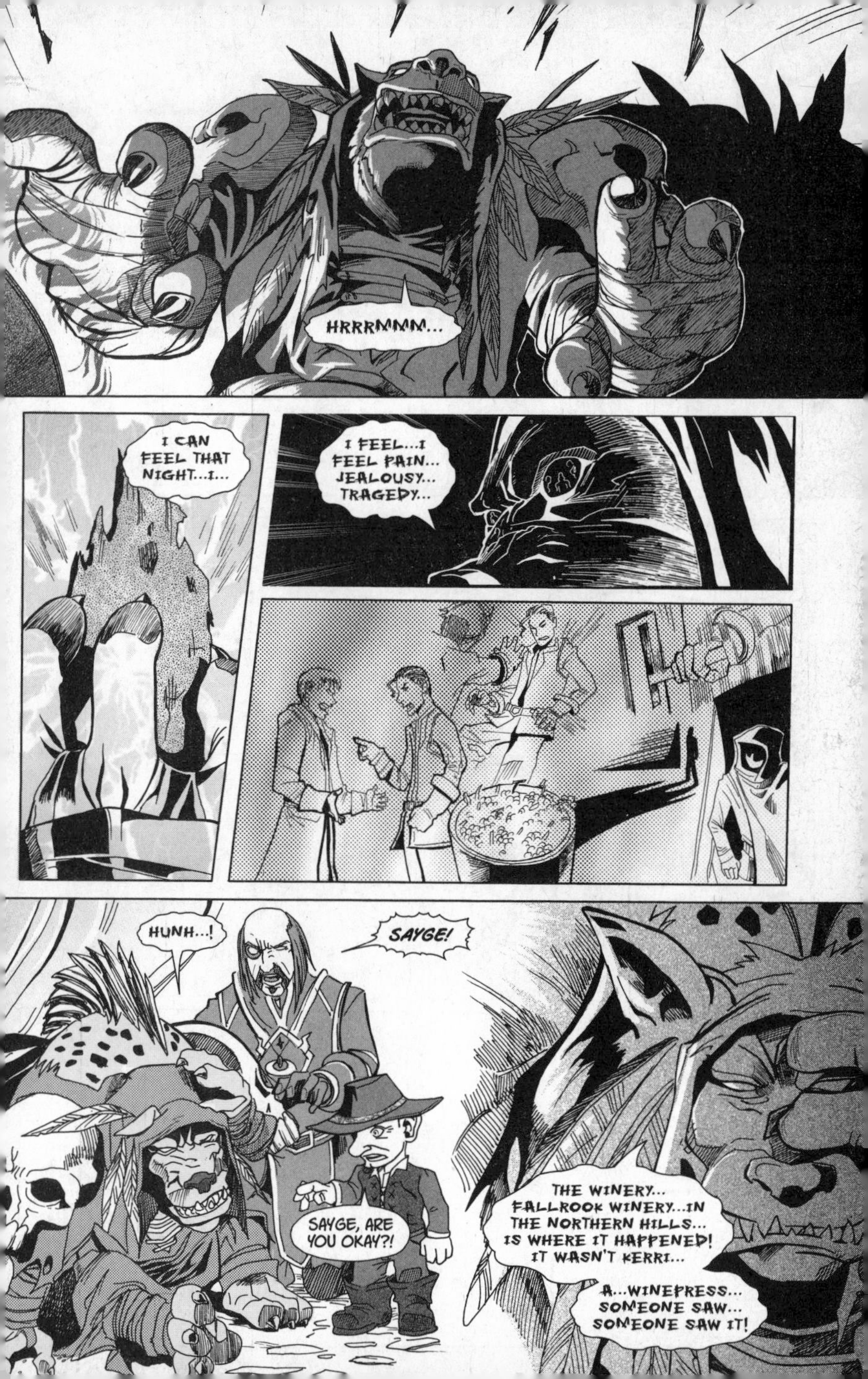
HRRRMMM...
I CAN FEEL THAT NIGHT...I...
I FEEL...I FEEL PAIN... JEALOUSY... TRAGEDY...
HUNH...!
SAYGE!
SAYGE, ARE YOU OKAY?!
THE WINERY... FALLROOK WINERY...IN THE NORTHERN HILLS... IS WHERE IT HAPPENED! IT WASN'T KERRI...
A...WINEPRESS... SOMEONE SAW... SOMEONE SAW IT!

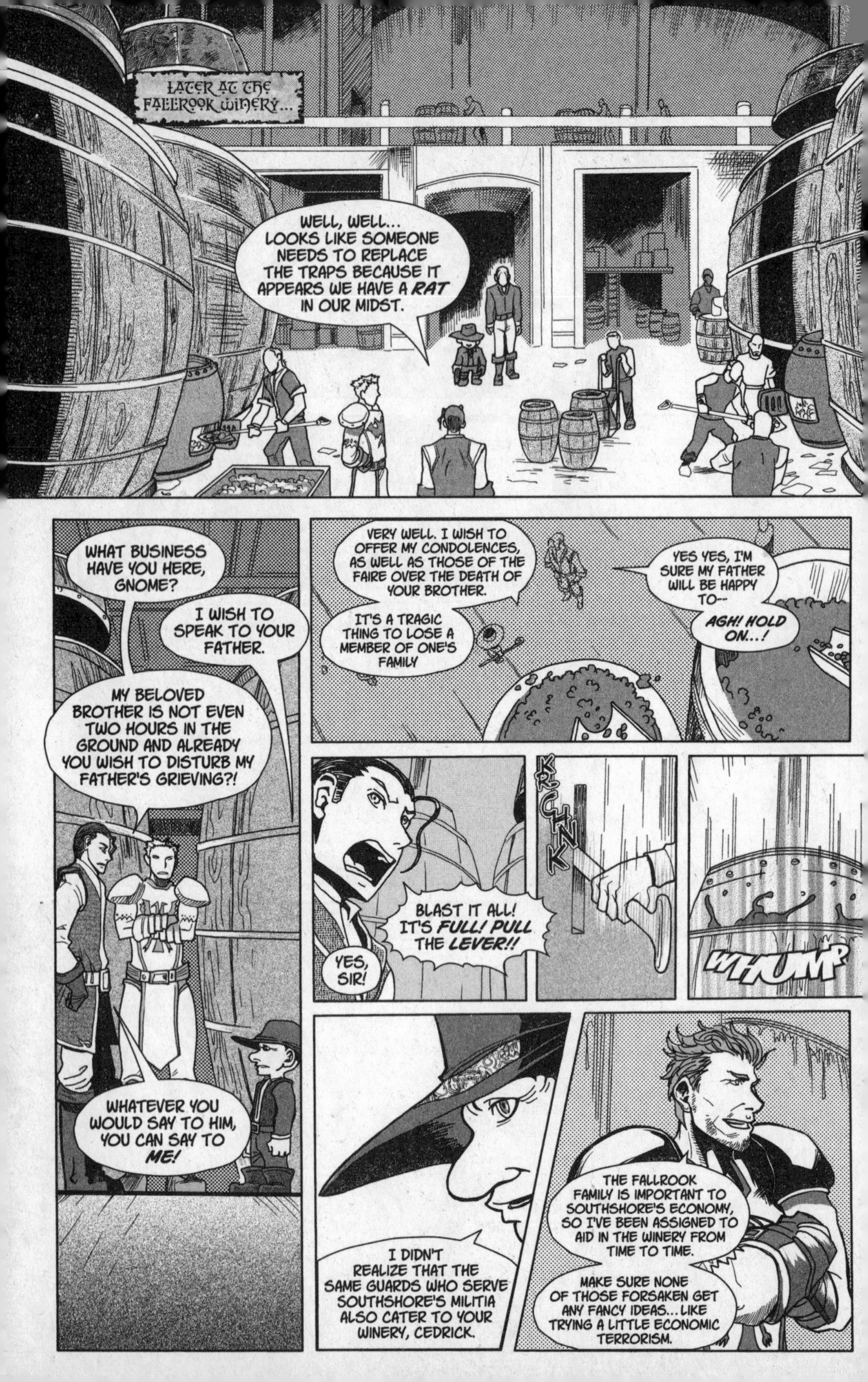
LATER AT THE FALLROOK WINERY...
WELL, WELL... LOOKS LIKE SOMEONE NEEDS TO REPLACE THE TRAPS BECAUSE IT APPEARS WE HAVE A *RAT* IN OUR MIDST.
WHAT BUSINESS HAVE YOU HERE, GNOME?
I WISH TO SPEAK TO YOUR FATHER.
MY BELOVED BROTHER IS NOT EVEN TWO HOURS IN THE GROUND AND ALREADY YOU WISH TO DISTURB MY FATHER'S GRIEVING?!
WHATEVER YOU WOULD SAY TO HIM, YOU CAN SAY TO *ME!*
VERY WELL. I WISH TO OFFER MY CONDOLENCES, AS WELL AS THOSE OF THE FAIRE OVER THE DEATH OF YOUR BROTHER.
IT'S A TRAGIC THING TO LOSE A MEMBER OF ONE'S FAMILY
YES YES, I'M SURE MY FATHER WILL BE HAPPY TO--
AGH! HOLD ON...!
BLAST IT ALL! IT'S *FULL! PULL* THE *LEVER!!*
YES, SIR!
KRCHNK
WHUMP
I DIDN'T REALIZE THAT THE SAME GUARDS WHO SERVE SOUTHSHORE'S MILITIA ALSO CATER TO YOUR WINERY, CEDRICK.
THE FALLROOK FAMILY IS IMPORTANT TO SOUTHSHORE'S ECONOMY, SO I'VE BEEN ASSIGNED TO AID IN THE WINERY FROM TIME TO TIME.
MAKE SURE NONE OF THOSE FORSAKEN GET ANY FANCY IDEAS... LIKE TRYING A LITTLE ECONOMIC TERRORISM.

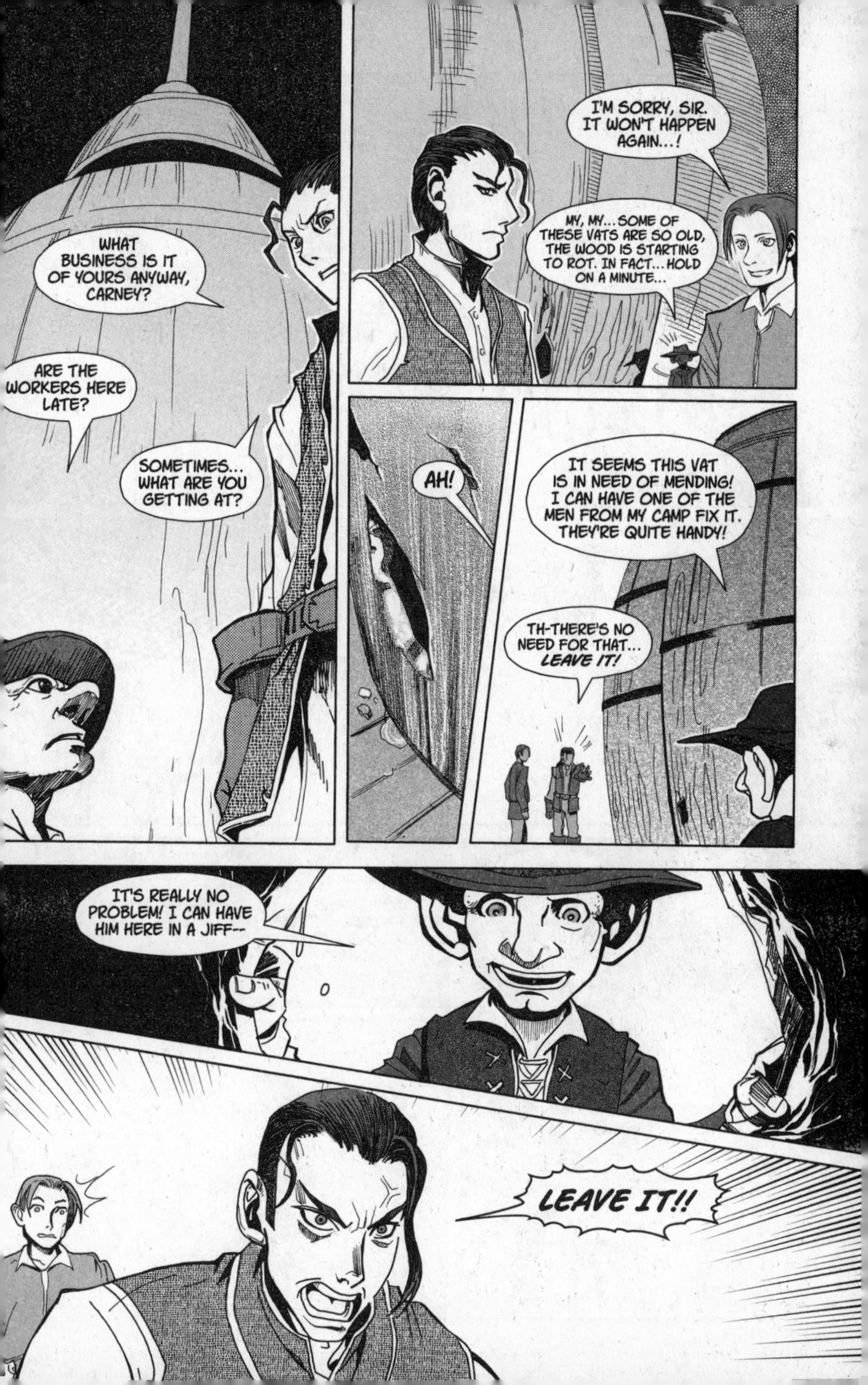
WHAT BUSINESS IS IT OF YOURS ANYWAY, CARNEY?
ARE THE WORKERS HERE LATE?
SOMETIMES... WHAT ARE YOU GETTING AT?
I'M SORRY, SIR. IT WON'T HAPPEN AGAIN...!
MY, MY... SOME OF THESE VATS ARE SO OLD, THE WOOD IS STARTING TO ROT. IN FACT... HOLD ON A MINUTE...
AH!
IT SEEMS THIS VAT IS IN NEED OF MENDING! I CAN HAVE ONE OF THE MEN FROM MY CAMP FIX IT. THEY'RE QUITE HANDY!
TH-THERE'S NO NEED FOR THAT... *LEAVE IT!*
IT'S REALLY NO PROBLEM! I CAN HAVE HIM HERE IN A JIFF--
LEAVE IT!!

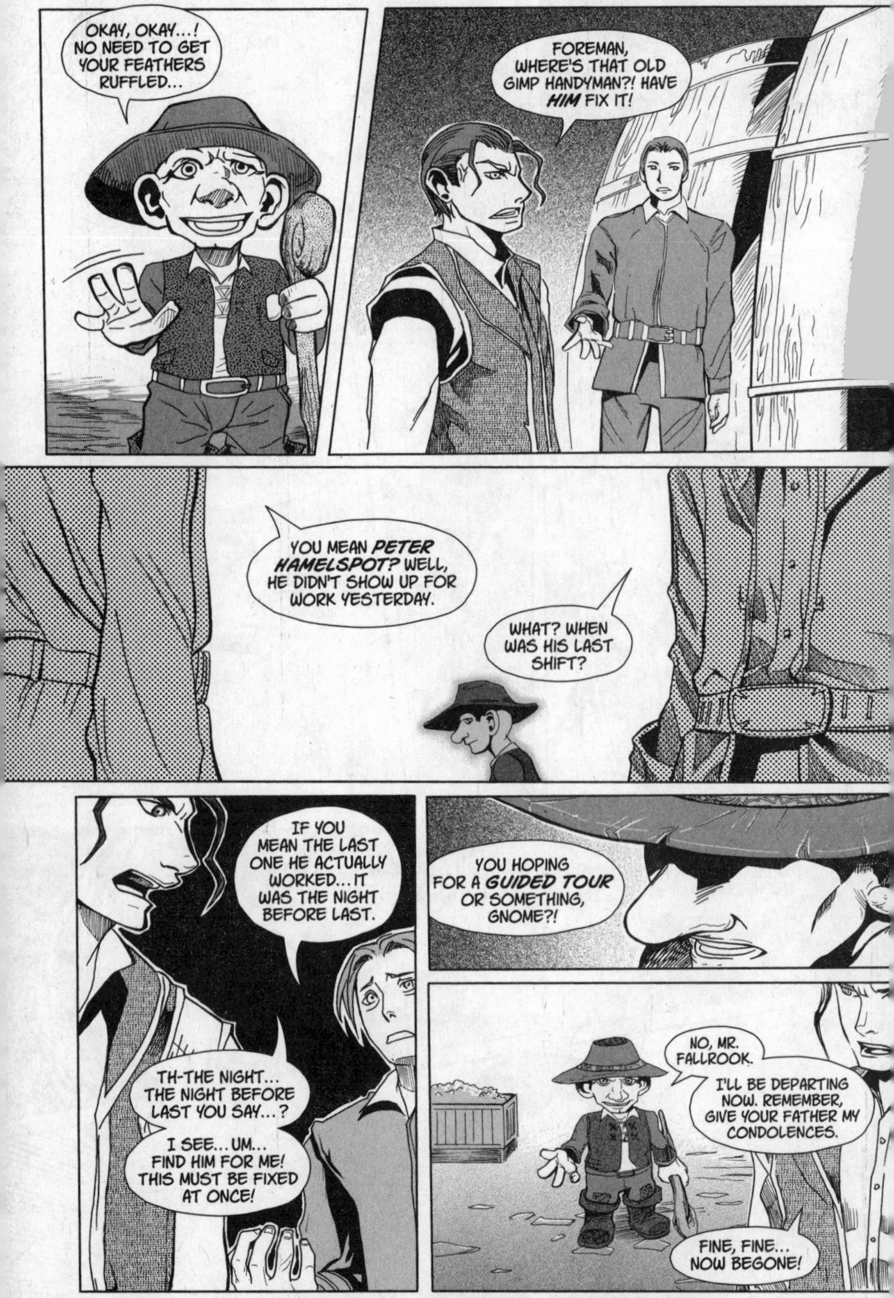
OKAY, OKAY...! NO NEED TO GET YOUR FEATHERS RUFFLED...
FOREMAN, WHERE'S THAT OLD GIMP HANDYMAN?! HAVE *HIM* FIX IT!
YOU MEAN *PETER HAMELSPOT?* WELL, HE DIDN'T SHOW UP FOR WORK YESTERDAY.
WHAT? WHEN WAS HIS LAST SHIFT?
IF YOU MEAN THE LAST ONE HE ACTUALLY WORKED... IT WAS THE NIGHT BEFORE LAST.
TH-THE NIGHT... THE NIGHT BEFORE LAST YOU SAY...?
I SEE... UM... FIND HIM FOR ME! THIS MUST BE FIXED AT ONCE!
YOU HOPING FOR A *GUIDED TOUR* OR SOMETHING, GNOME?!
NO, MR. FALLROOK.
I'LL BE DEPARTING NOW. REMEMBER, GIVE YOUR FATHER MY CONDOLENCES.
FINE, FINE... NOW BEGONE!

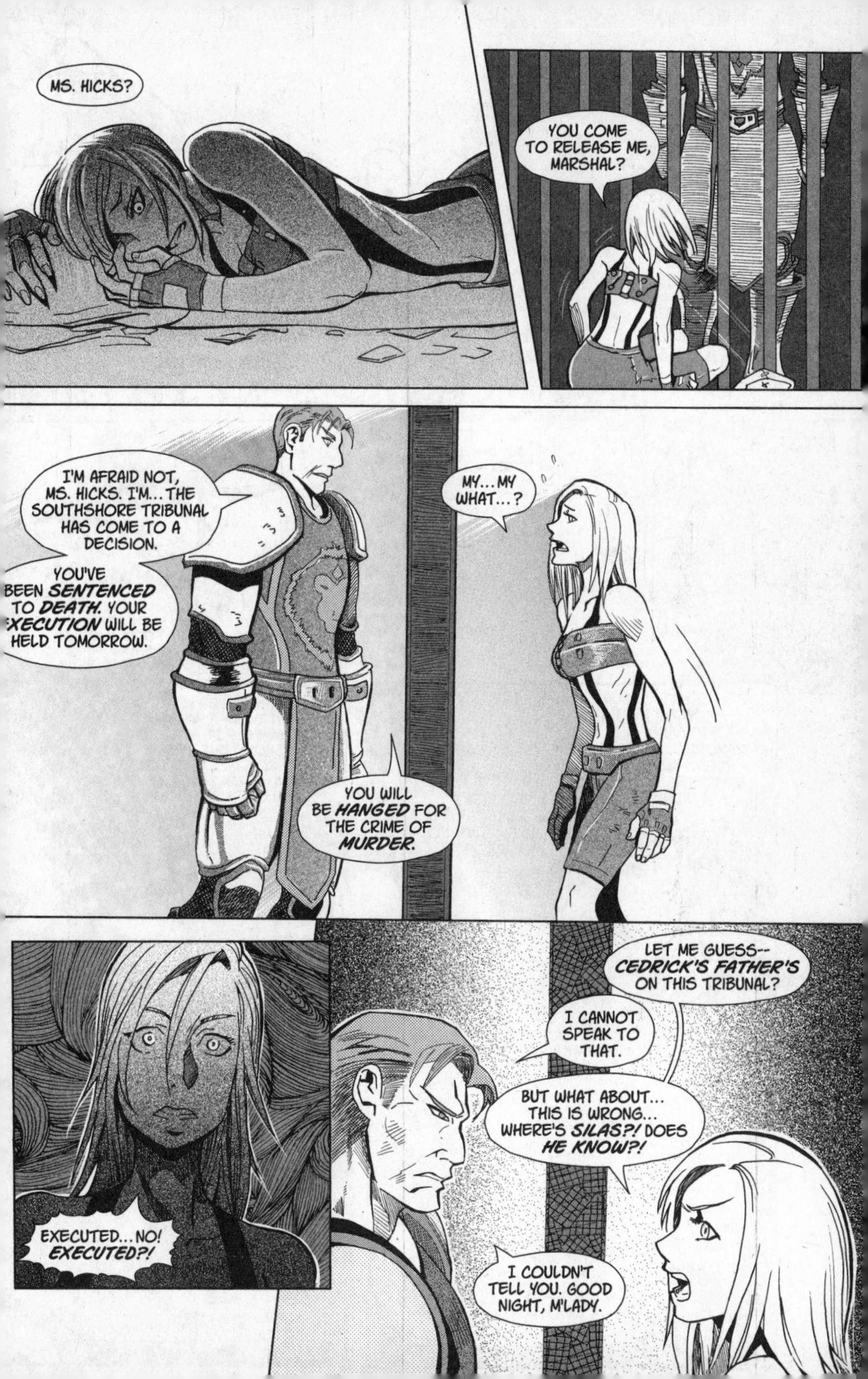
MS. HICKS?
YOU COME TO RELEASE ME, MARSHAL?
I'M AFRAID NOT, MS. HICKS. I'M... THE SOUTHSHORE TRIBUNAL HAS COME TO A DECISION.
YOU'VE BEEN SENTENCED TO DEATH. YOUR EXECUTION WILL BE HELD TOMORROW.
YOU WILL BE HANGED FOR THE CRIME OF MURDER.
MY... MY WHAT...?
EXECUTED... NO! EXECUTED?!
LET ME GUESS-- CEDRICK'S FATHER'S ON THIS TRIBUNAL?
I CANNOT SPEAK TO THAT.
BUT WHAT ABOUT... THIS IS WRONG... WHERE'S SILAS?! DOES HE KNOW?!
I COULDN'T TELL YOU. GOOD NIGHT, M'LADY.

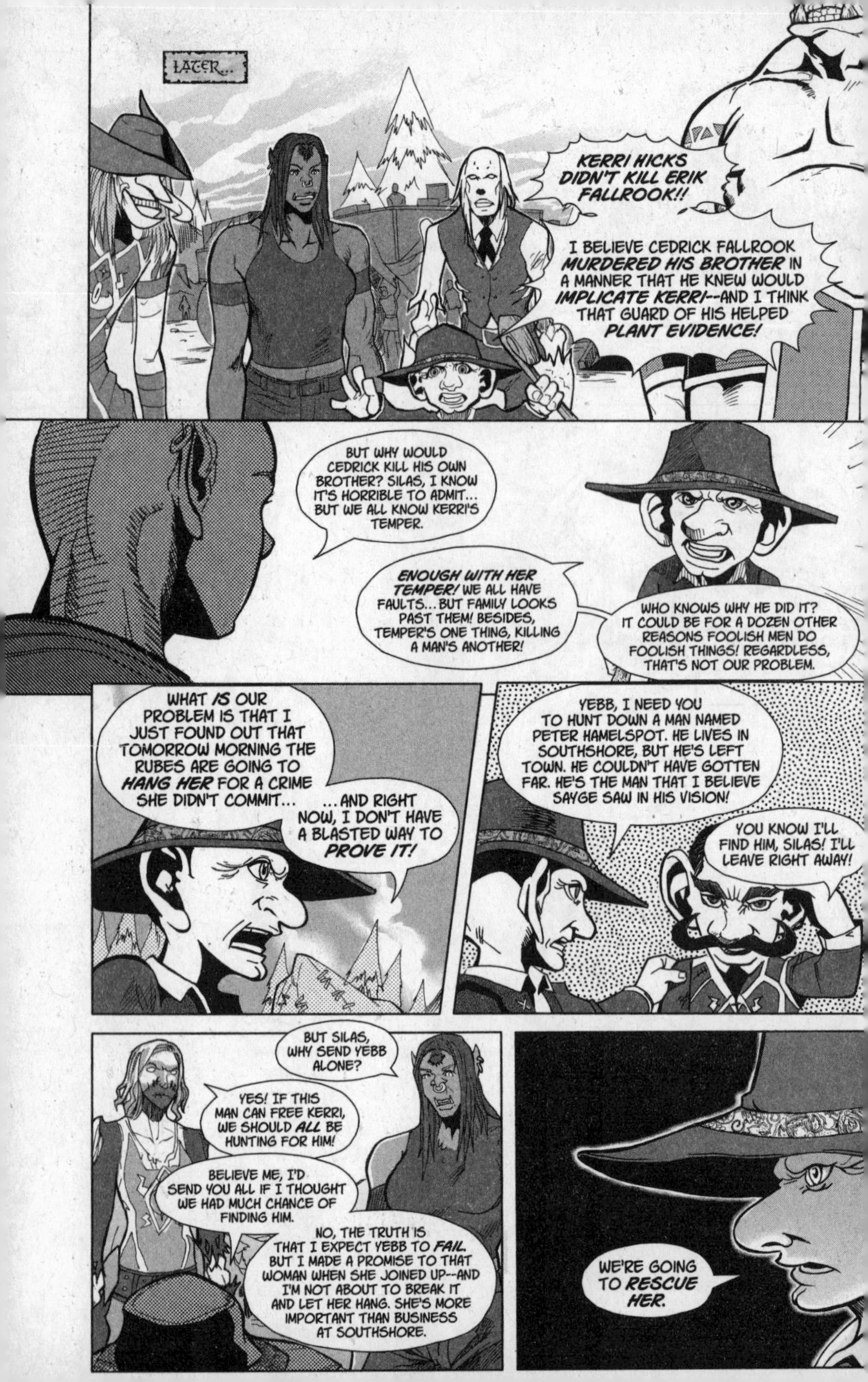
LATER...
KERRI HICKS DIDN'T KILL ERIK FALLROOK!!
I BELIEVE CEDRICK FALLROOK MURDERED HIS BROTHER IN A MANNER THAT HE KNEW WOULD IMPLICATE KERRI--AND I THINK THAT GUARD OF HIS HELPED PLANT EVIDENCE!
BUT WHY WOULD CEDRICK KILL HIS OWN BROTHER? SILAS, I KNOW IT'S HORRIBLE TO ADMIT... BUT WE ALL KNOW KERRI'S TEMPER.
ENOUGH WITH HER TEMPER! WE ALL HAVE FAULTS... BUT FAMILY LOOKS PAST THEM! BESIDES, TEMPER'S ONE THING, KILLING A MAN'S ANOTHER!
WHO KNOWS WHY HE DID IT? IT COULD BE FOR A DOZEN OTHER REASONS FOOLISH MEN DO FOOLISH THINGS! REGARDLESS, THAT'S NOT OUR PROBLEM.
WHAT IS OUR PROBLEM IS THAT I JUST FOUND OUT THAT TOMORROW MORNING THE RUBES ARE GOING TO HANG HER FOR A CRIME SHE DIDN'T COMMIT...
...AND RIGHT NOW, I DON'T HAVE A BLASTED WAY TO PROVE IT!
YEBB, I NEED YOU TO HUNT DOWN A MAN NAMED PETER HAMELSPOT. HE LIVES IN SOUTHSHORE, BUT HE'S LEFT TOWN. HE COULDN'T HAVE GOTTEN FAR. HE'S THE MAN THAT I BELIEVE SAYGE SAW IN HIS VISION!
YOU KNOW I'LL FIND HIM, SILAS! I'LL LEAVE RIGHT AWAY!
BUT SILAS, WHY SEND YEBB ALONE?
YES! IF THIS MAN CAN FREE KERRI, WE SHOULD ALL BE HUNTING FOR HIM!
BELIEVE ME, I'D SEND YOU ALL IF I THOUGHT WE HAD MUCH CHANCE OF FINDING HIM.
NO, THE TRUTH IS THAT I EXPECT YEBB TO FAIL. BUT I MADE A PROMISE TO THAT WOMAN WHEN SHE JOINED UP--AND I'M NOT ABOUT TO BREAK IT AND LET HER HANG. SHE'S MORE IMPORTANT THAN BUSINESS AT SOUTHSHORE.
WE'RE GOING TO RESCUE HER.

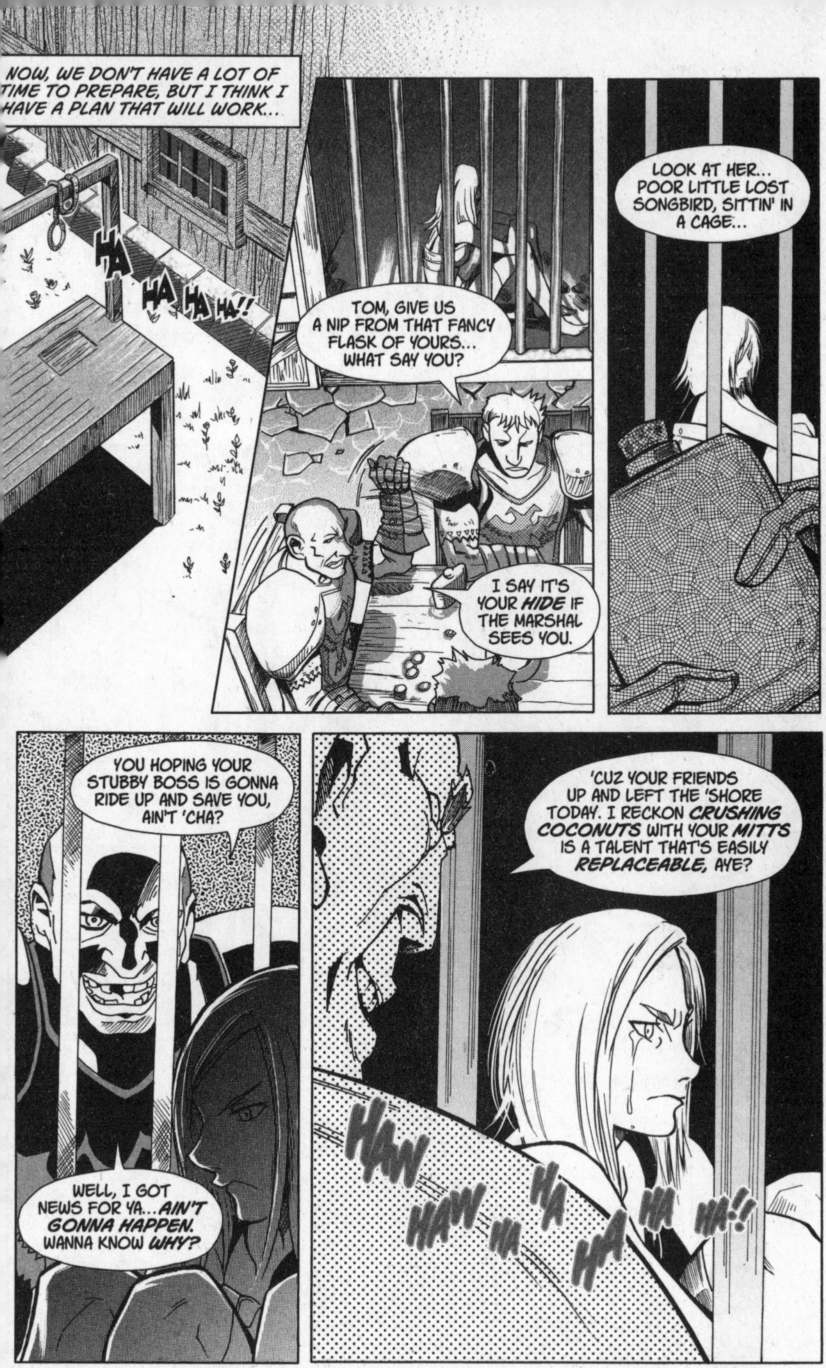
NOW, WE DON'T HAVE A LOT OF TIME TO PREPARE, BUT I THINK I HAVE A PLAN THAT WILL WORK...
HA HA HA HA!!
TOM, GIVE US A NIP FROM THAT FANCY FLASK OF YOURS... WHAT SAY YOU?
I SAY IT'S YOUR HIDE IF THE MARSHAL SEES YOU.
LOOK AT HER... POOR LITTLE LOST SONGBIRD, SITTIN' IN A CAGE...
YOU HOPING YOUR STUBBY BOSS IS GONNA RIDE UP AND SAVE YOU, AIN'T 'CHA?
WELL, I GOT NEWS FOR YA... AIN'T GONNA HAPPEN. WANNA KNOW WHY?
'CUZ YOUR FRIENDS UP AND LEFT THE 'SHORE TODAY. I RECKON CRUSHING COCONUTS WITH YOUR MITTS IS A TALENT THAT'S EASILY REPLACEABLE, AYE?
HAW HAW HA HA HA HA HA HA!!

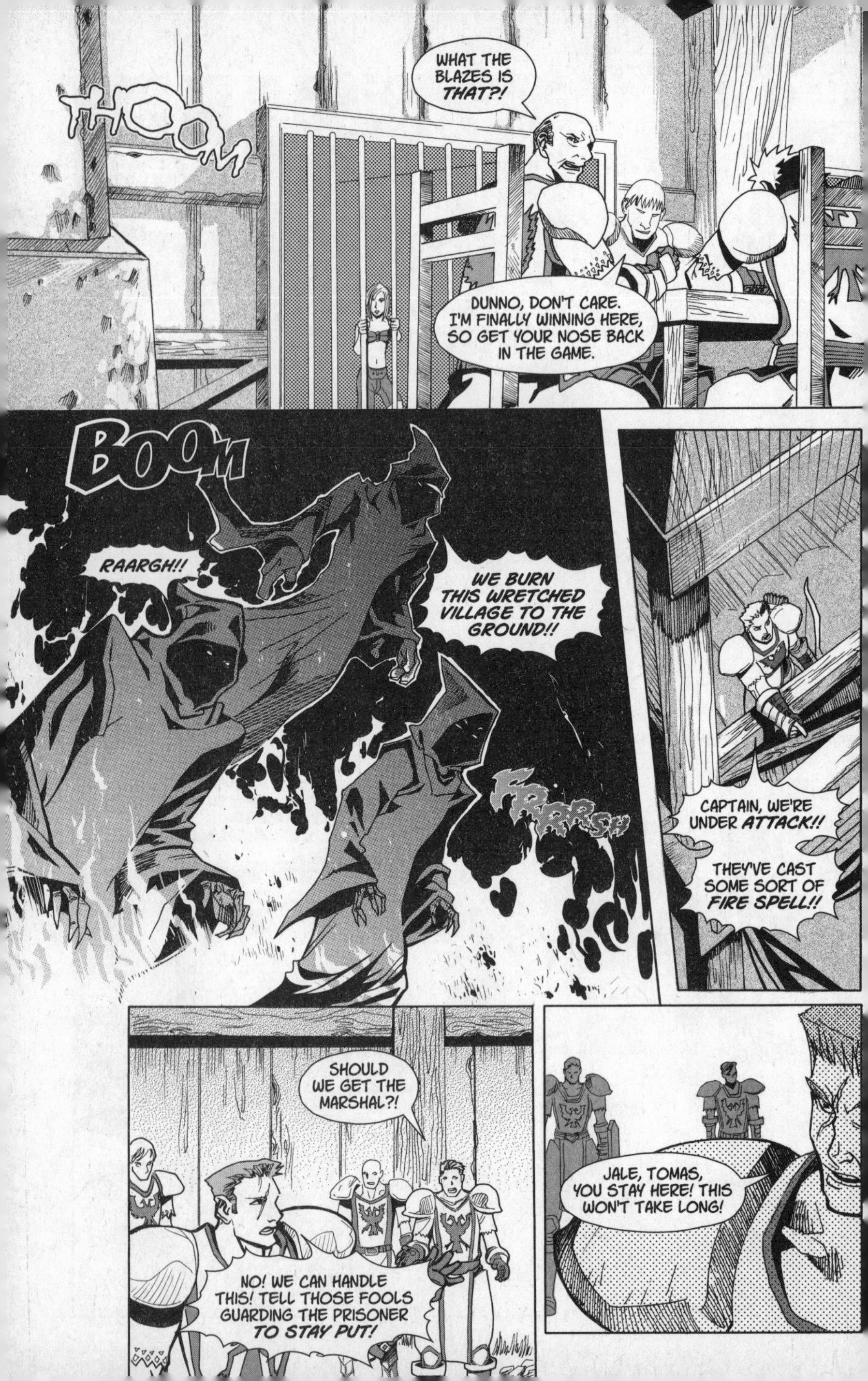
THOOM
WHAT THE BLAZES IS THAT?!
DUNNO, DON'T CARE. I'M FINALLY WINNING HERE, SO GET YOUR NOSE BACK IN THE GAME.
BOOM
RAARGH!!
WE BURN THIS WRETCHED VILLAGE TO THE GROUND!!
FRARSH
CAPTAIN, WE'RE UNDER ATTACK!!
THEY'VE CAST SOME SORT OF FIRE SPELL!!
SHOULD WE GET THE MARSHAL?!
NO! WE CAN HANDLE THIS! TELL THOSE FOOLS GUARDING THE PRISONER TO STAY PUT!
JALE, TOMAS, YOU STAY HERE! THIS WON'T TAKE LONG!

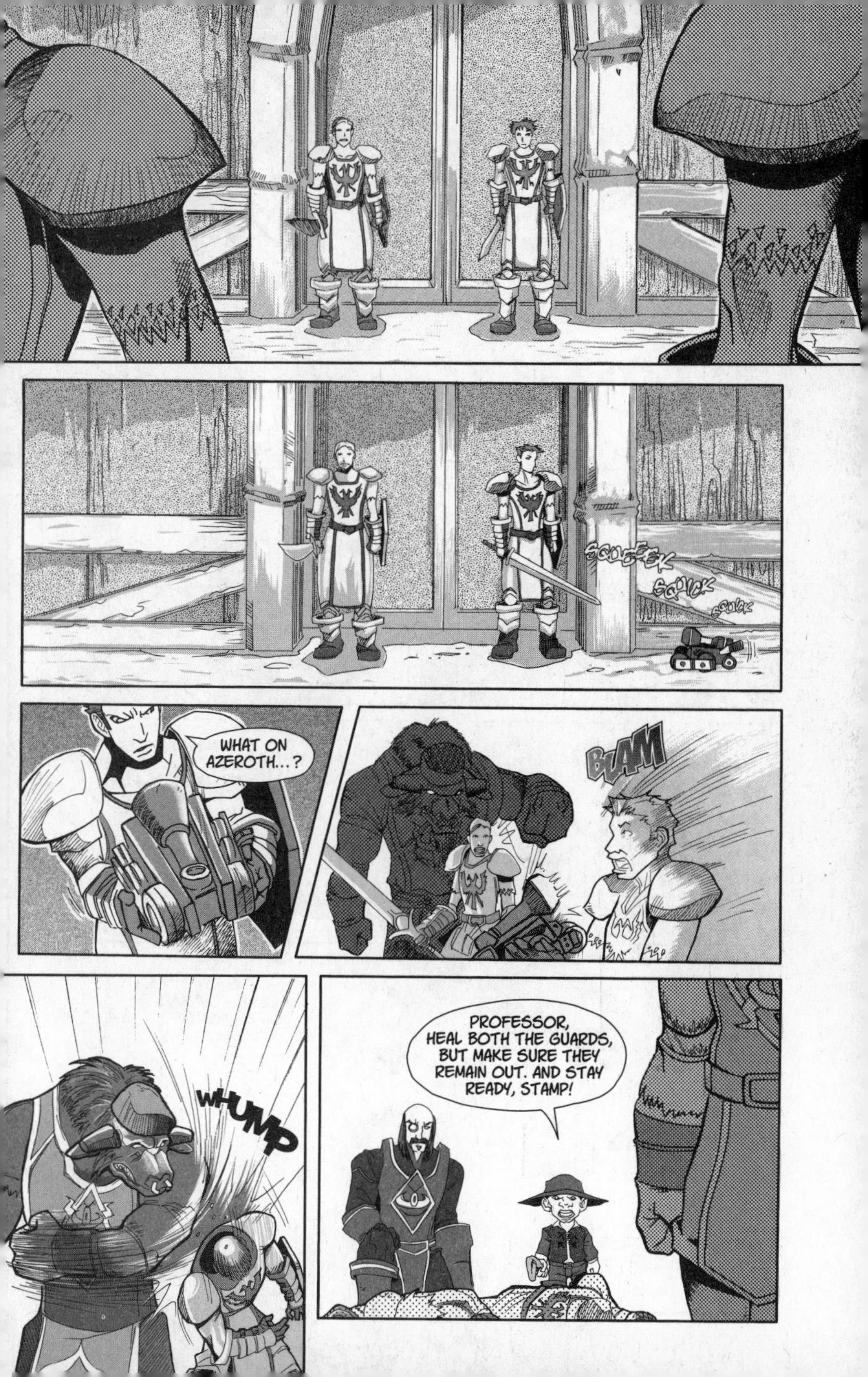
SQUEEEK
SQUICK
SQUICK
WHAT ON AZEROTH...?
BLAM
WHUMP
PROFESSOR, HEAL BOTH THE GUARDS, BUT MAKE SURE THEY REMAIN OUT. AND STAY READY, STAMP!

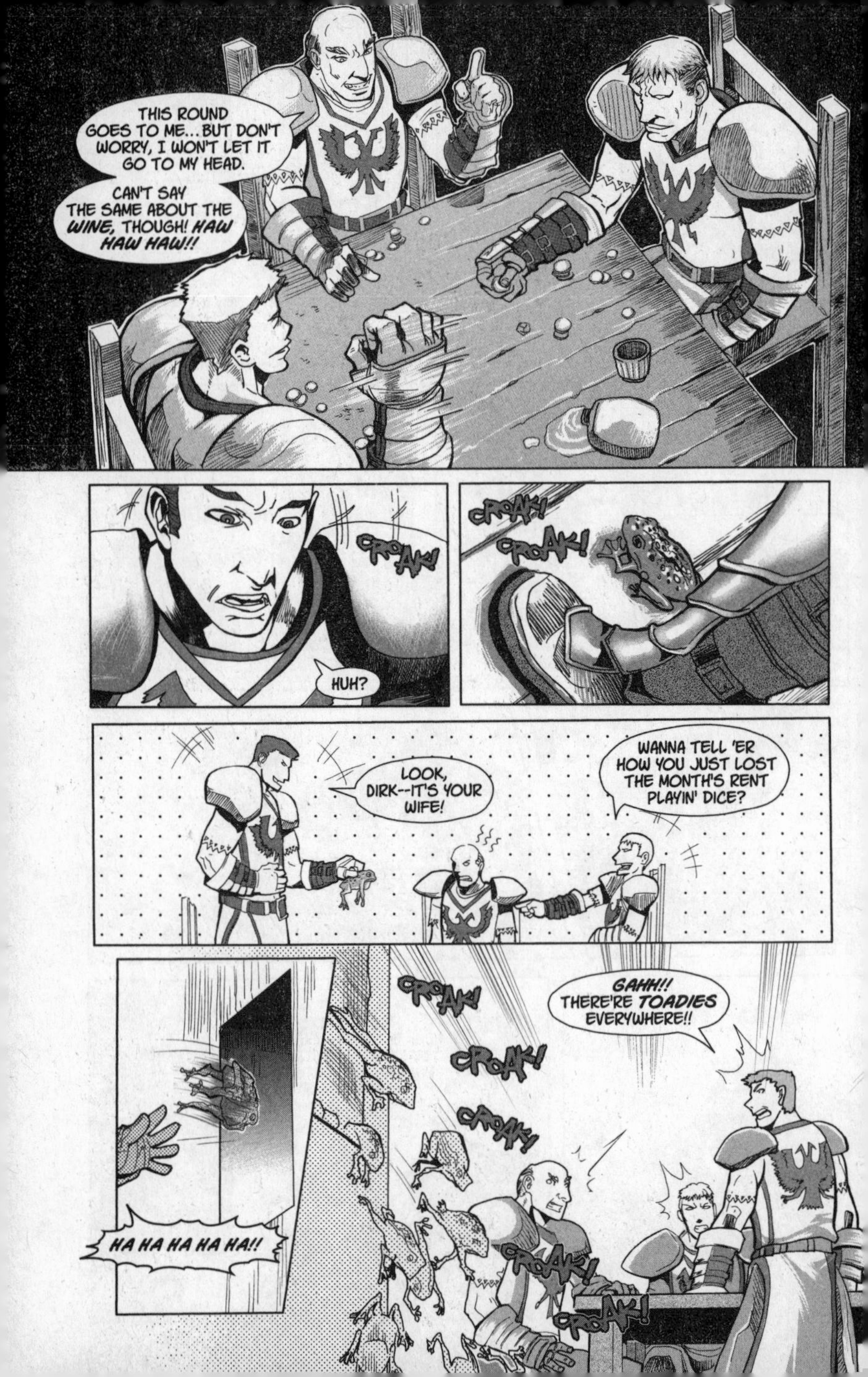
THIS ROUND GOES TO ME... BUT DON'T WORRY, I WON'T LET IT GO TO MY HEAD.
CAN'T SAY THE SAME ABOUT THE WINE, THOUGH! HAW HAW HAW!!
CROAK!
HUH?
CROAK!
CROAK!
LOOK, DIRK--IT'S YOUR WIFE!
WANNA TELL 'ER HOW YOU JUST LOST THE MONTH'S RENT PLAYIN' DICE?
HA HA HA HA HA!!
CROAK!
GAHH!! THERE'RE TOADIES EVERYWHERE!!
CROAK!
CROAK!
CROAK!
CROAK!

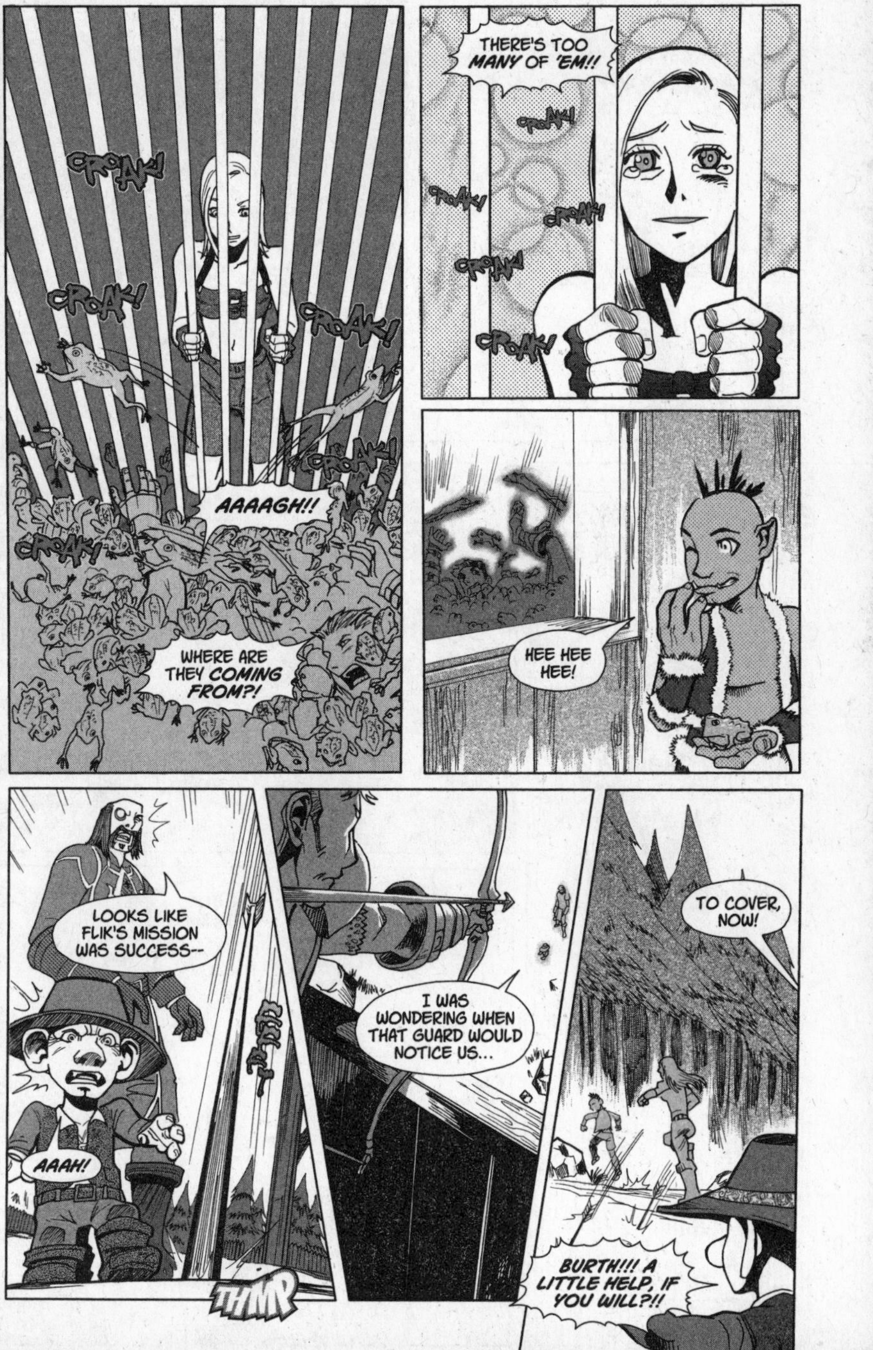
CROAK!
CROAK!
CROAK!
CROAK!
CROAK!
AAAAGH!!
WHERE ARE THEY COMING FROM?!
THERE'S TOO MANY OF 'EM!!
CROAK!
CROAK!
CROAK!
CROAK!
CROAK!
HEE HEE HEE!
LOOKS LIKE FLIK'S MISSION WAS SUCCESS--
AAAH!
THMP
I WAS WONDERING WHEN THAT GUARD WOULD NOTICE US...
TO COVER, NOW!
BURTH!!! A LITTLE HELP, IF YOU WILL?!!

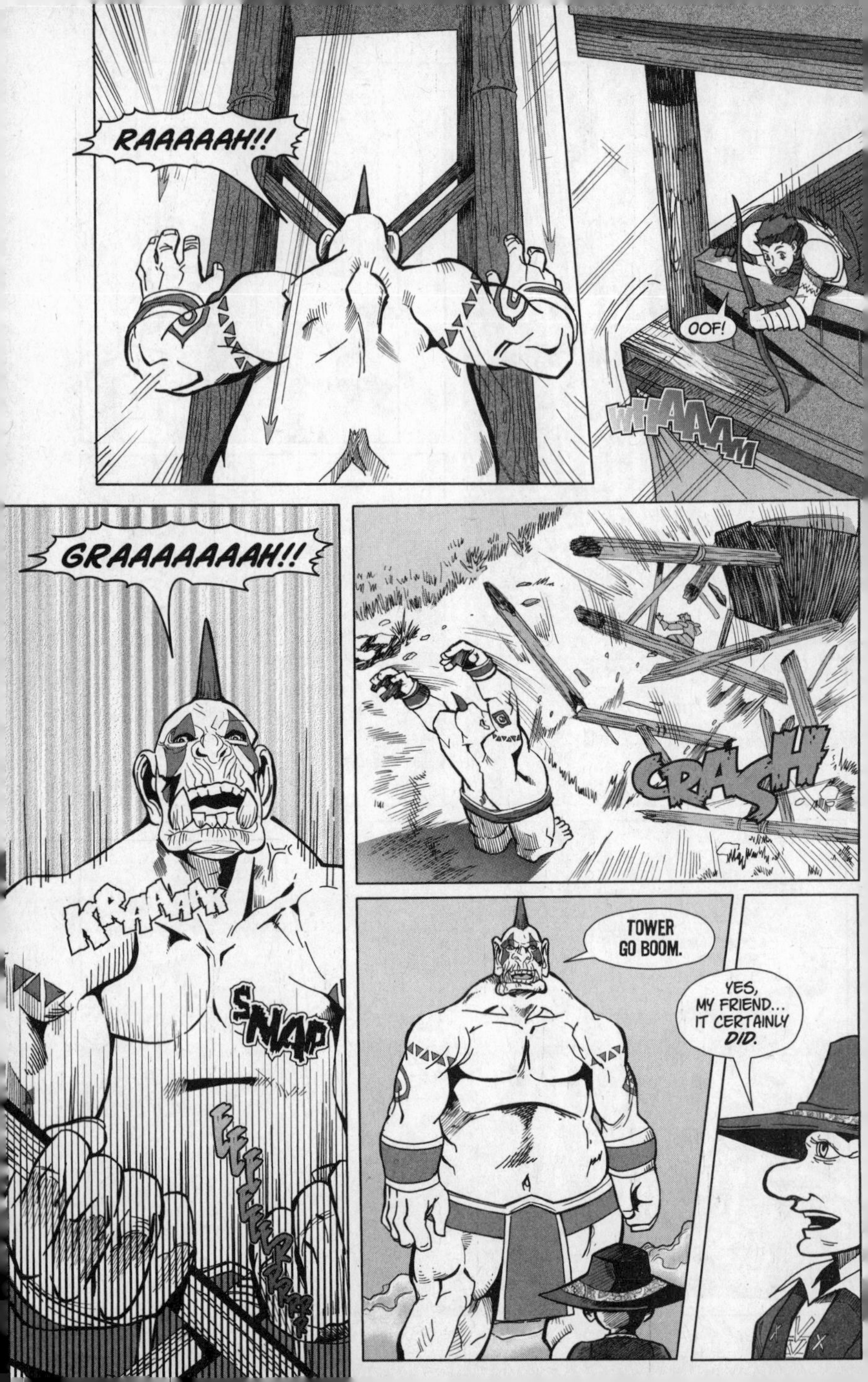
RAAAAAH!!
OOF!
WHAAAAM
GRAAAAAAAH!!
KRAAAAK
SNAP
EEEEEERAAAA
CRASH
TOWER GO BOOM.
YES, MY FRIEND... IT CERTAINLY *DID*.

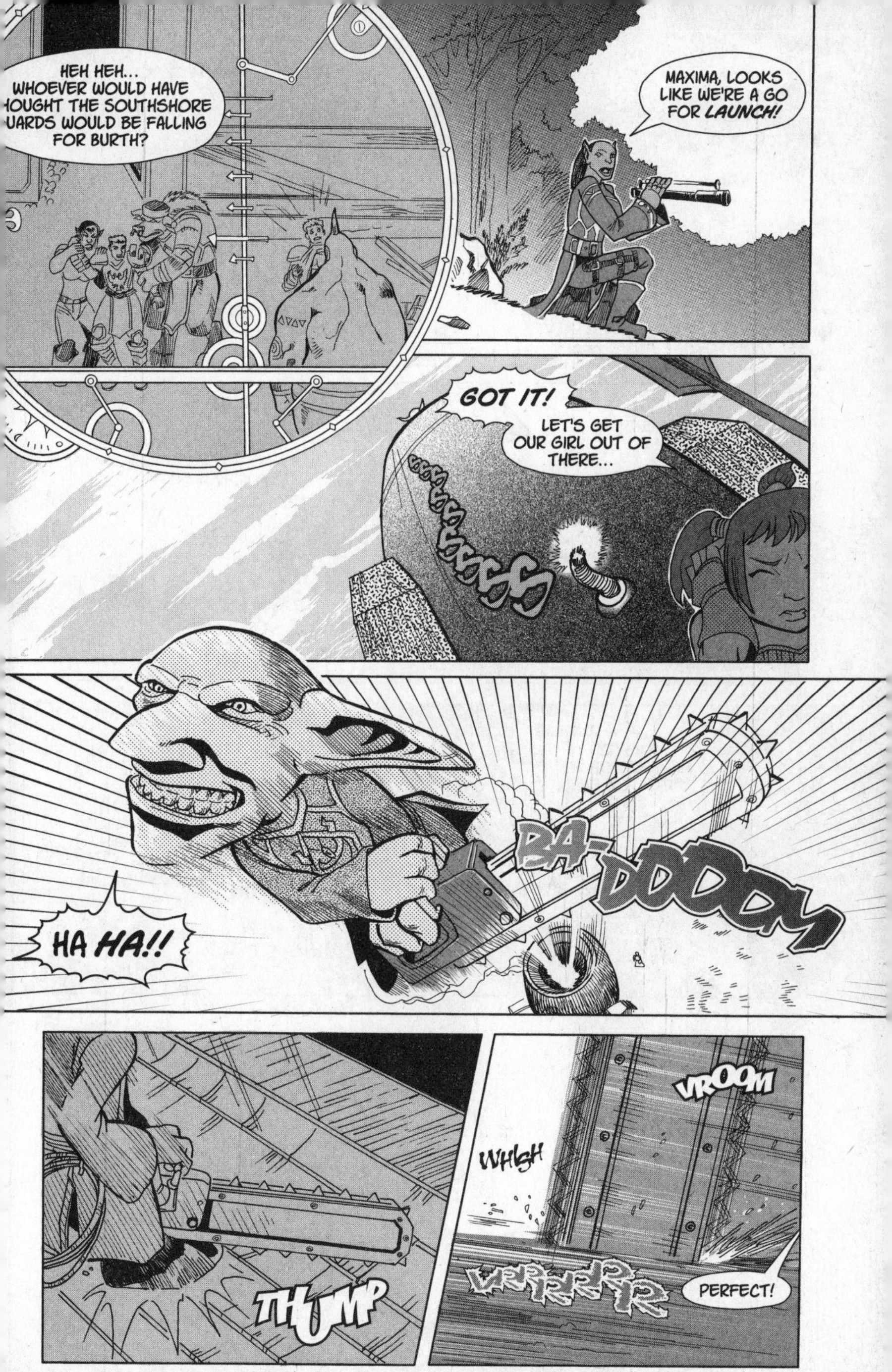
HEH HEH... WHOEVER WOULD HAVE HOUGHT THE SOUTHSHORE UARDS WOULD BE FALLING FOR BURTH?
MAXIMA, LOOKS LIKE WE'RE A GO FOR LAUNCH!
GOT IT!
LET'S GET OUR GIRL OUT OF THERE...
HA HA!!
BA-DOOOM
THUMP
VROOM
WHSH
PERFECT!

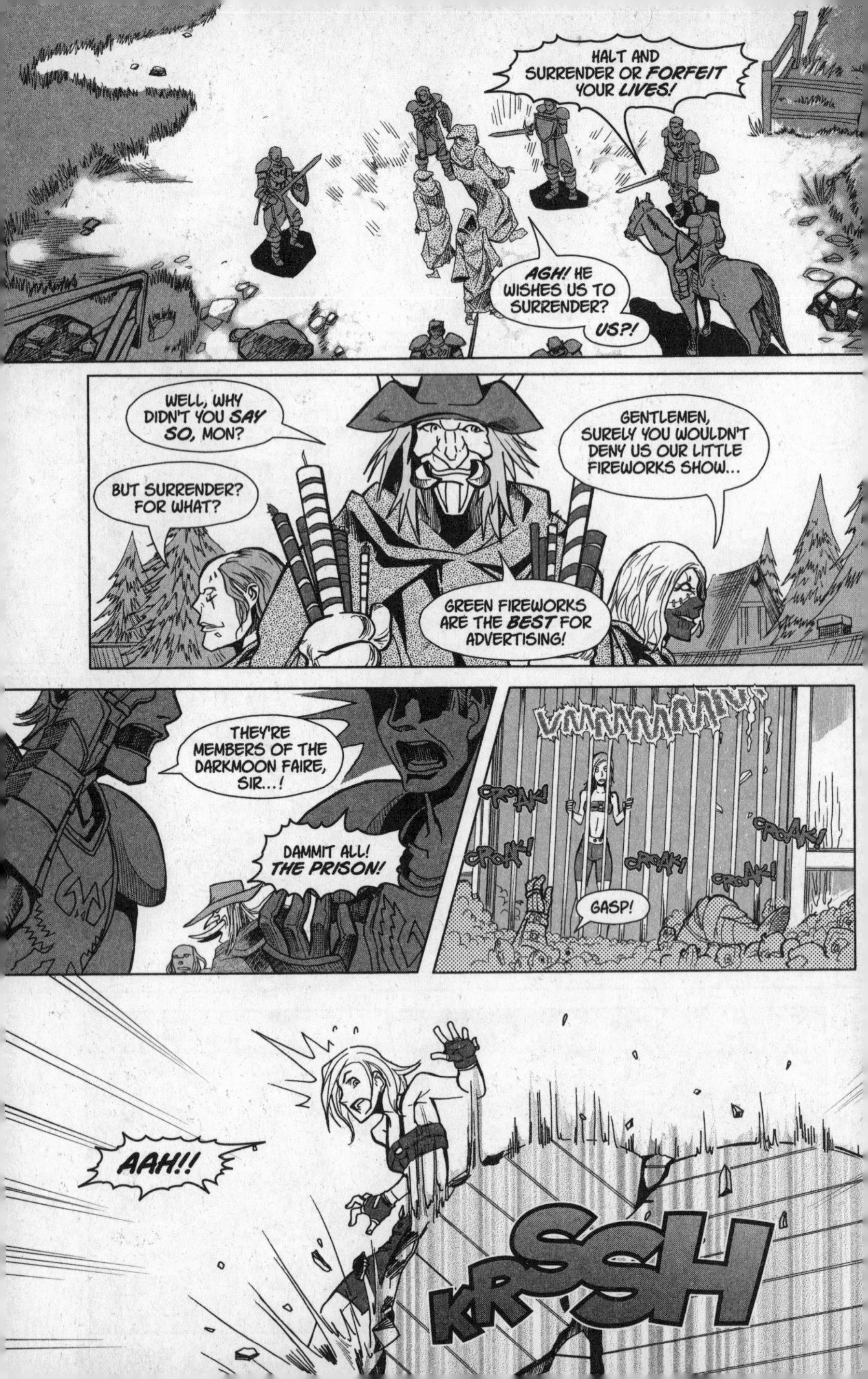
HALT AND SURRENDER OR FORFEIT YOUR LIVES!
AGH! HE WISHES US TO SURRENDER? US?!
WELL, WHY DIDN'T YOU SAY SO, MON?
BUT SURRENDER? FOR WHAT?
GENTLEMEN, SURELY YOU WOULDN'T DENY US OUR LITTLE FIREWORKS SHOW...
GREEN FIREWORKS ARE THE BEST FOR ADVERTISING!
THEY'RE MEMBERS OF THE DARKMOON FAIRE, SIR...!
DAMMIT ALL! THE PRISON!
VMMMMMM
CROAK!
CROAK!
CROAK!
CROAK!
CROAK!
GASP!
AAH!!
KRSSH

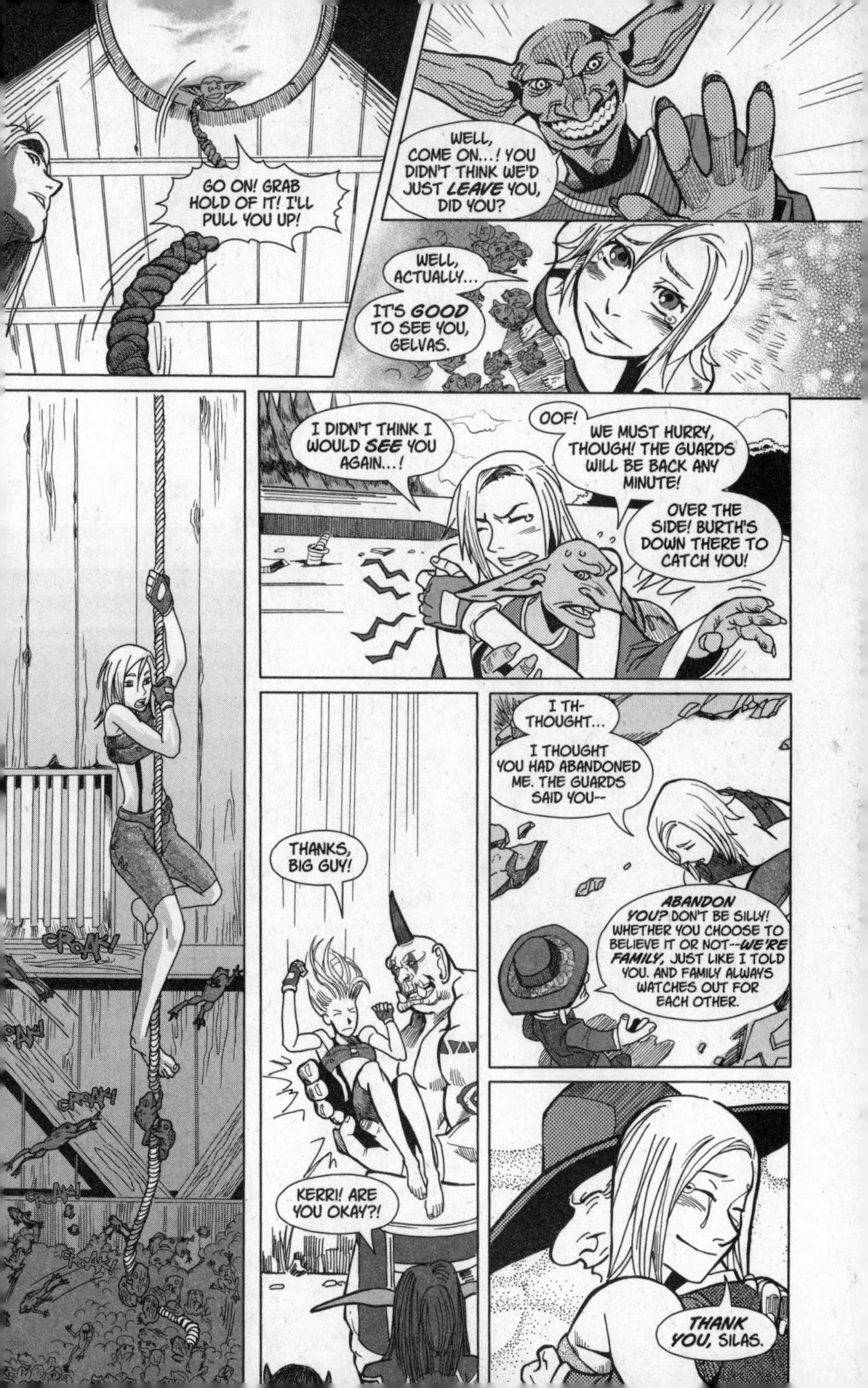
GO ON! GRAB HOLD OF IT! I'LL PULL YOU UP!
WELL, COME ON...! YOU DIDN'T THINK WE'D JUST *LEAVE* YOU, DID YOU?
WELL, ACTUALLY...
IT'S *GOOD* TO SEE YOU, GELVAS.
CROAK!
CROAK!
CROAK!
I DIDN'T THINK I WOULD *SEE* YOU AGAIN...!
OOF!
WE MUST HURRY, THOUGH! THE GUARDS WILL BE BACK ANY MINUTE!
OVER THE SIDE! BURTH'S DOWN THERE TO CATCH YOU!
THANKS, BIG GUY!
KERRI! ARE YOU OKAY?!
I TH- THOUGHT...
I THOUGHT YOU HAD ABANDONED ME. THE GUARDS SAID YOU--
ABANDON YOU? DON'T BE SILLY! WHETHER YOU CHOOSE TO BELIEVE IT OR NOT--*WE'RE FAMILY,* JUST LIKE I TOLD YOU. AND FAMILY ALWAYS WATCHES OUT FOR EACH OTHER.
THANK YOU, SILAS.

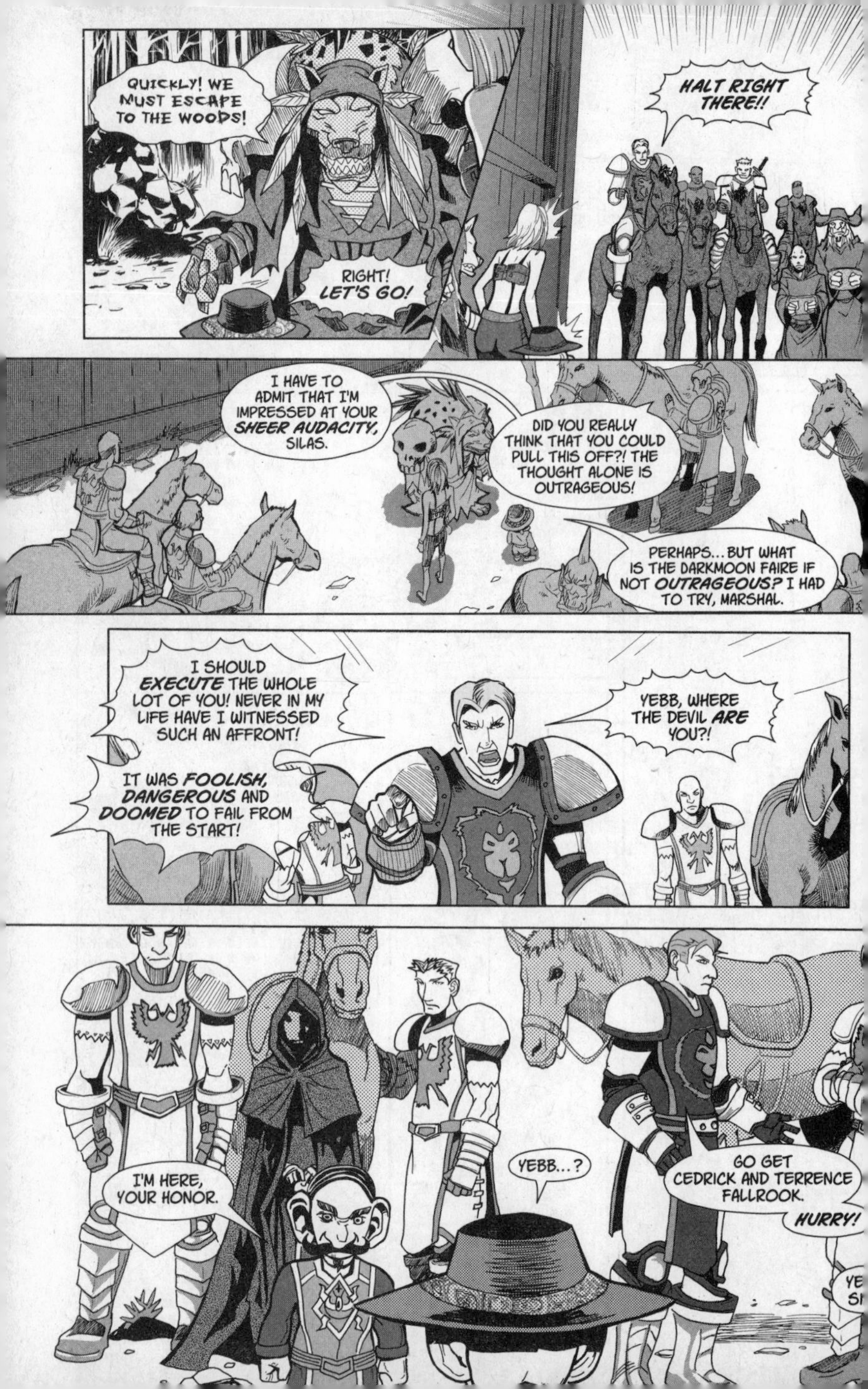
QUICKLY! WE MUST ESCAPE TO THE WOODS!
RIGHT! LET'S GO!
HALT RIGHT THERE!!
I HAVE TO ADMIT THAT I'M IMPRESSED AT YOUR SHEER AUDACITY, SILAS.
DID YOU REALLY THINK THAT YOU COULD PULL THIS OFF?! THE THOUGHT ALONE IS OUTRAGEOUS!
PERHAPS... BUT WHAT IS THE DARKMOON FAIRE IF NOT OUTRAGEOUS? I HAD TO TRY, MARSHAL.
I SHOULD EXECUTE THE WHOLE LOT OF YOU! NEVER IN MY LIFE HAVE I WITNESSED SUCH AN AFFRONT!
IT WAS FOOLISH, DANGEROUS AND DOOMED TO FAIL FROM THE START!
YEBB, WHERE THE DEVIL ARE YOU?!
I'M HERE, YOUR HONOR.
YEBB...?
GO GET CEDRICK AND TERRENCE FALLROOK.
HURRY!

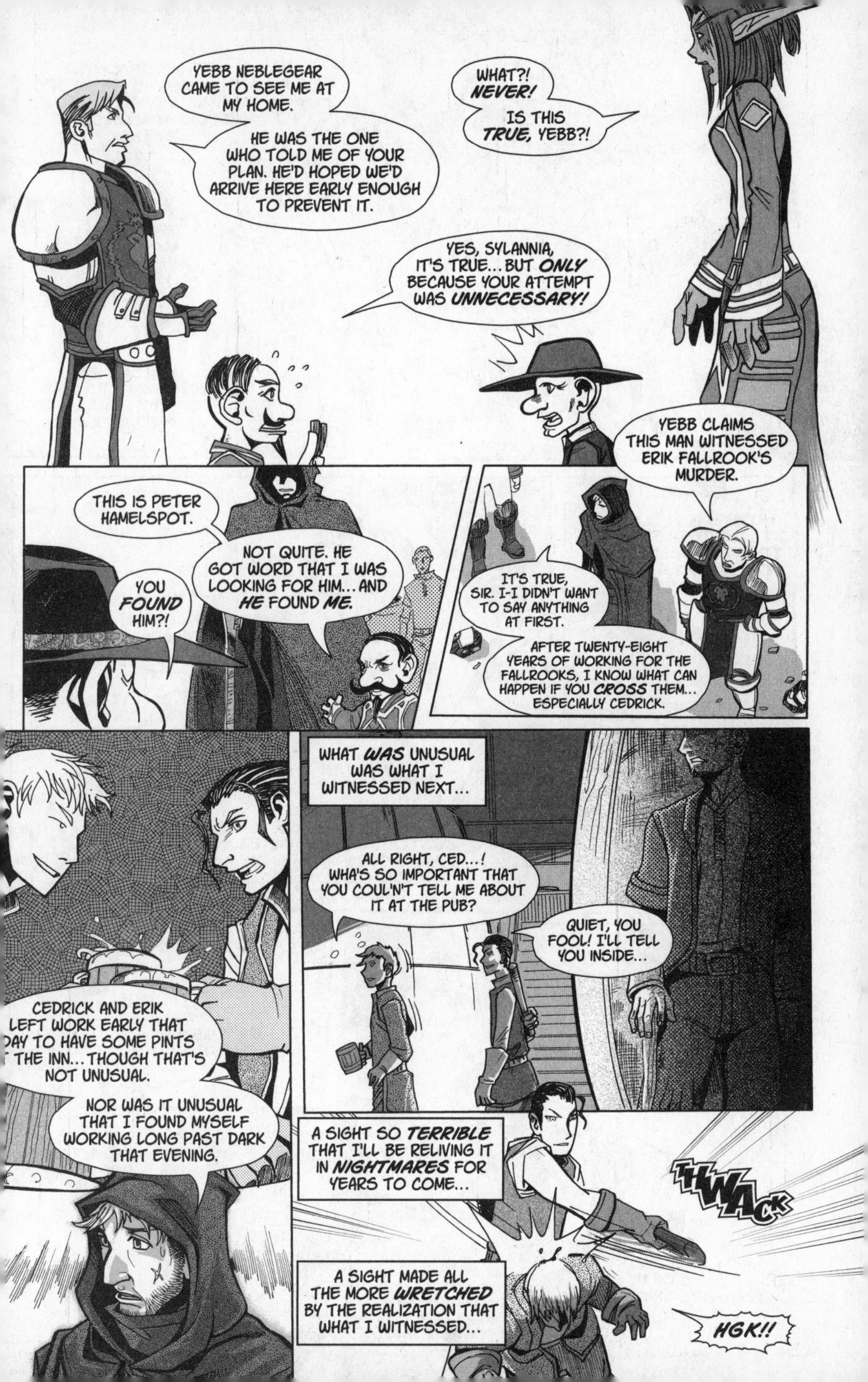
YEBB NEBLEGEAR CAME TO SEE ME AT MY HOME.
HE WAS THE ONE WHO TOLD ME OF YOUR PLAN. HE'D HOPED WE'D ARRIVE HERE EARLY ENOUGH TO PREVENT IT.
WHAT?! ***NEVER!***
IS THIS ***TRUE,*** YEBB?!
YES, SYLANNIA, IT'S TRUE... BUT ***ONLY*** BECAUSE YOUR ATTEMPT WAS ***UNNECESSARY!***
THIS IS PETER HAMELSPOT.
YOU ***FOUND*** HIM?!
NOT QUITE. HE GOT WORD THAT I WAS LOOKING FOR HIM... AND ***HE*** FOUND ***ME.***
YEBB CLAIMS THIS MAN WITNESSED ERIK FALLROOK'S MURDER.
IT'S TRUE, SIR. I-I DIDN'T WANT TO SAY ANYTHING AT FIRST.
AFTER TWENTY-EIGHT YEARS OF WORKING FOR THE FALLROOKS, I KNOW WHAT CAN HAPPEN IF YOU ***CROSS*** THEM... ESPECIALLY CEDRICK.
CEDRICK AND ERIK LEFT WORK EARLY THAT DAY TO HAVE SOME PINTS T THE INN... THOUGH THAT'S NOT UNUSUAL.
NOR WAS IT UNUSUAL THAT I FOUND MYSELF WORKING LONG PAST DARK THAT EVENING.
WHAT ***WAS*** UNUSUAL WAS WHAT I WITNESSED NEXT...
ALL RIGHT, CED...! WHA'S SO IMPORTANT THAT YOU COUL'N'T TELL ME ABOUT IT AT THE PUB?
QUIET, YOU FOOL! I'LL TELL YOU INSIDE...
A SIGHT SO ***TERRIBLE*** THAT I'LL BE RELIVING IT IN ***NIGHTMARES*** FOR YEARS TO COME...
THWACK
A SIGHT MADE ALL THE MORE ***WRETCHED*** BY THE REALIZATION THAT WHAT I WITNESSED...
HGK!!

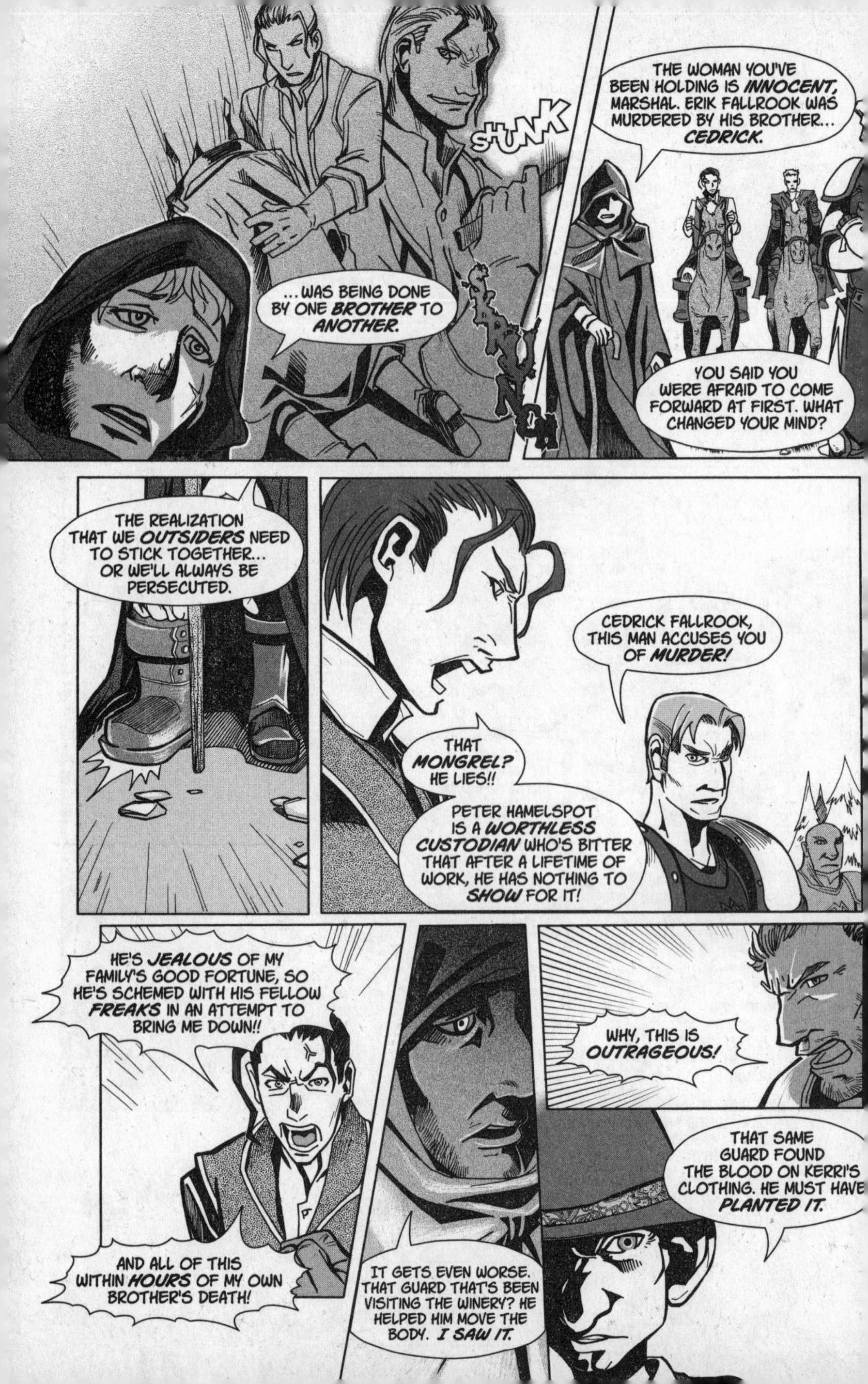
SHUNK
...WAS BEING DONE BY ONE BROTHER TO ANOTHER.
THE WOMAN YOU'VE BEEN HOLDING IS INNOCENT, MARSHAL. ERIK FALLROOK WAS MURDERED BY HIS BROTHER... CEDRICK.
YOU SAID YOU WERE AFRAID TO COME FORWARD AT FIRST. WHAT CHANGED YOUR MIND?
THE REALIZATION THAT WE OUTSIDERS NEED TO STICK TOGETHER... OR WE'LL ALWAYS BE PERSECUTED.
CEDRICK FALLROOK, THIS MAN ACCUSES YOU OF MURDER!
THAT MONGREL? HE LIES!!
PETER HAMELSPOT IS A WORTHLESS CUSTODIAN WHO'S BITTER THAT AFTER A LIFETIME OF WORK, HE HAS NOTHING TO SHOW FOR IT!
HE'S JEALOUS OF MY FAMILY'S GOOD FORTUNE, SO HE'S SCHEMED WITH HIS FELLOW FREAKS IN AN ATTEMPT TO BRING ME DOWN!!
AND ALL OF THIS WITHIN HOURS OF MY OWN BROTHER'S DEATH!
IT GETS EVEN WORSE. THAT GUARD THAT'S BEEN VISITING THE WINERY? HE HELPED HIM MOVE THE BODY. I SAW IT.
WHY, THIS IS OUTRAGEOUS!
THAT SAME GUARD FOUND THE BLOOD ON KERRI'S CLOTHING. HE MUST HAVE PLANTED IT.

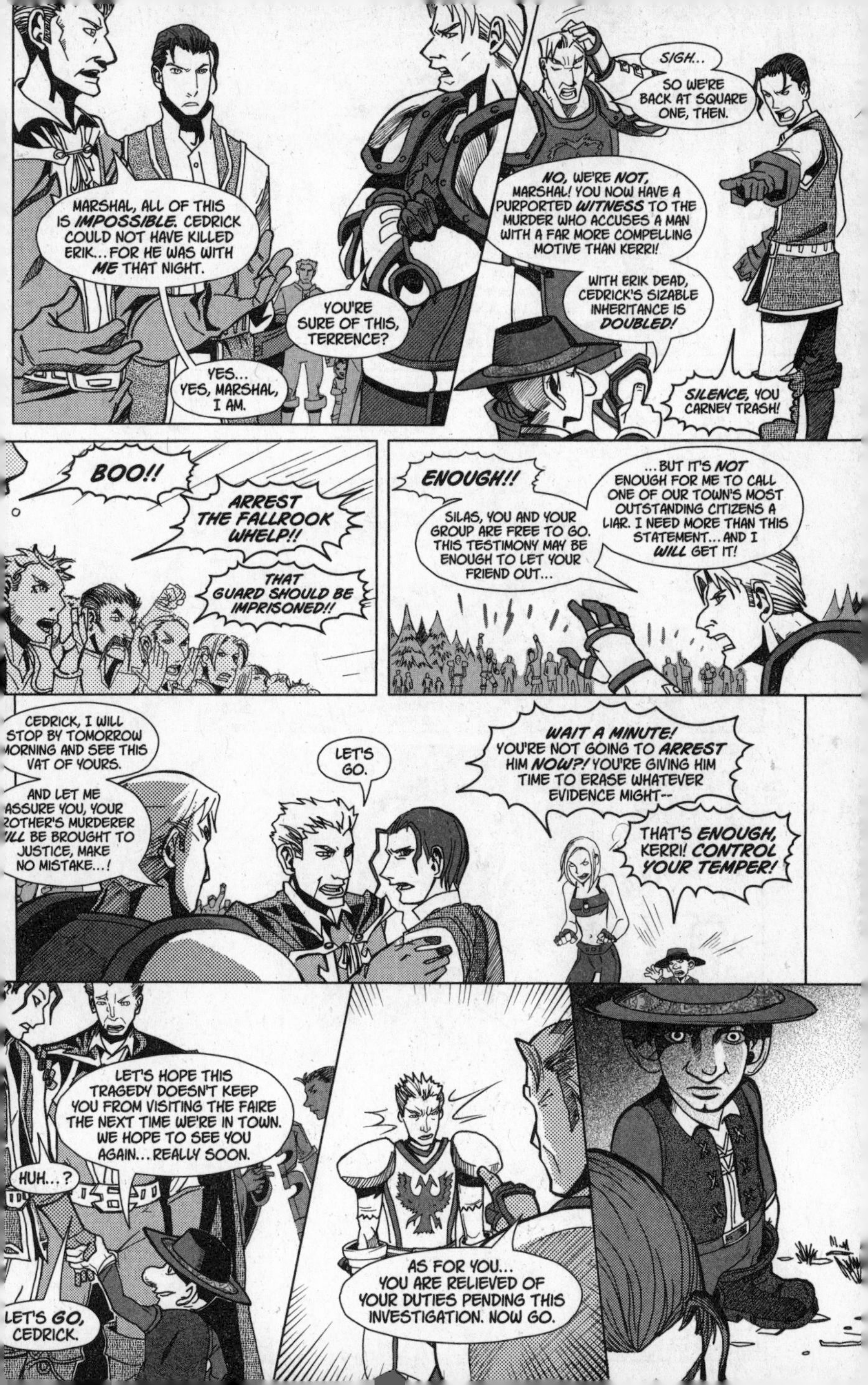
MARSHAL, ALL OF THIS IS IMPOSSIBLE. CEDRICK COULD NOT HAVE KILLED ERIK... FOR HE WAS WITH ME THAT NIGHT.
YOU'RE SURE OF THIS, TERRENCE?
YES... YES, MARSHAL, I AM.
SIGH... SO WE'RE BACK AT SQUARE ONE, THEN.
NO, WE'RE NOT, MARSHAL! YOU NOW HAVE A PURPORTED WITNESS TO THE MURDER WHO ACCUSES A MAN WITH A FAR MORE COMPELLING MOTIVE THAN KERRI!
WITH ERIK DEAD, CEDRICK'S SIZABLE INHERITANCE IS DOUBLED!
SILENCE, YOU CARNEY TRASH!
BOO!!
ARREST THE FALLROOK WHELP!!
THAT GUARD SHOULD BE IMPRISONED!!
ENOUGH!!
SILAS, YOU AND YOUR GROUP ARE FREE TO GO. THIS TESTIMONY MAY BE ENOUGH TO LET YOUR FRIEND OUT...
...BUT IT'S NOT ENOUGH FOR ME TO CALL ONE OF OUR TOWN'S MOST OUTSTANDING CITIZENS A LIAR. I NEED MORE THAN THIS STATEMENT... AND I WILL GET IT!
CEDRICK, I WILL STOP BY TOMORROW MORNING AND SEE THIS VAT OF YOURS.
AND LET ME ASSURE YOU, YOUR BROTHER'S MURDERER WILL BE BROUGHT TO JUSTICE, MAKE NO MISTAKE...!
LET'S GO.
WAIT A MINUTE! YOU'RE NOT GOING TO ARREST HIM NOW?! YOU'RE GIVING HIM TIME TO ERASE WHATEVER EVIDENCE MIGHT--
THAT'S ENOUGH, KERRI! CONTROL YOUR TEMPER!
LET'S HOPE THIS TRAGEDY DOESN'T KEEP YOU FROM VISITING THE FAIRE THE NEXT TIME WE'RE IN TOWN. WE HOPE TO SEE YOU AGAIN... REALLY SOON.
HUH...?
LET'S GO, CEDRICK.
AS FOR YOU... YOU ARE RELIEVED OF YOUR DUTIES PENDING THIS INVESTIGATION. NOW GO.

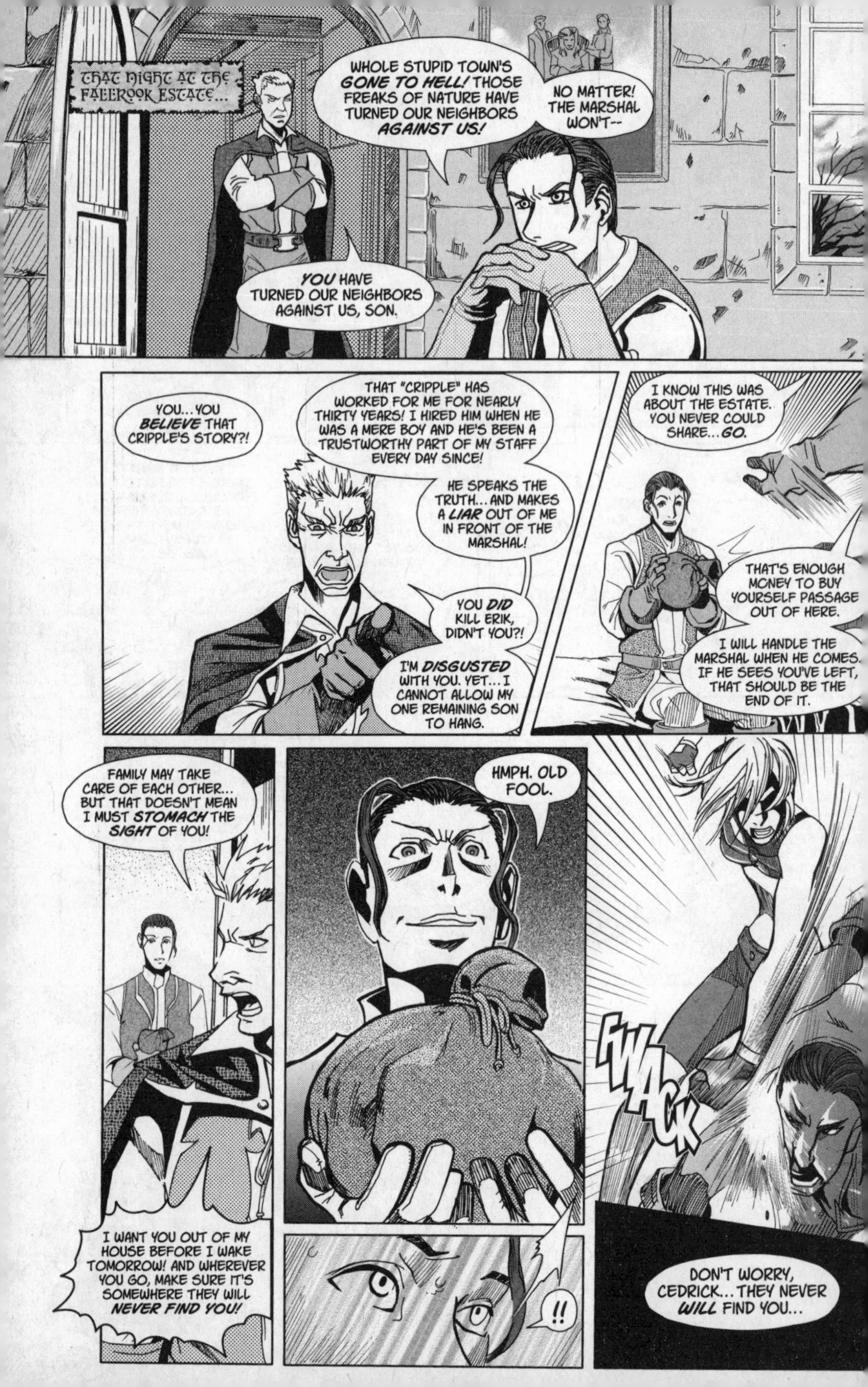
THAT NIGHT AT THE FALLROOK ESTATE...
WHOLE STUPID TOWN'S GONE TO HELL! THOSE FREAKS OF NATURE HAVE TURNED OUR NEIGHBORS AGAINST US!
NO MATTER! THE MARSHAL WON'T--
YOU HAVE TURNED OUR NEIGHBORS AGAINST US, SON.
YOU... YOU BELIEVE THAT CRIPPLE'S STORY?!
THAT "CRIPPLE" HAS WORKED FOR ME FOR NEARLY THIRTY YEARS! I HIRED HIM WHEN HE WAS A MERE BOY AND HE'S BEEN A TRUSTWORTHY PART OF MY STAFF EVERY DAY SINCE!
HE SPEAKS THE TRUTH... AND MAKES A LIAR OUT OF ME IN FRONT OF THE MARSHAL!
YOU DID KILL ERIK, DIDN'T YOU?!
I'M DISGUSTED WITH YOU. YET... I CANNOT ALLOW MY ONE REMAINING SON TO HANG.
I KNOW THIS WAS ABOUT THE ESTATE. YOU NEVER COULD SHARE... GO.
THAT'S ENOUGH MONEY TO BUY YOURSELF PASSAGE OUT OF HERE.
I WILL HANDLE THE MARSHAL WHEN HE COMES. IF HE SEES YOU'VE LEFT, THAT SHOULD BE THE END OF IT.
FAMILY MAY TAKE CARE OF EACH OTHER... BUT THAT DOESN'T MEAN I MUST STOMACH THE SIGHT OF YOU!
I WANT YOU OUT OF MY HOUSE BEFORE I WAKE TOMORROW! AND WHEREVER YOU GO, MAKE SURE IT'S SOMEWHERE THEY WILL NEVER FIND YOU!
HMPH. OLD FOOL.
!!
FWACK
DON'T WORRY, CEDRICK... THEY NEVER WILL FIND YOU...

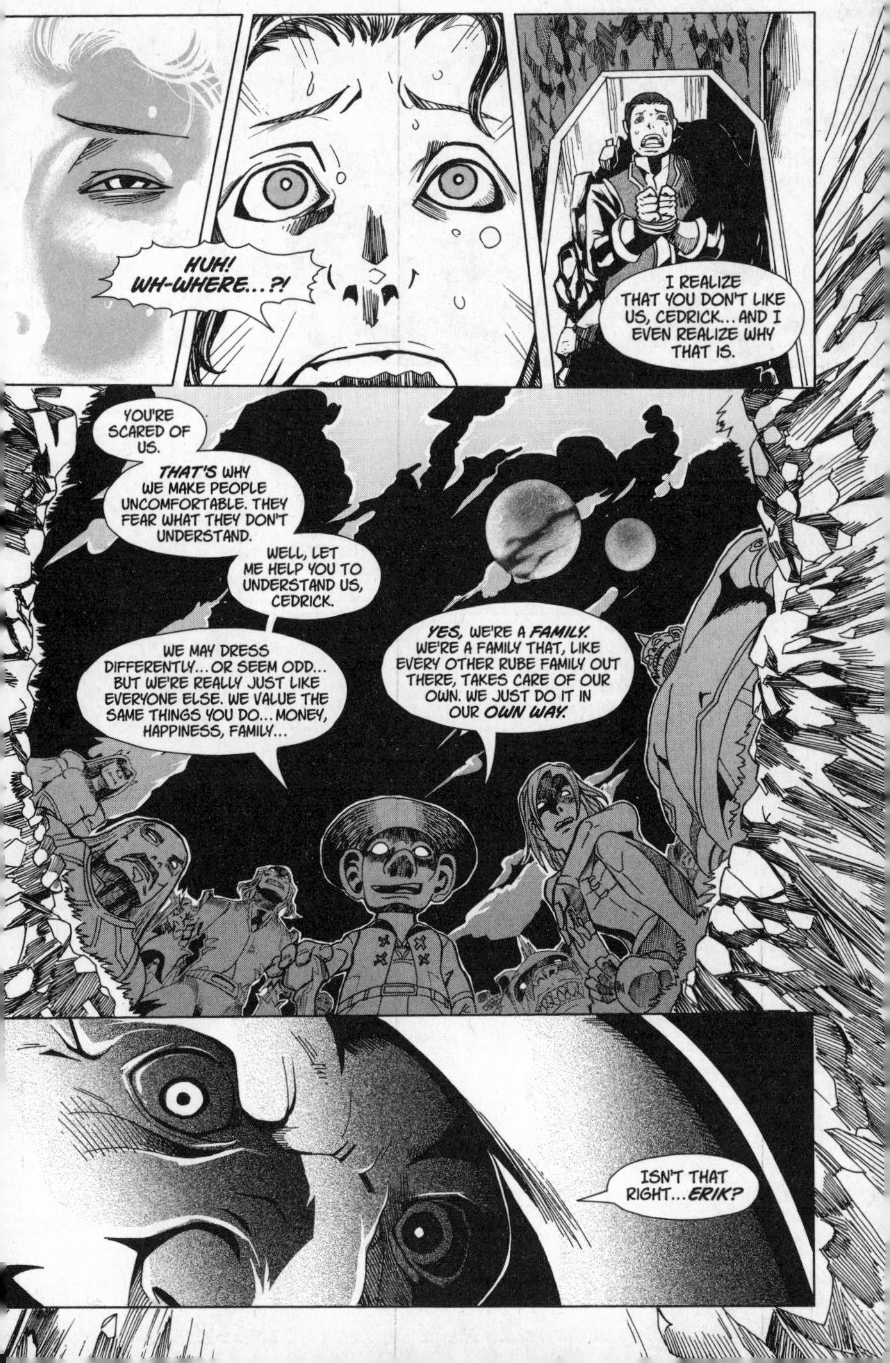
HUH! WH-WHERE...?!
I REALIZE THAT YOU DON'T LIKE US, CEDRICK... AND I EVEN REALIZE WHY THAT IS.
YOU'RE SCARED OF US.
THAT'S WHY WE MAKE PEOPLE UNCOMFORTABLE. THEY FEAR WHAT THEY DON'T UNDERSTAND.
WELL, LET ME HELP YOU TO UNDERSTAND US, CEDRICK.
WE MAY DRESS DIFFERENTLY... OR SEEM ODD... BUT WE'RE REALLY JUST LIKE EVERYONE ELSE. WE VALUE THE SAME THINGS YOU DO... MONEY, HAPPINESS, FAMILY...
YES, WE'RE A *FAMILY.* WE'RE A FAMILY THAT, LIKE EVERY OTHER RUBE FAMILY OUT THERE, TAKES CARE OF OUR OWN. WE JUST DO IT IN OUR *OWN WAY.*
ISN'T THAT RIGHT... *ERIK?*

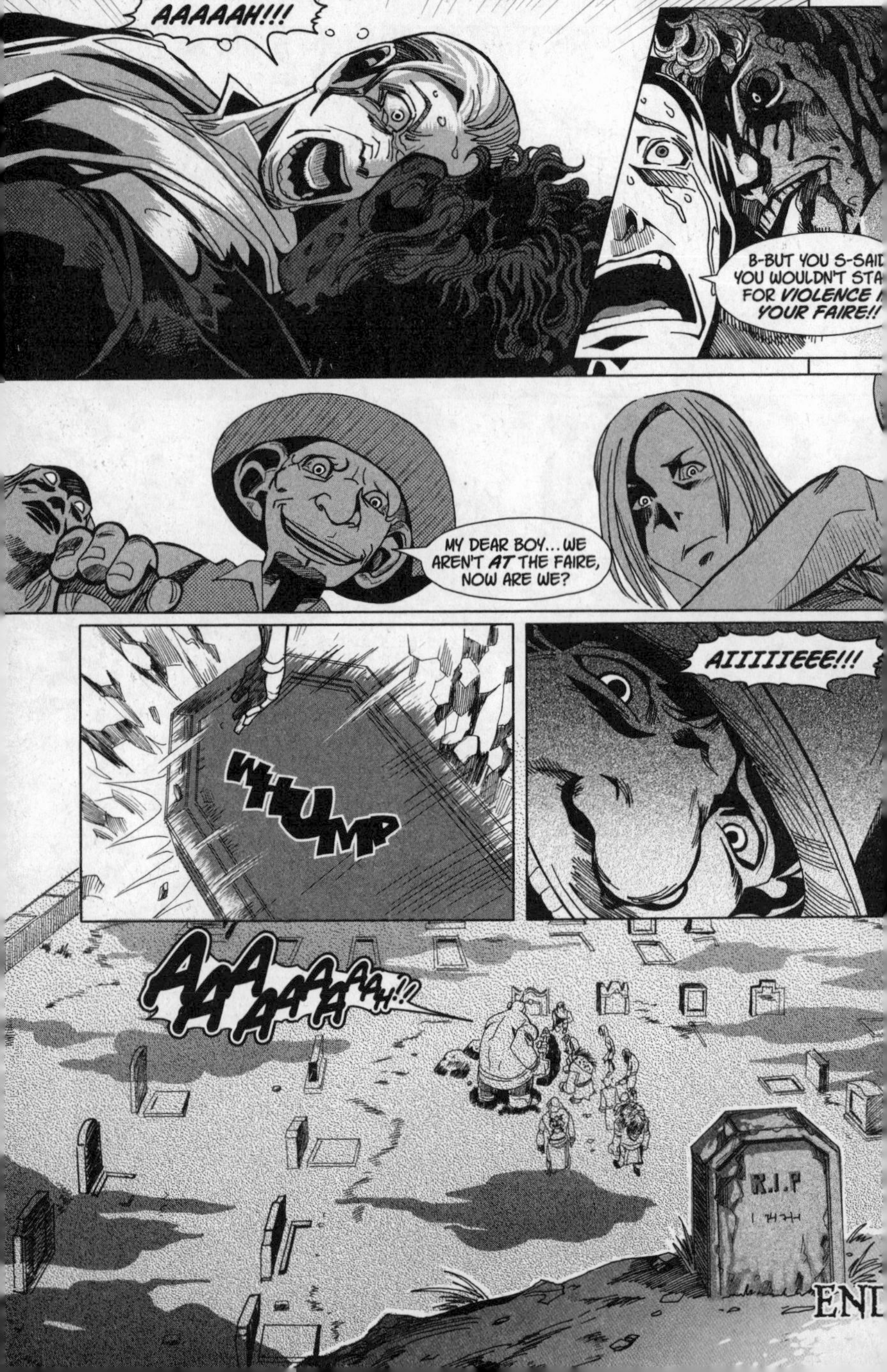
AAAAAH!!!
B-BUT YOU S-SAID YOU WOULDN'T STA FOR VIOLENCE I YOUR FAIRE!!
MY DEAR BOY... WE AREN'T AT THE FAIRE, NOW ARE WE?
WHUMP
AIIIIIEEE!!!
AAAAAAAAAH!!!
R.I.P
END

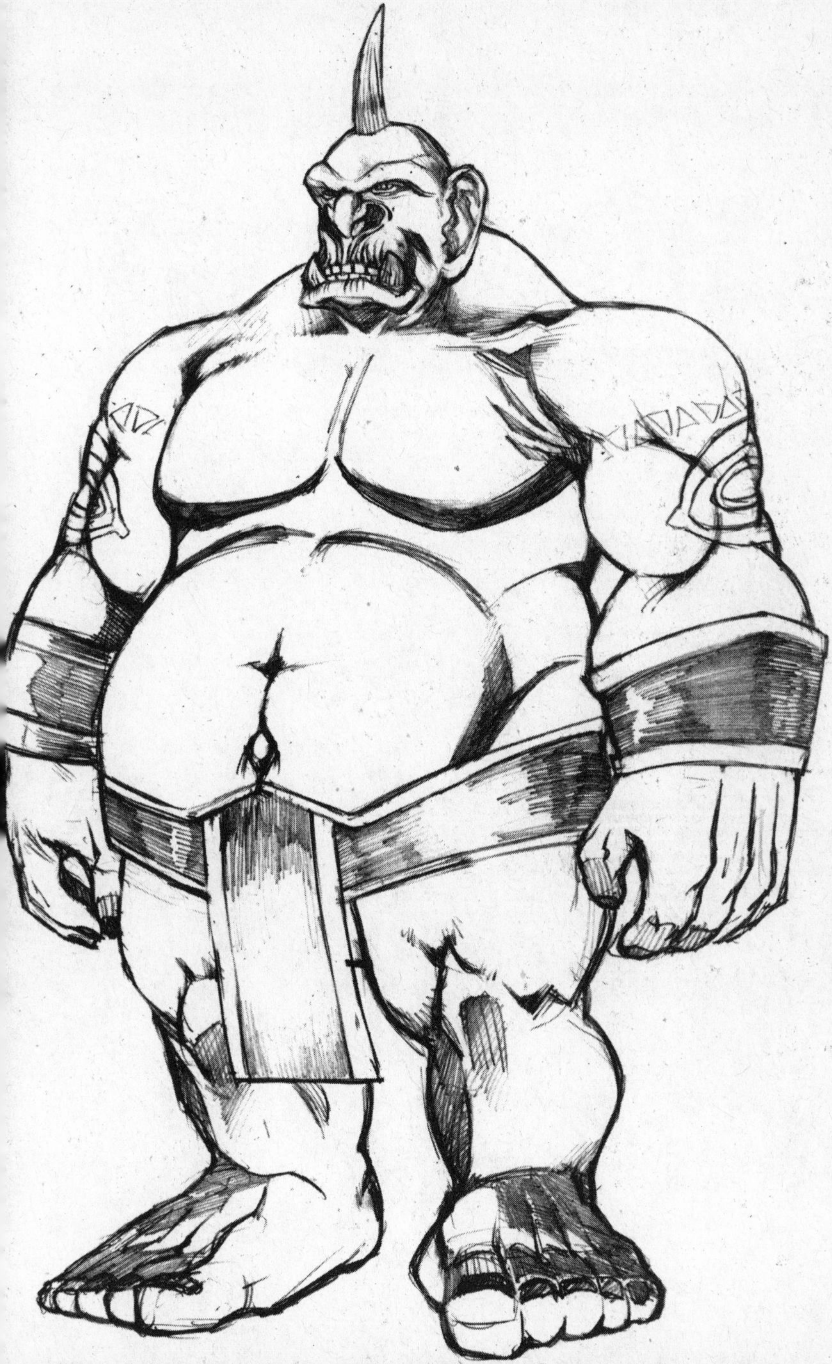

WARCRAFT
LEGENDS
VOLUME FOUR

A WARRIOR MADE--PART 1

WRITTEN BY CHRISTIE GOLDEN

PENCILS BY IN-BAE KIM
INKS BY IN-BAE KIM & MI-JIN BAE
TONES BY MARA AUM

CONTRIBUTING EDITORS: HYUN JOO KIM & JANICE KWON
LETTERER: MICHAEL PAOLILLI

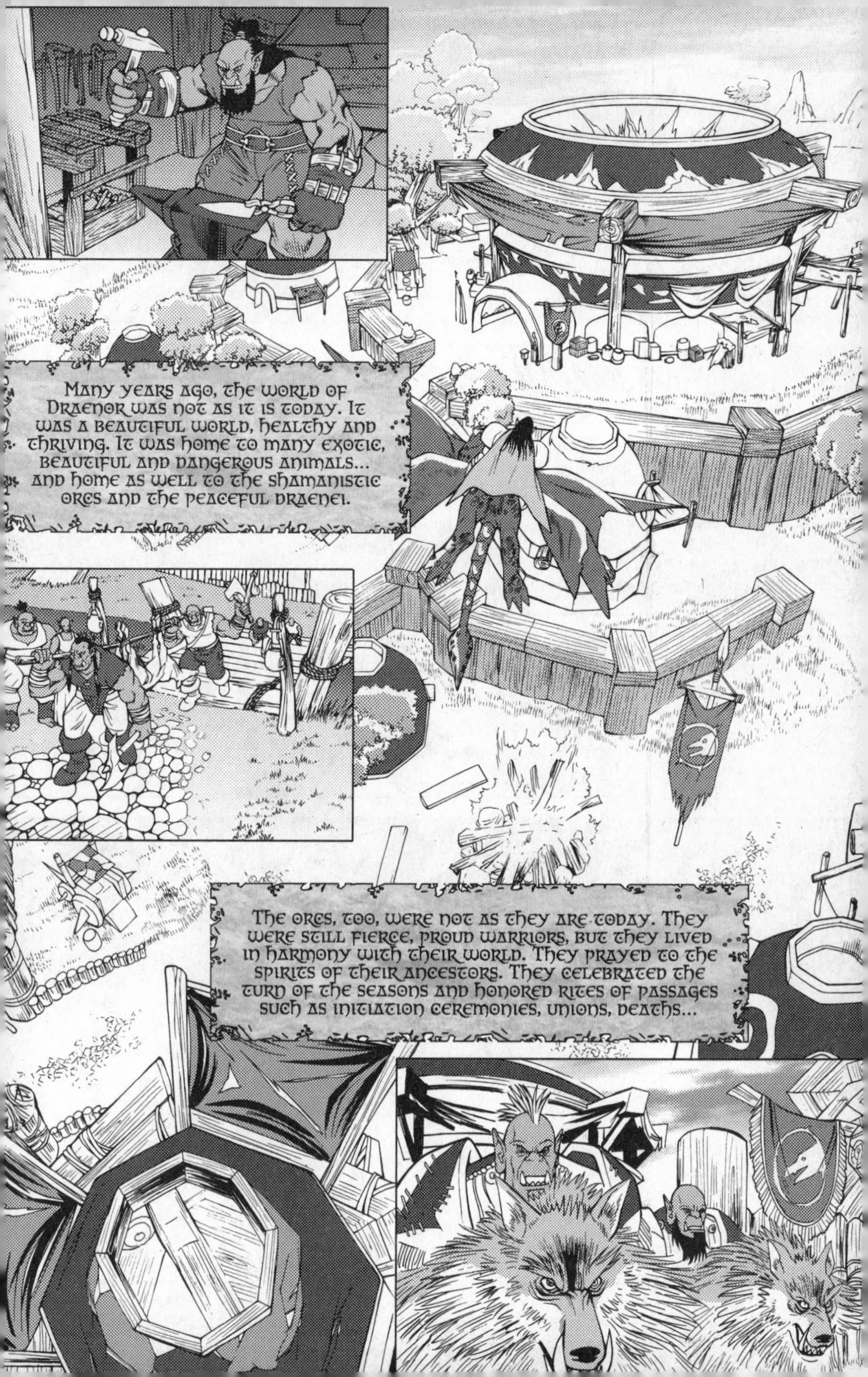
MANY YEARS AGO, THE WORLD OF DRAENOR WAS NOT AS IT IS TODAY. IT WAS A BEAUTIFUL WORLD, HEALTHY AND THRIVING. IT WAS HOME TO MANY EXOTIC, BEAUTIFUL AND DANGEROUS ANIMALS... AND HOME AS WELL TO THE SHAMANISTIC ORCS AND THE PEACEFUL DRAENEI.
THE ORCS, TOO, WERE NOT AS THEY ARE TODAY. THEY WERE STILL FIERCE, PROUD WARRIORS, BUT THEY LIVED IN HARMONY WITH THEIR WORLD. THEY PRAYED TO THE SPIRITS OF THEIR ANCESTORS. THEY CELEBRATED THE TURN OF THE SEASONS AND HONORED RITES OF PASSAGES SUCH AS INITIATION CEREMONIES, UNIONS, DEATHS...

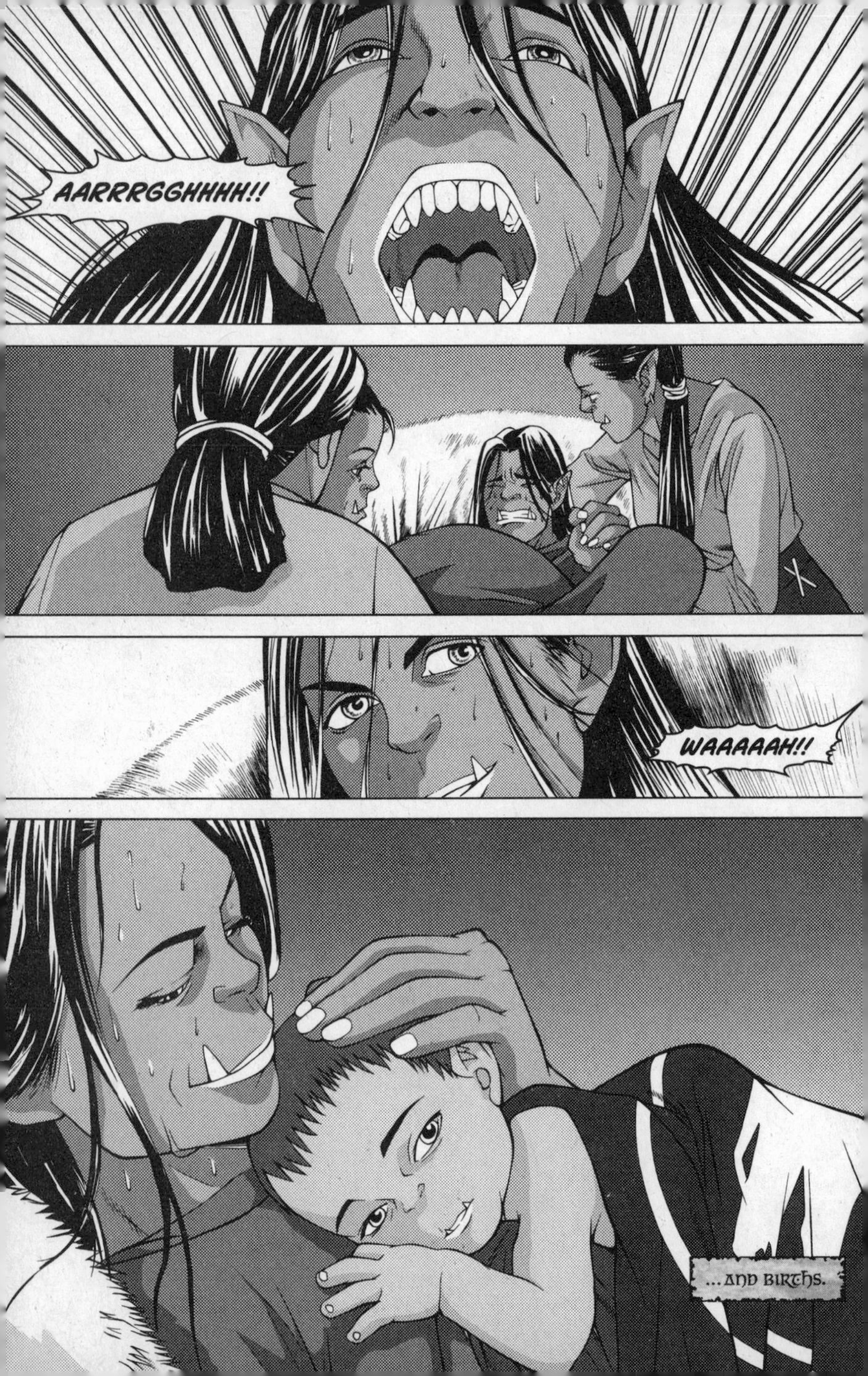
AARRRGGHHHH!!
WAAAAAAH!!
...AND BIRTHS.

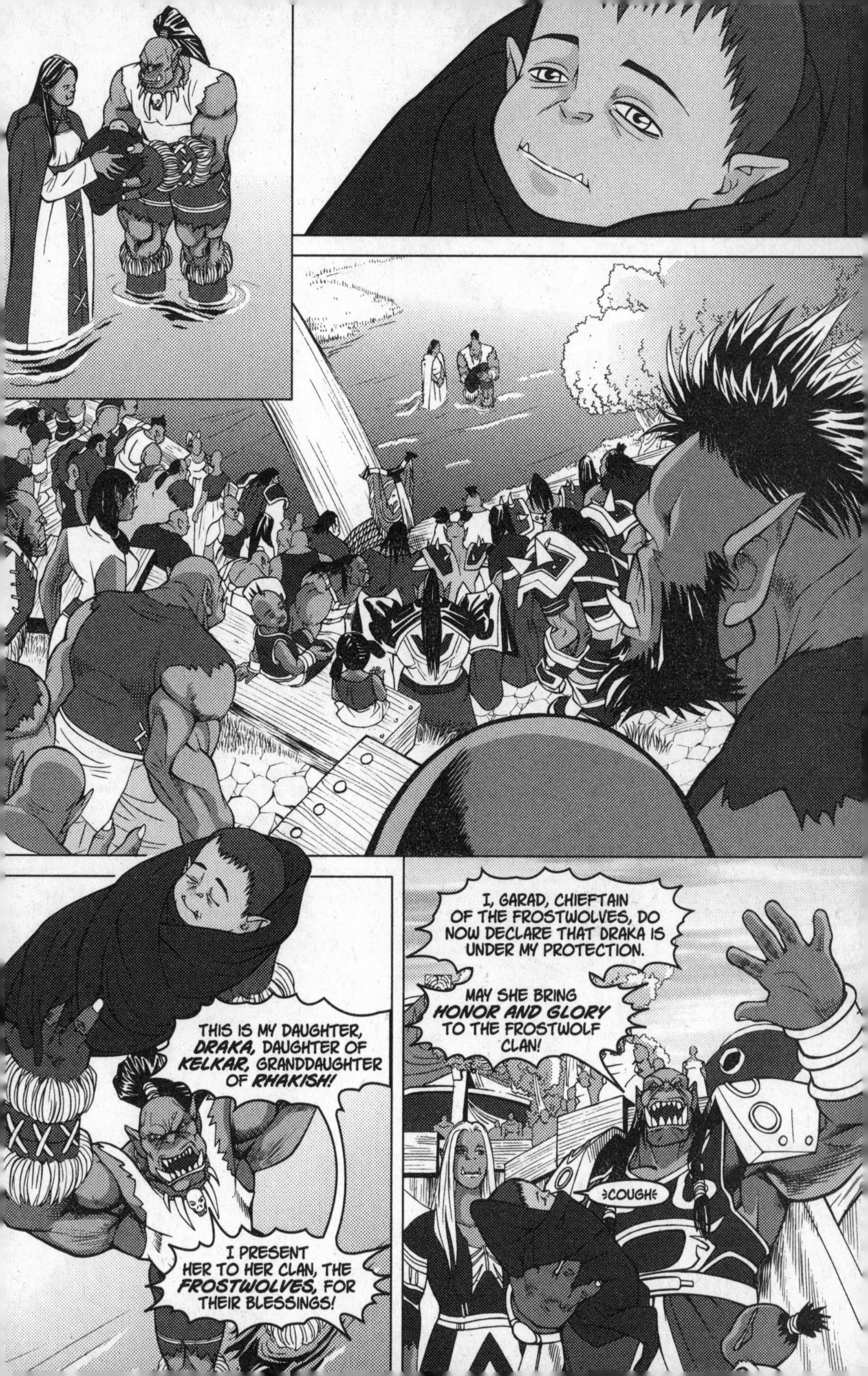
THIS IS MY DAUGHTER, ***DRAKA,*** DAUGHTER OF ***KELKAR,*** GRANDDAUGHTER OF ***RHAKISH!***
I PRESENT HER TO HER CLAN, THE ***FROSTWOLVES,*** FOR THEIR BLESSINGS!
I, GARAD, CHIEFTAIN OF THE FROSTWOLVES, DO NOW DECLARE THAT DRAKA IS UNDER MY PROTECTION.
MAY SHE BRING ***HONOR AND GLORY*** TO THE FROSTWOLF CLAN!
COUGH

SHE'S...KINDA *SCRAWNY*, ISN'T SHE?

DUROTAN! GIVE HER A BLESSING, SON.

UH...I HOPE THAT YOU GROW UP *STRONG* AND *HEALTHY*. AND *FIGHT* REALLY WELL!

≥COUGH COUGH≤

BUT YOUNG DUROTAN WAS NOT ALONE IN HIS OBSERVATION...

...SO FRAGILE... *TOO* FRAGILE...

DID YOU SEE HOW *PALE* SHE IS? HER SKIN IS *FAWN-COLORED*, NOT A GOOD, SOLID, HEALTHY *BROWN* LIKE THE REST OF US...

POOR LITTLE THING... IT'S GOING TO BE *HARD* ON HER...

THAT *CONSTANT COUGH*...IT DOESN'T BODE WELL AT ALL...

GOOD THING SHE WASN'T BOR[N] BONECHEWER...TH[EY] HAVE *DROWN[ED]* HER AT BIRTH

BUT ONE AMONG THEM WAS NOT SO QUICK TO JUDGE...

PERHAPS YOU *ARE* TOO FRAIL, CHILD. OR MAYBE THE ANCESTORS AND THE ELEMENTAL SPIRITS HAVE SOME *SPECIAL PLAN* FOR YOU, EH?

I ASK THE BLESSING OF THE SPIRITS OF EARTH, AI[R] FIRE, WATER AND THE WILDS UP[ON] THIS CHILD. MAY ANCESTORS WATCH OVER HER!

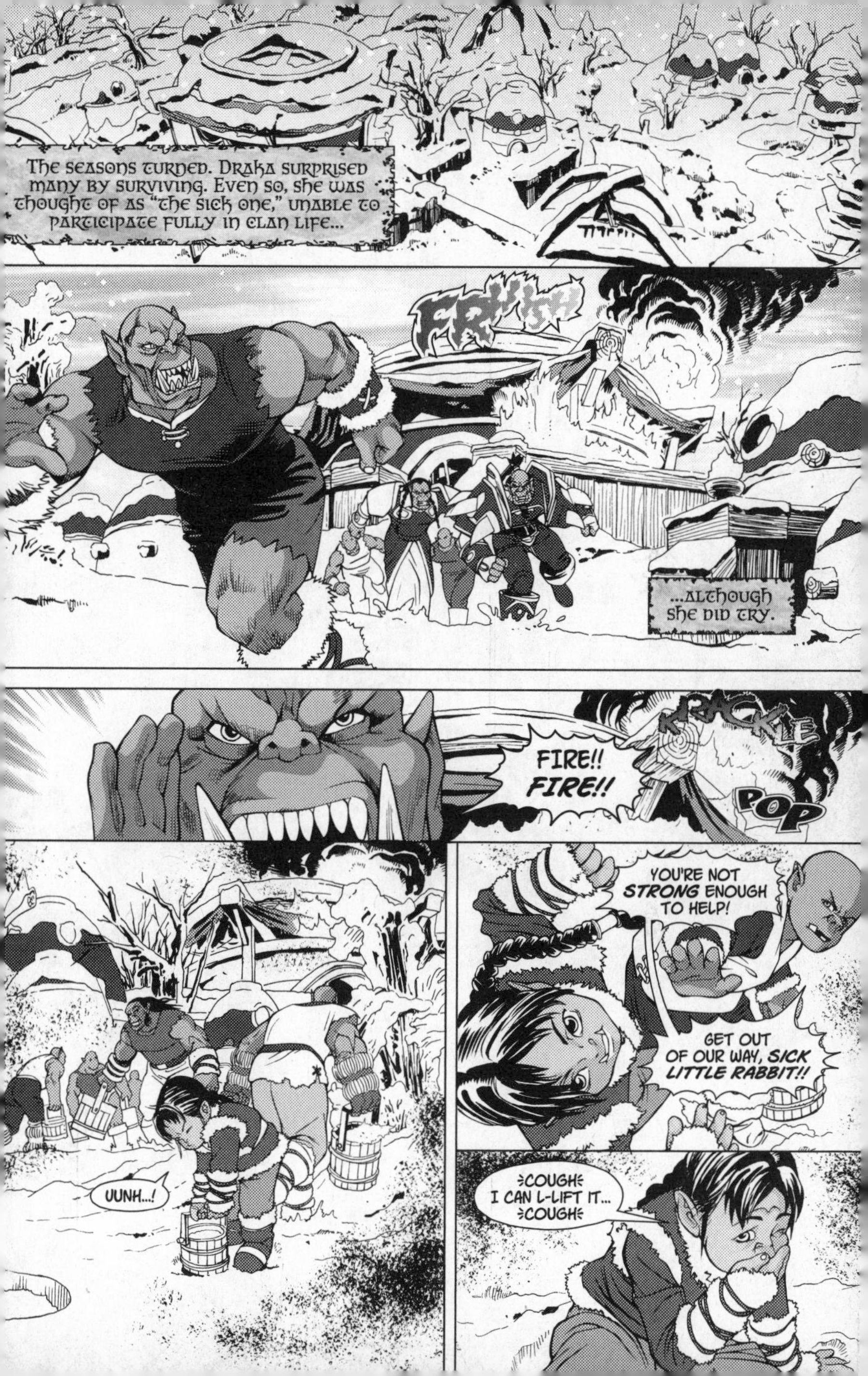
The seasons turned. Draka surprised many by surviving. Even so, she was thought of as "the sick one," unable to participate fully in clan life...
...although she did try.
FIRE!! FIRE!!
KRACKLE
POP
UUNH...!
YOU'RE NOT STRONG ENOUGH TO HELP!
GET OUT OF OUR WAY, SICK LITTLE RABBIT!!
COUGH I CAN L-LIFT IT... COUGH

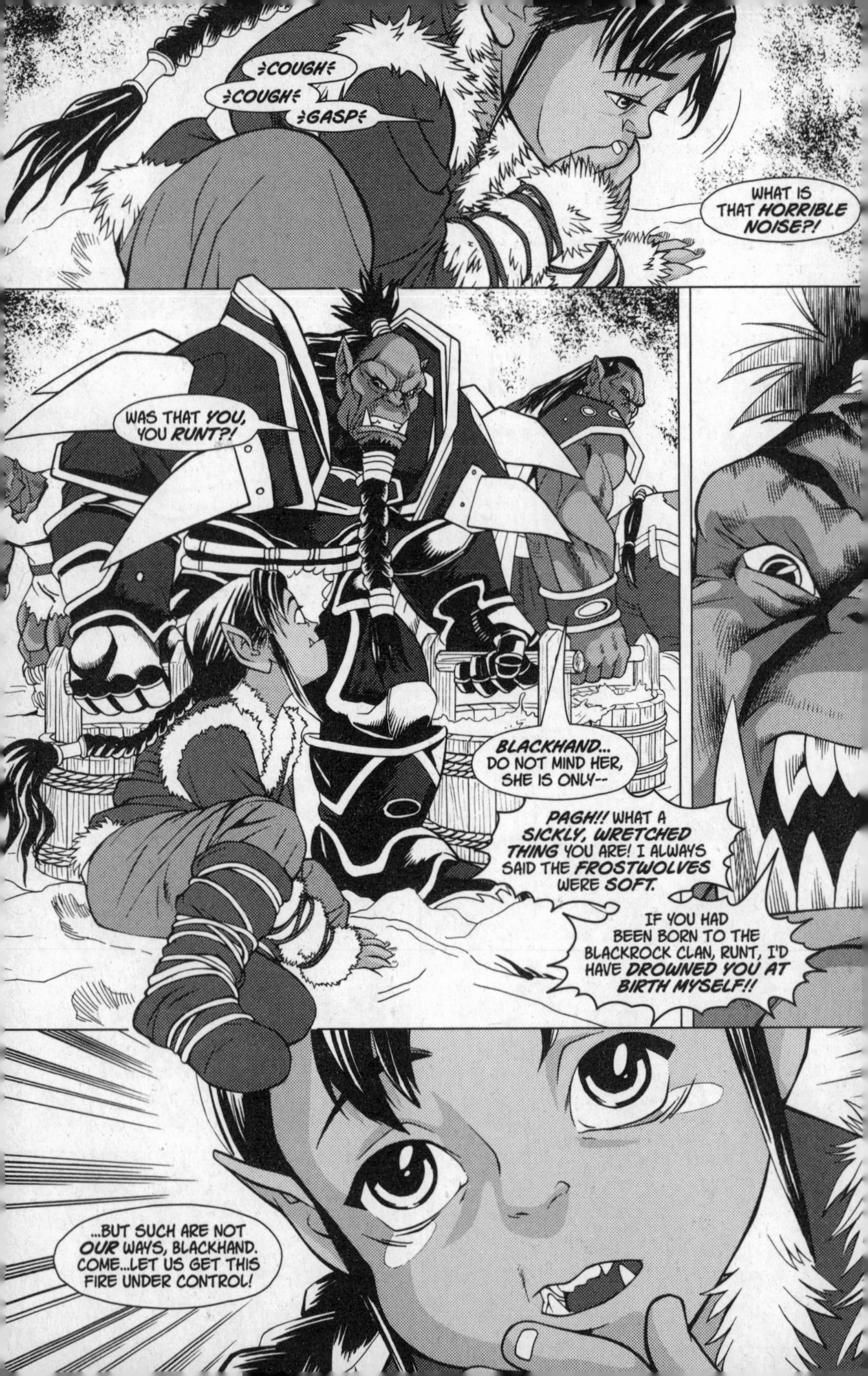

COUGH
COUGH
GASP
WHAT IS THAT HORRIBLE NOISE?!
WAS THAT YOU, YOU RUNT?!
BLACKHAND... DO NOT MIND HER, SHE IS ONLY--
PAGH!! WHAT A SICKLY, WRETCHED THING YOU ARE! I ALWAYS SAID THE FROSTWOLVES WERE SOFT.
IF YOU HAD BEEN BORN TO THE BLACKROCK CLAN, RUNT, I'D HAVE DROWNED YOU AT BIRTH MYSELF!!
...BUT SUCH ARE NOT OUR WAYS, BLACKHAND. COME...LET US GET THIS FIRE UNDER CONTROL!

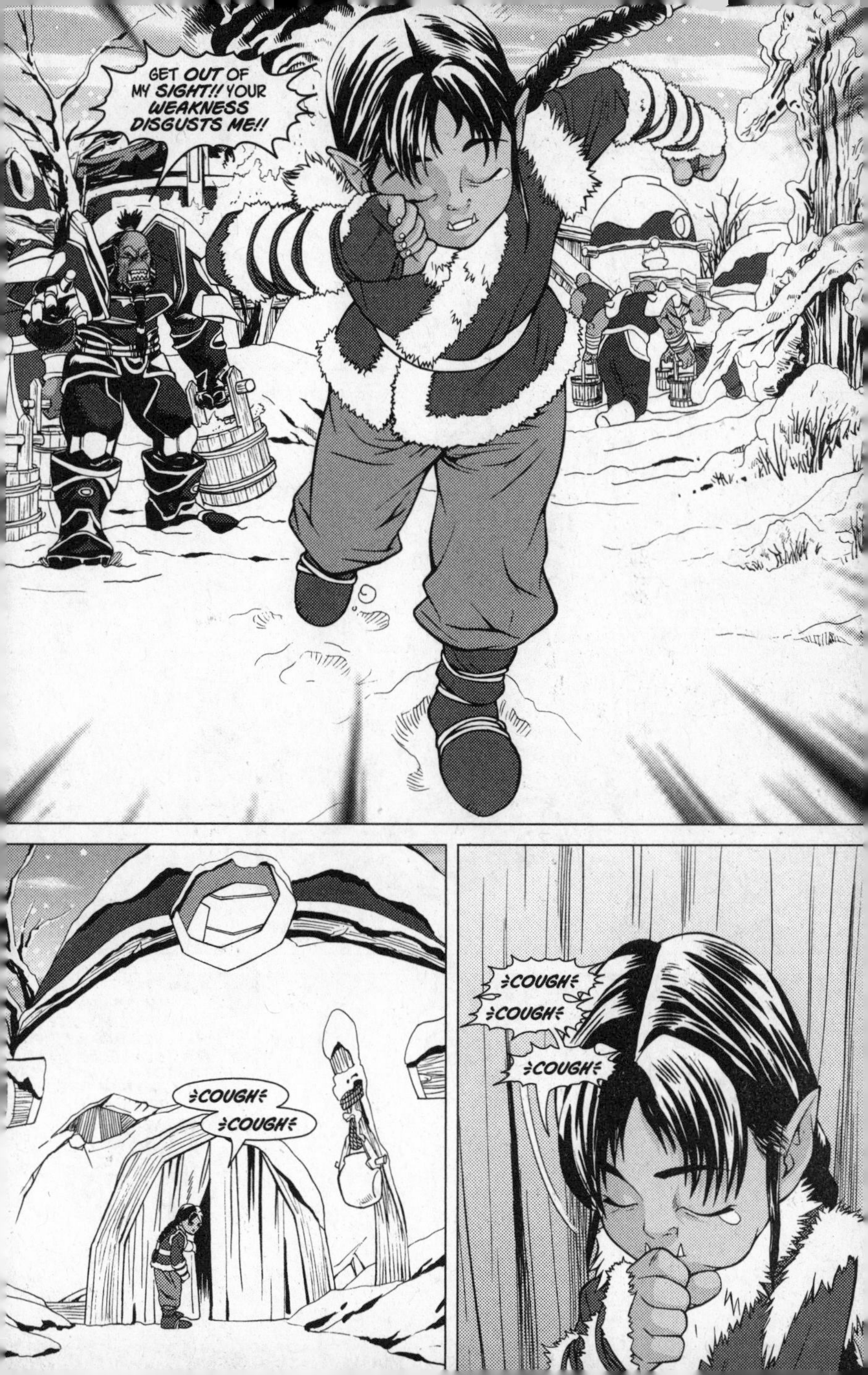
GET OUT OF MY SIGHT!! YOUR WEAKNESS DISGUSTS ME!!
COUGH
COUGH
COUGH
COUGH
COUGH

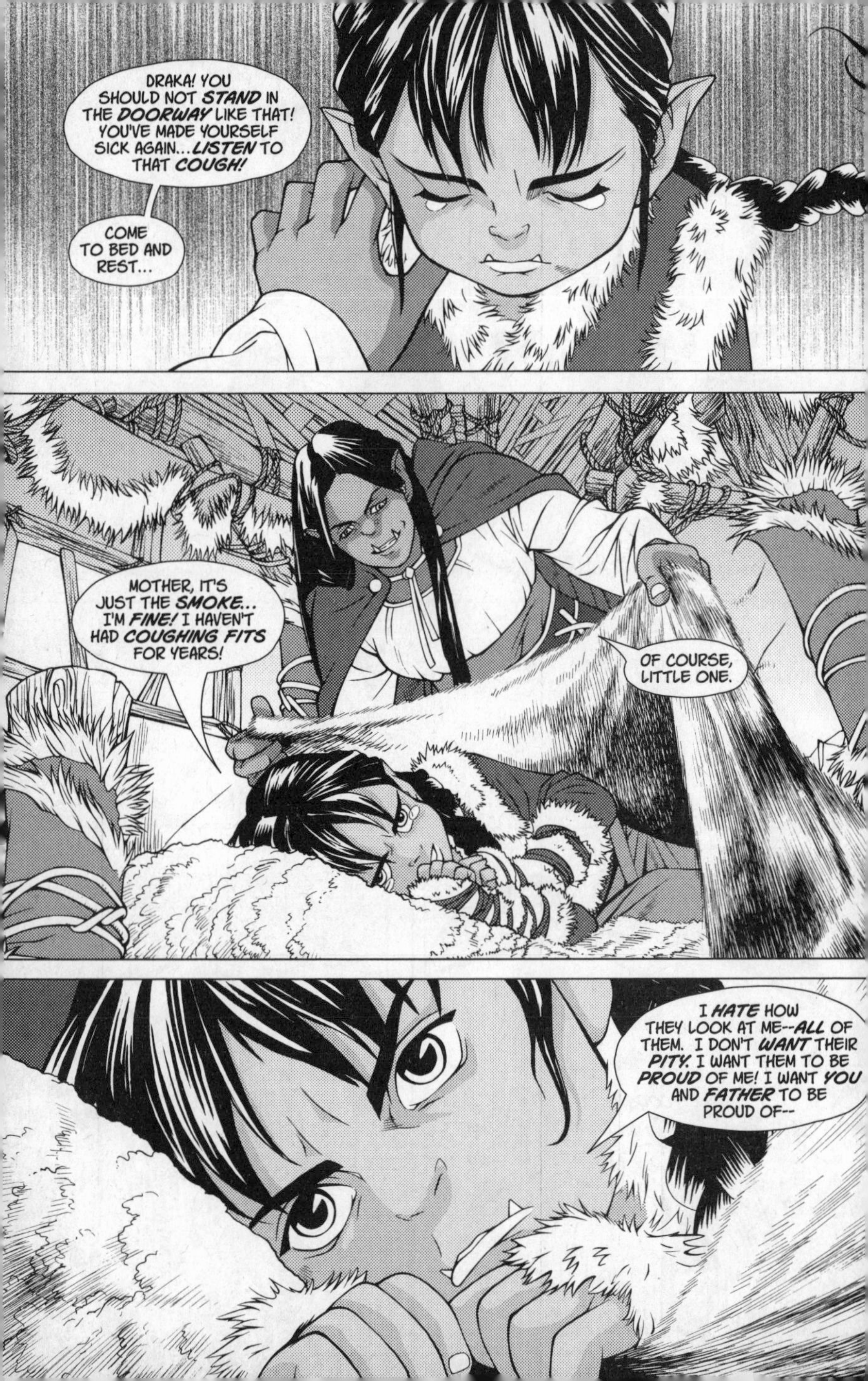
DRAKA! YOU SHOULD NOT STAND IN THE DOORWAY LIKE THAT! YOU'VE MADE YOURSELF SICK AGAIN... LISTEN TO THAT COUGH!
COME TO BED AND REST...
MOTHER, IT'S JUST THE SMOKE... I'M FINE! I HAVEN'T HAD COUGHING FITS FOR YEARS!
OF COURSE, LITTLE ONE.
I HATE HOW THEY LOOK AT ME--ALL OF THEM. I DON'T WANT THEIR PITY. I WANT THEM TO BE PROUD OF ME! I WANT YOU AND FATHER TO BE PROUD OF--

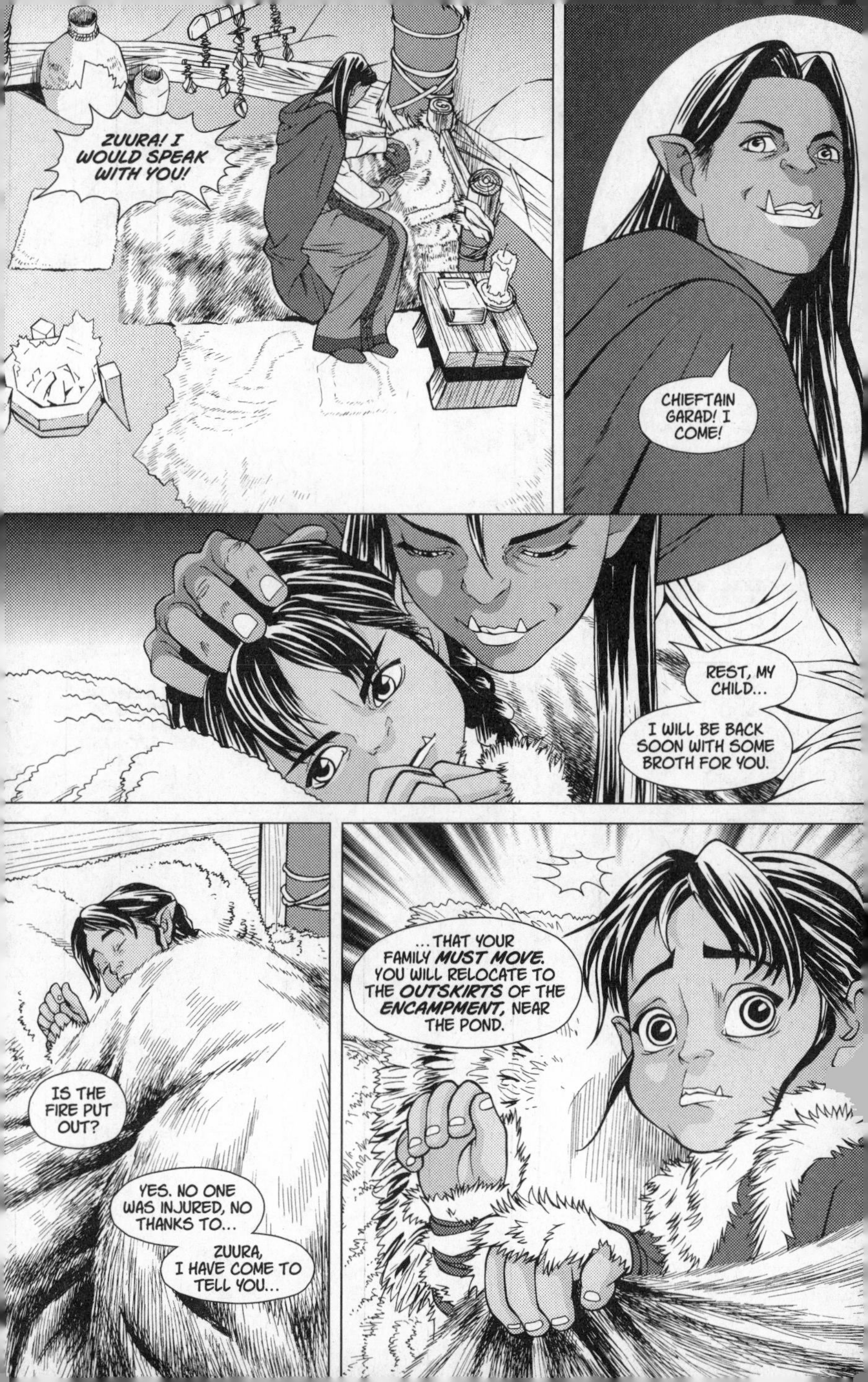
ZUURA! I WOULD SPEAK WITH YOU!
CHIEFTAIN GARAD! I COME!
REST, MY CHILD...
I WILL BE BACK SOON WITH SOME BROTH FOR YOU.
IS THE FIRE PUT OUT?
YES. NO ONE WAS INJURED, NO THANKS TO...
ZUURA, I HAVE COME TO TELL YOU...
...THAT YOUR FAMILY MUST MOVE. YOU WILL RELOCATE TO THE OUTSKIRTS OF THE ENCAMPMENT, NEAR THE POND.

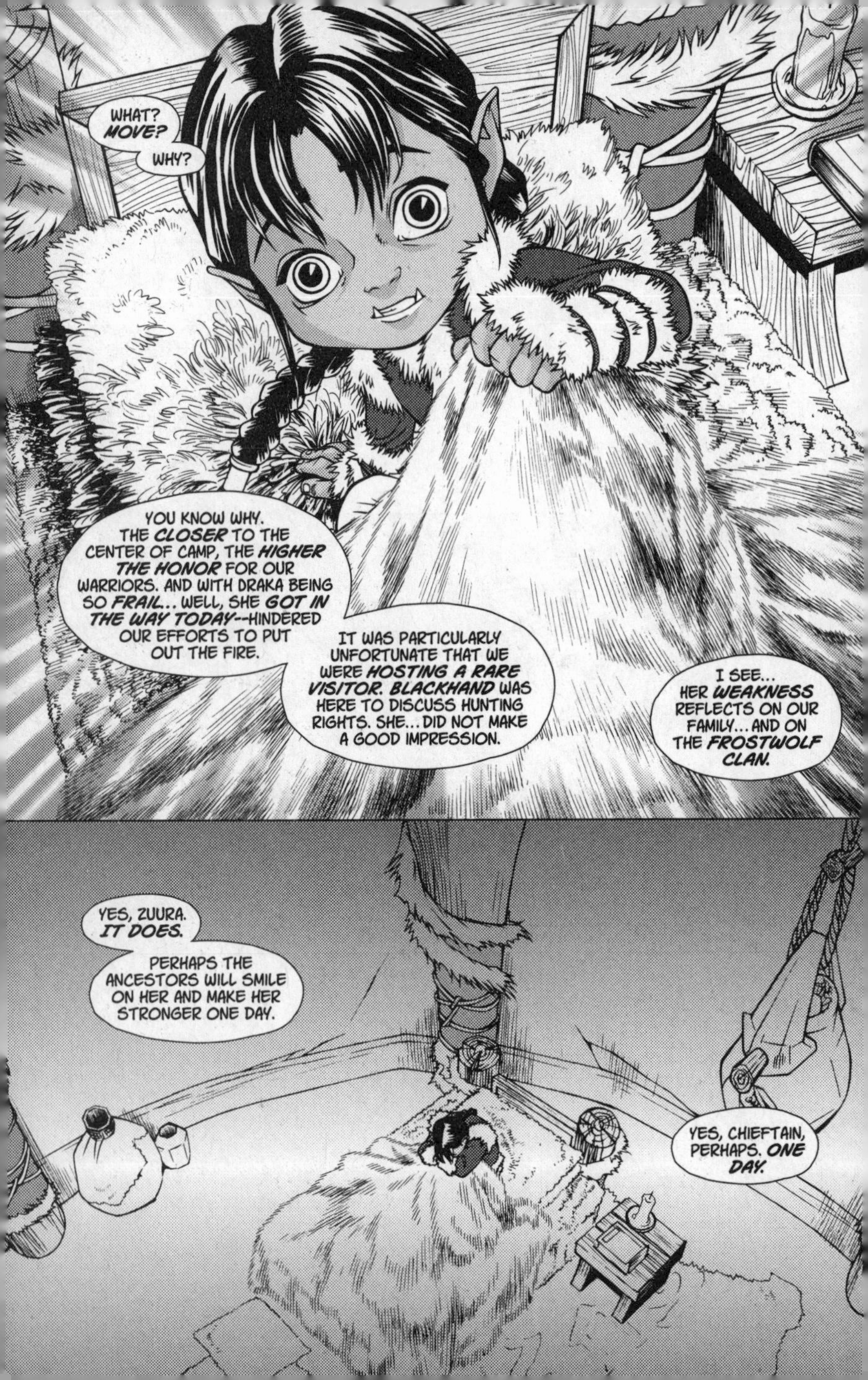
WHAT? MOVE?
WHY?
YOU KNOW WHY. THE CLOSER TO THE CENTER OF CAMP, THE HIGHER THE HONOR FOR OUR WARRIORS. AND WITH DRAKA BEING SO FRAIL... WELL, SHE GOT IN THE WAY TODAY--HINDERED OUR EFFORTS TO PUT OUT THE FIRE.
IT WAS PARTICULARLY UNFORTUNATE THAT WE WERE HOSTING A RARE VISITOR. BLACKHAND WAS HERE TO DISCUSS HUNTING RIGHTS. SHE... DID NOT MAKE A GOOD IMPRESSION.
I SEE... HER WEAKNESS REFLECTS ON OUR FAMILY... AND ON THE FROSTWOLF CLAN.
YES, ZUURA. IT DOES.
PERHAPS THE ANCESTORS WILL SMILE ON HER AND MAKE HER STRONGER ONE DAY.
YES, CHIEFTAIN, PERHAPS. ONE DAY.

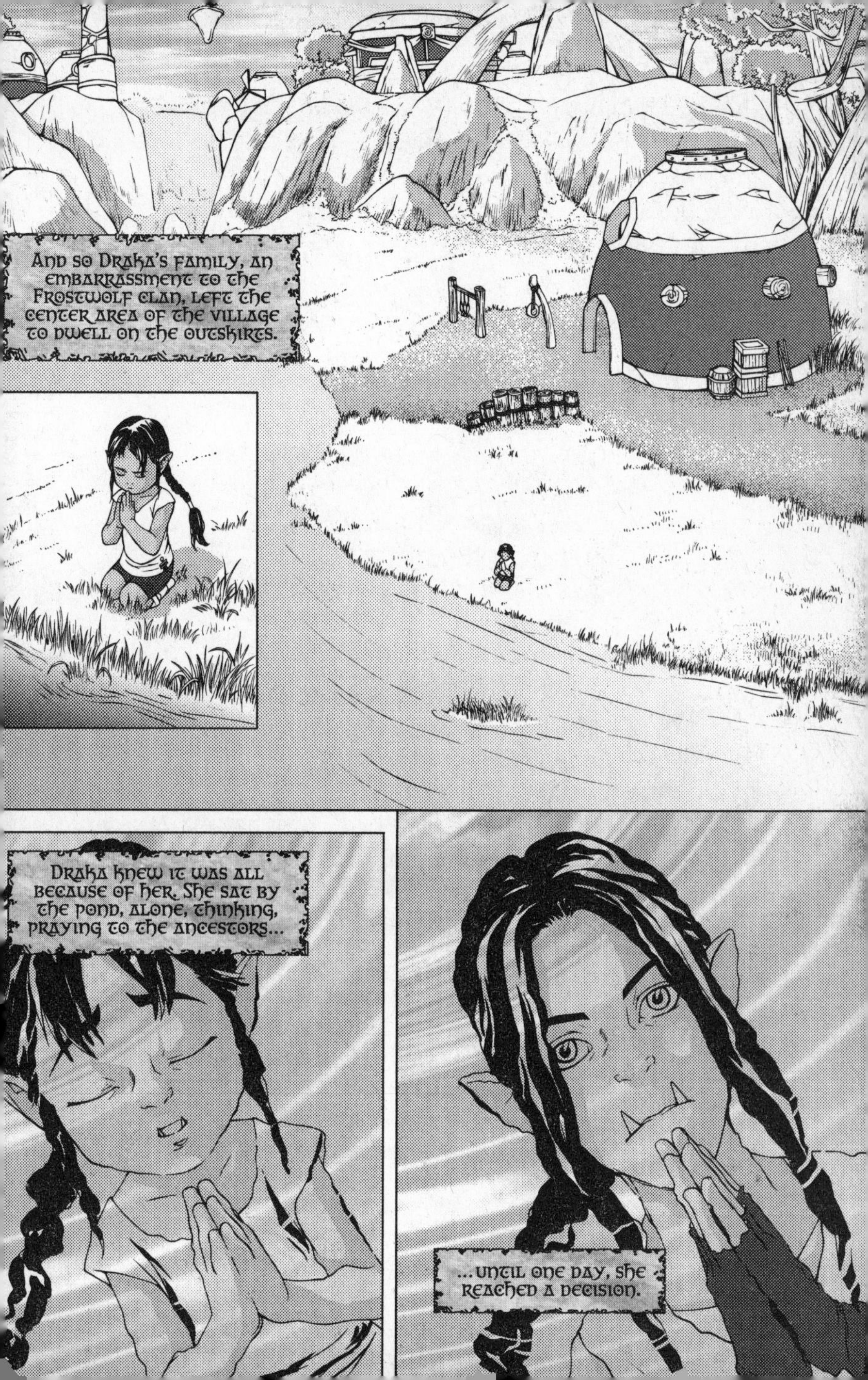
And so Draka's family, an embarrassment to the Frostwolf clan, left the center area of the village to dwell on the outskirts.
Draka knew it was all because of her. She sat by the pond, alone, thinking, praying to the ancestors...
...until one day, she reached a decision.

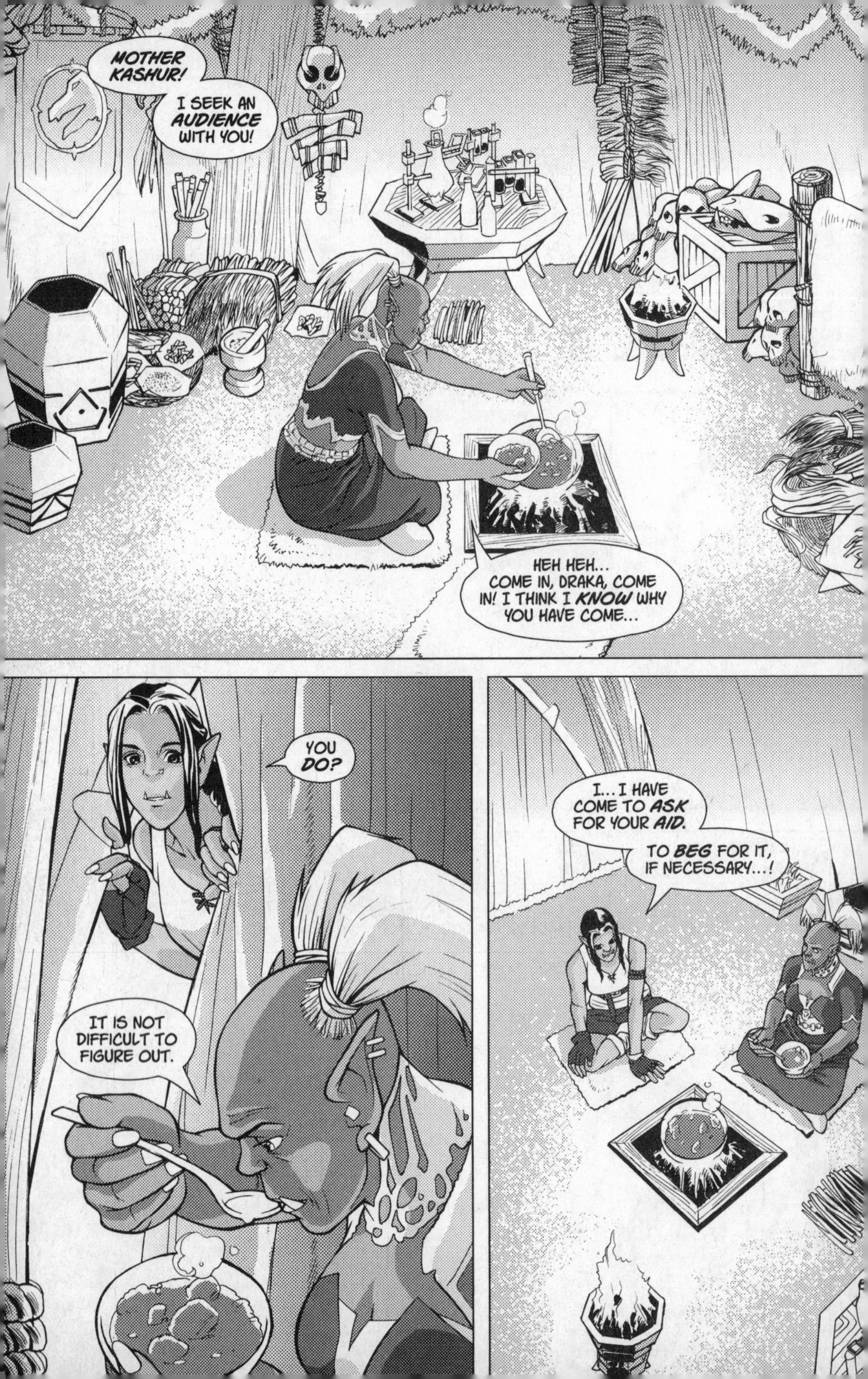
MOTHER KASHUR!
I SEEK AN AUDIENCE WITH YOU!
HEH HEH... COME IN, DRAKA, COME IN! I THINK I KNOW WHY YOU HAVE COME...
YOU DO?
IT IS NOT DIFFICULT TO FIGURE OUT.
I... I HAVE COME TO ASK FOR YOUR AID.
TO BEG FOR IT, IF NECESSARY...!

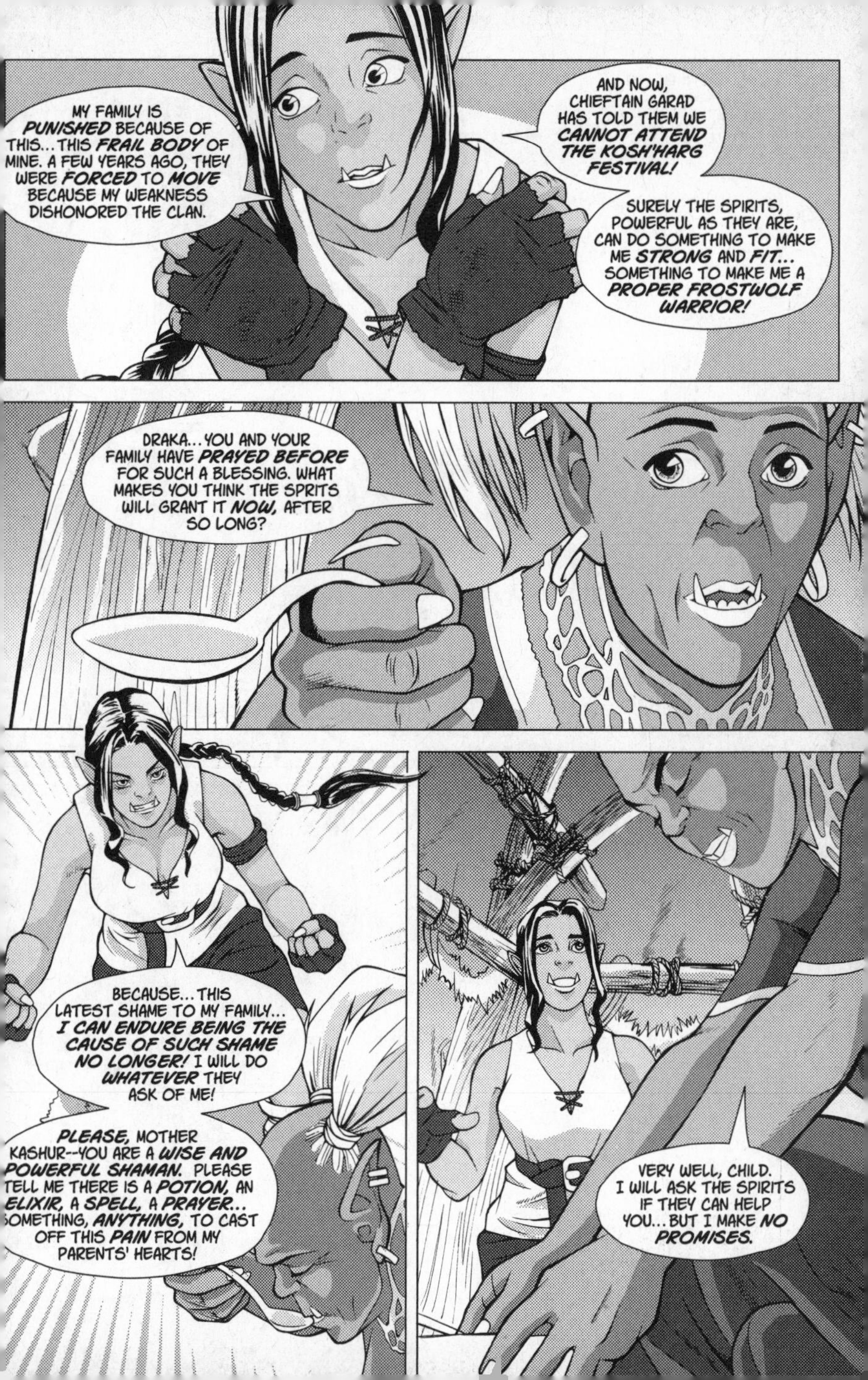
MY FAMILY IS PUNISHED BECAUSE OF THIS... THIS FRAIL BODY OF MINE. A FEW YEARS AGO, THEY WERE FORCED TO MOVE BECAUSE MY WEAKNESS DISHONORED THE CLAN.
AND NOW, CHIEFTAIN GARAD HAS TOLD THEM WE CANNOT ATTEND THE KOSH'HARG FESTIVAL!
SURELY THE SPIRITS, POWERFUL AS THEY ARE, CAN DO SOMETHING TO MAKE ME STRONG AND FIT... SOMETHING TO MAKE ME A PROPER FROSTWOLF WARRIOR!
DRAKA... YOU AND YOUR FAMILY HAVE PRAYED BEFORE FOR SUCH A BLESSING. WHAT MAKES YOU THINK THE SPRITS WILL GRANT IT NOW, AFTER SO LONG?
BECAUSE... THIS LATEST SHAME TO MY FAMILY... I CAN ENDURE BEING THE CAUSE OF SUCH SHAME NO LONGER! I WILL DO WHATEVER THEY ASK OF ME!
PLEASE, MOTHER KASHUR--YOU ARE A WISE AND POWERFUL SHAMAN. PLEASE TELL ME THERE IS A POTION, AN ELIXIR, A SPELL, A PRAYER... SOMETHING, ANYTHING, TO CAST OFF THIS PAIN FROM MY PARENTS' HEARTS!
VERY WELL, CHILD. I WILL ASK THE SPIRITS IF THEY CAN HELP YOU... BUT I MAKE NO PROMISES.

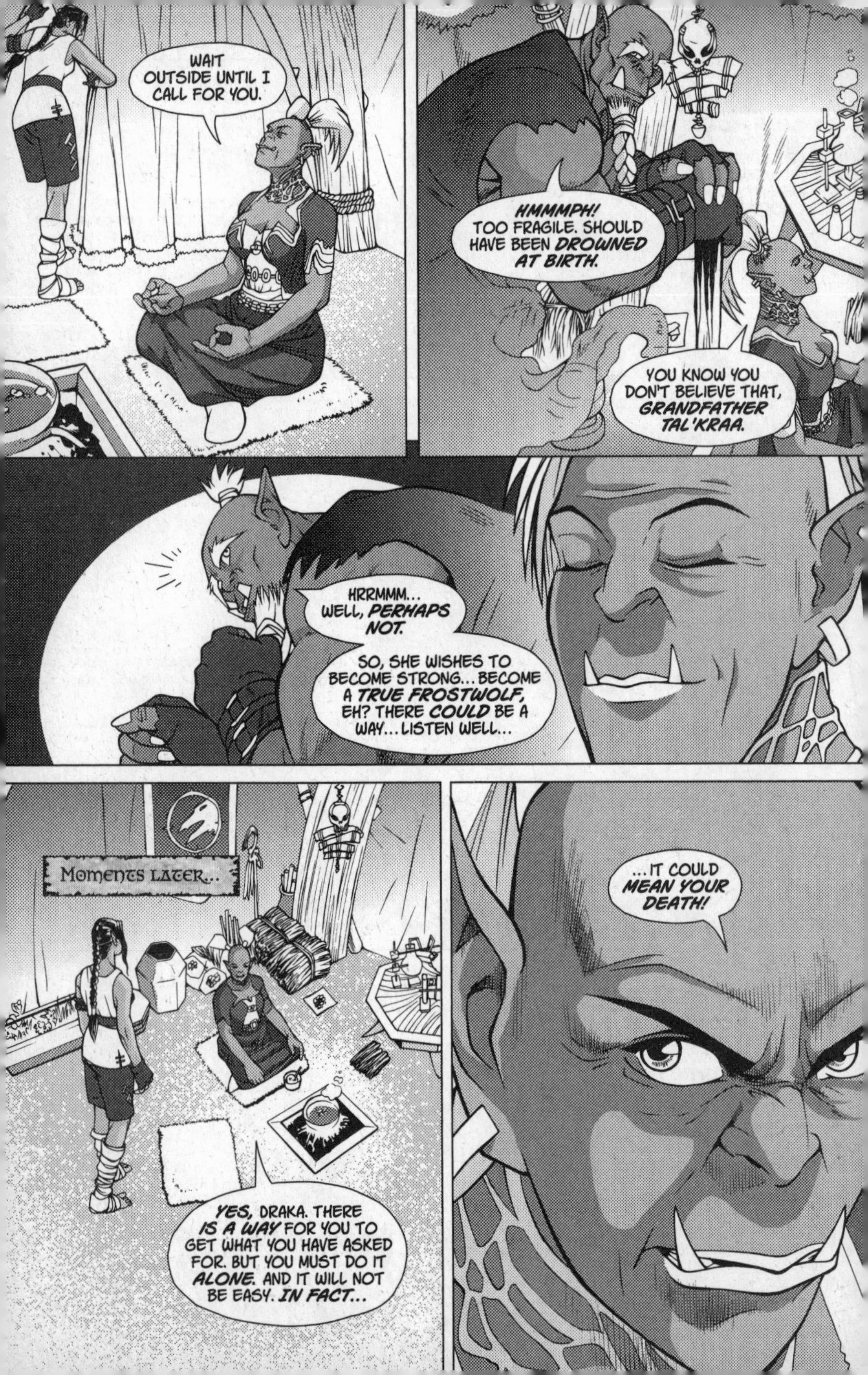
WAIT OUTSIDE UNTIL I CALL FOR YOU.
HMMMPH! TOO FRAGILE. SHOULD HAVE BEEN DROWNED AT BIRTH.
YOU KNOW YOU DON'T BELIEVE THAT, GRANDFATHER TAL'KRAA.
HRRMMM... WELL, PERHAPS NOT.
SO, SHE WISHES TO BECOME STRONG... BECOME A TRUE FROSTWOLF, EH? THERE COULD BE A WAY... LISTEN WELL...
MOMENTS LATER...
YES, DRAKA. THERE IS A WAY FOR YOU TO GET WHAT YOU HAVE ASKED FOR. BUT YOU MUST DO IT ALONE. AND IT WILL NOT BE EASY. IN FACT...
...IT COULD MEAN YOUR DEATH!

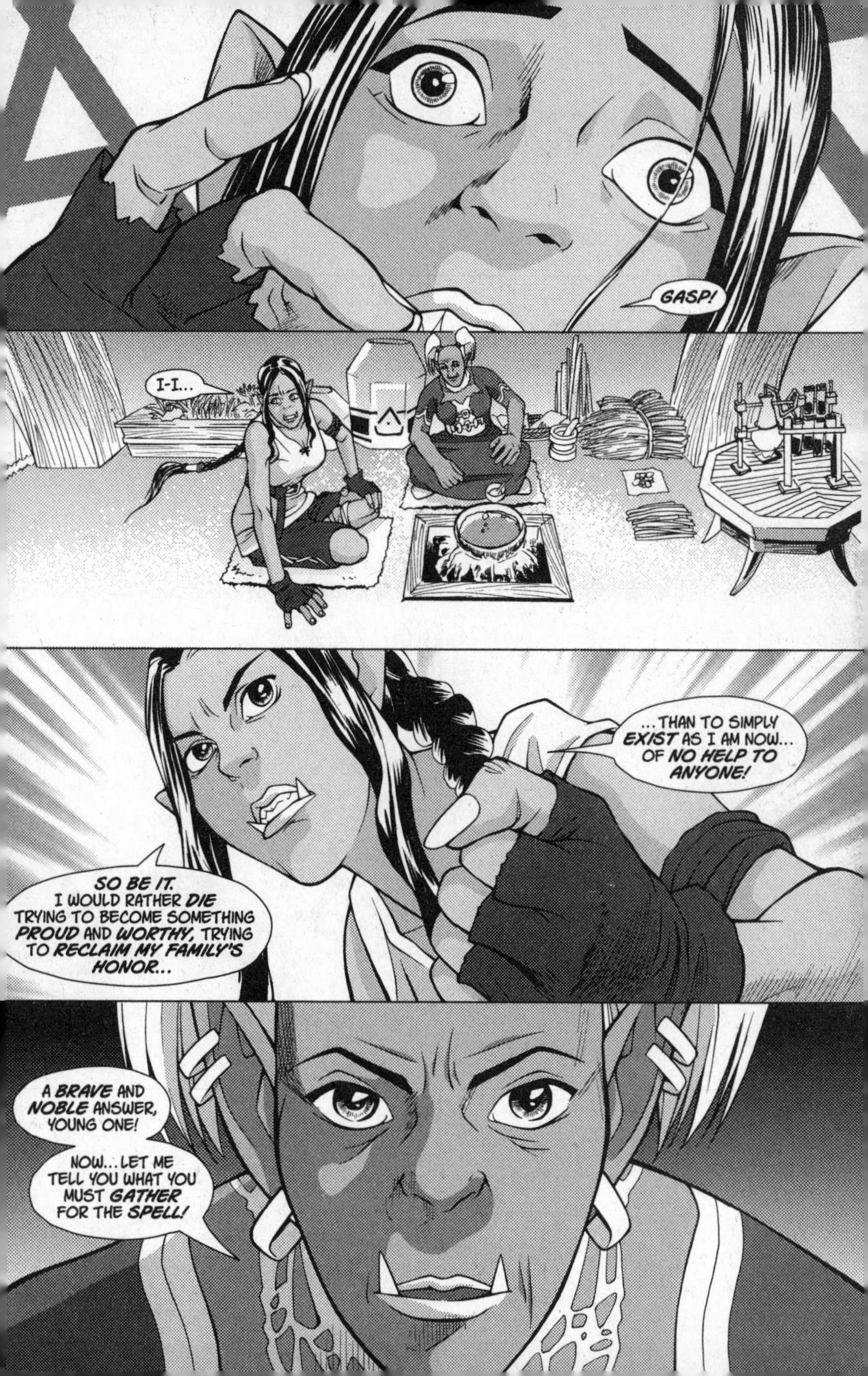
GASP!
I-I...
SO BE IT. I WOULD RATHER DIE TRYING TO BECOME SOMETHING PROUD AND WORTHY, TRYING TO RECLAIM MY FAMILY'S HONOR...
...THAN TO SIMPLY EXIST AS I AM NOW... OF NO HELP TO ANYONE!
A BRAVE AND NOBLE ANSWER, YOUNG ONE!
NOW... LET ME TELL YOU WHAT YOU MUST GATHER FOR THE SPELL!

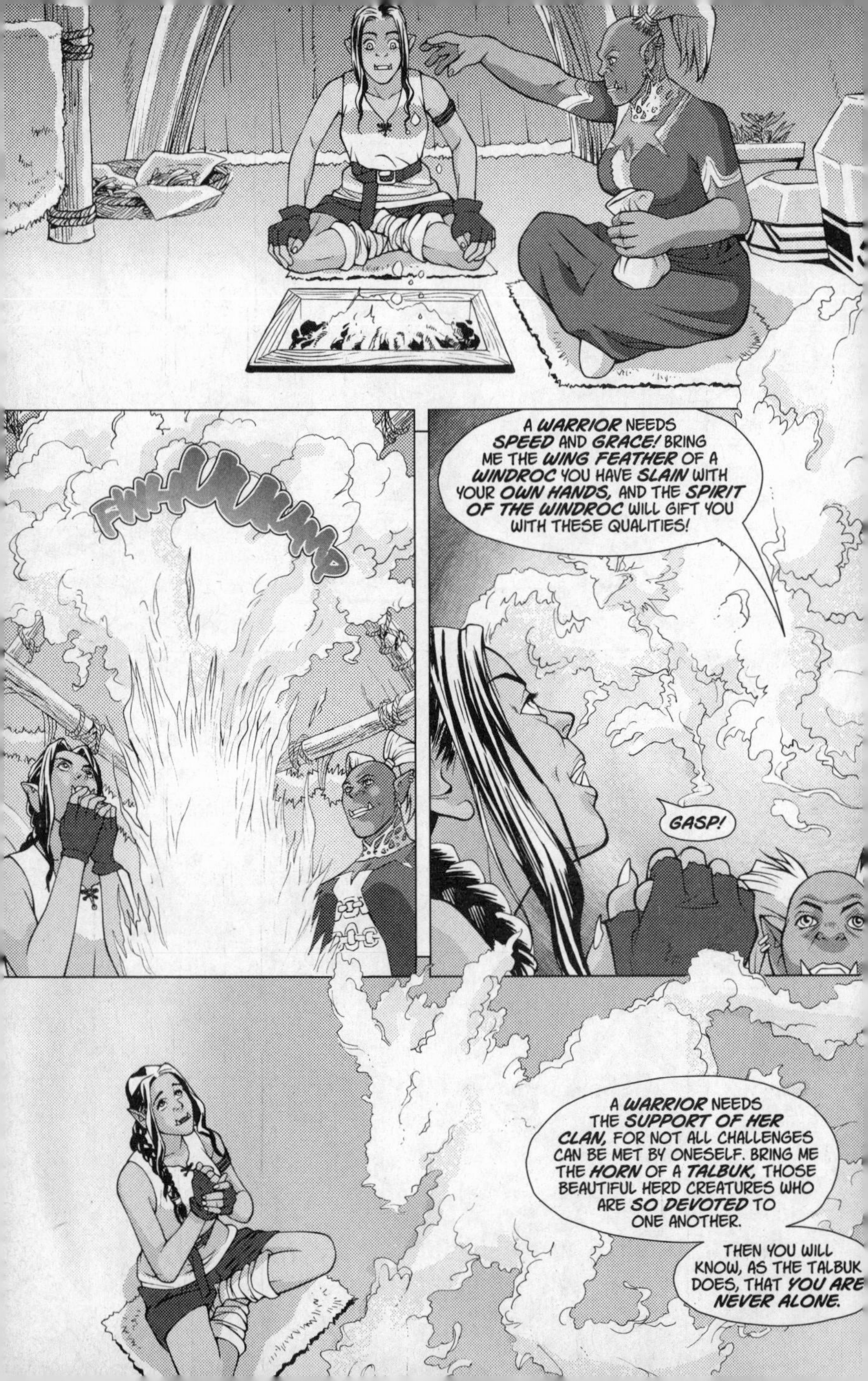
FWHUUUMP
A WARRIOR NEEDS SPEED AND GRACE! BRING ME THE WING FEATHER OF A WINDROC YOU HAVE SLAIN WITH YOUR OWN HANDS, AND THE SPIRIT OF THE WINDROC WILL GIFT YOU WITH THESE QUALITIES!
GASP!
A WARRIOR NEEDS THE SUPPORT OF HER CLAN, FOR NOT ALL CHALLENGES CAN BE MET BY ONESELF. BRING ME THE HORN OF A TALBUK, THOSE BEAUTIFUL HERD CREATURES WHO ARE SO DEVOTED TO ONE ANOTHER.
THEN YOU WILL KNOW, AS THE TALBUK DOES, THAT YOU ARE NEVER ALONE.

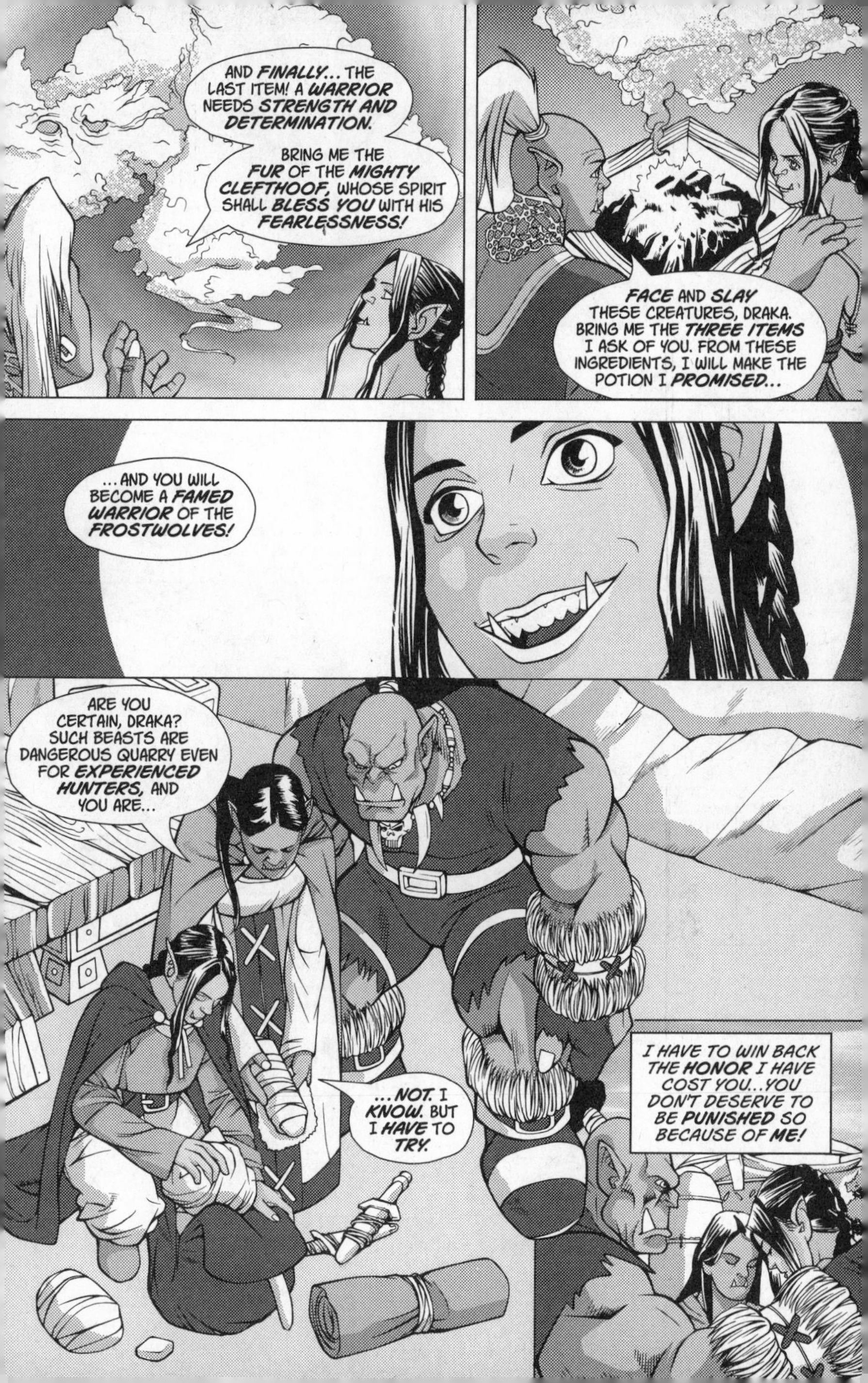
AND FINALLY... THE LAST ITEM! A WARRIOR NEEDS STRENGTH AND DETERMINATION.
BRING ME THE FUR OF THE MIGHTY CLEFTHOOF, WHOSE SPIRIT SHALL BLESS YOU WITH HIS FEARLESSNESS!
FACE AND SLAY THESE CREATURES, DRAKA. BRING ME THE THREE ITEMS I ASK OF YOU. FROM THESE INGREDIENTS, I WILL MAKE THE POTION I PROMISED...
...AND YOU WILL BECOME A FAMED WARRIOR OF THE FROSTWOLVES!
ARE YOU CERTAIN, DRAKA? SUCH BEASTS ARE DANGEROUS QUARRY EVEN FOR EXPERIENCED HUNTERS, AND YOU ARE...
...NOT. I KNOW. BUT I HAVE TO TRY.
I HAVE TO WIN BACK THE HONOR I HAVE COST YOU...YOU DON'T DESERVE TO BE PUNISHED SO BECAUSE OF ME!

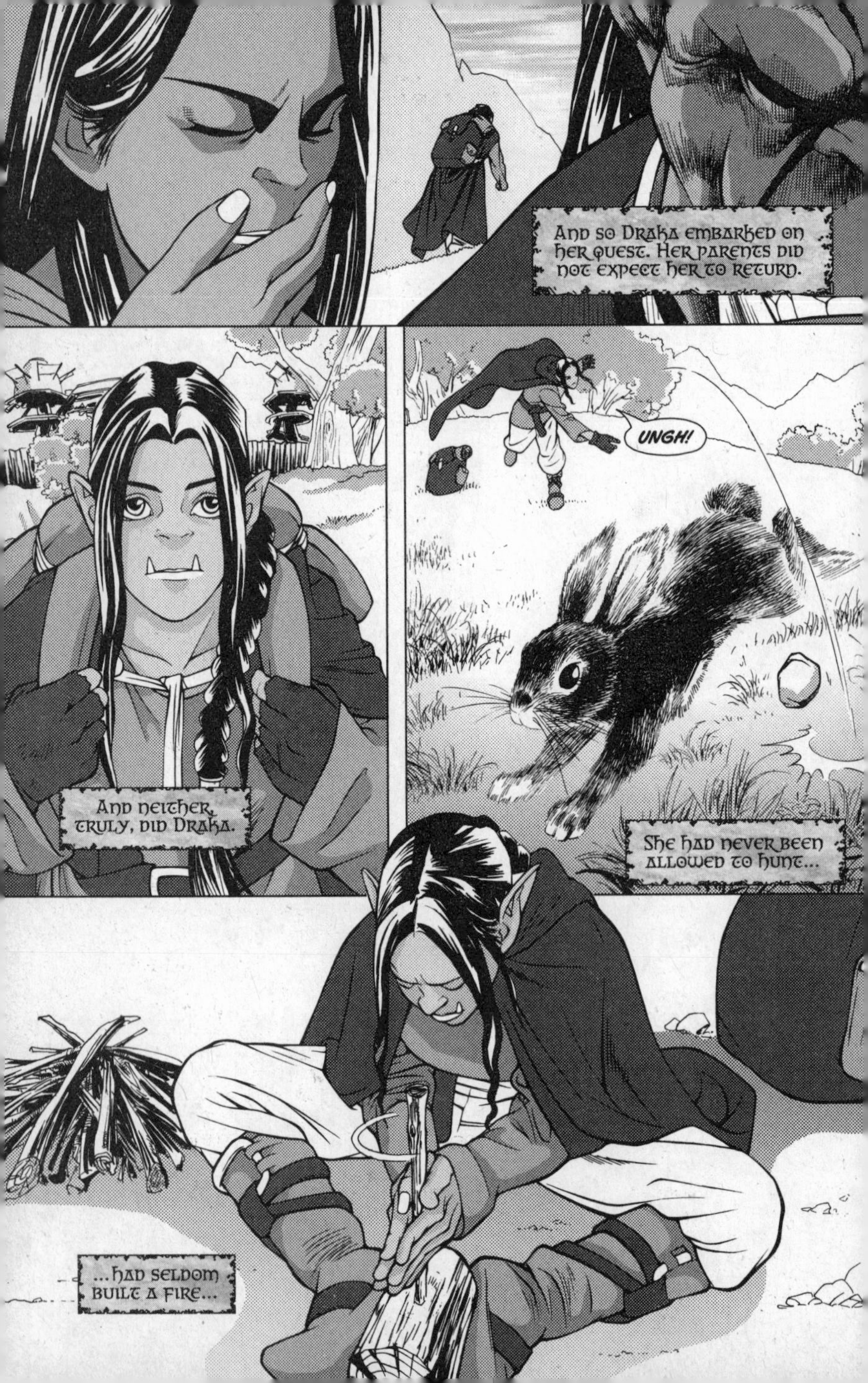
And so Draka embarked on her quest. Her parents did not expect her to return.
And neither, truly, did Draka.
UNGH!
She had never been allowed to hunt...
...had seldom built a fire...

BOOOOM

KRRSSH

GASP!

AAAAAH!

KRAAAAAAACK

BOOOOM

PANT...

GASP...

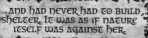

...AND HAD NEVER HAD TO BUILD SHELTER. IT WAS AS IF NATURE ITSELF WAS AGAINST HER.

IF SHE COULD NOT DO THESE SIMPLE, BASIC THINGS...

...HOW COULD SHE COMPLETE SO DAUNTING A TASK AS THE ONE SHE HAD BEEN SET?

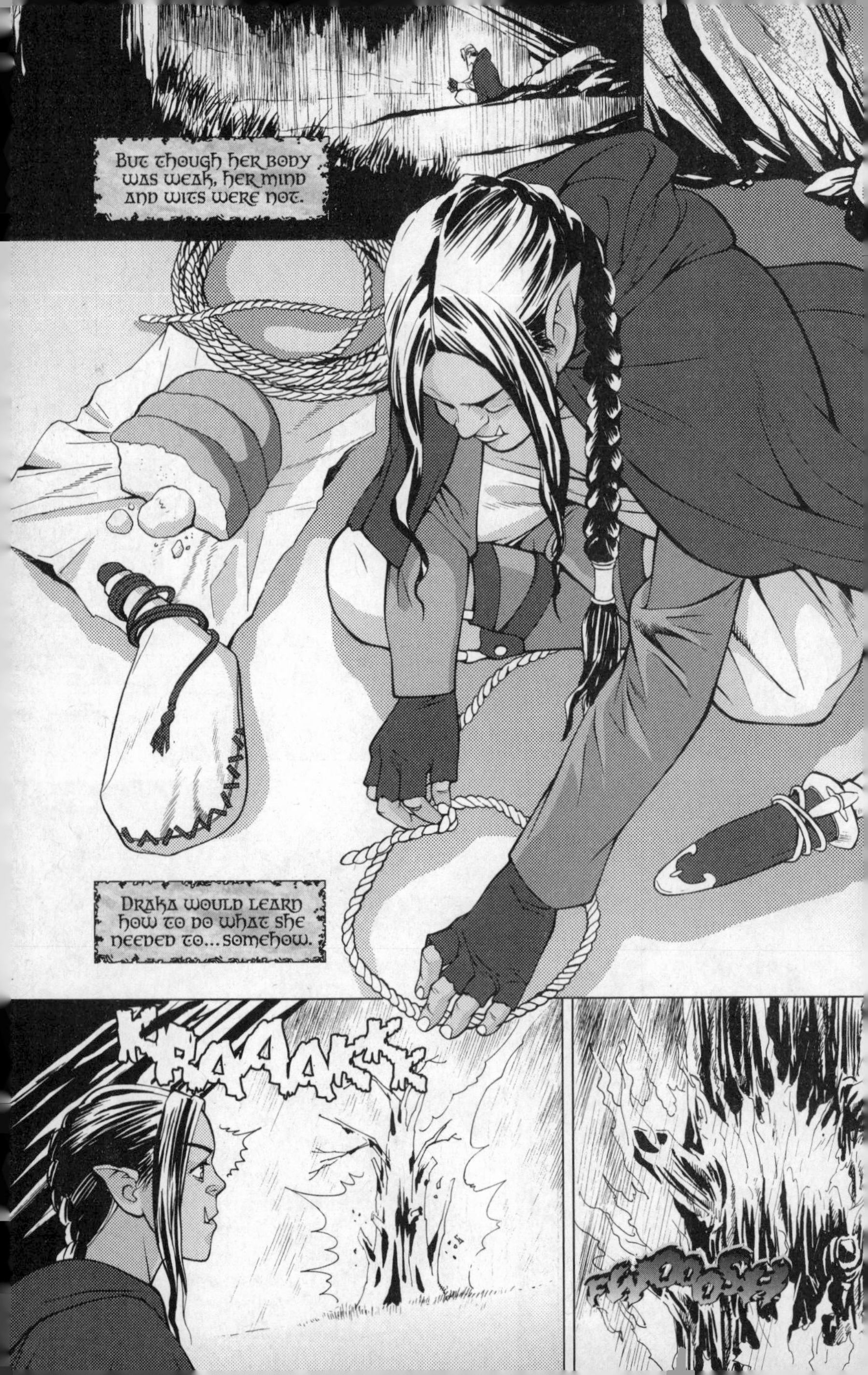
BUT THOUGH HER BODY WAS WEAK, HER MIND AND WITS WERE NOT.
DRAKA WOULD LEARN HOW TO DO WHAT SHE NEEDED TO... SOMEHOW.
KRAAAKK

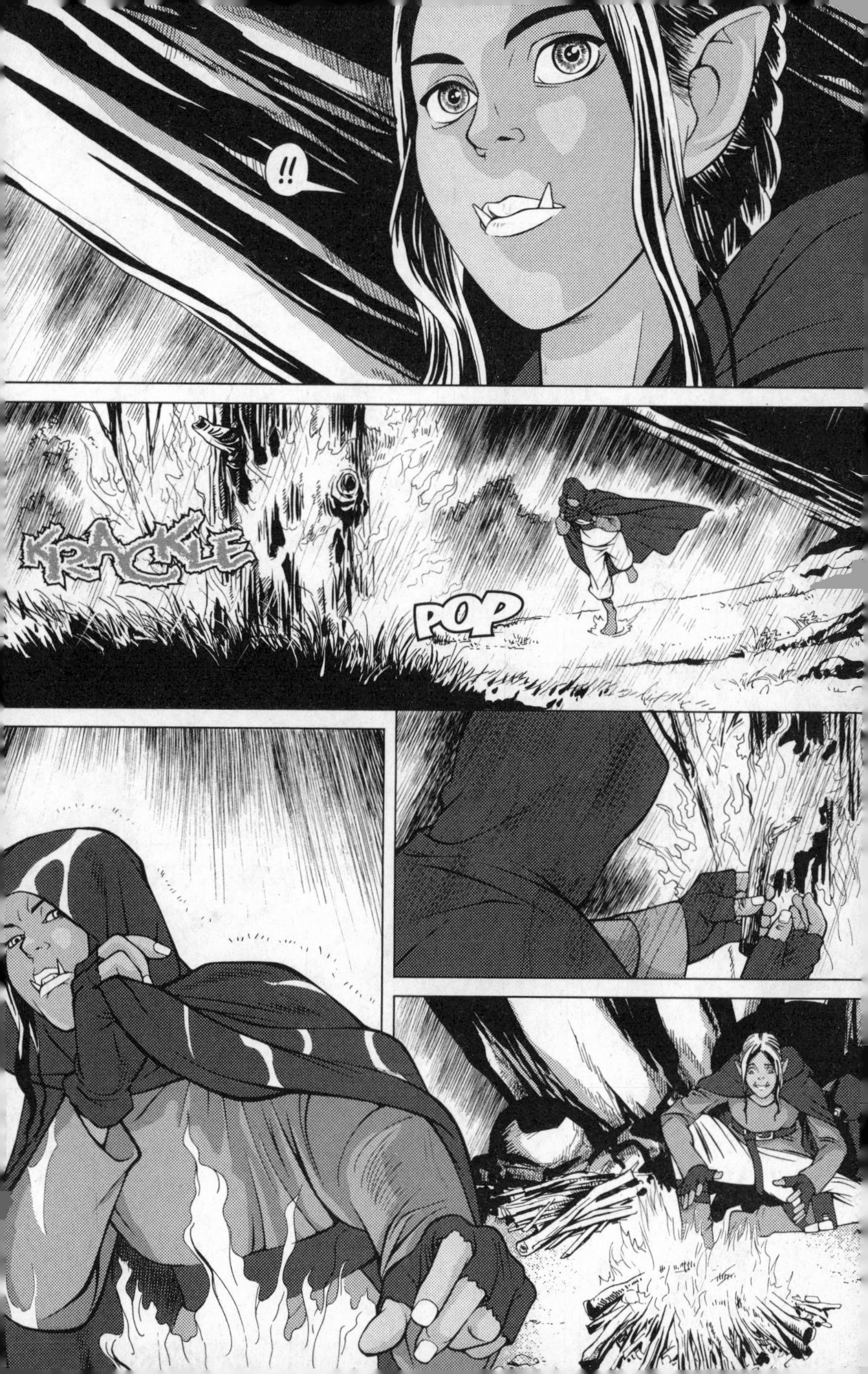
!!
KRACKLE
POP

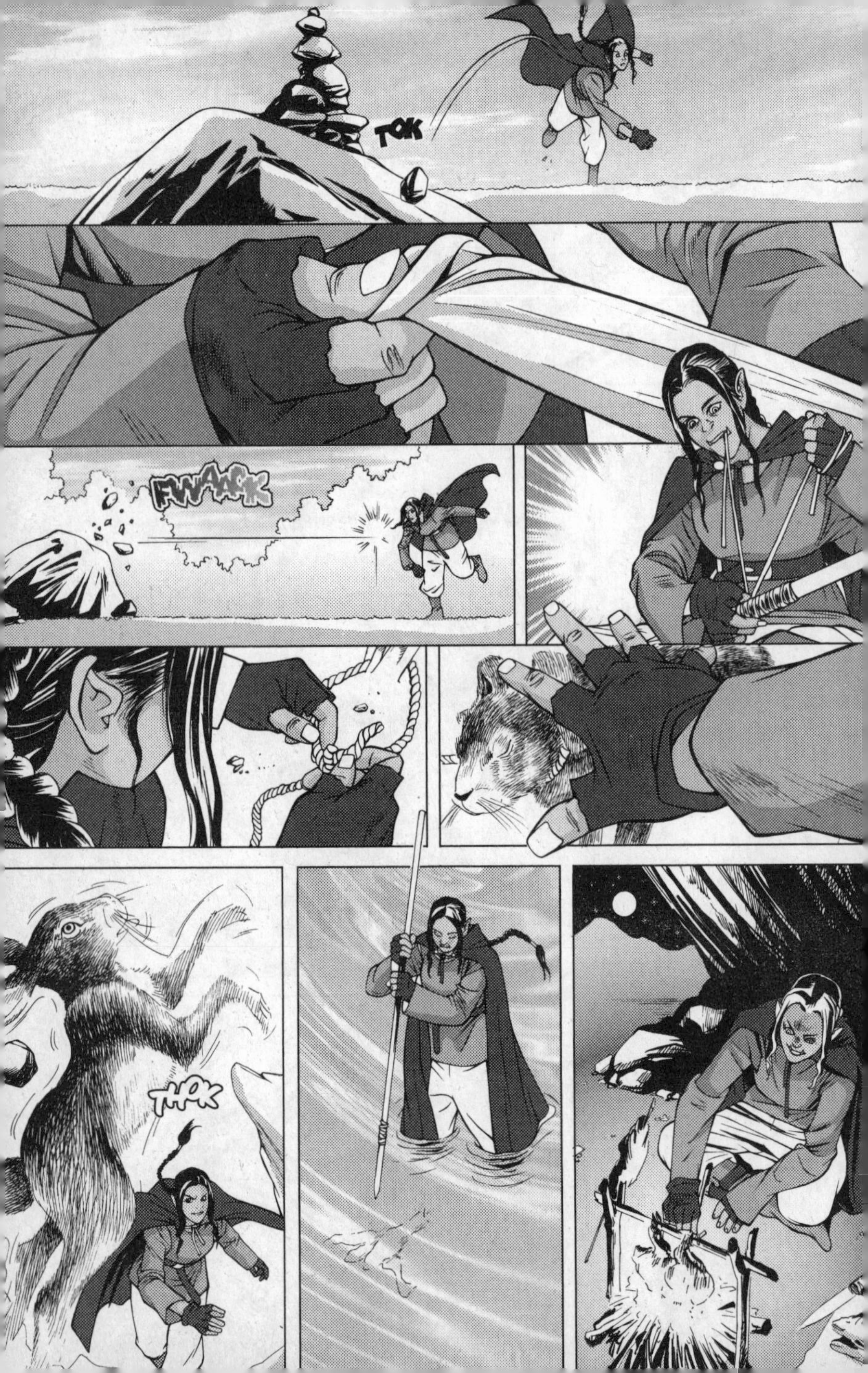
TOK
FWAACK
THOK

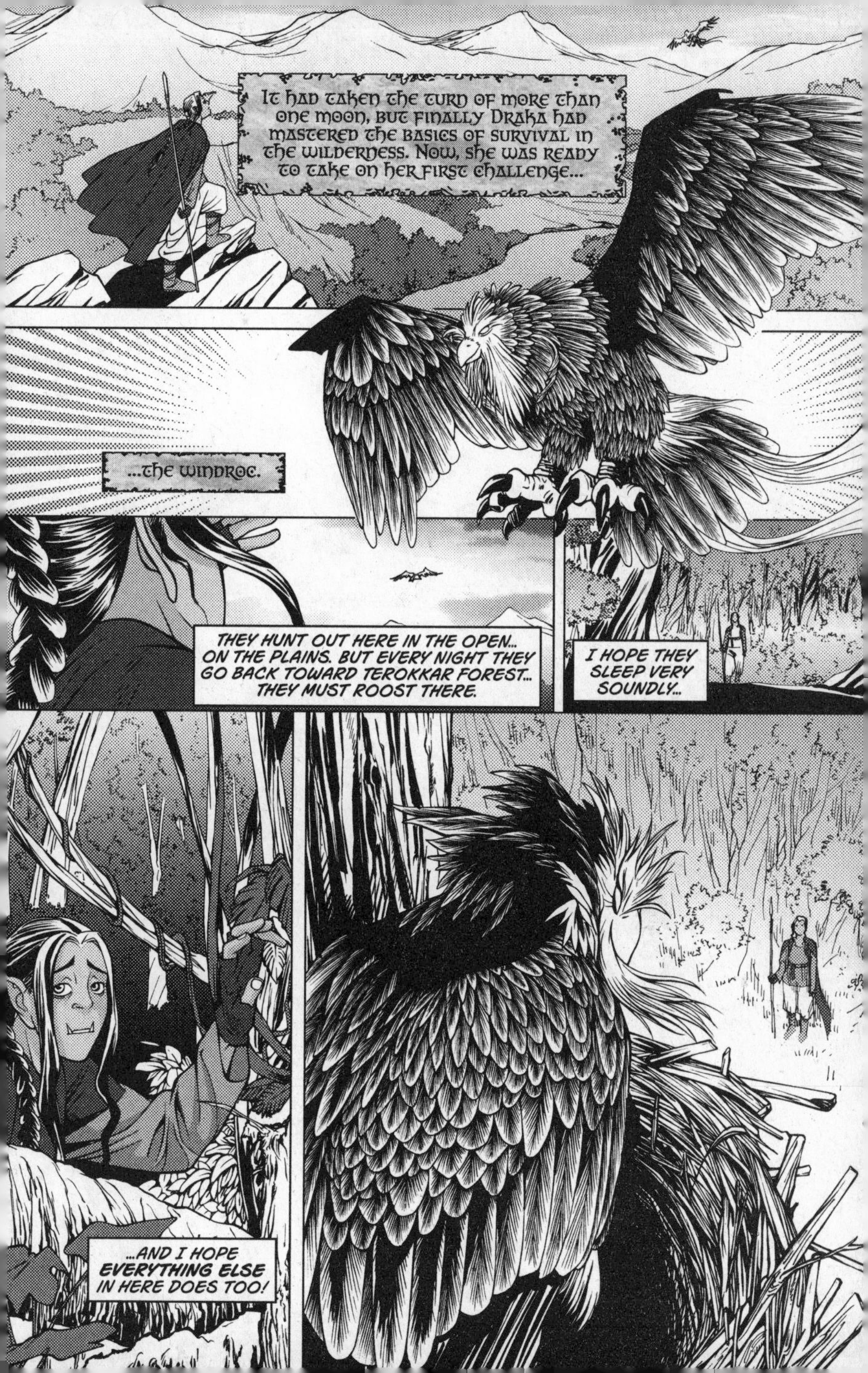
It had taken the turn of more than one moon, but finally Draka had mastered the basics of survival in the wilderness. Now, she was ready to take on her first challenge...
...the windroc.
THEY HUNT OUT HERE IN THE OPEN... ON THE PLAINS. BUT EVERY NIGHT THEY GO BACK TOWARD TEROKKAR FOREST... THEY MUST ROOST THERE.
I HOPE THEY SLEEP VERY SOUNDLY...
...AND I HOPE EVERYTHING ELSE IN HERE DOES TOO!

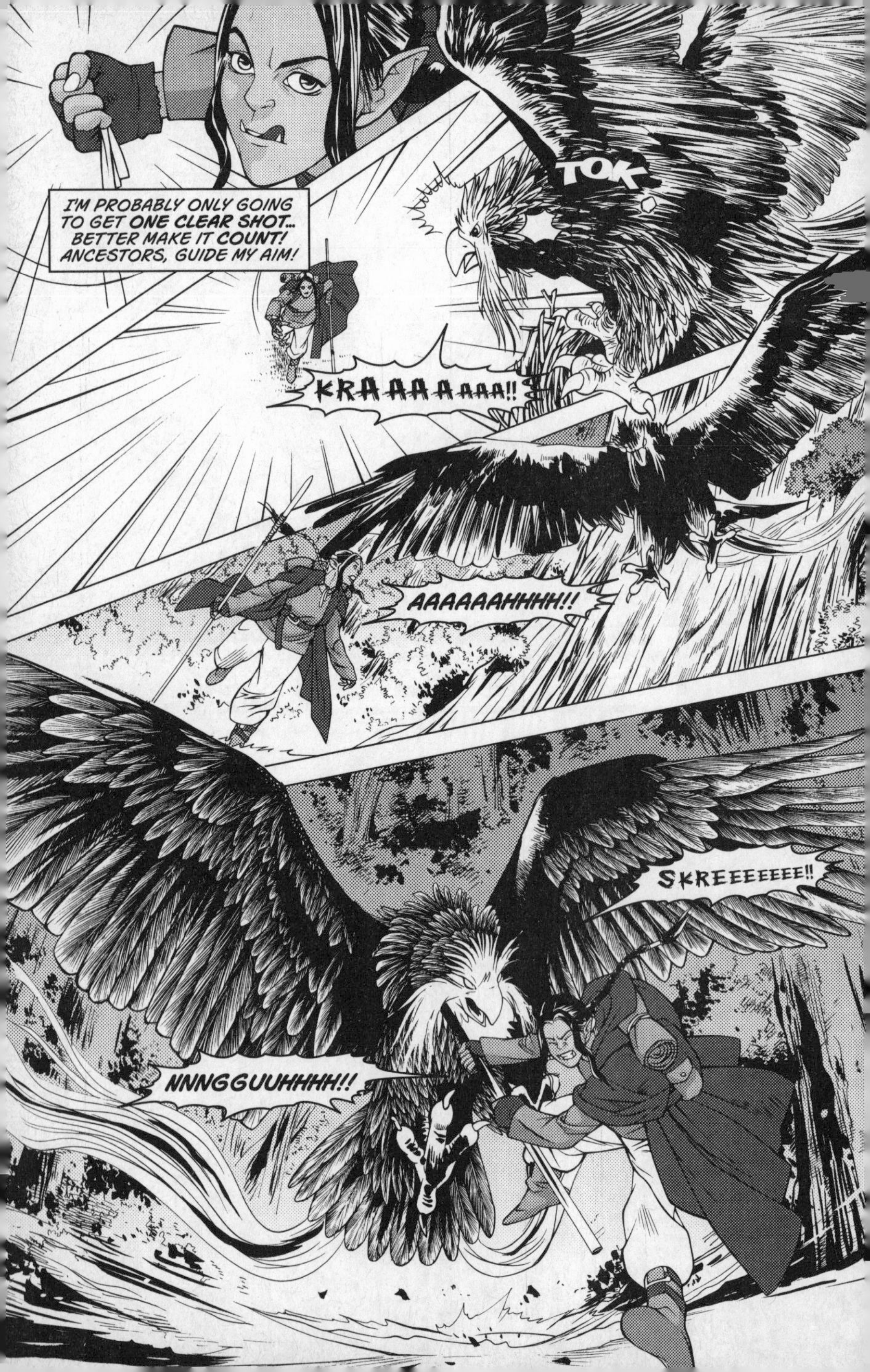
I'M PROBABLY ONLY GOING TO GET ONE CLEAR SHOT... BETTER MAKE IT COUNT! ANCESTORS, GUIDE MY AIM!
TOK
KRAAAAAAA!!
AAAAAAHHHH!!
SKREEEEEEE!!
NNNGGUUHHHH!!

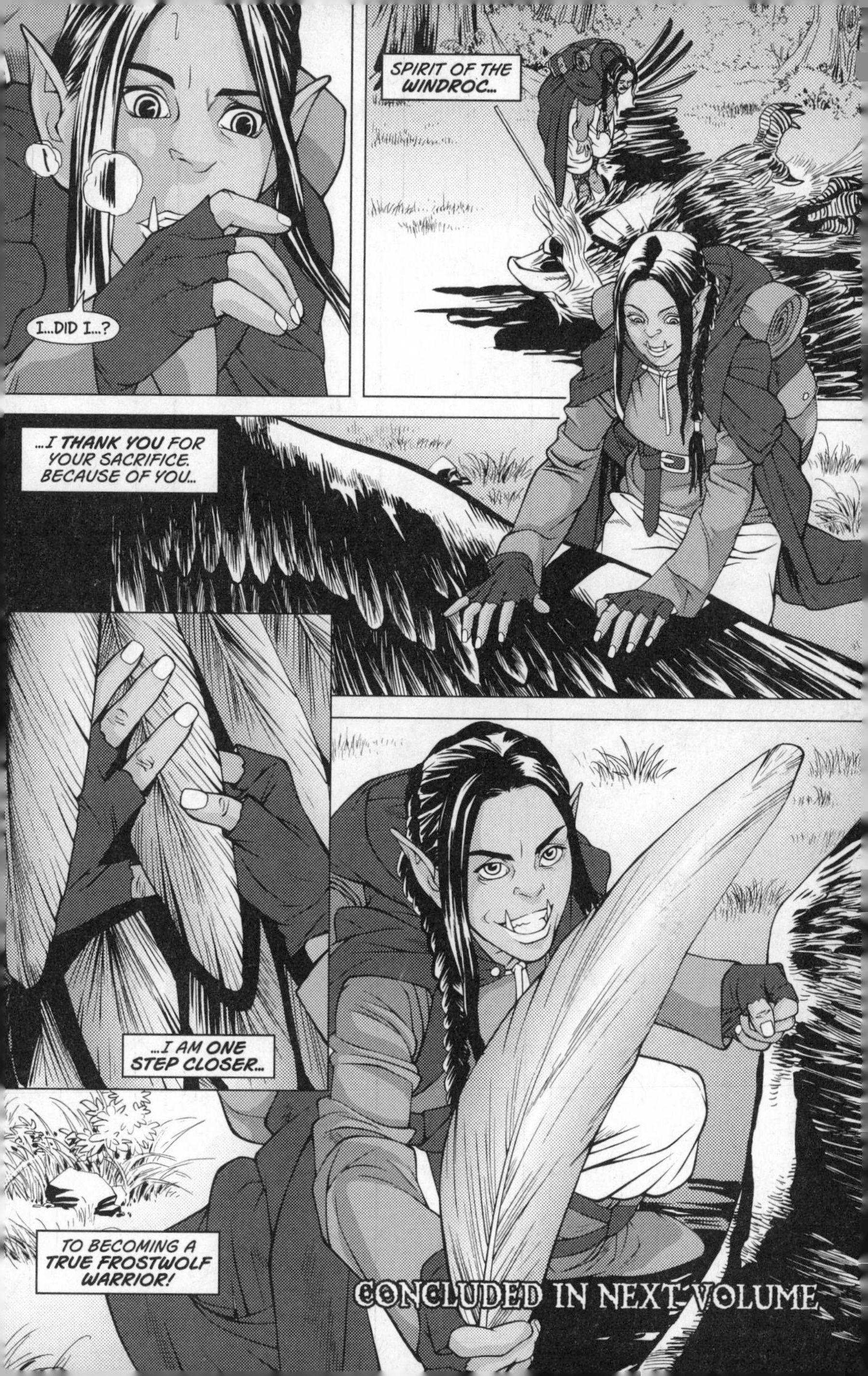
I...DID I...?
SPIRIT OF THE WINDROC...
...I THANK YOU FOR YOUR SACRIFICE. BECAUSE OF YOU...
...I AM ONE STEP CLOSER...
TO BECOMING A TRUE FROSTWOLF WARRIOR!
CONCLUDED IN NEXT VOLUME

ABOUT THE WRITERS

RICHARD A. KNAAK

Richard A. Knaak is the New York Times bestselling fantasy author of 40 novels and over a dozen short stories, including *The Legend of Huma & The Minotaur Wars* for Dragonlance and the *War of the Ancients* trilogy for *Warcraft*. In addition to the TOKYOPOP series *Warcraft: The Sunwell Trilogy*, he is the author of its forthcoming sequel trilogy, *Warcraft: Dragons of Outland*, as well as four-part short story featured in *Warcraft: Legends* Volumes 1-4 (concluded in this volume). Richard will also have a short story entitled "Nightmares" featured in the upcoming *Warcraft: Legends* Volume 5. His latest Warcraft novel, *Night of the Dragon*, is a sequel to the best-selling *Day of the Dragon*. He also recently released *The Fire Rose*, the second in his *Ogre Titans* saga for Dragonlance. To find out more about Richard's projects, visit his website at www.richardaknaak.com.

DAN JOLLEY

Dan Jolley is the author of multiple books for TOKYOPOP, including the young adult prose novel series, *Alex Unlimited*, and the bestselling *Warriors* manga trilogies based on the hugely popular Erin Hunter novels. Dan authored "How to Win Friends," "Miles to Go" and "Crusader's Blood," short stories for *Warcraft: Legends* Volumes 1-3, as well as the forthcoming TOKYOPOP manga *Warcraft: Death Knight*. Much more information about Dan can be found at his website, www.danjolley.com.

TIM BEEDLE

Tim Beedle is a writer, editor and comic book geek who once co-edited the very series you're reading. He was also the editor of such popular TOKYOPOP titles as *Return to Labyrinth*, *Legends of The Dark Crystal*, *Priest* and *East Coast Rising*. Currently, Tim is writing the *Muppet Robin Hood* miniseries for Boom! Entertainment and recently completed an issue of *Marvel Adventures Spider-Man*. He's also editing *The Color of Water* for First Second and finishing *Coin-Operated Boy*, an illustrated novella that he's collaborating on with artist Whitney Leith.

CHRISTIE GOLDEN

Award-winning author Christie Golden has written over thirty novels and several short stories in the fields of science fiction, fantasy and horror. She has written over a dozen Star Trek novels, several original novels, the *StarCraft: Dark Templar* trilogy and three *Warcraft* novels, *Lord of the Clans*, *Rise of the Horde*, as well as *Arthas: Rise of the Lich King*, which was released in April 2009. Christie is currently hard at work writing a yet-to-be titled *Warcraft* novel, as well as three of the nine *Star Wars: Fate of the Jedi* books (in collaboration with Aaron Allston and Troy Denning). *Omen*, her first book in the series, is slated for release in July 2009. Christie has also written two short manga stories, "I Got What Yule Need" and "A Warrior Made," for the TOKYOPOP manga *Warcraft: Legends* Volumes 3, 4 and 5.

ABOUT THE ARTISTS

JAE-HWAN KIM

Born in 1971 in Korea, Jae-Hwan Kim's best-known manga works include *Rainbow, Combat Metal HeMoSoo* and *King of Hell*, an ongoing series currently published by TOKYOPOP. Along with being the creator of *War Angels* for TOKYOPOP, Jae-Hwan is the artist for TOKYOPOP's *Warcraft: The Sunwell Trilogy*, as well as its sequel trilogy, *Warcraft: Dragons of Outland*, which will be available in 2009. Jae-Hwan is also the artist for Richard Knaak's four-part short story featured in *Warcraft: Legends* Volumes 1-4.

FERNANDO FURUKAWA

Born in Argentina, Fernando is the son of a German father and a Japanese mother. Fernando has been drawing since he was a small child and furthered his artistic education under the tutelage of local art professors, Pier Brito and Feliciano Garcia Zecchin. He began his professional artist career at age nineteen and was published in several local magazines. This led to him publishing his own series (along with writer Mauro Mantella and artist Rocio Zucchi) *TIME: 5*. His recent works include his job as lead artist for an online web series, drawing the TOKYOPOP manga *Tantric Stripfighter Trina*, drawing two stories for TOKYOPOP's *Warcraft: Legends* anthology series, as well as being the artist for the upcoming *StarCraft: Ghost Academy* series, also from TOKYOPOP.

RYO KAWAKAMI

Born in Miyako Island, Japan, Ryo he lived there until 1990, after which he and his family moved to the United States. Ryo currently resides in Greenville, N.C., where he studied Fine Art for two years at Coastal Community College. Ryo's first published work is the TOKYOPOP manga *Orange Crows*, which is available in stores now.

IN-BAE KIM

In-Bae made his Korean manga debut in 1998 with *Tong-hwa-joong* (On the Phone). He followed that with several webzine short manga including "Film Ggengin Nar" (The Day I Blacked Out Drinking) and "Call Me." His serialized manga, "Bbuggoogi" (Cuckoo Bird), has been featured in several newspapers. In-Bae was also the artist for "Family Values," a short manga story featured in *Warcraft: Legends* Volume 2.

FORGING A PAGE

If I said it once to the voice in my head, I'll say it again--creating manga art ain't like making a hamburger (though really bad art *can* give you indigestion). It is a complex process, in which the promise made by a script is brought kicking and screaming into the world. And even though developing the page can prove to be a daunting task, with proper nourishment and guidance it can grow into something quite beautiful.

The following is one such example of this...page 36 from "Blood Runs Thicker" was what I call "ninja art"--in that it was a seemingly easy page in the script, but quickly morphed into a stealthy schedule assassin, in that the dense text, limited space and shot selection all required several revisions to get just right. But it is also an example of how teamwork between the artist and editor can conquer any sequential mountain, no matter how steep.

THUMBNAIL

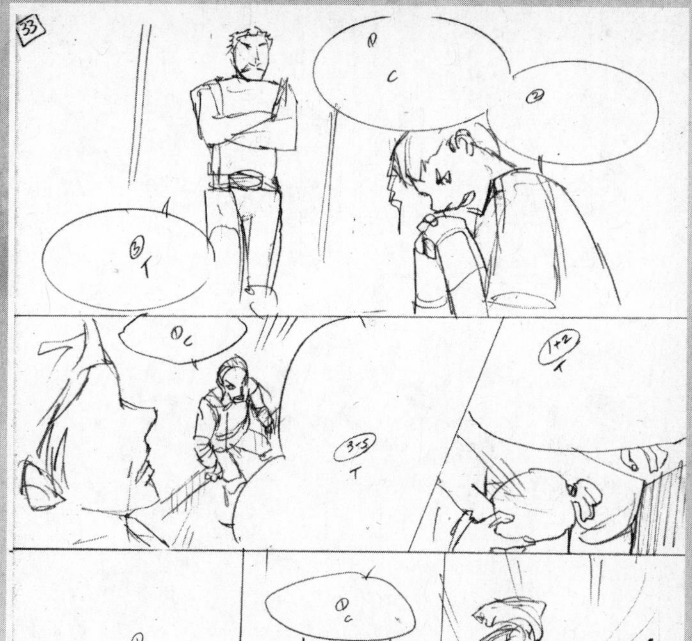
33
*ADDED THIS PANEL TO SHOW CED NOTICED SOMEONE WAS ABOVE HIM.

The thumbnail stage is the artist's first crack at the page. We're concerned less with actual character design at this point, and more with the actual page flow in terms of staging the scene and choosing the best angles. The key thing here is deciding in each panel what the focus should be, and why.

PENCIL DRAFT 1

In this first version of the pencil, you can see a dramatic improvement from the thumbs. Obviously the designs are clearer and more fleshed out, but beyond that some of the shots have changed. But there are still problems with this page: in panel 1 and 2 the décor is too modern (do they even have tea cups in Azeroth?), in panel 2 Cedrick only has one line of dialogue yet he is the focal point of the panel, in panel 3 we need to see where that money bag actually came from (instead of magically flying in from seemingly nowhere) and in panel 5 while the angle is great, we need to lower the bag to see Cedrick's sneer (as well as make him look a bit more villainous). Which leads us to...

PENCIL DRAFT 2

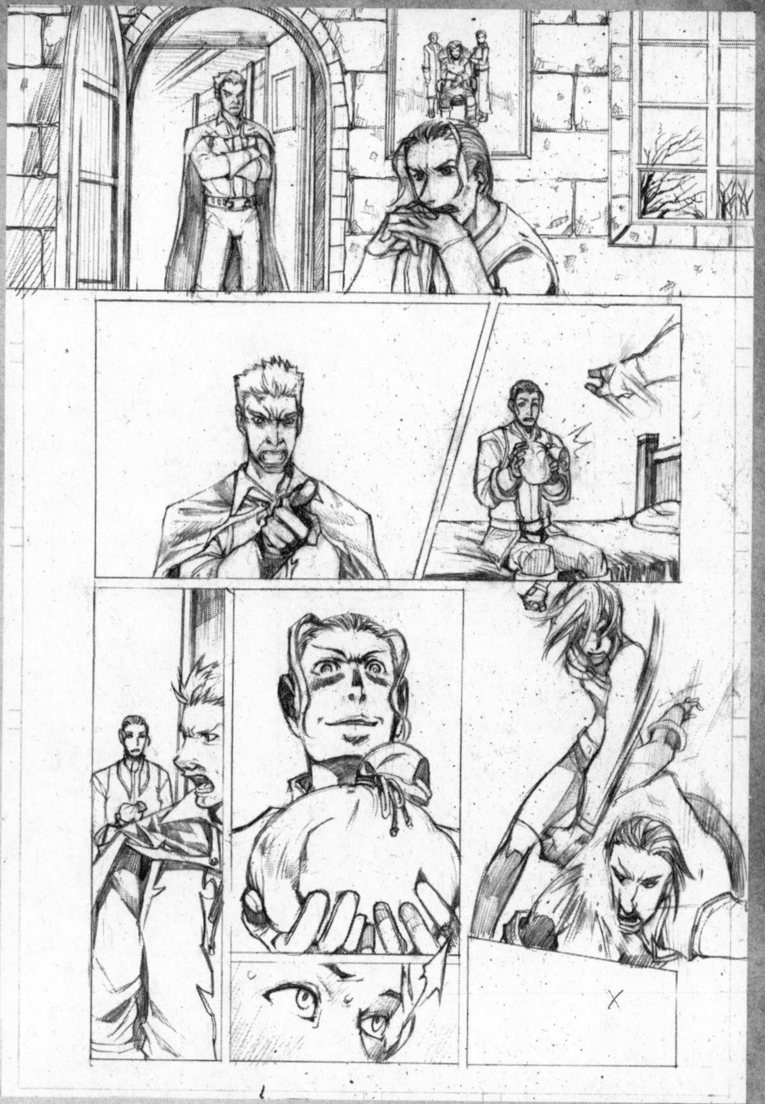

...the final version of the pencil! All the issues have clearly been addressed, in that each panel is focused and conveys the right dramatic beat.

INKED PAGE

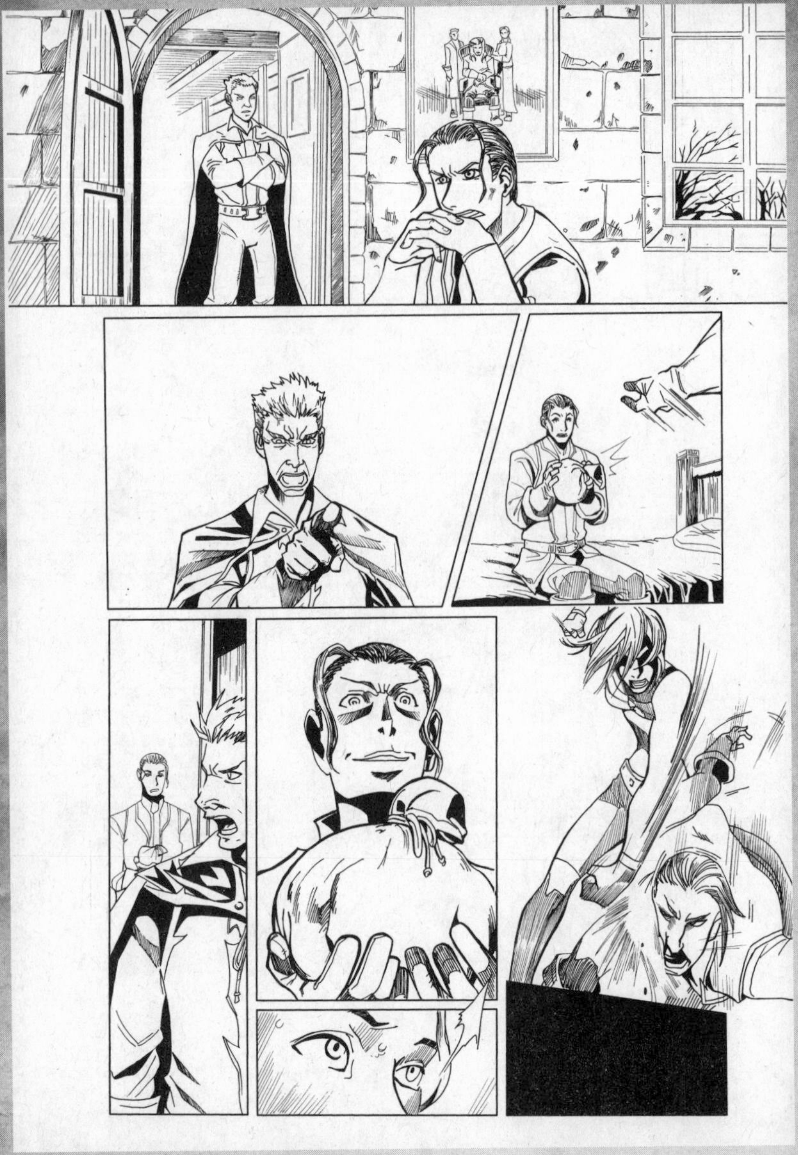

And now that the car has passed inspection, it's time to give it a bit o
"detail"...in the form of inks...

TONED PAGE

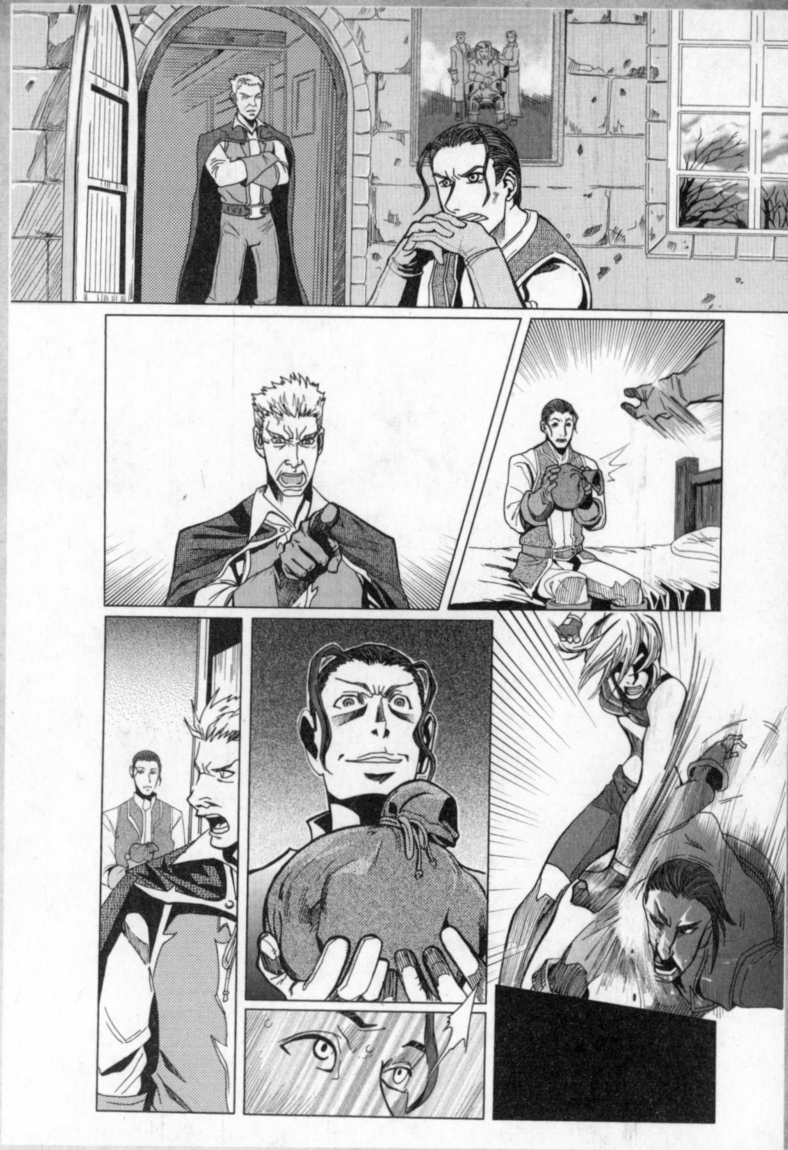

...and tones. Presto! A shiny new manga page, ready for print. Mr. Kawakami, take a bow, sir!

FORGING A HERO

But what would a page be without great looking characters to populate it? The process of creating the right character is often just as complex, if not more, than creating a single page of sequential art. Character is everything, since it's why you care about the story in the first place. The following is an example of how heroes can grow into men (literally in this case).

First up is Fernando's first pass at Jimmy, Liam and Bram. The script didn't specify an exact age, and only indicated that they were young adolescents. In this sketch Jimmy and co. are much, much younger than as they appear in the story...a bit *too* young, actually. Additionally, Jimmy's boots are too modern and not "Warcraft" enough.

Fernando tweaked the age of the boys here, but now they are a bit too old for the story. It was a tricky thing, as we needed to convey thier gradual transition into men, but it had to be a bit more subtle, as they were with the Bloodsails for only a few months at best. On to the next draft...

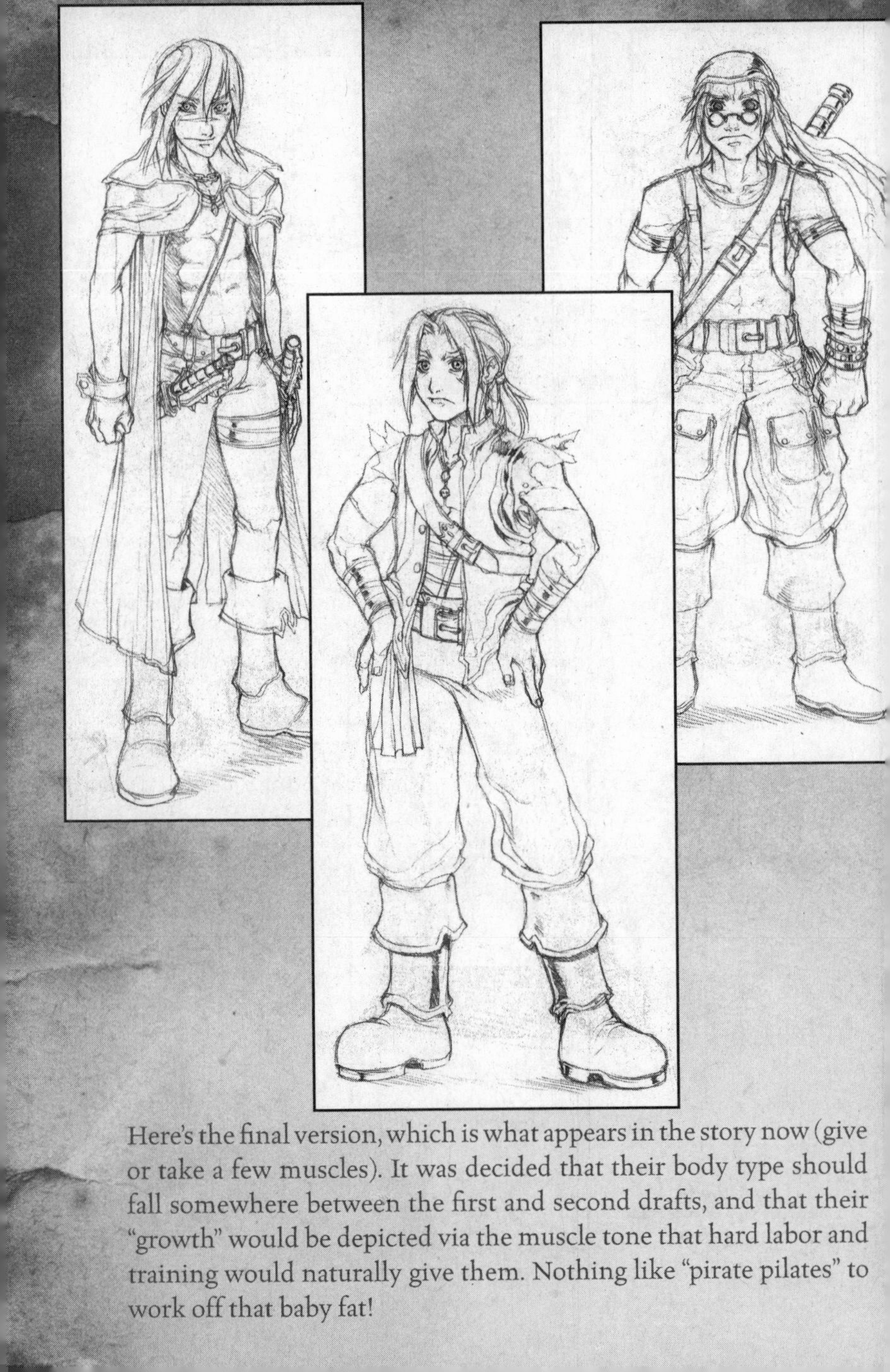

Here's the final version, which is what appears in the story now (give or take a few muscles). It was decided that their body type should fall somewhere between the first and second drafts, and that their "growth" would be depicted via the muscle tone that hard labor and training would naturally give them. Nothing like "pirate pilates" to work off that baby fat!

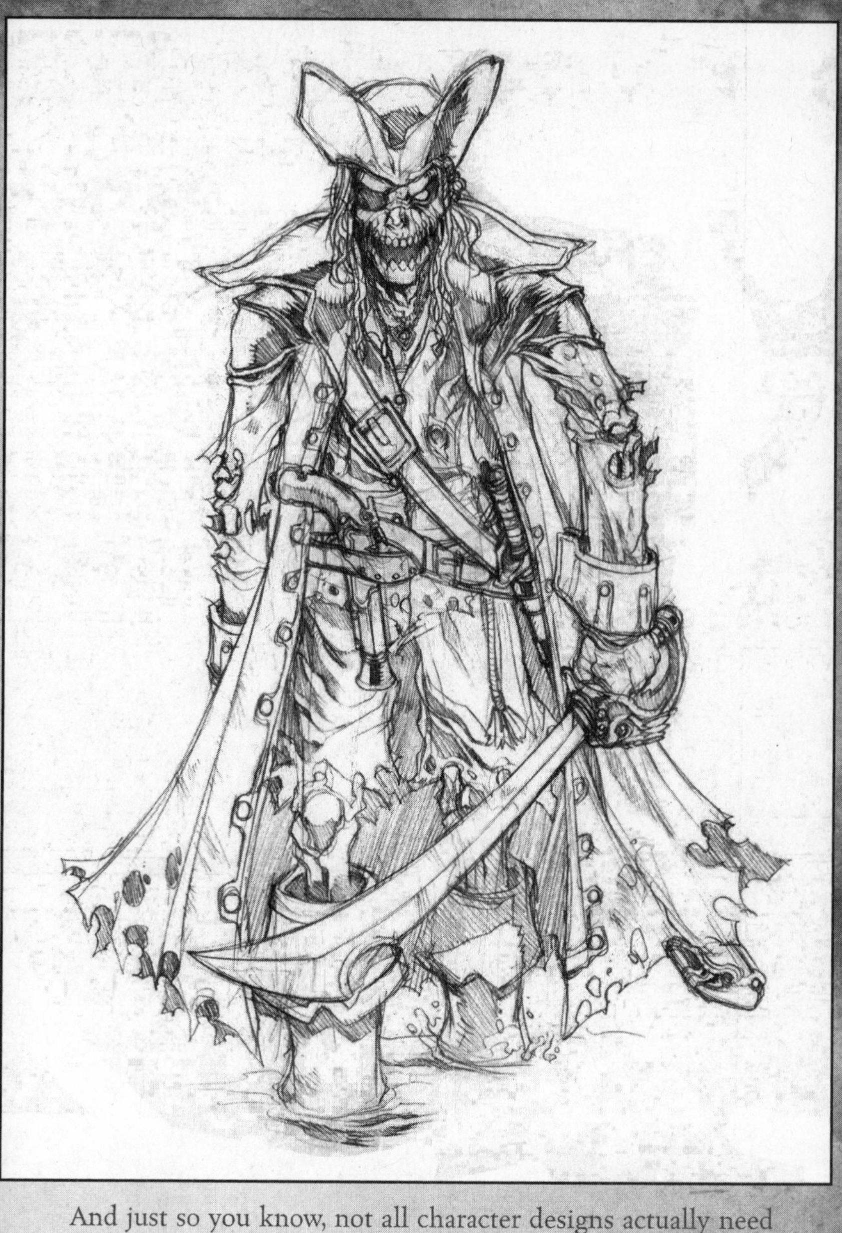

And just so you know, not all character designs actually need revising. Fernando hit this one outta the park on his first try! Amazing work, brutha!

We really hope you enjoyed Volume 4 of *Warcraft: Legends* as much as we enjoyed creating it! This of course includes the talented writers and artists, as well as the hardworking development teams at TOKYOPOP and Blizzard.

Speaking of, none of these manga would be possible without the assistance and guidance of key Blizzard team members: Jason Bischoff, Micky Neilson, Rob Tokar, James Waugh, Evelyn Fredericksen, Samwise Didier, Tommy Newcomer and of course, Chris Metzen. Their dedication to giving *Warcraft* fans an authentic and entertaining experience never ceases to amaze and impress.

On the TOKOYPOP side, we'd like to single out Michael "Iron Mike" Paolilli, layout artist, letterer and creative consultant for all things *Warcraft* and *StarCraft*. Mike never complains and always embraces the challenge (which are numerous and daily) with a smile. Though, he seems to smile a lot more when we would ask him to hop into the game to snag a screen grab for us. We wonder why...heh heh...

Lastly, though we mentioned them already, we can never mention them enough--*big* thanks to all the writers and artists who contributed to this volume, without whom this book wouldn't exist. You all endured harsh deadlines and revision lashings without complaint or hesitation, and though some of you were nearly overtaken by the overwhelming craving to play WoW and *not* draw (wink wink) you still managed to make it across the finish line, squealing tires and all.

And while there is only one more volume of *Warcraft: Legends* to come, there are still many more volumes of *Warcraft* manga to look forward to (including *Warcraft: Dragons of Outland*, the three volume sequel series to the critically acclaimed *Warcraft: The Sunwell Trilogy*, as well as *Warcraft: DeathKnight*, which we have a special preview of after the next page). So stay tuned for what TOKYOPOP and Blizzard has in store for the coming year.!

Also, don't forget to pick up Volumes 1 and 2 of our other Blizzard anthology series, *StarCraft: Frontline*, both available in stores now.

And if you enjoyed this volume, don't forget to pick up Volume 5 of *Warcraft: Legends*, available in September 2009!

Troy Lewter
Editor

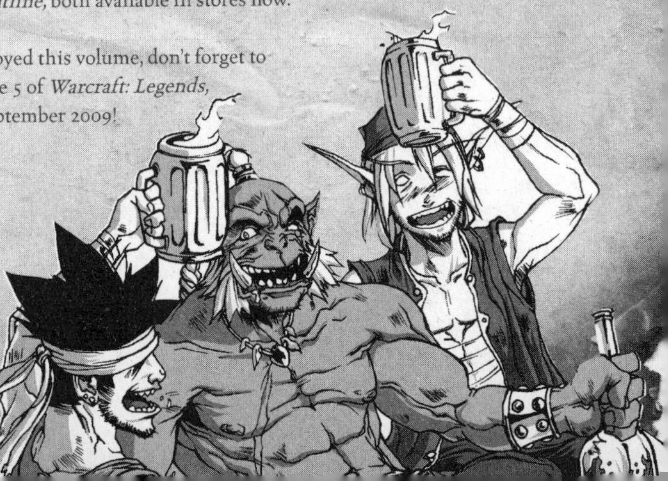

IN THE NEXT VOLUME

Like moths to the flame, to this book ye did flock, now take a gander below at what tales we have next in stock...

Draka's journey to find the ingredients needed to become a strong warrior comes to a dramatic conclusion...

Three legendary warriors–orc Warchief Thrall, Mage Jaina Proudmoore and King Magni Bronzebeard–are all forced to face their innermost fears and darkest dreams...

In Azeroth's ancient past, a secret council of magi discovers an unlikely hero in their battle against a demon...

Two twin sisters journey to the cursed Tower of Karazhan to rescue their long lost father...

A Scarlet Crusader's heartless obsession with cleansing Azeroth of the undead leads to his rebirth...as the Headless Horseman. His never-before-revealed origin will finally be told...

The stories be the honey, your local bookstore the hive, so be sure to journey there for the sweetness that is Volume 5!

WARCRAFT: LEGENDS VOLUME 5
COMING SEPTEMBER 2009

A MESSAGE FROM DAN JOLLEY, AUTHOR OF WARCRAFT: DEATH KNIGHT

Hi all--Dan Jolley here. We've got some great stuff to show you from the upcoming TOKYOPOP manga Warcraft: Death Knight (written by yours truly and drawn by the super-talented Rocio Zucchi), and to go along with the preview, the good folks at TOKYOPOP and Blizzard asked me to document a few thoughts and observations on the process as a whole.

I'm actually taking some time out from leveling my tauren shaman to put this together. I finally got my blood elf mage to 80, and the shaman's at 77, and my guildmates are all like, "Come on! You can do it! You can do it! Only three more levels!"

Ahem.

Anyway. Some of you may be aware that I've written a few shorter stories for *Warcraft: Legends*. It was right after I turned in one of those that I got the call about doing *Warcraft: Death Knight*; this was back when *Wrath of the Lich King* was still in beta, but fortunately, I'd been part of the testing since friends-and-family alpha, so I already knew a thing or two about death knights. And when I heard what Blizzard wanted to do with the book--namely, provide a backstory for Thassarian, a supremely cool death knight I had previously encountered in the game--I was all over it. I mean, it would've taken a lot to keep me away from this project. I was even willing to challenge Richard Knaak to some hand-to-hand combat if necessary. (Thank goodness it *wasn't* necessary. I'm a little taller than Richard, but he's fast as a cobra, and I suspect he'd fight dirty.)

So please join me in December 2009 as we get to know Thassarian, his mom Vivian and his sister Leryssa, everyone's favorite taciturn blood elf death knight, Koltira Deathweaver, and a horde (no pun intended) of other characters, both good and evil.

And pack some warm clothes. Northrend is freaking *cold*.

Dan Jolley

Cary, North Carolina

March 2009

FORGING A COVER

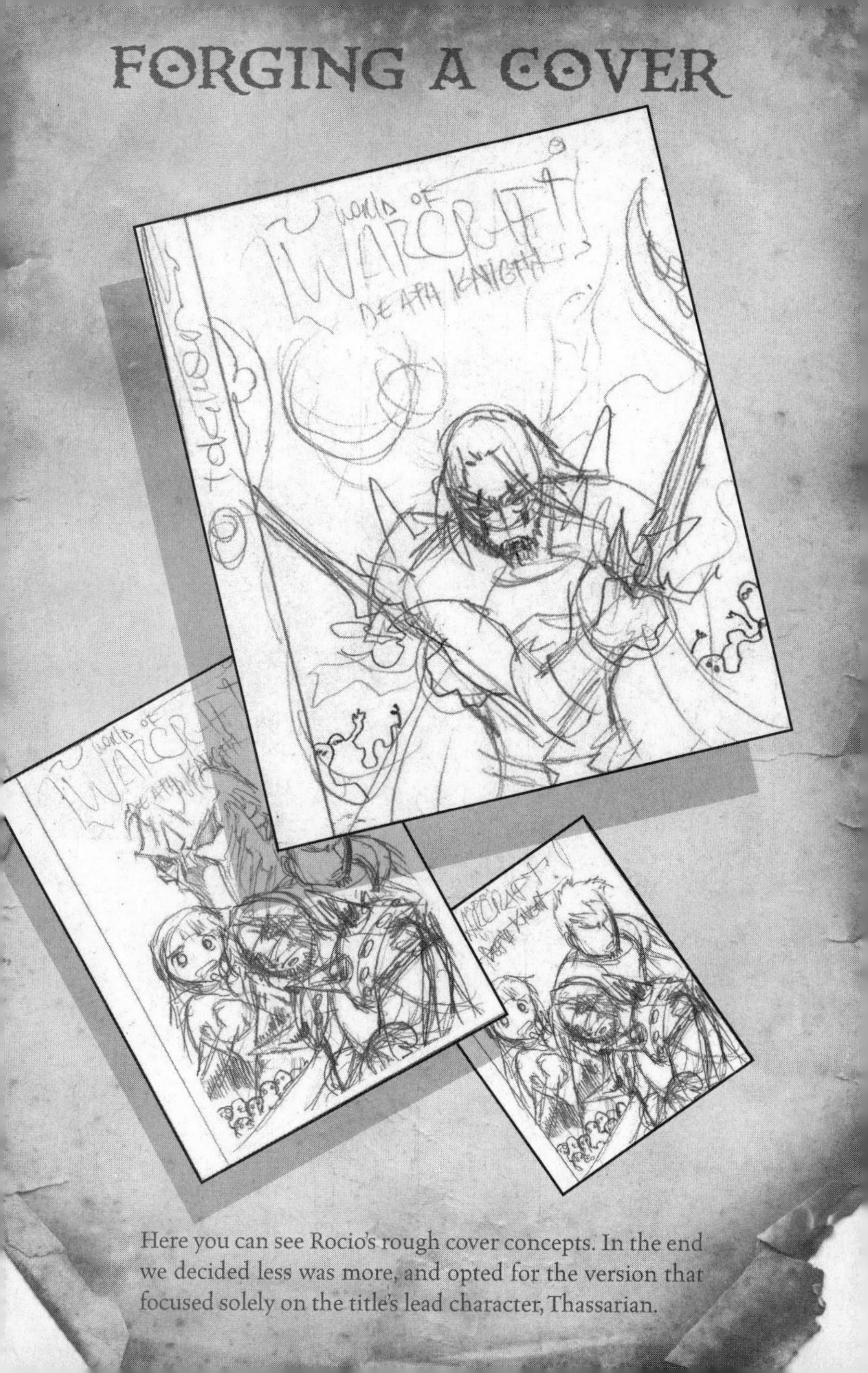

Here you can see Rocio's rough cover concepts. In the end we decided less was more, and opted for the version that focused solely on the title's lead character, Thassarian.

Now that the basic design had been picked, it was time for Rocio to move on to the pencils...

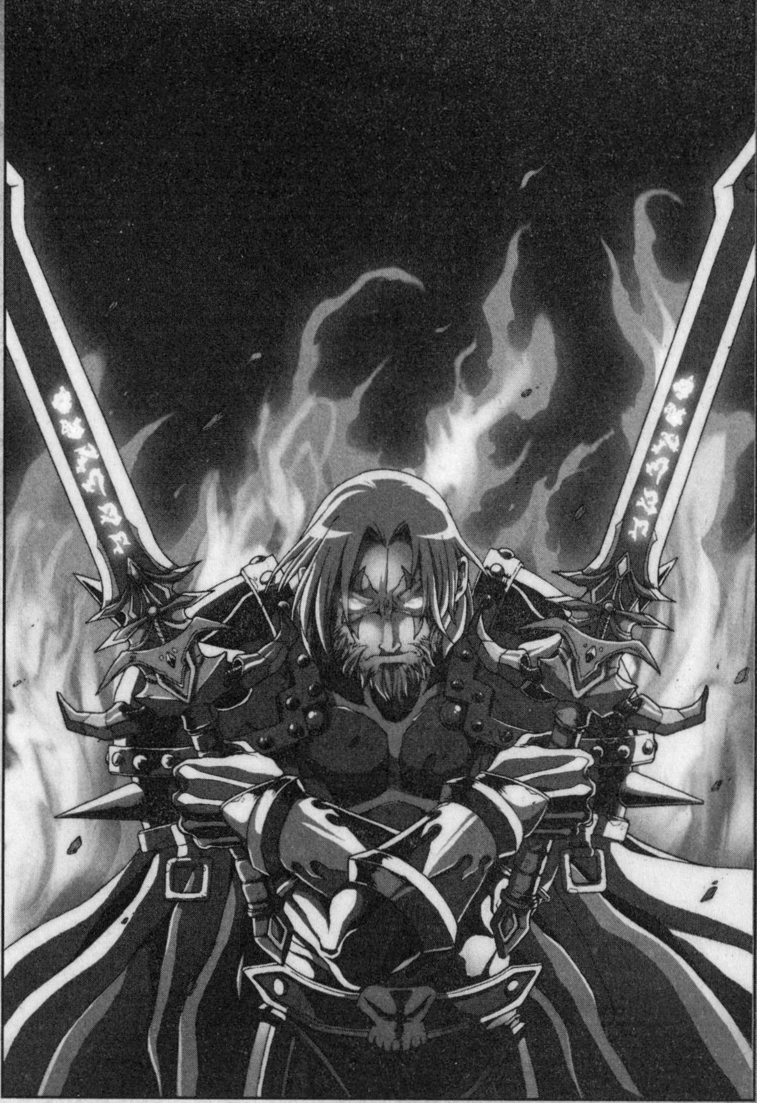

...and then the final cover. And while this tease is in black & white (and still plenty badass), just wait until you see the final color version in all its flaming glory in December!

FORGING A CAST
THASSARIAN

If it ain't broke, why fix it? Since Blizzard and TOKYOPOP want to give fans the most authentic experience possible, Thassarian's armor design was lifted directly from the game. The above is the second death knight armor set he wears in the game (and in the story).

VIVIAN

And while *Warcraft: Death Knight* is essentially Thassarian's story, it features many other characters from WoW lore. Here we have Vivian, Thassarian's loving mother. It just goes to prove even the most cold-blooded warrior has a mother at home to knit him socks.

LERYSSA

Leryssa is Thassarian's younger sister, and like any siblings, they are constantly bickering. Even so, at the end of the teasing and taunts, they still love each other all the same.

ARTHAS

But without a doubt the biggest "supporting" character is Arthas/
the Lich King. He is the ultimate catalyst for Thassarian's tragic fate.
It was absolutely essential that Rocio nailed Arthas before the fall...

THE LICH KING

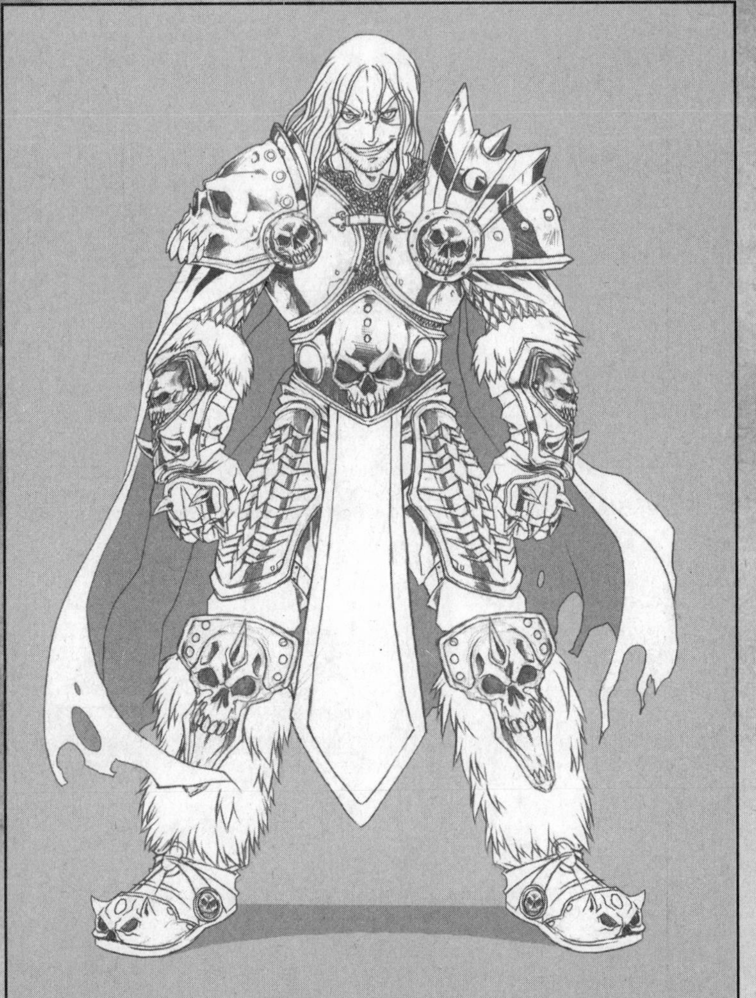

...and Arthas as he becomes the Lich King. This armor design was very difficult, as it is so iconic and recognizable to fans around the world, so every detail had to be exact...but Rocio totally rocked it!

FROSTMOURNE

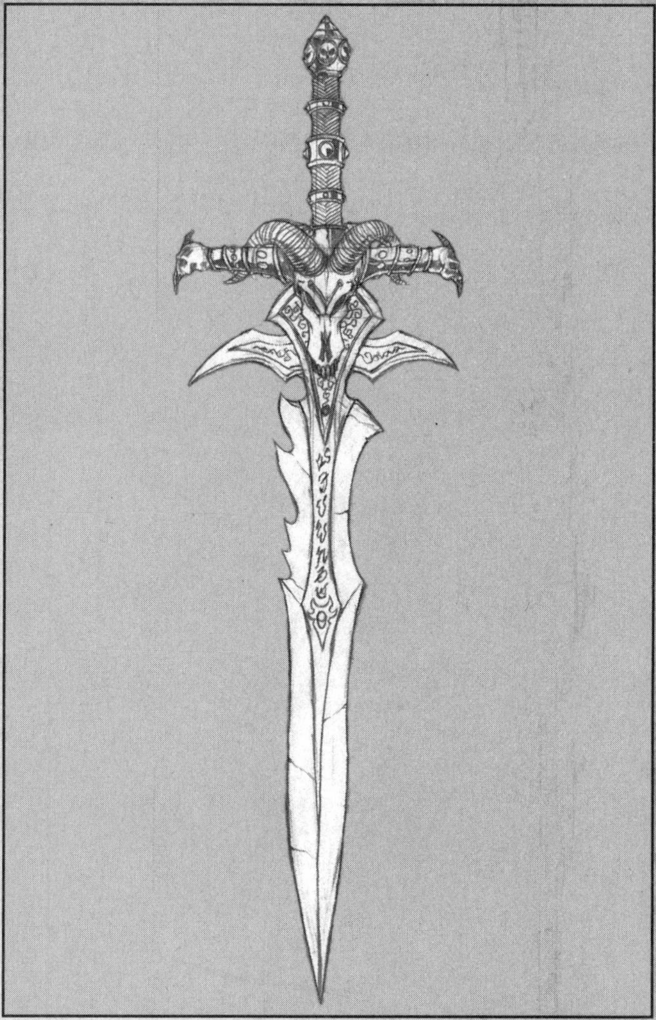

Speaking of iconic, equally important was nailing the Lich King's weapon of mass destruction...Frostmourne.

THE PAGES WE WIELD

Warcraft: Death Knight is as much a story about death and corruption as it is about rebirth and hope. The challenge Rocio faces is that on any given page she will have to tackle intense drama, intense action—and very often both at the same time. But much to our delight she is more than up to the challenge, as the following exclusive first look at *Warcraft: Death Knight* sequential pencils will show!

First off we have the above splash page, showing a very distraught Vivian cowering from some unseen threat. Could it be a Scourge? Or perhaps even a death knight? Or...

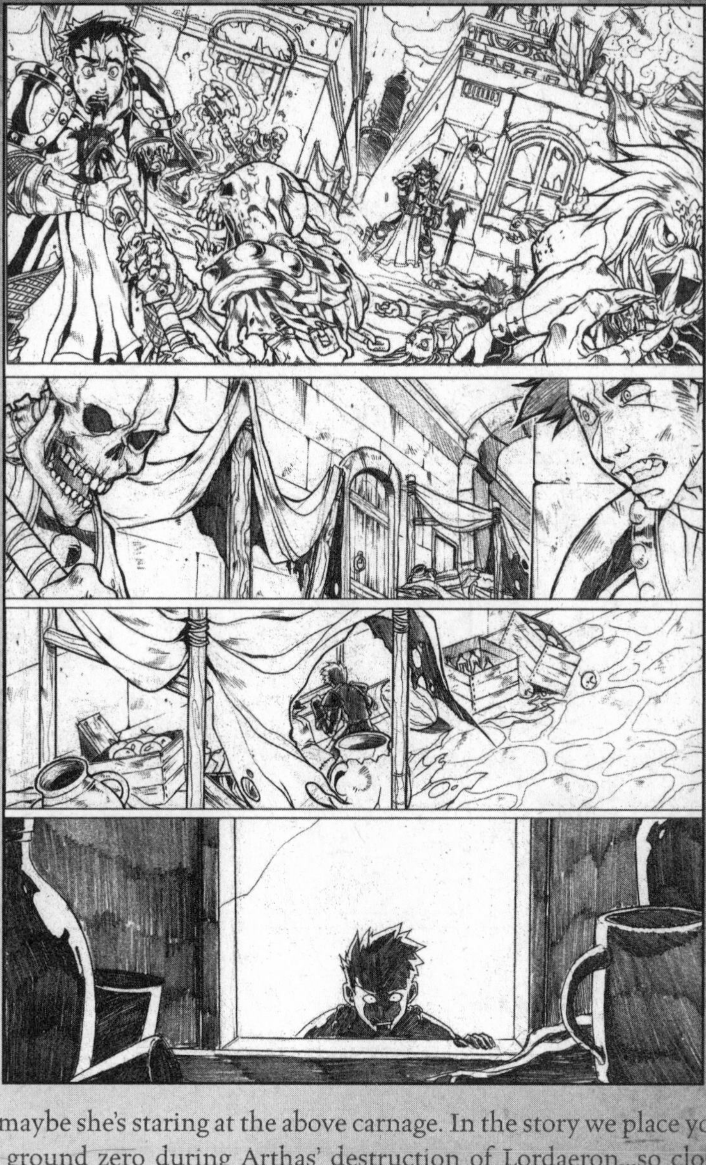

...maybe she's staring at the above carnage. In the story we place you at ground zero during Arthas' destruction of Lordaeron...so close you can virtually feel the blood in the gutters soaking your feet. And though this page is a work in progress, we can still see at this early stage how intense the action will be.

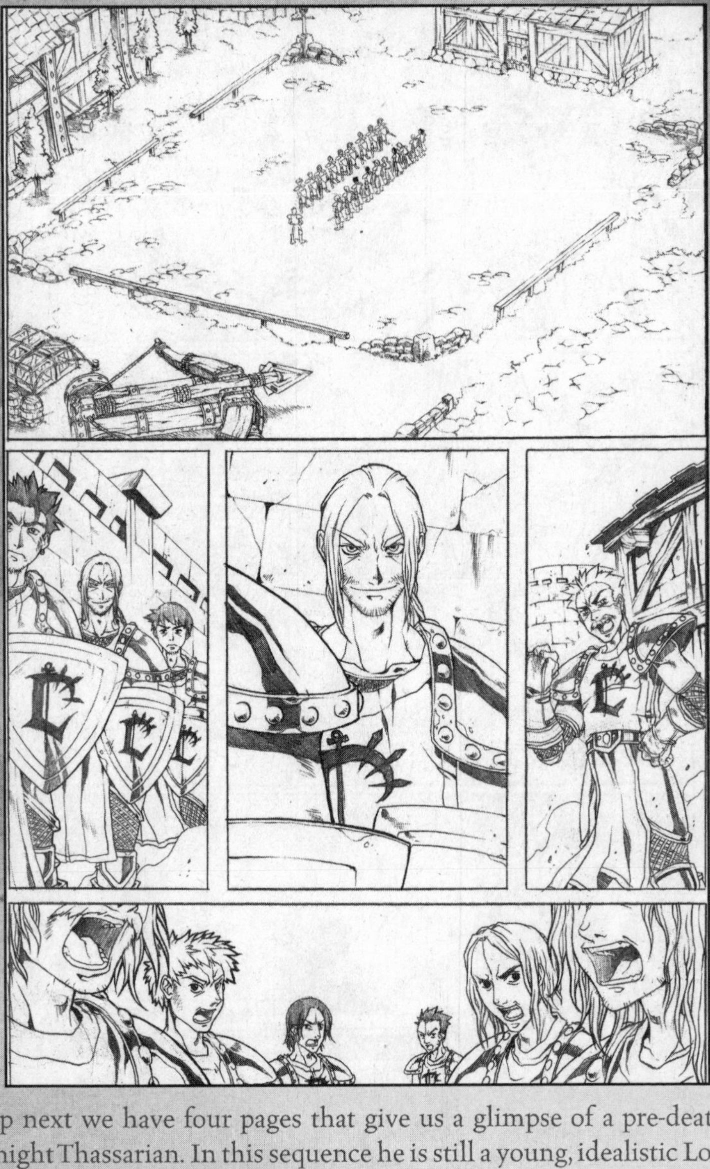

Up next we have four pages that give us a glimpse of a pre-death knight Thassarian. In this sequence he is still a young, idealistic Lordaeron soldier, brimming with aspirations of impressing his superiors and moving up in the ranks.

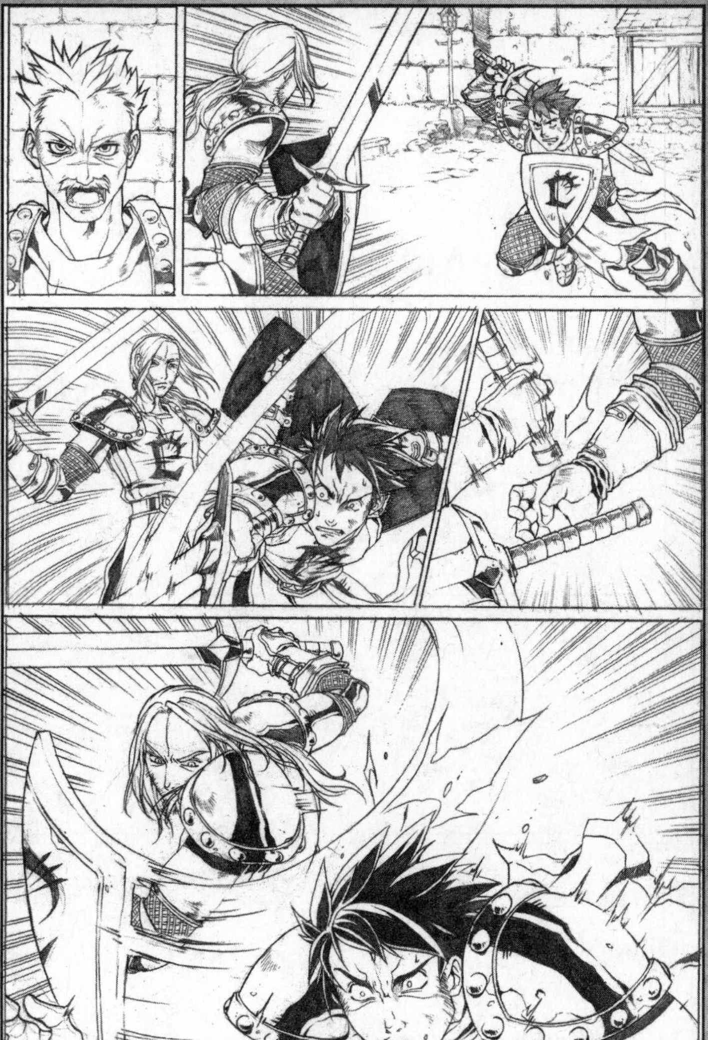

Thassarian has intensely studied the combat rule book and knows every offensive and defensive move and counter...

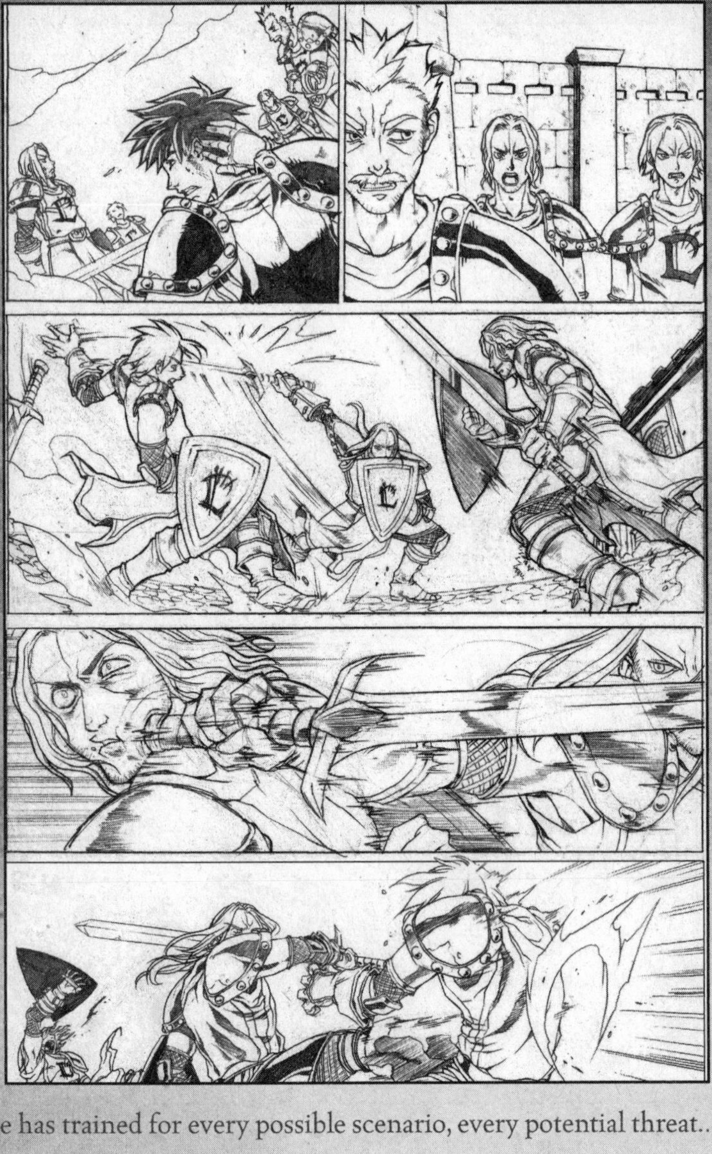

He has trained for every possible scenario, every potential threat...

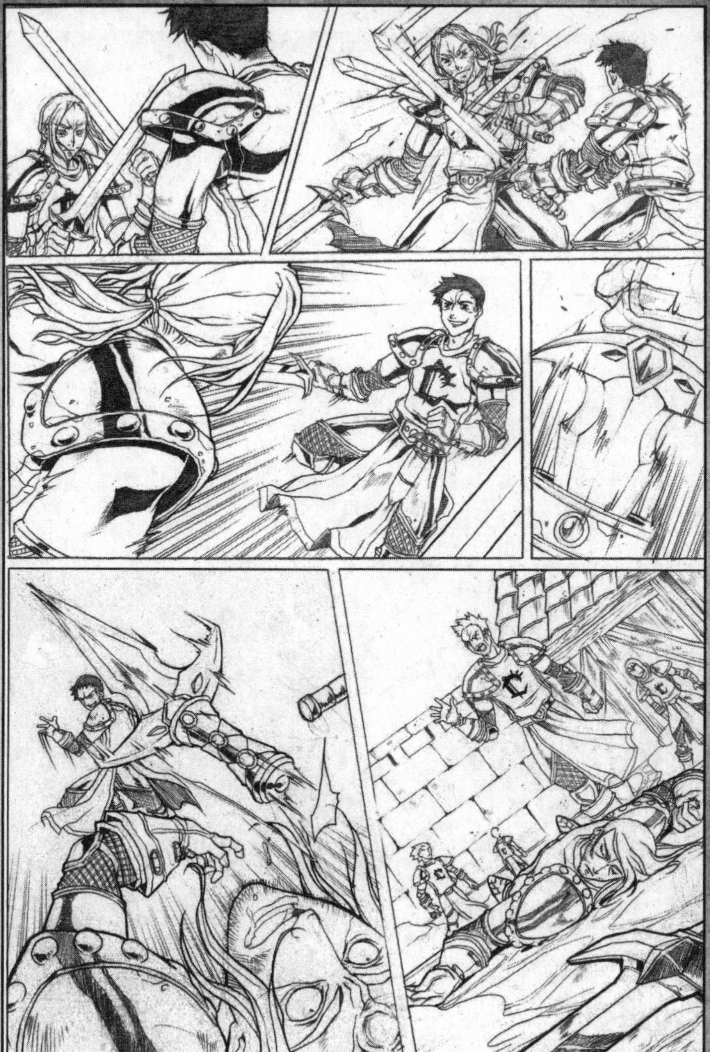

That said, as he learns here the hard way, even the fiercest lion can be undone by the sneakiest snake!

We hope you enjoyed this glimpse behind the death knight curtain. Be sure to pick up *Warcraft: Death Knight,* storming bookstores December 2009!

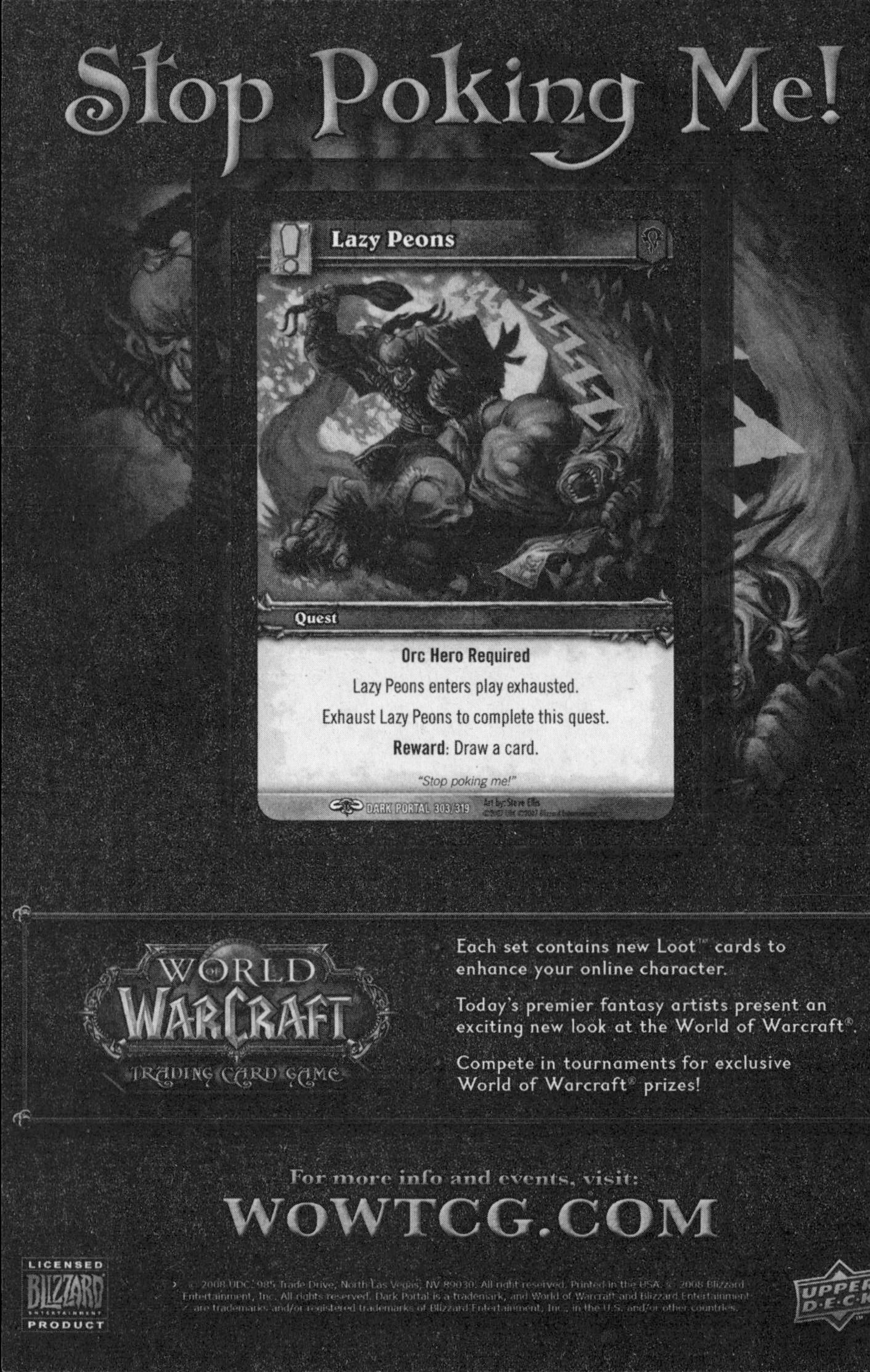
Stop Poking Me!
Lazy Peons
Quest
Orc Hero Required
Lazy Peons enters play exhausted.
Exhaust Lazy Peons to complete this quest.
Reward: Draw a card.
"Stop poking me!"
DARK PORTAL 303/319
Art by: Steve Ellis
WORLD OF WARCRAFT
TRADING CARD GAME
Each set contains new Loot™ cards to enhance your online character.
Today's premier fantasy artists present an exciting new look at the World of Warcraft®.
Compete in tournaments for exclusive World of Warcraft® prizes!
For more info and events, visit:
WOWTCG.COM
LICENSED
BLIZZARD
ENTERTAINMENT
PRODUCT
© 2008 UDC. 985 Trade Drive, North Las Vegas, NV 89030. All right reserved. Printed in the USA. © 2008 Blizzard Entertainment, Inc. All rights reserved. Dark Portal is a trademark, and World of Warcraft and Blizzard Entertainment are trademarks and/or registered trademarks of Blizzard Entertainment, Inc., in the U.S. and/or other countries.
UPPER DECK

MMO GAMING MOUSE

World's first
gaming mouse
designed exclusively
for World of Warcraft®

Incredible customization options:

- 6 million illumination choices
- 15 programmable buttons
- Custom macro creation

Intuitive, ergonomic design and
premium components ensure superior
performance, comfort and control

Available Q4 2008

LICENSED
BLIZZARD
ENTERTAINMENT
PRODUCT

�> steel**series**

Actual Gameplay.

NO. I'D RATHER KILL RATS.

With millions of players online, World of Warcraft has made gaming
history — and now it's never been easier to join the adventure.
Simply visit **www.warcraft.com**, download the FREE TRIAL and join
thousands of mighty heroes for ten days of bold online adventure.
A World Awaits...

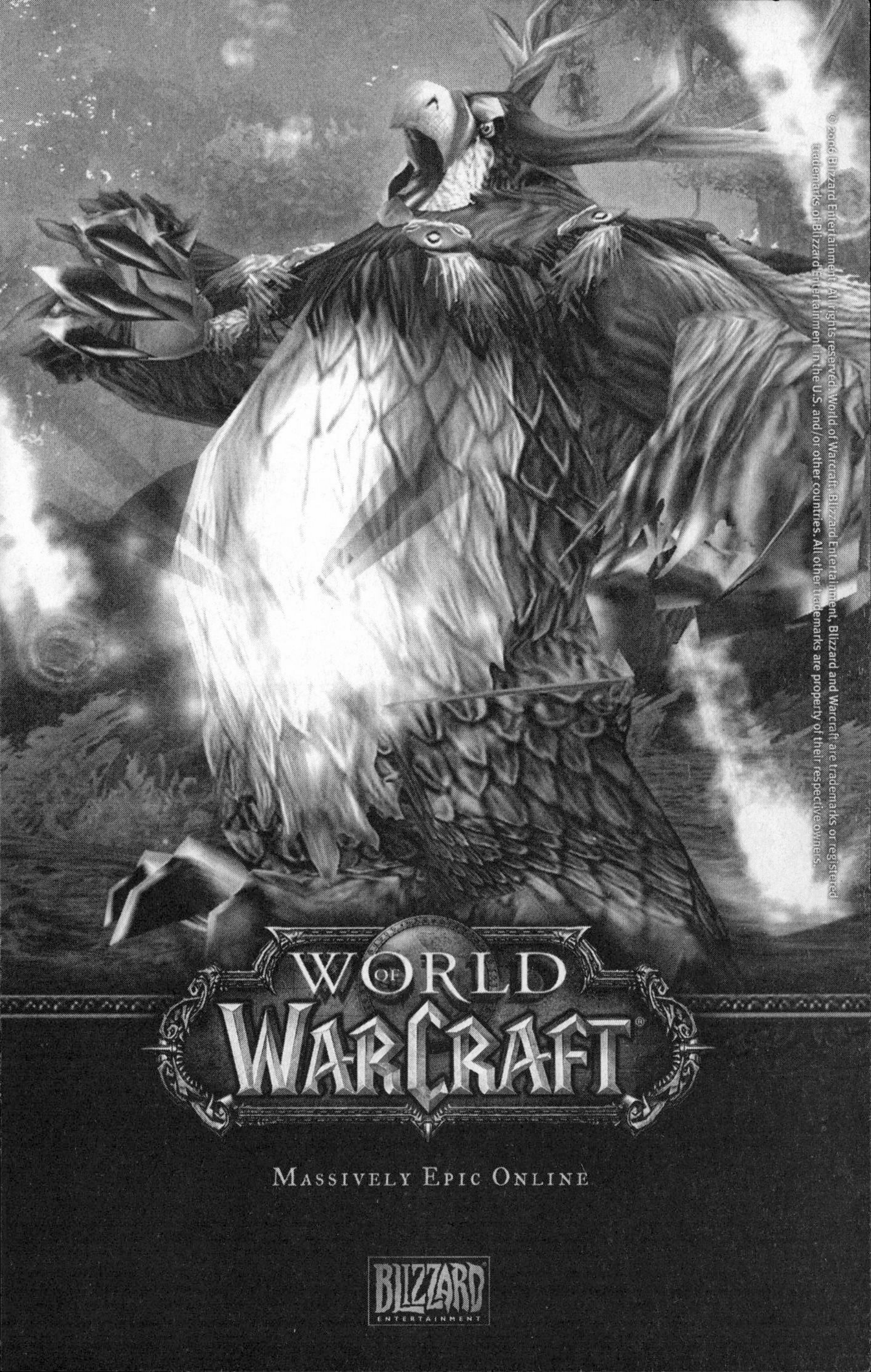